INNER RECESSES OUTER SPACES

INNER RECESSES OUTER SPACES

Memoirs

KAMALADEVI CHATTOPADHYAY

INDIA INTERNATIONAL CENTRE

NIYOGI BOOKS

Published in collaboration with the India International Centre, New Delhi.

Published by
NIYOGI BOOKS
Block D, Building No. 77,
Okhla Industrial Area, Phase-I,
New Delhi-110 020, INDIA
Tel: 91-11-26816301, 26818960
Email: niyogibooks@gmail.com
Website: www.niyogibooksindia.com

ISBN: 978-93-83098-39-2
Publication: 2014
Reprint: 2018

Printed at: Niyogi Offset Pvt. Ltd., New Delhi, India.

'My world will light its hundred different lamps with thy flame and place them before the altar of thy temple.'

RABINDRANATH TAGORE

KAMALADEVI CHATTOPADHYAY

Foreword

Inner Recesses Outer Spaces, first published in 1986, has been out of print. A second edition was long overdue. Those who knew Kamaladevi wanted to re-read the book, and those who did not, wanted to acquaint themselves with the life of this remarkable woman who had shaped the lives of many. They wanted to hear her voice. *Inner Recesses Outer Spaces* is that authentic voice of one who believed in the extraordinariness of the ordinary.

Raja Rao, the great writer of rare sensitivity and insight, known for his many works, particularly the *Serpent and the Rope*, knew Kamaladevi over a long period, especially before Independence. He has written a very insightful preface to the first edition. There is little for me to add as I cannot match his friendship with the author, nor do I belong to that generation. Nevertheless, it is my privilege to situate Kamaladevi in the India International Centre as the institution which is now republishing the work.

Kamaladevi is remembered by a host of old timers as that gracious presence, immaculately dressed, sitting in the last-but-one row in the Auditorium, watching performances and making an incisive comment. More, she is fondly remembered by the cook, the *mali*, the old colleagues, N.H. Ramachandran, Premola, Kutty, and of course the Directors, particularly Eric Gonsalves and, most of all, the Trustees, especially Professor M.G.K. Menon and the late Dr. L.M. Singhvi.

A close associate of Dr. C.D. Deshmukh and Durgabai Deshmukh, Kamaladevi guided the activities of the IIC in his absence. She has left an indelible mark on the institution, its character, its commitment to 'values', and to its vital role in providing a forum for articulating concerns over a large canvas, ranging from the political to the social, the artistic, on which she brought to bear her vast experience, her unflinching commitment and her effortless courage and, above all, a total negation of self centeredness. The new wing of the IIC—the 'Kamaladevi complex'—named after her, commemorates her memory, but in so doing, it reminds, or should remind, this generation and the generation to come, that there was one who broke barriers and fought battles with extraordinary ease and felicity.

Her world was as local as universal. She knew every nook and corner of this country, but also others in the East and the West. With unassuming ease she could converse with the villagers, the craftsman, the puppeteers, the musicians, the dancers, the social workers, the women's groups and, of course, politicians as also scientists. With ease she asked Einstein how he felt when the atom bomb fell on Hiroshima. Without flinching, she could write a letter to General Zia-ul-Haq to return the innocent boy who had unknowingly strayed into Pakistani territory. With intensity of purpose, she drove to Meerut to rescue a girl who was burnt for lack of dowry.

Her commitment to the cause of the handicrafts and handlooms is today legendary. The all-India cooperative movement was her brain child, the establishment of the All India Handicrafts Board a result of her advocacy.

She gave dignity and value to hand-made crafts. This was a logical sequence of Gandhiji's call for *khadi* and *swadeshi*. This is not the occasion to recount all this and more examples of her untiring effort to not only revive craft tradition, but also to give prestige to the arts of puppetry, masks, and much else.

Understandably, she was the Vice Chairperson of Sangeet Natak Akademi. She returned to the SNA as Chairperson with inspired fresh vigour and new energy. As Chairperson of the Centre for Cultural Resources and Training she was responsible for making a link between the hundred other areas for which she is remembered, and will be remembered. The second edition of the volume will no doubt refresh our memories.

And finally, I recall an incident which is pertinent in the context of the title. With some reluctance I share this. The memory of that moment has never been erased. I live and relive that telephone call, 'Kapila, please come immediately'—I drove as fast as I could to find her lying on the floor with blood oozing out from the skull. She was not thinking of her wound; instead, she commanded: 'Where is the title of the book?' In an instant I suggested 'Inner Recesses Outer Spaces'. The doctor arrived only after she remarked, 'Yes, I agree that is an appropriate title.'

New Delhi
19 March 2014

Kapila Vatsyayan

Preface

Srimati Kamaladevi is perhaps the most august woman on the Indian scene today. Firmly Indian and therefore universal, highly sophisticated both in sensibility and intelligence, she walks with everyone, in city and country with utter simplicity. And so natural her movements, she crosses India constantly, trying to help some troupe of traditional dancers in Manipur (and brings them back to Delhi) or goes to a miserable village near Khutub to help poor families make decorations for an honourable living. This is how in fact the whole world began to know and use Indian handicrafts. Once walking with her in Paris, taking her to see a play of Sartre (I think the 'NO EXIT') she seemed as familiar there as she would have been in the streets of Bombay or Delhi. There is indeed something utterly elevated about her presence, so that one wishes one could only live and breathe at her level of existence. I think too her patience with us seems to come from pride as her devotion to handicrafts arises out of compassion. Thus, I feel, in her Memoirs, she has been understanding and fair to everyone. I have never found any statement here which, with all the complexity of Indian political and social existence, is a single petty remark. And that is saying a great deal in the context of our present day world.

Born into a fairly comfortable upper class family, with a mother as wise as she was courageous, who gave her daughter at once protection and freedom, understanding and education; offering, too, space for sports, dance, to act in plays, against all social conventions too. Then the girl goes out because of some *Yakshini's* guidance, to meet the proper people, learning organisation from Dr. Hardiker's *Seva Dal* and meeting the Karves and Pandita Ramabai in Pune, trying to see what should be done to lessen the humiliation and suffering Indian women silently bear because of some ununderstood and often outmoded customs. Then with Mrs. Cousins, she works for the All India Women's Conference, and becomes without wanting, a leading figure in Indian reform movements, a woman talking to women as a woman, were she the formidable Begum of Bhopal or the sweet Vicerine, Lady Irwin. But soon she enters the giddy universe of Gandhiji and the Nehrus, and works through time and distance, it seems to me, with miraculous ease—to live in the atmosphere of politics, without, as it were, politics. And she finds herself again at an international conference as for example in Berlin, where each group of delegates hoisted their flag, but India having no flag at that time, at Kamaladevi's instance three women tore a sari each and made up a flag, of red, green and white and stuck the flag in its proper place—may be the first such flag of India at any international conference. Thus there she meets ardent revolutionaries like Viren Chattopadhyay (her brother-in-law) and Madame Cama, that fiery Indian nationalist, of whom the British were so afraid. And that other, the American Agnes Smedley, once a wife to Viren Chattopadhyay, then a hero in Communist China.

Kamaladevi seemed to have asked for nothing and so received everything, position and praise from those who understood worthiness. At her age she looks truly beautiful as only an artistic temperament could shape and keep a woman. Significantly, therefore, she starts her memoirs with flowers gathered in her mother's garden.

Throughout all this, however, Kamaladevi never forgot the poor, their traditional riches of festive dances, their sense of colour and their handicrafts. In fact in Shantiniketan, Tagore and she speak of this, the riches of our countryside and one day the Poet is so moved by this innocent and inspiring young lady, he invites her to listen to him sing, and then talks to her of nature, of rhythm, the rhythm that runs through the mystery of creation. It seems to me, reading these memoirs, there is a similar magical rhythm and naturalness to Kamaladevi's life. For what astonishes one indeed is the spontaniety with which events occur, as if a magic wand took her through the extraordinary, seeing it all as natural, the quotidian appearing as the truly creative.

There is too, a great gravity about Kamaladevi's story, which to me proves, what any serious and disinterested being realises little by little, that to forget oneself is to live the miraculous, something that Gandhiji has reminded us again and again in our own time. All this, may I say, is the wisdom and meaning of India. And it is, of course, with this creative naturalness, the book ends in sheer poetry, the nobility of which will be discovered one day as among the most beautiful pages written in the India of today.

For, in the heart of the human is the *abhuman*. (In the heart of the *abhuman* however is not the human—there can be no duality in the *abhuman*.) The dancer becomes the dance. Often in the deep human identification with another, in the deep courage Kamaladevi reveals, almost by a terrible attraction she seems to feel towards the awesome, the impossible (the *abhuman*), she plunges into the forgetfulness of herself, which appears to throw her into a state of exhilaration, the dance. For example when she is in Ethiopia in the midst of a civil war, or in Kashmir against the Pakistani marauders, she wants to face the adversary (for, to her, 'Bandits are human too') but the commander will not allow her so near the danger zone. The visit to Palestine while the battle raged and flight into Chung-King while bombs rained. Actually that is the extraordinary aspect of such courage, as Gandhiji would say, nothing evil ever happens if you have rare courage, everybody welcomes her. 'She is from Gandhi's country' . . . the bandits of Ethiopia cried out and she was treated as an honoured guest.

This is the strange fact about Kamaladevi; she touches the limits of herself only to drink of its purity, I almost said, of its sweetness. And so it is when she meets the extraordinary humans she has met, almost in every field of human activity open themselves to her and reveal their most secret natures. There is, for example, Vincent Sheen she meets at Gandhiji's funeral. He knew, he says, that Gandhiji was going to be shot—so he had to be there on the spot, as it was. But how did he know the event was going to be. 'To me', Vincent Sheen says, 'My inner eye saw it as my sixth sense became keenly aware of it.'

But it is when she touches all, that she dips into herself most naturally. Drawn always by music and the spontaneous images that music creates, she discusses this with O.C. Gangoly and remarks, 'I grasped his belief that the reality lies behind external appearances.' And then she asks, almost like a child, 'how does one conjure up this reality' and he answers 'why through the very air around' and she says to him 'Only Indian art draws its inspiration from a single core, the universe as a totality...There is no basic difference in the various divergent manifestations of life such as human, animal, vegetable worlds, because a single life line is running through them all.'

So that when she meets Balasaraswati, the great dancer, Kamaladevi's whole universe of feeling is opened up. When the dancer's eye caught her presence 'What they roused were not fires but an inner quiet that comes from a sense of fulfilment. It was almost like (the) two (of us) floating together.' Later they become very great friends and one day when Kamaladevi was visiting the dancer, Balasaraswati was playing with her grandchild. 'She (Balasaraswati) was just a woman happily watching the child trying to be the big Bala, seeking approval, a happy nod from a smiling face . . . a giant of an artist, yet at heart a sweet simple woman.' The dancer is the dance. That is what this memoir is *all* about.

That she would ask me to write this preface, is the gift of a great privilege, so I have been utterly honest.

Dhvanyalaka
Manasagangotri
Mysore
December 31, 1985

RAJA RAO

Contents

1

Does man make the age or the age make the man, is a question that has dangled tantalisingly before us over the ages, more as a provocation than to find an answer. Would my life have been different had I been born in another age rather than the early part of this century? We think the 20th century is the most exciting. We like to flatter ourselves as superior to those who went before us. But those with any concept of history realise this is an absurd delusion. For man has been a creature of daring, adventure, invention, changing and adding, rejecting and destroying. When one looks back one is overwhelmed by the vast panorama of the history of man.

Nearer home India too has a refulgent history, marred no doubt as all history is, by dark patches, for nature itself around us is a scene of light and shadow.

It is in this context that I wish to narrate a little page from this big tome, the social history of our time, illustrated through my life and that of some others who filled its momentous pages. I feel greatly privileged that I can talk of some of the significant events and of some of the personalities not as distant historical figures cast on an imaginary screen but as part of my own life and my own contemporaries with whom I shared some of the adventures, hopes, fears, sorrows, from whom I drew inspiration, sustenance, above all, warm companionship.

Mine has been perhaps an eventful life, crowded with some usual and some unusual experiences. But it is neither possible nor necessary to narrate or to project every detail. Moreover as it touches the lives of other personalities it is necessary to be objective and dispassionate, something not too close, yet not too wide off the mark. Whatever the modern trend may be, I do not think that in a life story one is required to lower the barriers of the discreet reticence which govern our everyday life and affairs. Life is like a landscape touched with patches of light and shadows as the day passes over it. There are moments when they leave a mark, other times they just touch and pass. I feel I am justified in deciding what seemed vital and what was not.

Whatever else I may have lacked, I have always received warm affection in abundance. It has not only overwhelmed me but made me very humble. The load of debt has weighed heavily on me always. But obviously one cannot name even all those who have been close to me or have meant a great deal to me as a story like this is not a catalogue. Their absence is not an omission. Like the stars they are all there pulsating in the sky though they may not all be discernible.

What I feel I think can be best expressed through this poem by Prem Kirpal :

> Inside my heart there are such people,
> glimpsed here and there in far-flung space,
> emerging from the flux of time,
> created in sweet fancy's flame.
>
> They are the best of my treasures,
> strong sources of my life's sustenance,
> companions of my dreary hours—
> dear radiant friends who can never fade.
>
> I bless these souls and bless myself
> and ask of the gods that be
> to grant such shrines of love and beauty
> to the lonely hearts wherever they be !

I like to think that though the circumstances of one's birth may be accidental, they can be made purposeful. True, had I not been born in the family and the social setting in which I was, I may never have been able to carve out the kind of life that I did. Nevertheless, the spanning of it had to be my own. And it was by no means an easy walkover at any point. I had to contend with considerable obstacles, if I may so describe my continuous and at times heart-breaking struggles.

The relations who influenced me the earliest were largely from my mother's side, for in her family the women had what seemed adequate education which was rather unusual then, for I am talking of the early 20th century. Even more important, they had cultivated what I may call their natural gifts and talents which to me were more exciting and great sources of perpetual delight. They could chant, recite and sing, were deft with their hands and could make a variety of functional objects and gorgeous decorations out of natural materials like grass, leaves, fibres, flowers, nuts, etc. for festive occasions. For each occasion called for special creations.

Flowers figured a great deal in our life. They had a special social symbol. Not only were they indispensible in ceremonies and worship as an embodiment of one's devotion and respect for the one to whom they were offered, they were also a synonym for courtesy. Whatever else you may offer to a guest, flowers had priority; and even before the tea or coffee was started, one had to make sure the floral offerings were there. If not, you dashed someone off to the bazaar for them. Normally a daily delivery was the prevailing custom, which showed how essential flowers were.

Festivities were natural happy occasions when the art instinct in everyone in the household came into full play. Even planning them was exciting; arranging existing things with a keen eye on achieving a total aesthetic; therefore pleasing effect. The emphasis was on homemade things. Now cheap artificial material objects are displayed under the glare of vulgar multicoloured lights, with loud music blaring through a megaphone—altogether a lurid experience repellent to all sensitivity.

An exciting task was preparing paper lanterns for Diwali. Each year new patterns had to be devised. Each household would vie with another for striking out the most spectacular. People would throng the streets moving from house to house to see what was new. Some houses attained a standing reputation for their variety.

In Dusserah, the ten days were full of excitement. The old dolls and artefacts were brought out for display and new ones were laboriously prepared out of the natural materials found in the garden. The banana tree was an inexhaustible treasure house from which an infinite variety of articles were made. For its fibres could be woven into numerous shapes. Treasured craft objects of exquisite workmanship were taken out reverently from their safe custody for display.

A most charming celebration was sailing boats on Makarasankranti day. The boats were made from the trunk of the banana tree cut into pieces with a depression made in each by scooping out a little to stick into it broomsticks with the tips wrapped in oil soaked wicks which were then lit. Then they were placed in an elegant wide mouthed vessel filled with water, where these delicate boats could sail. The water itself was decorated with many coloured flowers and the scene became a fairyland.

Janamashtami was another occasion when the creative talent was stimulated. Some women celebrated it elaborately over a week. Each day a scene from Krishna's life was laid out in a tableau form with small statues, figurines, profuse use of flowers, fruits, nuts, grass, scented roots, all ingeniously manipulated to form a variety of forms and many different attractive scenes. Lighting effects were cleverly contrived just with small earthen and brass oil lamps, lit up with wicks, for there was no electricity in those days. The occasion called for creative genius and mental ingenuity to get the large variety of scenes aided by the magic of lights. Fabulous costumes were prepared using simple fabrics turned into little rainbows through the tie-dye process and patchwork stitching. In several houses, the scenes were changed every day and drew crowds for viewing, as do current exhibitions.

The month of Shravan, glistening with gentle showers, provided us a different but equally stimulating pursuits. Every Friday and Sunday young girls poured out into streets almost ravaging every flower garden to fill their baskets. Here the ingenuity lay in weaving the flowers into different kinds of garlands and posies with blades of fresh green stalks stuck in to embellish them. After offering them to the Tulsi plant, these garlands were offered to the elders of the family to seek their blessings, then to friends to wish them well. In my memory the hunt for the flowers was as exciting as weaving them into garlands or tying them into posies.

For the actual participation in these festivities we had to dress up, even adorn ourselves with jewellery, for every festival was that important.

The Tulsi plant became the centre of rituals once a year when Tulsi's marriage was performed and the platform was lit up with little clay lamps. The Tulsi plant had a permanent artistically structured platform which was decked and rituals performed on it through the entire month of Shravan when we too decked ourselves. This has tied me to the

Tulsi plant with an emotional link and made it a close companion. I would feel a sense of emptiness without it in my garden.

The Gauri puja was one of my favourites. This particular Gauri used for the occasion was drawn in dark lines on a plain sheet of paper, the head and hair being indicated by jet black strokes. It was never painted over in colour and yet made one of the most explicit pictures in folk style. The face had large wide eyes whose depths seemed to be pools of affection and had a kind of luminosity. This paper-Gauri was placed flat on a cushion made of banana leaves, stuffed with grass and tied with banana tree fibre. The fibre strings in turn made definite patterns as they went winding round the package. If one did not have the time to make the cushion it was available for sale. Today that delicate Gauri and leaf cushion have vanished, leaving us the poorer for it. Instead a garish face in multi-colours stuck on a cardboard piece is what is on sale. At that time every festive occasion was a provocation for creativity, for beautifying was a compelling custom. Decorations on the floor in front of the house and where one squatted to eat, or on the walls, varied according to the season and the occasion. After one learnt the basic elements of this customary art, one could copy fresh ones from books, or innovate, keeping to the alphabet and observing its grammar.

There was a lot of fun and frolic even on solemn occasions, and a variety of home entertainments and diversions. Take the marriage, at which today the prestigious fare offered outside of eats is a serious music or dance performance, often indifferently listened to or watched. The time I am talking about, jokes were played on some chosen victims, one of whom had to be the bridegroom, who had to be provoked to a battle of wits. A popular game was to accuse the bridegroom either of stealing or masquerading, ultimately leading to the summons of a community panchayat to try the accused or alternately the modern court scene with professionalised legal battles when the bridegroom was very much on his test. Or, a valuable object belonging to the bride was hidden, some mysterious hints were dropped as to the spot where it was hidden. Then the hunt would start. If the groom could not spot it, he was in disgrace and expected to hang his head and apologise to the bride for his unworthiness.

To me the best was the story telling by professionals. Occasionally scenes from folk plays were enacted, some well known actor being the big draw. Puppet shows were most popular with young and old alike. What a far cry from the wedding of today where gifts, particularly if they are of foreign make, are exhibited as a worthy diversion, notwithstanding the deadly shadow of dowry and the dread aftermath that may follow, hanging over the glitter of lights.

In our resentment to the several unhappy customs of the past, one is apt to forget some of the nicer ones. For instance, girls were taught to be self-reliant in their domestic domain. The home crafts were a must; stitchery, embroidery and culinary products, all of which also provided ample stimulus to their imagination and inventive faculties. True, they were emotionally moulded and mentally conditioned to be wives, mothers, housewives, which meant they had to fulfil enormous physical and social responsibilities. But are most girls of today psychologically so very different ?

For while a few may train for professions, the vast majority set their sails for the conventional marriage career. The main difference is that the girls of today enjoy a much longer childhood while in the past the girls were called upon to shoulder family burdens very much earlier. Towards this however they were consciously trained, physically and psychologically.

I had come to learn from experience in my own family that where the man proved unreasonably obstinate and the wife made all effort to adjust, she was often not a weak character; in fact she was strong in herself and proved a tower of strength to the other family members, winning their confidence and respect. I recall an aunt of mine—though now gone in age, still had an ethereal kind of beauty, petite in stature, with a glow on her face. She had had a thin married life; the husband having become mad early and died, leaving her with a small brood of children to rear on slender resources. Yet she was a reservoir of strength to the entire family. She was sought out in a crisis, sent for in any serious illness. I did that myself when I felt depressed or was in trouble. We felt a kind of strong power radiating out of her. Ironically enough she was the only one in the family who carried the obvious signs of widowhood. She explained to me that her husband's family was blindly orthodox and had insisted on the ugly disfigurement. She had resisted but had ultimately struck a bargain with them, for the alternative was quitting the house, leaving the children behind. Legally she could claim nothing. She indicated she would stay on their terms, but she would brook no further interference; she would live the way she wanted, bring up her children her own way. At some stage my father discovered her plight and helped her to set up on her own, guiding her to handle her limited resources and the children's education. But the experience seemed to have burnt into her, leaving a patch of bitterness that was carefully hidden. Before me she would burst into a rage more out of sorrow than anger. She confessed she felt utterly humiliated, but she saw no purpose in taking it out on anyone. I often dwell on that little figure, with its sweet, powerful voice which sang, recited, narrated fabulous stories with a captivating allure. She had the strength to salvage something of her personality, be able to give strength to the weak, solace to the disconsolate, even though she looked like any custom-ridden widow. I realised what that meant, for the word 'widow' was then used as a term of *abuse*. 'You son of a widow' was a term of withering contempt.

I could fill pages about my rich experiences, learning about seasons, flowers, trees, the journey of the sun to the north, then the south, what effect it had on us, our habits, food, clothing, why these cosmic changes were important enough to be noted in our calendars. We recited the beauties and significance of each season. The month of Ashad even today tingles me with exhilarating memories of a world overcast with jet black clouds, their distant roar as they approached to empty themselves in sheets. The day the *Mrigasirsha* star reigned would be the rainiest day. The star was so named because on that day the weight of the torrential showers would press down the head of the animal. Thus in my young imagination, a link was struck between the stars and the creatures on the earth.

I have known no experience comparable to the thrill of the strange darkness which enveloped the bright day when the fierce south-west monsoon was about to break, the stunning sound of falling water, which could go on for days with no break. In my emotional make up, it is an experience with few parallels and one that has left an indelible mark, something I could relive over and over again, with the same excitement. It is such experiences that teach one not to be overawed or to feel defeated by the powers of Nature, but urge one to try to come to terms with them. No wonder early man defied these challengers, making them benefactors instead.

Like in the village, in different sections of my home-town, there was a raised platform built around what was considered a sacred tree, usually the peepul. It would indeed be a large spreading tree, throwing a wide shade. Generally in the afternoons people from the neighbourhood, most of them women, gathered here to listen to old books being read, old texts interpreted, at times devotional songs sung to the accompaniment of little bells and castanettes and a drum. The narratives, whether stories read or related, or just discourses, were usually made current by likening them to present events or sometimes lending a personal touch to the episodes. As there was one such platform, locally called *Katta* beside the house of my aunt, it became normal for me to slip into this assembly whenever I went visiting her or if I was alerted of a special function. On festive occasions the place used to be decorated with green mango leaf garlands, the gorgeous palm leaf flowers and a host of others, while it glittered with tiny wicks nestling in clay cups, like nesting glow-worms. The *Katta* otherwise served as a community centre, where the householders of the neighbourhood could get together. It was also a shelter for wayfarers, for the magnificent peepul tree offered protection as well as mental relaxation. Water was always provided in two big vessels, to drink, bathe the face, wash the feet. A generous household also kept a block of jaggery, for it was believed this helped when a heated body had to consume a lot of cold water. It added a gentle flavour to the water so unlike the stringent tastes the bottled drinks offer. The wayfarers could sit or recline, even have a short nap. One of the finest aspects of this was the fact that both the givers and the partakers remained equally anonymous. No ringing the doorbell, to try to establish one's identity, above all bonafides, for everyone today, seems a suspect, known or unknown.

The *katta* has faded away from the community life as a common shelter. In me it has left a tinge of regret for nothing quite like it has evolved or emerged as a substitute. It has hardly a place in the harsh bustle of today. Card parties for the women of leisure and coffee houses for the youth have sprung up like hybrid growth to while away time that seems to hang heavily.

My memory of those days is also filled with numerous aunts, for elderly ladies were always aunts. They usually made surprise visits, for in those days no appointments were made over telephones, now a frustrating experience that kills the joy of expectancy. The unexpectedness itself had a thrill of its own. Often a long dull evening would be enlivened by such a visitor. For there would be narrations of humorous skits, posing of conundrums, puzzles and the excitement of finding answers and a whole lot of lively activities, each opening up a fresh new experience. Or the old books were brought out to continue from where we had last left off, or start on a new epic, or a new period of history.

I shy away today as I see children gorge on the comics. The usual facile comment that counters our displeasure is "It is the generation gap". Why was there no generation gap when I was young ? In fact, in my generation we matured naturally, painlessly, free from the nervous tensions both generations are subjected to in seeking companionship. Why did we love, treasure and cling to elders ? How we relished what they gave us !

I believe the physical surroundings are as significant as the personal in moulding us. I grew up in a most beautiful countryside. It seemed like a well designed landscape. Nestling right under the rising Western Ghats, the town carried their stamp on it, its roads rising and falling. Two rivers encircling it, each holding one side in its arms. Across the beach was the Arabian Sea. An unbelievable combination of all one could ask for. So thickly wooded was the region when one looked down from the hilltop at the town, that one saw nothing but thick greenery, not a trace of a structure, as though the bustling town had vanished by the waving of some magic wand.

This is part of the land reclaimed from the sea by Parsurama, who is the first known land reclaimer. One should look beyond the mythical story to learn how he made the sea recede back to throw up the present West Coast.

Later in the 18th century Hyder Ali conquered and turned the picturesque port into a naval arsenal and dockyard for the entire coast. Tippu Sultan, his son, improved on it, docked even big warships, each mounted with over 50 cannons.

Equally scintillating was its early history. Over the centuries this Dakshina Kannada district, whose historical name was Tuluva or Tulu Nadu, a patch tinier than the palm of a little hand in the huge body of India, has had great religious waves pass over it—Buddhism, Jainism, Catholicism. Jainism still continues to be a force, vividly projected through its magnificent temples, one of them with thousand pillars of exquisite carvings and significant inscriptions; above all is the awe-inspiring sixty-foot high statue of Gomata or Gomateswara, whose sanctity is still kept alive through fantastically elaborate rites performed periodically, drawing devotees from all over the world. Catholicism is an educational and cultural stream while one of its monumental churches—St. Alousius with its exquisite frescoes is a testimony to its antiquity.

Historical records prove TulaNadu's ports traded with far-off lands suchas Greece, Rome, Egypt, the Mediterranean and later with the Arab countries, the last still going on. It also came under the suzerainty of varied dynasties : the Kadambas, a Brahmin ruling clan who planted a Kadamba tree before their house; Chalukyas, Pallavas, Rashtrakutas, Hoysalas and finally the Vijaynagar empire. Through all this the region once known as Tulu Nadu comprising of small kingdoms, contrived to retain its own identity, with its own succession of dynasties, only paying tribute when pressed, to an overlord. Women also figured as rulers and some even led armies and fought successful battles. The most outstanding was Abbaka Devi who won resounding fame while she was queen of Ullal, today a suburb of Mangalore city, who powerfully resisted the Portuguese invaders for nearly three decades, refusing to pay any tribute to them.

The basic culture of Tulu Nadu still holds sway, notwithstanding the ponderous external pressures exerted on it, and life centres around the Bhuta religion. (It is too substantial and pervasive to be termed as a *cult*). This .is not to be mixed up with demonolatry which is reduced to witchcraft or propitiation of devils. Bhuta still continues to receive impressive participation of the public, most of whom also worship the orthodox Hindu pantheon. Several of their old wooden temples are renovated with more durable material. Seva (offerings) are made by votaries at festivals, now disturbingly through a profusion of electrification! What is more, the votaries increase, consequently contributions increase proportionately, which proves that this folk religion satisfactorily serves large communities. We cannot but conclude that it must have tremendous vitality not merely to survive but dominate like a hardy perennial.

Because of our superficial knowledge of the primitive forms of religion, we are too often misled by the expressions used by those who practise them to define their beliefs. Their vocabulary too, often finds no parallel expressions in our own to operate on the same plane, so to say. We therefore find it hard to forge precise transcriptions of some of their terms. Their phraseology being limited becomes all the more exact. One has therefore to conjure up images rather than outline them verbally. One such is the concept of "Bhuta".

In Dakshana Kannada every village has a special place for its Bhuta known as Bhutasthan. The officiating pujari (priest) is a Billava, of the fisherman's caste.

The concept of Bhuta is however rather complex for it is also tied with ancestors. In fact, the term 'Bhuta' literally means a ghost, the spirit of the departed. The innumerable shrines scattered throughout the district are dedicated to the spirits of deceased celebrities who in their lifetime had acquired a more than local reputation as benefactors or for heroic deeds whose memory is thus kept green. There are also the spirits or Bhutas of the jungle, diseases and pestilence; others whose business seems to be only to play tricks and make themselves a nuisance; there are Bhutas who protect and guard the villages, especially the boundaries, very crucial in the old days. Some seem to evoke fear and awe like those representing dangerous diseases and have to be propitiated by various rites.

Inside the Bhutasthan are found wooden images of human shapes, or of various creatures from the tiger to the fowl, like the ox, the horse, the pig, as also a giant. These Bhutas have a legion of names. The most dreaded is Kalkutti, whose name lingers on the lips of the local people as one fearsome and indomitable. Kalkutti (meaning stone sculpture) according to local legend, carved the famous sixty-foot high Gomateswara, the Jain deity located in the district.

Local people of all castes believe in the Bhutas. Therefore one naturally finds strands of Hinduism in the Bhuta tales. For instance, one of the most important amongst the Bhutas is Brahmeru which is regarded as a corruption of Brahma. Some are regarded as the Ganas (attendants) of Siva and the Shaivite influence can also be traced in their song build-up, which mainly concerns Shiva and Parvathi. One kind of worship is a community one to which the public subscribe and share, named Kola, a private ceremony held in a house is Dema.

The main performer in this rite is the dancer, carrying a beautiful sword with a handsomely carved handle which he shakes and flourishes, jumping and dancing and trembling all the while.

The original Bhuta temples were of wood, constructed in a special style, very few of which survive. In the course of my hunt for traditional crafts, I found one of them still stacked with the marvellous giant size figures, 16 to 18 feet high, life size elephants, horses and other animals. I was horrified to find several such Bhuta figures lying out in the open, thrown away as they had decayed and could not be worshipped. Even in the damaged condition the faces looked alive, each projecting a different character. I succeeded in buying all of them and carting them to the Handicrafts Board Museum in Delhi.

This visit left me in a turmoil of anxiety, apprehensive of the sad fate which awaited those magnificent carvings. They were so strikingly powerful, boldly modelled, breathing vitality. The experts' verdict on them was: this style of carving was very distinctive, very rare and the figures would be *at least* 800 years old. Were these treasures to be left to pass into oblivion? Haunted by this thought, I revisited the temple and struck a bargain with the temple authorities. They were to hand over all the figures we selected for the Crafts Museum in Delhi and in return I offered to have them replaced with new figures in the same style. For we had found that the local craftsmen were excellent and could still turn out the same types. This was agreed to, for I reminded them that the Bhulis would be destroyed when they ceased to qualify for worship.

The new figures were completed most satisfactorily, but the exchange of the old and the new coincided with my leaving the Handicrafts Board and I found to my dismay that I had left behind a hornet's nest. The senior officers in the Handicrafts Board were hauled over the coals by audit, for what they defined as blatantly robbing the government. Rotten old figures literally thrown away as only fit for fuel, had been taken over for the museum, whereas the new figures made from fresh wood were bartered away to the temple. Incidentally, some local politicians, in particular legislators, decided to dabble in this spicy situation. On the one hand they sent an accusation against me to the Prime Minister that I was taking away sacred images from ancient temples, bluffing the owners. On the other hand, the temple authorities were stirred up by being ridiculed for so foolishly giving away precious antiques costing lakhs, for almost nothing. The temple authorities were now enraged believing they were tricked and would not allow the old figures to move out even though the new beautiful ones had been installed.

I was called upon to resolve this situation and I found myself between these cross-fires, a criminal twice over. To cap it all, Dr. Stella Kramrisch, the noted American Indologist, borrowed two of these ancient Bhuta sculptures for a prestigious exhibition, to travel all over the United States, insuring them for US $ 10,000. I faced a knotty situation, for all these transactions had been conducted verbally with no documents with signatures. One of the senior trustees of the temple who had been my colleague in the political struggle, successfully resolved the tangle. The Stella Kramrisch incident successfully silenced the audit.

As elsewhere, in this district too, the village community was, and still is, composed of numerous castes each having its own hereditary occupation or profession. Though in the early days the boundaries of the caste distinctions were more marked and the occupational monopoly of each caste was generally not encroached upon by others, the folk religion Bhuta seems to have helped promote a sense of social belonging among persons of various castes. Functionaries of each caste forming part of the village community had specific duties to perform at the time of the Bhuta festivals. This infused among the caste-fellows a sense of self importance with regard to the service they rendered to the community. At the time of the observance of periodical Bhuta festivals, the equality of all castes was reasserted, as it were, for on all such occasions the differences in rank and status were ignored. The institution of trance and oracle provided to one and all a sort of psychological security, for all those affected by problems, irrespective of the nature of such problems, strongly believed they could obtain divine guidance from the Bhuta. Contravention of caste rules, inter-caste disputes and intrigues could also be brought up before the presiding Bhutas and solutions obtained. Thus, the Bhuta faith established in the rural community a stable equilibrium economically, socially and culturally. Furthermore it provided encouragement for the continuance and development of certain rural sports which as in all old societies also included a mingling of arts and sports.

The ritual cock fight had gradually become a popular sport. Similarly, the ritual of Kambala, the buffalo race, also developed into a popular sporting event of the district. The general belief among the votaries that Yakshagana Bayalata (literally a play performed in the field) would appease the Bhutas, provided much needed sustenance and encouragement to these arts. It is presumed that this folk religion initially inspired the growth and development of the more stylised Yakshagana, the current popular dance-drama of Karnataka and Andhra.

It has already been explained that each caste had its own distinct identity and functions, and thereby developed its own distinct cultural forms and expressions. The three outstanding castes are : Nalke, Panas and Koragas. Each has its own style of music, musical instruments, dances and related properties, costumes, headgears, ornaments, etc. Their main role is to propitiate a certain category of Bhutas through rituals. These are performed to certain dances, chief among them to the accompaniment of songs : Paddanas (song offerings). The heavy bells, tied at the ankle, 'gaggare' fill the air with musical resonance.

The Panas, Paravas and Pambadas too perform some of the Bhuta rituals to music and dances of their own. The Pana and Nalke have their own dance-dramas built around the Bhuta rituals which surprisingly enough have become quite stylised, far removed from the crude and primitive.

The Koragas, considered the lowest in the social rung, are really the most colourful of them all, as also the most important, for even to this day it is their drummers that lead in the front when the temple deity is taken out in a procession, which proves that originally caste at all levels was *functional*, giving equal importance to every socio-economic section of society, each of which had its own significant contribution to make, before the present rigid divisions and distortions were brought in. They have their own pantheon of deities to whom they perform their own rituals to the accompaniment of their own vigorous group dances. They decorate themselves gaily with wild flowers and ornamental leaves tied round their waists and perform to drums played by elders who could not dance any more. Music is rendered by a slender delicate flute carved out of a bamboo stump to which they sing melodies, punctuated by *le le le le—le le le le*. To this day those tunes haunt me, with the joyous *le le* entwined with a soft strand of melancholy.

Besides these there were other vital cultural forces in my background that nurtured me into what I now am.

Behind our house were fields that were an extension of the wide five-acre land on which the house stood. These provided me the exhilaration of watching the ceaseless cycle of sowing, the sprouting of the emerald rice shoots, their ripening into the golden yellow, with each successive season, each exciting in its own way.

After harvest when the fields were cleared there were even more exciting scenes, the field becoming the natural theatre, which presented a variety of folk performances, including the now noted and more sophisticated Yakshagana also known as Byalata (play in the fields). Mother, our family members and I were deeply interested in these indigenous forms. We showed them to visitors with great pride.

Yakshagana literally means a style of music, now turned into a dramatic theme worked out through dances with their own pattern of footwork to which are added flowing, flowery and often witty dialogues by the different characters in the play, a good part being extempore to highlight current events. The tints of the costumes distinguish the romantic and the villainous characters. The turbans have a special lotus form, while the size and shape of each is determined by the status and importance of the wearer.

The show was announced by beating on a sonorous drum whose sound could reach a long distance to alert and call the spectators who arrived carrying mats to squat on or for short naps as the climax came only just before dawn. Yet the audience sat on getting tenser as the crisis approached. Even children sat wide-eyed, and proved how deeply the audience got involved in the spectacle. Such dramatics moved my very depths.

While I had a physical background of natural beauty and cultural romance, I had an equally stimulating home. The house itself had large grounds, thickly clustered trees, palm groves, climbing creepers which converted the setting into an enchanting woodland. My family too was equally invigorating.

In my imagination my grandmother, mother's mother, was a colossus who strode across my life. She was one of the several unusual women that our country has produced from time to time. Though a mother of seven, she seemed emotionally rather detached as though settled on a mountain top, while her progeny and their own brood with a myriad problems tossed around below. This capacity to be still, to be relaxed, full of a silence that was pregnant not empty, which stirred me, my mother explained, came of deep meditation. I was stirred by an interest in it, hoped this would soothe my restless spirit, and Mother tried to guide me. It did me help.

Grandmother's absorbing interest was in books and learning. The main hall served as a library where every afternoon she sat with a few sagacious looking gentlemen, as one of them read from the books piled up. Then they went into discussions. The scene fascinated me and I liked to sit in the group wanting to be one of them though I could not follow them. When no one was around I would struggle with one of the books and pretend to read it, and it gave me rare pleasure. Seeing my keen interest, grandmother encouraged me with a broad smile. "Books are lifelong friends," she said, "and will stay with you in faith, teach you many truths, and enrich your mind." Gradually she tried to open up my mind with short chats "taste the tiny drop of its essence and you will continue to linger on it," as she put it. It was only later that I grasped the full import of it, for I realised the "tiny drops" as she described were the real essence of our philosophy, the foundation from which flowed a way of life. Thus was I provided a lasting background of tradition to lend value and flavour to the varied facets in my life.

She was amongst the unusual in other ways too. Earlier she had travelled all over the country with her husband and though she was now alone and well advanced in age, she still continued her travels. visiting her daughters. The railway lines were only just being laid and had come within a hundred miles of us; nevertheless, she travelled alone by boat, by bullock cart, and even on foot ! The journey from home started by crossing a river in a boat, usually by night, stretching out through the length of the boat and going off to sleep. The boatmen were Moplahs, a sturdy and fiery community generally forbidding looking. Further there were infact several more rivers to be crossed as also jogging in bullock carts. She came back from these trips in radiant spirits, though physically rather wan. "Some women think that I am a bad woman because I go alone and put myself in the hands of the Moplahs," she once told me. She described the boatmen as also cart drivers as gallant who took care of her with respect for her age. Today as I travel by plane, train or car and get mercilessly pushed around, I tell myself I should be a teeny, weeny chip of that old block.

One indelible last memory I have of her is when her only son died. She sat dry eyed, aloof, a figure of strength, while all the sobbing and wailing went on around.

My mother was probably the closest to her, for they both shared a love for books, and an almost insatiable hunger for knowledge. But my mother, while she was interested in philosophy, sought it through modern teachers like Ramakrishna, Vivekananda, Swami Ram Tirth. Though born earlier, she was emotionally and intellectually of the 20th century and an involuntary social crusader. Even as a girl she exhorted her companions to study. Several elderly women confessed that but for her exhortation, they would have remained totally uneducated. She visited homes and read social literature to the women, dilating on their low position, discriminatory laws. Of crucial importance was her reading newspapers to them. Even more important, to encourage those who could read, young and old, to get and read the right kind of material, particularly current newspapers and magazines as they proved extremely stimulating and educative and opened up new vistas and widened their world. She kept projecting before them pictures of struggles by women in other parts of India and countries beyond. This began to make visible impact especially on those who were rather cloistered physically. Their burden lightened when their problems were shared with women over the world. In her town she was the first to set up a women's association, the Mahila Sabha, largely to propagate women's rights. This still continues as one of the premier bodies in the district.

She had however equally strong cultural tastes. She could play several instruments and learnt Hindustani, Karnatak, as also Western music through the piano, very rare in her time. She was proficient in several Indian languages which enabled her to keep up an ever widening cosmopolitan circle of companions as also a fairly wide correspondence. Her avid passion to learn something new never abated, and she never felt too old to master a language or an instrument at any age. For instance she continued with her music when I was learning as though making up for the opportunities and facilities she had missed in her early days.

I did not inherit this zeal but I was stirred by a social awareness as she kept her accent on the low position to which women had been depressed and the many grave injustices they laboured under. She was sometimes bitter about it, though sourness was not a constant element in her composition. She drew before me a vivid panorama of the women of the early Puranic period, but did not stress the conventional line of holding them up as model husband-worshippers. In fact they were presented as *personalities* with individualities of their own. She described learned Puranic women such as Gargi and Maitreyi, the former challenged the famous learned sage Yagnavalkya to a debate and the latter, who was his wife, demanded that he share his knowledge with her.

But largely her heroines were the current fighters for women's freedom. For instance, Pandita Ramabai was described as of unusual calibre and put one in mind of Gargi. She often reminded me that she was from our district and that I could become a crusader like her. She admired Annie Besant equally warmly and once when the latter was visiting our town took me to her and asked her to bless me that I may become a freedom fighter like her. Of course, years had to roll by for me to grasp what that wish meant.

She had a strong streak of fearlessness in her and she tirelessly tried to imbue this spark into me. She saved me from the usual fear children have of the dark, of ghosts and such superstitions. As soon as I could travel alone, she encouraged me to take trips by myself. She would go to pujas, bhajans, harikathas alone at night with a lantern, returning at midnight, scoffing at stern warnings.

Once when I was attending school, a crude-looking, unkempt man began to try to accost us girls as we walked home. After a couple of days when I happened to be alone I spotted him and taking courage in both my hands I walked slowly leading him by keeping close, towards the Chowk where the police guard was on duty. Then I turned facing him and he put out his hand to snatch my chain, thereupon I raised an alarm running towards the policeman who rushed hearing the alarm and leapt on the thief and caught him. When I told mother of my exploit she gave me a pat, with a proud look in her eyes, a very rare experience for me. I hardly ever seemed to measure up to her expectations.

Mother had started the first women's body in the town, Mahila Sabha, to bring women together and make them discuss their problems, their disabilities and seek ways of resolving them. She also made available to members her large collection of books, journals, newspapers. The discussions were later lightened by music, vocal or instrumental. Later outdoor modern games, such as badminton were added and I took to it with great zest. The Mahila Sabha is still going strong and just celebrated its 75th year.

Mother was reserved and of retiring disposition, rarely indulged in gossip, never talking unless she had something to say. I am equally unconcerned, even as my mother was, of some of the conventions which are a must, like attending formal functions and parties because one is told one must be seen at such gatherings if one wishes to survive socially. Half a century has passed by since, and I still find that those who need me seek me, and those I want, I seek them.

She was a stern disciplinarian and subjected me to severe do's and dont's in my daily life. Some of her own ways and habits probably shaped my disposition and mental attitudes.

Today I am amused when people wonder how mother allowed me to actively participate in Civil Disobedience, did not she panic, considering how over careful she was while bringing us children up. On the contrary when I was in jail, she went in for picketting herself, the only activity in which she could participate.

Mother taught me at a very early age to read and write two Indian languages outside my mother tongue, each with a totally different script. It was done through letter writing, not text books. I was deeply depressed and lonely when my sister to whom I was closely attached, left me periodically after her marriage. She had endeared herself to me by playing with me as though she were a little girl herself, even though years senior. Mother seeing the situation braced me up by suggesting that instead of fretting for the far off dear ones, I could keep up communication with them simply through letters. First, the letter was written on a slate until I mastered the alphabet. Later, my sister used the same method to encourage me to write compositions, narratives, experiences, imaginary tales. A stimulus was there to communicate with a dear one far away. By and by I began to write when I felt moved to do so, and fill exercise books. Like reading, it has served me not only as a fruitful preoccupation but also a relaxation. Today no matter how great the depression or tension, writing melts it away. I have never known boredom.

Though I could now read myself, hearing the ancient tales read was still more exciting with the reader bringing each character alive with a vividness which the reader evoked. Parts were chanted, some stanzas sung, making each tale a kind of drama.

I however disliked school and loved to wander in the large grounds which held an endless allure for me. Here I could watch the sunlight penetrating through little broken patches like a fugitive seeking a pathway, glistening on the damp leaves, offering me an enthralling sight.

Equally thrilling was the warbling of birds, sounds that changed from season to season, and which had a special fascination for me. In fact I had this bird singing captured by recording it. To make it even more exciting, the wood had its share of snakes, one of them occasionally finding its way to nestle on the cool floor of the bathroom. We children were however warned not to dread snakes, for many were not poisonous and rarely harmed unless threatened. We were therefore alert to any rustle under dry leaves when we walked.

In this seclusion, one tends to build a dream world of ones imagination that has no relation to any reality. Time-space-events seem to span centuries—characters that had become faded memories came alive. I clothed and embellished them. I became one with heroes, martyrs, devotees, common folk. Out of the churning of all the ingredients an element of lasting value would emerge, not related to any particular period or place to take me out of all constraining limitations, in fact fill me with a fresh sense of fullness. To tear away from this to sit cooped up in a classroom became a dreaded spectre. Father protected me for a long time from the school. He believed children should have freedom to develop their innate talents and not to be put into a straitjacket.

Besides the woods, I had one other favourite spot, the cowshed which fortunately for me was large, airy and sunny for I loved to be with the cows. They fascinated me, in fact they still do. The Indian cow to me is the most beautiful creature, and I have seen cows all over the world. What I felt was different from my feelings for animal pets, and we had quite a menagerie of them from a monkey to guinea pigs and rabbits. But to me the cow was the dearest, it was a human, with whom I enjoyed a unique companionship. When I talked to the cows, their eyes showed a quiet understanding. I confided to them my little problems which of course became bloated in my childish mind, and through those extraordinarily expressive eyes they showed sympathy and invariably nodded their heads. I envied the calf who nestled close to its mother and of course plucked lovingly at the teats. Completely emotionally overcome I once tried to do that and as invariably happens, I was caught at it by mother. The most horrifying part of the aftermath was having my mouth disinfected—from the sublime to the ridiculous !

As time passed however, mother became desperate over my cutting school. She was fully convinced that women never came into their own except by their own effort and for this a strong foundation of education specially professional, was indispensible, for that alone would make them economically independent. So one morning I was enticed out seemingly to see some festivities but driven straight into the school, which I soon found had its own stimuli, excitement, and an outlet for whatever creativity I possessed. Here was my introduction to western music, eurhythmic dances, above all, dramatics. I was not only encouraged to learn western music but also to sing in public. I loved to act and seemed to possess some talent for it. I was given important parts in the plays, an experience that brought me deep satisfaction.

It was not all play, song, act. The nuns enforced strict discipline but I have no memory of harshness or cruelty. If rules were broken, there was an effort to get behind why this happened. Punishment did not evoke revolt or resentment, though some of it struck me as foolish. For instance, a repeated offender was made to stay back after class hours to fill up an exercise book or sheets of paper with repetition of some rigmarole, which it seemed to me would make the culprit resentful rather than contrite. It seemed extraordinary how a rational community like these nuns could indulge in such irrationality.

The contact with the nuns however was beneficial in a wider sense on my burgeoning personality, for some of those school experiences left indelible touches on me. The nuns though highly professional were nevertheless very warm, friendly and human. If any day my usual bright self seemed dull, a nun noticing it would talk to me, subtly, unobstrusively, to find out what troubled me. Every talent I possessed was spotted and encouraged. Each of us was individually handled, never *en masse*, a visible respect for the individual.

A new element that was subtly injected into me by the nuns was voluntarily but consciously submitting oneself to severe discipline, such as exercising control over one's impulses, physical cravings, hunger, thirst, also physical pain and mental restlessness, observing silence and controlling speech. This was to be practised strictly within certain fixed hours to gain mastery, gradually trying to expand the limit. I tried to be as relaxed as possible during these practices and realised after a time I could stay relaxed and experience a sense of inner strength. In later years this exercise stood me in good stead, especially in the traumatic days of the political movement and the long periods in prison when I could withstand without breaking, the heavy demands made on my physical and psychological framework. In fact these stern practices have helped me to keep myself physically fit, endure long physical and mental strain. Even when I feel I am at a breaking point, I never show cracks, I look poised and at ease, though I may be in tumult within. I always remember my days with the nuns with deep gratitude.

Another abiding element of those days that left a mark on me was the life and personality of Jesus. He was not a character out of a story, or a myth. He was one of us, belonged to the suffering human community. The nuns with their singular devotion to Him made Him a living force. I had been very deeply moved by the elaborate, touching ceremony of young girls taking the veil, first dressed in resplendent bridal clothes, then lying on the floral cross, symbolising their dying to the worldly life and then appearing in the sombre habit of the nunnery. I remember in particular a bright radiant youthful girl, a gay companion of mine lying on the cross. When she left it, quite involuntarily I picked a fern and a red rose from the cross as a keepsake of a memorable experience. There still stands above my bed a simple wooden crucifix, an image that continues to mean so much to me. Though emotionally very deeply moved, I could not accept the idea of conversion of faith through a ritual or that baptism alone saved one's soul, which seemed to be more a superstition than a spiritual concept. I believe that if there is an ultimate liberation it can and should come through one's own conscious effort.

There were, however, apart from these elevating experiences other wide variants between the school and the home. I learnt the *English* English, which in fact was more than a mere medium. Unlike the English taught in English medium schools today, we learnt it through English teaching materials used in schools in England. When I learnt English it meant also absorbing English topics, descriptions and pictures of English countryside, homes, family life, in short a good deal of the English atmosphere.

We were compelled to speak only in English; use of the Indian language was banned by a rule. One may conclude that any trait of Indian culture was virtually blacked out. The dominant place in history was assigned to English history. The Indian history we learnt was a book by one Marsden, dyed deep in the Imperial Faith, according to whom Indians had been primitives, worshipping stones, trees, snakes, visually depicted by pictures of scantily clad, wild looking figures, prostrate before blocks of stone, stone snakes, etc. Shivaji was a brigand who looted people, and lots more of similar revolting stuff. Marsden's history continued in our schools even when my son went to school. By then revolt was in the air. He refused to buy this history book or learn from it. So he was sent out when history class started. This he did on his own, no prompting from anyone. I remember a foreigner questioning me once in my school days on Indian economy, and my startling the questioner by my answer : 'Indian economy, never heard of it !' That about summed up what I was learning of India in school.

There were also other overtones in the school's daily routine. A steady patriotism for England was generated and maintained specially through songs like 'Rule Britannia' in which warm tributes were paid to Britain, praying that she ever rule over wide lands and wider oceans, and 'Britons never shall be slaves', assuming it was their divine right to enslave others. All these paeans to British rule however left me cold, for my home influence was too strong. Mother was a staunch nationalist and had a lot of political literature around the house. I was told stirring tales of the heroes who sacrificed their lives for the country's freedom. Tilak's journal *Kesari* was like a Bible, and I was filled with agony and shame at his cruel incarceration, conjuring up his image languishing in Burma in the Mandalay prison. Many years later when I visited Mandalay and the cell where he was confined and wrote his commentaries on the Gita, that sharp, sad current seemed to run through me again.

The school brought a new and unexpected emotional element into my life. I started working seriously on western music at school. Unaccountably, from my childhood I had suffered from a strange diffidence to sing and therefore shied away from music. But the nuns had a way with them. Almost unconsciously they were able to help me overcome this handicap and after some practise I was called on to sing first at school assemblies and later, to my surprise, even at public gatherings. As I began to take music more seriously, I took up piano very earnestly with a professional teacher.

The shedding of my diffidence in singing gave me a sense of release and I started to learn Hindustani music, both to sing and to play the *Sarangi*—a predominantly male monopoly ; for me however it was the only instrument to render Hindustani music faithfully. My teacher for both was a pupil of Abdul Karim Khan and his renderings had dim echoes of the great master. In his easygoing manner he straight-away plunged me into *Khayal.* He could not be bothered starting with basic notes or any fundamentals of music. When Mother worried at what she termed slipshod teaching, his impatient retort was "Is it not enough if I make your daughter sing in Abdul Karim Khan's style ?" Mother promptly got me a Karnatak music teacher who of course started me like I was an infant, on the primary notes. I resented being forced to go through very elementary lessons. Soon however I saw that Karnatak music was well structured with a definite grammar while Hindustani seemed more governed by each Gharana style. Gradually I felt as though the ground were opening up and tender shoots taking root. I felt blessed and I still continue to count it amongst the many blessings life has conferred on me. For the first time I was learning the roots and intricacies of Indian music.

The social awareness that mother had evoked in me on discrimination against women began to take on wider dimensions as I started to view the society around me. I would visit the houses of the workers living nearby, noting the difference in their life and ours. A big question mark now kept teasing me, why this ? A keen desire that I should try to narrow this gap in my own living stirred up : simplify my apparel, food, walk to school rather than ride in the horse carriage, a point on which mother and I had strong disagreement, but I held out.

In school I became conscious of some girls who seemed timid, retiring, unwilling to mix freely with others. I discovered after considerable effort, that they were the daughters of what are known as professional women. This was the first venture of their families to expose them to society outside their exclusive circle. They would go with me for walks to secluded places and in course of time open out and talk haltingly. Mother explained that this was a purely economic problem and if other avenues of living were provided through professional training, they would happily settle down. I felt distressed to think of these girls as helpless vict.ms of an established custom. Later whenever I came across the socio-literary term 'oldest profession' I recoiled at this cynicism, for it seemed to be something taken for granted, like washing floors. I did however see in my life-time some of these girls go in for higher education and take up other 'professions'.

The caste distinctions bothered me equally. Those lower down the social rung had their own culture, rituals, and way of life. Why were some termed depressed classes ? Too many questions confronted my enquiring mind. When I challenged them, I was asked vehemently whether a girl in her teens could catch orthodoxy by its neck and shake it out of its comfortable posture. All this however only goaded me to resolve I should take them on some day as a life mission.

The first blow that shattered my idyllic life was my father's death as the Halley's comet appeared in the sky and news came of King Edward's death. 'When Dhumketu (Halley's comet with a tail) becomes visible, prominent persons are struck down, whispered people, visibly overawed by this comet with its long white tail and forecasts of disasters.

An unexpected chapter unfolded before me. No will was found among Father's papers. Nobody could explain how it happened. We learnt that according to a family settlement now arrived at, the house we lived in and income from some small properties would be mother's income for her life time, with nominal amounts for the girls, a little extra for me as a minor. This almost brought mother's world crashing, for unlike father, a self-made man who rose to a high administrative position, she came from a landed aristocratic family with a fair amount of liberal spending and sophistication.

Until now we had a large household, several dependent relations around, as was the custom then. Poor students from rural areas unable to afford schooling and hostel fees, were provided for in this sprawling house. There were no students' hostels then.

Most of this establishment had to be disbanded, the house routine drastically altered. But it was Mother's self-esteem as a woman that was deeply hurt, a wound that rankled for a long time. All the vast property the largesse to no part of which we, the girls, qualified because of our sex, all went to a stepbrother whom we hardly knew except as a tycoon in a large faraway city. I woke up as from a daze. This was what mother had been alerting me about. Women had no rights and we should qualify to stake our claims and assert them. The question was not one of possessions but of principle.

Overnight I got transformed into a responsible woman on whom rested, so it seemed to me then, not only my own burden but a share also of the burdens of millions of other women like me. I felt as youngsters do, I must take up the banner and start on my march !

Mother's personality underwent very great cnange. ѕne assumed her role as head of the family in her husband's place with a deep sense of responsibility, although most of what this involved was completely new to her. She also had now to deal with the knotty problems of the properties. She did not relish being an absentee owner. She visited the cultivators on her property regularly, concerning herself with their problems. I saw how they could get out of their obligations and dues when they chose, appealing to her compassion. Years later when she sold off the properties, to leave the town, they wept like kids. In those days women of mother's circle were not known to do their own marketing, it was considered a man's job. Mother broke the convention. There were shocked comments. 'She goes to the bazaar like a man.' She shrugged it off. But before long others, the younger women first, took it up, confessing they found it more profitable and obviously equally enjoyable and instructive, and with 'You know men never really understand these things' was whispered aside.

2

Life had grown lonely for me after I lost my father. Emotionally my father had been my closest companion. He was of a gentle disposition, with a compassionate understanding of my rather rebellious spirit, patient with my wanderings and escapades. Above all, protecting me from having to attend school. "Let her commune with Nature in the woods, and dream. Now is the only time she will be carefree to dream," was his answer to my mother's strong protests. He was not fully right about the dreaming habit for it stayed with me all my life, often to cause disasters if not complete frustration. Now my affection began to twine around anyone who conjured up a father image.

At first it was my maternal uncle, who was a noted social reform leader of his time. As enthusiatic support, for womens' education and freedom grew, he began to take an affectionate interest in me because he found, as he said 'a bright and serious student'. He got me select books and encouraged fruitful reading. Because of his heart ailment, uncle began to lead a more retired life and even though I was still young he enlisted me for some of his secretarial work as also to play hostess to his innumerable guests. This brought me some of my most exciting and inspiring experiences. The visitors included several noted personalities of his time such as Gopalkrishna Gokhale, Srinivas Sastri, Bhandarkar, Sir Chandavarkar and his wife, Justice Ranade and his wife, Ramabai, Sir Tej Bahadur Sapru, Sir Sankaran Nair and his family and a whole lot of lesser known social workers. I was treated by one and all as though I were grown-up because of my position with my uncle. For I dealt with his letters, his meetings with visitors, programmes of his guests, etc. It was a great education to meet them and hear their discussions, and at meal times have talks with them. Alas it all ended when my uncle passed away.

After an interval an old family friend came to fill this void. Ramalingam was a more conventional person and his sensibility may have sometimes been disturbed for I was then at an age when I took pride in proving myself a social rebel. He was however uniformly kind and thoughtful, accepted my youthfulness with patience. With infinite delicacy and persuasiveness he started channelling my bubbling restlessness into fruitful channels. He initiated me into the organising and running of cooperatives. I attended important conferences with him to get a wider view of this field, from Cobbler's Coops to large Land Mortgage Banks. Cooperation as a way of life seemed to satisfy some social hunger within me, because of the two basic elements in its component : independence and self-reliance. But I was to adventure into cooperation in a big way only much later.

He was among the pioneering leaders in the cooperative field. Unlike today the cooperative field of that time was of a fine adventurous nature, attracting workers with idealism and a spirit of service. Unlike the present, they were committed to cooperation as a way of life and not a stepping stone to a political career.

The seed sown then however was to burgeon later when I cut new ground and initiated adventurous experiments in cooperation.

Then came Pithaji as I called him and as he was to me from the moment he accepted me into his family. This reminds me of Mira Behn telling me how she came to Gandhiji. 'I wrote to ask if I may come to him and he said "Yes". When I arrived I stood at his door and he called out to me, "Come my daughter", and I knew I had come home.' This is how I felt with Pithaji when I first came to him. Unfortunately my coming introduced later a storm into his life, for he was a senior Indian Civil Service official. When I became active in politics he was repeatedly warned by the authorities to disassociate himself from me. One of their strong arguments was that I was neither his daughter nor a relative and there seemed no justification for our close association. When I was imprisoned in the city, where he held office, they withheld even books which he sent me. I shall never know how grave was the harassment he was subjected to. But he firmly refused to break with me, for, he said, it was a matter of conscience. He had called me his daughter and he could not shut me out. Fate however intervened and he died in his sleep and was gone beyond the pale of any embarassment by the authorities.

This touched my very depths. I understood what genuine affection and friendship was. He did not however quite orphan me, he left a part of his inmost core, his daughter Sarojini. We have remained very close to each other, one may almost say nurture each other, for each draws strength and hope from the other. When I am weary and tired even a little time with her restores my normal balance. I feel a flood of warm affection flowing from her into my veins.

As part of the Mahila Sabha activities, outdoor games were also introduced. In those days it was not normal for young girls to indulge in outdoor games. Mother who favoured this wanted to encourage them just as she encouraged music, talks, debates. Mother provided badminton and I took enthusiastically to it.

As the Sabha concentrated on women's education and social problems, a ladies' club was set up in the town for recreation and games, including tennis, which became my game. I was the only member who played everyday with a college boy student from next door, who braved the jokes of his friends for being an active member of a ladies' club ! This interest of mine led me into taking part in matches and tournaments, which took me to Kerala which adjoined our district.

Quite unexpectedly this region opened out to me during my sports visits, a wonder world of performing arts, which were more numerous and varied than ours. It would take volumes to describe them. Apart from Thyayyam which corresponded to our Bhuta dance, there were scores of well established, greatly cherished folk forms—Kalis, as they were called, and precious remnants of ancient days, still surviving, were enacted in temples. Kudiyattam in Sanskrit dance drama, dating back to the 10th century A.D. performed by professional men actors called Chakyars and, women actresses, Nanghyars who recite the verses to which the Chakyars act.

Much is being written on the special significance of this ancient drama form. I would only like to stress the magnetic effect it has as one watches the performance. One is stunned into a kind of pregnant silence by the drama, the mere play of the face muscles, the many gambols of the eyes to the accompaniment of the subtle artistry of the hand gestures. The very absence of a dialogue adds power to these movements.

Krishnattam, the Krishna story, also in Sanskrit, is presented in a lighter vein through verses sung in Sopana traditional style music embellished by dance and simple gestures. It was dramatisation of a vision of Balgopal that the Prince Manaveda of Calicut had. To me it was an equally ecstatic experience.

Kathakali, comparatively the most modern and sophisticated of these performing arts impressed me more as an intellectual dramatic experience. It is both universal and ageless, speaking in a set stylised gesture language. Each face is frozen of identifying a certain *type.* The action alternates between the immobility of the mask-face and the galvanic air created by the super sensitive hand gestures, finished by the incredible delicacy of the foot work.

As I watched all these, I felt I had entered a long endless cave where one came upon treasure after treasure. They enriched my concept of drama and the theatre, for even though they were old, nevertheless fresh and dynamic.

The high water mark for me came with an invitation from Mahakavi Vallathol, the noted Malayalee poet. Kalamandalam, his centre for the revival of Kathakali, was then unknown to the outside world. I was excited to see his effort to make the traditional theatre current. True, several decades had to lapse for this to happen. In fact our 'colonial' minds detected the beauty of our past mainly after the 'superior' West began to seek them out. Vallathol was an imposing person, a magnificent figure with a massive head and a powerful body. He could easily be taken for a landed gentry from one of the Tharawad mansions. He had an air of freedom, no pose or put on airs, none of the sleek smoothness that hides mountains of tensions. He was easy to converse with and had quick ready answers, but in a kindly tone.

How did he come to attempt resurrecting Kathakali which was going into disuse, if not exactly dying? "It must have been a tremendous effort, for I find apathy and indifference towards traditional culture", I ventured to ask Vallathol. "It was a difficult venture. But I was confident of succeeding because of the innate strength and vitality in this form. It can never die. It is as you know, comparatively a newer evolution of the old. It has certain in-built characteristic qualities that remain ageless. Not only Kerala, not only India but the whole wide world will one day pay homage to this great art. Mine is no idle empty illusion, I feel it here inside me", he asserted. His soft gentle eyes which spoke of a simple nature, rather strange for a man of his physique and iron will, now flashed. He became quite dramatic, expressing more meaningfully with gestures, rather than words. It made one quite unmindful of the weakness of his hearing power. "I am going to give you a little taste of what I say", he added. After dinner we sat in the courtyard to watch 'Poothana Moksha', a familiar theme. But what I witnessed made me hold my breath. Watching Kalyani Kutty, now an Akademi award winner, then a youthful artist, do the ogress Poothana preparing to kill baby Krishna was an unforgettable experience. This story had always meant for me a bald cruel plot in which an ogress would naturally perpetrate her contemplated crime with ease.

But what I now witnessed was not that familiar story, but the very essence of man's daily struggle. Poothana is lured by the baby Krishna as she begins to feed him at her breast and she groans with pangs. The dual forces in each of us are perpetually locked in a struggle, tamely described as good and bad. This, the crux of life, was being enacted superbly. When it ended it were as though a vision had faded away leaving a lingering glow that stayed. Vallathol had given me the answer I needed.

When he invited me for his 60th birthday I was able to see the rendering of his poetic Miriam (Mary Magdalene), an exquisitely moving piece. It also revealed his socio-religious liberal bias in choosing an unorthodox non-Hindu theme.

This was also the first time I saw Mohini Attam, the special feminine dance of Kerala, executed by the famous Thangamani. It was an exquisitely gentle Lasya form in a Shringara Rasa which Natya Shastra describes as King among Rasas. An obvious characteristic of this dance is a unique graceful swaying of the torso, a soft completely feminine movement which seemed to blend itself in the undulating melodic rhythm of the drum - Edaka.

Sometime later I was able to have Vallathol's troupe perform in Bombay, but unfortunately in a modern closed theatre. Nevertheless much of its inner power caught the audience which sat spellbound. I saw that Kathakali had definitely caught on and come to stay.

One of my pleasant experiences in Kerala was getting to know some of the members of the Cochin Royal Family, especially the Consort, as the wife of Maharaja was known, and other ladies. Though they did not have the modern formal education, they were versed in the traditional knowledge, Sanskrit, music, dance, familiar with the ancient performing arts. The Maharaja too was a learned man, and I was privately told in confidence he knew sufficient English for a dialogue but deliberately muffed in his dialogues with the British officers, so that an interpreter had to be enlisted. In particular discussions like over the launching of the Cochin harbour and its complex, the Dewan confessed that he saw the enormous advantage the Maharaja enjoyed by this, for he insisted on the clear paraphrasing of those many ambiguous words and phrases in which the English language abounds and offers itself ideally as a perfect language for *diplomacy*. The Maharaja seems to have made many a clever central bureaucrat wipe his forehead in confusion.

The Royal household looked like a little kingdom to me, scattered over a large area, members living in houses of varying sizes, but mostly diminutive.

The intimate royal household was extraordinarily simple and the inmates amazingly unostentatious so different from the usual picture I had of Indian royalties.

A few years ago when I was doing a survey of Family Planning among women, I visited the Cochin palace grounds and expressed a wish to meet the young women. I was delighted to find a batch of bright, vivacious, self-possessed women. They were graduates, or specialising in various disciplines, all holding jobs or scholarships. They had not yet moved completely away from the tradition as they still lived in the same precincts. The old scene had however faded away as life moved on.

Annie Besant whom mother had held up to me as a guiding star, for a long time she had been striding across India's public life. She became the first woman to preside over the Indian National Congress in 1917. She had by now risen as one of the most outstanding world figures of her time. Even historically she has few women equals.

Though nurtured in a rigid conservative family she seemed to have soared into the very skies. Over a senseless execution of some Irish patriots, "legalising a judicial crime" as it was described, she came to henceforth support many human causes, as she confessed 'The flame of passionate love of liberty burst in my heart and has never flickered since.'

In her own life she went through a series of personal crises. Her baby daughter's serious illness ultimately ended her long stifled doubts in a blind religious faith and with that came her break with her bigoted Church husband. There followed several dark periods, including starvation. "I am glad I did experience it", she confesses, "for I now know the pangs of hunger."

She then threw herself into many worthy causes like feminism, civic rights, labour problems, unemployment, educational reform; crusaded against war, imperialism, capital punishment; started the New Malthusian League and was prosecuted for advocating birth control, turned to Socialism, but got frustrated. For everywhere she encountered hatred, while she was moved by a deep burning love of humanity. The lonely quest finally led her to Theosophy and to India. She describes how her trail ended in India : "I felt this was my home and realised for the first time I belonged to the people."

She threw herself into the Indian vortex with sincere passion and fervour. She travelled widely throughout India lauding in vivid terms Indian tradition and philosophy; to arrest the moving tide of westernisation and help the nation regain its own culture, encourage swadeshi, she established a network of national schools and colleges throughout the country, directed imaginatively and purposefully.

"Schools in England were the nurseries of patriotism," she declared. "Indian boys could not learn this from lives of Wellington or Clive. . . Let us not rob our boys of their heritage, nor turn their eyes away from the star-studded sky that arches over Bharatvarsha. Patriotism, the seed he brings with him at birth, must be nurtured into vigorous life. Patriotism grows in the nursery and the school, let our women teach it to our boys and girls — the young properly educated will make India strong."

She concentrated on the youth, promoting active youth leagues, youth gatherings to practise parliamentary affairs, provide public civic education by free discussion on problems of national interest. In this awakening, Indian womanhood found its rightful place, in furtherance of which she started the Women's Indian Association, a pioneering body which largely contributed to the modern Indian women's movement.

Her activities had been working on my heart and mind powerfully. Later actively working as Secretary of the Women's Conference, I had several opportunities to personally meet Mrs. Besant and come to know her. I was always pleasurably struck by her feminine appearance and a youthful buoyant spirit that made her seem young even as she aged in years. She was meticulously dressed, every little detail attended to, and wore light pastel shades that made her a unique personality.

Once while visiting her, she found me look ill, hot with fever. She got me to stay with her at the Theosophical Society and took great care of me.

We then had many quiet talks. I quoted how Bernard Shaw, a close friend and admirer of hers had described her as a woman of swift decisions. What had she to say? "From that arduous and painful struggle into which I entered in defense of my social training, with the sole desire to help the poor and the suffering, I have learned to stand alone, unmindful of ill-informed or self seeking opinion, to face approbrium for the sake of principle, social ostracism for the sake of duty, hatred for the sake of love". I asked her how she came to almost uncannily time her public speaking, how she mastered her emotions so that the ideas marched steadily and words flowed with no break, pause or propelling. She gave a gentle laugh, "You may not believe it but I prepare my speech with care, study, thought." I was surprised, for it sounded so spontaneous, with its free natural flow.

Inspired by Mrs. Besant's activities Mother placed at her disposal her own mansion in Mangalore with a request that a girls high school be set up there. It had been my dream to join one of these schools but unforeseen fate intervened to launch me on a very different course.

Tilak, a practical politician, had advocated the image of Home Rule as India's goal in 1895, but it was only in 1915-16 that Mrs. Besant resurrected it, vigorously exhorting leaders all over, even villages, stimulating the masses to demand Home Rule, self-government, undaunted by government warnings. Her slogan was 'a nation is ready for freedom the moment it is prepared to assume it'. To further this she formed the Home Rule League which several influential Congressmen including Pandit Jawaharlal joined. When the Government reminded her of the World War raging, she retorted 'What is the War for?' To her the war had infected urgency for national freedom. For her defiance Mrs. Besant was arrested and interned in June 1917; the result was more open defiance with even moderates joining the League. To stall a worsening internal turmoil, Mrs. Besant with her two aides were released, followed by a declaration that Britain's goal for India was 'Responsible

Government', a vague nebulous phrase. Mrs. Besant brushing it aside continued to build up the movement for self-government.

Through the Home Rule League a whole constitution for India was formulated to provide a clear picture of a free India based on local self-government on indigenous lines. She however aimed at a Commonwealth to replace the existing Empire, and not India's break with England.

When the long awaited Reforms came in 1920, the Home League could not accept them. On top of it came heavy repression ending in the conflagration of Jallianwalla Bagh. The peoples' mood underwent a transformation. The situation called for a fresh leadership and a new strategy.

My deepening interest in Mrs. Besant had also roused my interest in Theosophy, which had come at that period like a new breeze attracting several of the intellectuals. Even more, Mrs. Besant's own personality drew learned savants, and even where they may not have joined the Society, they were to be found in her circle. What drew me was Mrs. Besant's effort to reassert the core of our ancient philosophy and teachings, as current and purposeful in practise, not distant and abtruse. So much of what was worthwhile in the past could be equally of value today. This was to me a worthy objective for I was attracted to many of the traditional things in clothes, ornaments, articles of everyday use, personal and exterior decor. Aesthetically they seemed more satisfying: the chaste lines, the elegant shapes, pleasant to the touch. Hand crafted objects to me have a special feeling. The startling blending of colours, none of which conformed to the new ideas and norms that English education was injecting into our systems, laying a heavy hand of disapproval across the past as primitive.

I formed many friends in the theosophical circle, with some of whom my ties endured. Many theosophists were at the time in the forefront of new trends and movements. I was exhilarated as new paths seemed to beckon us to fresh pastures, burgeoning out afresh in a rather jaded old world that India had become in those days. We were now in the fast emerging renaissance era as we proudly called it.

My sister had become very ill as the result of mishandling of a small operation by an eminent English surgeon. As a last resort we took her to the Miraj Mission Hospital. Miraj was then what Vellore is today, noted for its doctors. While I was attending on my sister the days seemed long and rather depressing with anxiety. To relieve this gloom the American doctor incharge suggested I take interest in some of the long term patients, visit and chat with them, study some of the unusual cases. I was thus invited even to watch what the doctor thought were exciting operations. He thought I could learn some principles of nursing and conducting a hospital. For me this opened up a new world and also gave me some knowledge of caring for the sick and hospital requirements.

Later this came of some use for me when I decided to set up a hospital ward in the women's wing of the Belgaum Central Jail when I was an inmate there. I realised however that it was one thing watching a well shaped, smoothly run hospital routine, but quite another setting up a make believe ward in an abandoned shed with half raised walls leaving open spaces. The floor was ordinary raw ground, with sand, stone, rubble with not even a mud coating. But there was no alternative. I slept on the floor as all prisoners had to, with one shepherd's blanket (they really were woven for shepherds, rough and heavy) to sleep on and another as cover. There were no accessories for the hospital. So I begged of those who were getting released to donate to this hospital some essentials like cotton, bandages, disinfectants, a stove, etc., in short, various hospital supplies. All that the prison provided daily were six tall bottles, each with a different coloured liquid that arrived from the main prison hospital, each supposed to be for a different ailment. I do not think I really could find out during a year and nine months. I was there, which colour was for what ailment. Miraculously everybody seemed to get relief. The crisis came however one day in the form of a typhoid case which I firmly refused to keep and arranged to be sent to the city hospital. But next day back came the patient insisting she preferred my improvised set up to the proper district hospital. She actually recovered, obviously more because of the love and affection she got than any treatment. She went home to be married but held up the ceremony until I was released and could be with her.

I had other problems in the hospital. A raving mad woman, though kept in a separate cell, was put in my charge to be kept under control. It were as though this troubled soul realised the dilemma in which I was placed, for though she could be pretty ferocious, she quietened down when I coaxed her.

One hospital job I had not been prepared for was delivering a child. Though normally I am not easily frightened, I certainly was when I had to face this in the make-believe hospital. I feared I would drown the baby when I was bathing it in the little basin which had to do duty for a tub. I insisted after this that no pregnant woman be brought to this hospital. This was acceded to, to my intense relief.

But I must not digress too much from my sojourn in the Miraj Hospital and the real great event that befell me in there in the course of my stay.

One morning the name of a new arrival at the hospital came to me. I looked at one with unbelieving eyes: Pandita Ramabai and her ailing daughter Manorama. My most delighted mother persuaded me to meet her without delay. With great hesitation I went to her cottage. How was I to introduce myself, a raw young woman, what excuse could I offer for disturbing her? No use even trying to forge a link through the accident of our birth in the same district, for her parents had left it while she was still a baby; that we were born in the same month and cherished similar aspirations seemed just vapour to intrude on for an entry to a personality.

My desperate desire however to meet and talk with her overcame my diffidence. She herself opened the door and asked me in with a smile. She was tall and slim, girlish enough to be Manorama's elder sister, with an unusually fair skin. I decided to speak in Marathi. It seemed more natural and intimate as that was her mother-tongue. I told her of my reason for meeting her, and the interest stimulated by her book 'The High Caste Hindu Women'. The book had aroused much controversy but had sold well and brought her a sizeable amount which she donated to printing children's books for handicapped and delinquent children. The book I referred to was a painful narrative of the humiliation and the sufferings the Indian women were subjected to and bitter condemnation of our several ugly customs. I knew she and her family had gone through traumatic experiences in her young years because of social prejudices against her family for not honouring some of the senseless observances.

A contemporary of Maharashi Karve and linked with him and his work, Ramabai was known as Pandita because of her great Sanskrit scholarship. In my estimation she is the greatest Indian woman of our time. I cannot think of anyone before or after her who can compare with her scholarship, high intellect, wide vision, compassion for humanity, overflowing with love, dedication to service. Though born in my district of Mangalore at the foothills of the Western Ghats near Gangamul, she had been launched into a wandering life very early. Having heard from mother her life story with zeal and admiration it had become one of the pointers in my life.

Ramabai's father, a Maharashtrian Brahmin, had incurred the wrath of his community for daring to teach his wife a *woman* Sanskrit, Deva-Vani (language of the gods). Unrepentent he became a wanderer with his family, giving discourses and earning his living. While in Madras the famine raging there snatched away the parents, later the brother too. She had a problem even getting her parents cremated for their caste was in doubt since they observed none.

Ramabai had become highly proficient in Sanskrit and her brilliant discourses drew crowds. The traditional Pandits in Calcutta, deeply impressed by her scholarship, conferred upon her the title of *Pandita Saraswati* at a grand function in the Senate Hall. A Bengali Harijan scholar befriended her and they married. Within two years he died. Tragically she was once again left alone with a baby girl. Undaunted she carried on with her impassioned exhortations to reform society and better the conditions for women. Social reformers of Pune, deeply impressed by her fervour, invited her to settle amongst them. Pandita Ramabai had a fascinating style of persuasion in her public address, making epic characters current and ancient incidents relevant. In Pune one of the earliest to befriend her was Ramabai Ranade, a fellow missionary.

The Arya Mahila Samaj she founded to give succour to women spread widely. She boldly went ahead participating in public activities which women had not so far ventured to. She created history when she appeared before an India Government Commission on Education, to demand larger, liberal facilities for girls' education. For those were days when according to orthodox prophecies, widowhood hung over education for if a girl just held a pen in her hand, death threatened the husband.

She was the first to realise the crucial importance of political power and was intensely nationalistic. She was a pioneer in urging women to become active in politics. She was the first Indian woman to join the National Congress as also to attend and participate in its annual session along with nine other women. She wished to address this mammoth gathering "to reach the multitude", as she put it. To draw women into the political arena she even sought permission from the government to permit wives of officials to participate in her activities. She also exhorted the people to work towards a common national language and advocated Hindi. She especially appealed to women to take up the medical profession. A 20-year old girl, Anandibai Joshi, impressed by this appeal went to America to study medicine as she could not do it here, and became the first modern Indian lady doctor.

To widen her horizon and knowledge Pandita Ramabai went to England and for the trip she raised money through the sale of her book 'Stree Dharma Nithi'. In England she maintained herself by teaching Marathi. Later Professor Max Mueller, impressed by her scholarship, got her a place to teach Sanskrit in a girls' college.

In 1886 Anandibai Joshi became a full-fledged doctor in America and invited the Pandita for her convocation since she owed this scholarship to her. While in America Ramabai keenly studied the local social welfare, interacted with people in various walks of life and reaped valuable experience.

Pandita's fame had spread far and wide and she got an invitation from Japan. She rated the Japanese meetings as the best she had addressed. The queen of Japan she saw was a great advocate of women's education and Japan had plenty of schools and colleges for girls. The queen had also tried to abolish several irrational social customs.

On her return to India Ramabai set up kindergarden schools like she had seen abroad, for the first time in this country.

In 1889 she established an institution for women, Sharda Sadan, the first of its kind in India, which was inaugurated with great pomp and ceremony in Bombay, then moved to Pune. To fortify it to face inevitable opposition, she enlisted the active support of noted social reformers like Ranade, Bhandarkar, Bodak, etc. Now the widows and orphan girls had a place to go to.

It was from this Sadan that Maharashi Karve chose his wife, a widow girl. He admitted that without Ramabai's good offices the marriage may not have come off. Later when I asked Ramabai about it, she laughed and explained that Karve was shyer than his bride, 'so

I had to play his role'. Maharashi Karve regarded Ramabai as some one very special. "Mother of modern Indian women" was how he described her to me.

Ramabai's conversion to Christianity however reacted adversely on her and her institution. The public anger was accentuated because a Brahmin lady well versed in the scriptures and religion had abandoned her heritage and encouraged young women to get converted. Her scholarship was indeed prodigious. She mastered Hebrew and Greek and translated the Bible from these languages into Marathi which became a monumental work. In fact, no woman had strode the Indian scholastic stage like a colossus as she did. Nor was any other woman so highly elevated and honoured at that time, nor proved such an iconoclast. Nevertheless, she was now isolated and rejected. Only one great social worker saw the reality behind this tragedy and blamed our society for her conversion; Shri Angarkar, a noted social reformer of that time.

To carry on her work quietly she moved with Sharda Sadan to Khedgaon, a village in the Pune region. Here she founded the Mukhti Mission. However, she kept moving around to any place which called for succour. In 1897 when Madhya Pradesh came under severe famine, she rushed for rescue work and brought away 3000 girls and women and housed them in her Khedgaon Ashram. She also visited hospitals and did publicity against the dirt and negligence there as well as the malpractices. She not only gave them publicity in the newspapers, but even got questions raised in British Parliament against the maltreatment of women patients.

Before Ramabai and I parted at the Miraj Hospital, it was decided that we continue our association by my visit to Khedgaon. She talked with enthusiasm and satisfaction of her current work among the girls and women which she had made the core of her activities. Manorama, her daughter, also extended to me a personal invitation to their home. I had been very much drawn to Manorama, by her affectionate and kindly disposition.

I am glad I did visit Khedgaon and see Ramabai in her own setting. It was for me heartwarming to be with them. Manorama seemed like Martha of the Bible, a veritable busy bee, managing the Kripa Sadan, an educational institution for girls. I was very impressed by their organisational ability, specially their great feeling for the poor and the oppressed women for whose emancipation they had devoted their entire lives.

It was obvious that Ramabai was deeply religious but to her serving the people was synonymous with worship. Christ to her was the symbol of unlimited love and compassion for the oppressed and the suffering. For her the girls and women of India needed Him because of a society that dreaded daughters, who were pushed out of the house with the utmost speed for no other sin except their sex. They also lost the right to live a normal life when the husband died. She must have been moved to hear Christ's call of love : "Suffer little children come unto me". Thus from the cruel jaws of this society she decided she would lead the young girls into the wide open arms of Christ, the embodiment of love. It is not surprising that a great soul like Maharashi Karve found in Ramabai a kindred mate and characterised her as fit to be included in the 'category of saintly personalities who live to serve others'. Thus inspite of our close comradeship I did not ever feel the need to touch on religion as a topic of discussion with her. I understood her.

This was to be my last meeting with them, for both passed away soon after.

Mother was feeling low and I was myself pretty shattered after my sister passed away. True, her life had been a veritable tragedy, tied to a brutal, sadistic husband. To make someone gentle, sweet and uncomplaining the target of ones perversities to me was cruelty beyond comprehension. Even on her death-bed we seemed helpless to product her. He neither supported her nor the children, Mother bearing the entire responsibility. Nevertheless, law and custom were all on his side, on whose altar so many victims like her were being sacrificed. To her the end may have been a merciful release.

Mother proposed that we visit some of her old friends and old haunts as that mightlighten our gloom. One was a visit to her old friend and comrade, Ramabai Ranade in Pune, who invited us to be her guests in the famous Seva Sadan, of which I had many glowing reports. It was later to play a big role in my life too.

I found Ramabai Ranade a handsome figure with a broad forehead which in the native interpretation means a large vision and a sound intellect. She also had an air of quiet inner strengtht. Though gone in age, she looked endowed with power and self-confidence. 'I was not as fortunate as your mother who always seems so learned. I was completely illiterate and would have remained so but for my husband', she said to me with a smile, when I mentioned that I had read her reminiscences, 'Some Memories from Our Life'. It was a moving yet heart-warming narrative that revealed her as an uncomplicated woman who from a simple background was called on to take up a married life at the age of eleven with a husband of 32, already a leading public figure, to face unthoughtof challenges and solve unexpected problems, all of which she seems to have done with a quiet innate dignity. To me hers was a saga typical of that time : from an unlettered girl to a commanding social reformist leader. I knew that she was being modest, for her education had been much wider and deeper.

After their marriage, Shri Ranade became his wife's tutor inspite of his family displeasure. Soon she had gained mastery over Marathi, Sanskrit and English. He encouraged her even more to read newspapers, familiarise herself with current public affairs and even international developments, and discussed with her topics such as the regeneration of women through education. Soon she mastered the art of public speaking which is crucial in public campaigning. Moreover, as Shri Ranade was a leading figure in political, religious, economic and educational activities, Ramabai gained immense wide knowledge which proved of great value to her. In the midst of this Shri Ranade passed away. She however became determined to actively carry on with her social work instead of going into the oblivion a widow is expected to. In fact she was now called on to take on many new tasks. She promoted a new institution for women called Seva Sadan.

This was historically a wonderful pioneering venture which did yeoman service to the regeneration and independence of women. It not only provided shelter and succour to destitutes, widows and deserted wives, but was a heaven to the oppressed, in short to all the long exploited, including the unwanted daughters-in-law, mothers-in-law, sisters-in-law, etc. The significant role of the Seva Sadan lay in morally bolstering up a wife who is continuously ill-treated, and enable her to give an ultimatum to the husband that either he behave himself or she would march off to the Seva Sadan. This did serve to sober many an overbearing male. To me its importance also lay in being a clean institution, free from the kind of adventurous exploiters who now tend to feed on such sanctuaries.

It provided a kind of *instant* coaching through condensed courses to give even the absolute illiterate some basic foundation in literacy, practical general knowledge and some skill to enable them to earn their livelihood.

When we were staying with Ramabai she took us to a women's meeting where I met some interesting women. Amongst them was Premlilaben Thackersay. Young and beautiful, she seemed someone apart. I was rather curious because for the wife of a multimillionaire she was very simply dressed in an ordinary cotton sari. Later I learnt that Gujarati women, rich and poor alike, wore plain white saris except for festive occasions.

Later through my association with Maharashi Karve I came to know her as the multifaceted personality she had moulded herself into as the wife of a prominent social leader. She related her story when I was once staying with her, by then she had become fully absorbed in educational activities. "I came from a remote rural place, grew up in a large family. Maybe that laid the foundation for the large responsibilities I, a village maiden, had to shoulder at a young age when I married," and laughingly she recounted some of the highly sophisticated roles she had to play as hostess at banquets, club parties, sports and riding meets, educational conferences, political and social meetings, and so the list went on. "My husband, however, was very gentle and kind and patiently guided me at every turn and I for my part was determined to become a worthy mate to him. You see, my father, unlike the fathers of those days, was in no hurry to marry me off until he found his choice and he did not mind waiting 18 long years !"

Sir Vithaldas and Premlila were greatly drawn to Maharashi Karve and his devoted service for women's education. Impressed by the women's university in Tokyo, they persuaded Karve to convert his Mahila Vidyapeeth in Poona into an exclusive women's university, fortified by a donation of rupees fifteen lakhs. Sir Vithaldas dedicated it to the memory of his mother, Shrimati Nathibai. Premlila lost her husband even before she reached her thirtieth year. She converted most of his wealth into a Trust to help needy women to get education. She went through a series of financial crises however in stabilising the Women's University but succeeded with her characteristic tenacity. In recognition of her continued contribution and service, she was elected Vice-Chancellor of the Women's University, officially known as Shrimati

Nathibai Damador Thackersay, popularly called SNDT, now well established and enjoying a fine reputation.

A relation of mine in Madras who was described as a spiritual-intellect used to visit Sri Aurobindo periodically and often talked of him with great elation. She confided that she got the most rare inspiration from him. I only knew him as a passionate, vigorous revolutionary who had now settled as an exile in Pondicherry, then a French colony. She enlightened me on the metamorphosis he had undergone and how he had transformed himself into a *rishi*. Yugantar, a political paper he had long edited from Calcutta, and later the Bande Mataram, described as the voice of Indian revolution, had been my links with his thoughts. Mother talked to me of Sri Aurobindo with a certain awe. He was the first known Indian political revolutionary to live in England and propagate India's cause in 1892 through the Lotus and Dagger Society. So I easily succumbed when the lady suggested I accompany her to the sage's retreat.

We were in the early twenties. Although Sri Aurobindo had started his Sadhana, he had not yet gone into complete retreat. The Ashram then was a single large habitation with few inmates, mainly those serving him, specially with his publication, Arya, the well known journal and the sage's books. The Mother had not as yet taken over the ashram.

I entered his room feeling very inadequate. To reap the best fruits of this important event, I had hastily tried to acquaint myself with his current thinking through some of his writings. However, I was too young to fully grasp the grandeur of his 'Life Divine' or 'The Synthesis of Yoga'. I had found his style rather involved and reading heavy going until I got used to the fact that he was only using new terms and phrases to reveal the old fundamentals. Then things became more illuminating.

An unusual element in his writings were the detailed and copious references to Ancient European history, especially of countries like Greece and Rome, drawing striking comparisons between them and India that revealed deep study, and in the *original*, I learnt that he wrote not only philosophical theses but even verses in these classical languages. When schooling in England from an early age he had developed special interest in these languages and their cultures and had won many scholastic prizes. There is a comic little incident connected with this. At British instigation Sri Aurobindo's house was searched by Pondicherry's French authorities, and what the hunters came upon beside philosophical writings, were manuscripts in Latin and Greek which none of them could read, and therefore roused their ire !

I had been equally struck by his unorthodox interpretations of several old traditions. For instance, caste *-varna-* for him was a symbolic and typal institution, based on the four cosmic principles: the Brahmin symbolising knowledge, Kshatriya power, Vaishya production, and Shudra service, not the conventional practising social set-ups with distorted levels and contours. He applied the same analogy to the concept of Purusha and Prakrati, the male and the female, again as a *symbol of perfect equality*. According to him, the distortions took place because we read our own coarse mentality into the symbols of our ancient seers and the result was 'barbarism'. Equally unorthodox was his rejection of the concept of Maya, for to him matter and spirit were but two phases of the same. These interpretations to my young unsophisticated mind were new, hence stimulating. I had also noted from his writings that he differed from most other Indian leaders except Gandhiji, by laying persistent emphasis on *self-development* as most basic to fashion, a perfect instrument to gain freedom.

I don't believe I had stepped into Sri Aurobindo's presence with any preconceived physical image of him. I was however surprised to see rather a small figure. I realised that what I had heard of his political and revolutionary exploits and then his stirring writings had conjured up for me a physically big man. But as I sat and watched him, he seemed to grow in stature, in strength; power seemed to pour out of him, his face aglow. This was probably what our ancients termed *Tejus*.

I sat dumbly listening to my companion and him talk. Suddenly she shook me and admonished me for my silence. "Don't be shy young lady, you can speak freely," he added with a smile which seemed to light up the air around. I began haltingly confessing how intrigued I had been by his drawing from Greek and Roman parallels in his writings on India which was unusual. 'Could you follow ?' he asked. 'Some of it, yes, for I had done in my school more ancient Greek and Roman history and indifferent or bad Indian history.' 'All our education has been so' was his comment. I wanted to know more about the 'Spiritual Age' he predicted in his writings. He answered promptly : 'It is not an original idea of mine. After all society is only an enlargement of the individual. We have gone through the Golden Ages when society was not fixed into rigid grades, religion was not stereotyped, education not confining thought forms into unchangeable frames, thought was not subordinated to authoritarianism. In short, no bar halted the onward march along the long, long path on which humanity once moved. These periods were appropriately named Satya Yuga, Krita Yuga and so on. When a stamp of finality is cast on man's life to strangulation, men of intellectual power rise and strike at the walls that crush life. A spiritual idea is a power only when it is creative. Symbols, spiritual or social, are meaningless unless realised in spirit, in action, realise God within man not in an imaginary heaven. Towards the arrival of this age of enlightenment, we have to exercise our intelligence, our faculties actively, for which the entire multitude has to act, not a few, save for civilisation the past gains of mankind, add to them, enlighten and raise the life of the whole, pursue all types of knowledge to experience the divine in the world, such a pursuit would be self-developing and self-finding. Yes, I believe in the coming of that spiritual age. It will set in when the common mind of man becomes attuned to these truths and lets itself to be guided by them so that human life will move from its present limits into larger and brighter vistas."

Because of my unfamiliarity with his phraseology I sought permission to take down the discourse verbatim.

I asked one more question: Had he abandoned political activities completely? Quick came a spirited reply: "No, I have not turned away from politics. But I do not wish to enter the world of action with my old ideas or inspirations. I seek a higher goal for which I need to build a fresh base to work from."

I have had occasion to visit the Aurobindo Ashram many times since this memorable visit. Though the buildings multiplied, activities proliferated, the real light that had glowed in that Centre had long gone out.

After my first visit to this seer an idea wafted through me that I should qualify intellectually as also observe societies outside India. Mother always ready to further my studies encouraged me. I sold off the jewellery I inherited and got ready to set sail for England — then the only obvious foreign land readily open to us.

In the meantime a new comet, this time a benevolent one, had risen in our firmament which was to become the missile to strike at the 'invulnerable' British Empire and the world was to view the red sun set on its imperial frontiers.

To those of my generation the real political history of India begins with the Gandhi era. All that went before in the shape of bomb throwing, political assassinations, attempted violence were sporadic eruptions, symptoms of desperation.

When Gandhiji entered the Indian political arena I was still a young student but becoming politically awake, perhaps earlier than the generations before, for great upheavals had begun to take place specially in the context of a global war.

As stated earlier, I was fortunate to have grown up in a keen politically and socially aware atmosphere. For, Mother was politically very alive and kept abreast of current affairs and our political hunger was continuously fed on highly surcharged literature. But freedom was still a vague term.

By now my unhappiness over social and economic inequalities had burgeoned into resentment embittering my life and injecting strain in my social relationships.

I was fascinated by the Champaran struggle conducted by Gandhiji. Here was something in which the real people of the country were involved. Through their organisation, will, determination and loyalty they could stand up to the oppression of the indigo planters backed by a foreign regime. Exploitation was no vague term, it was concrete and meaningful to my own growing sense of the ills in our society. I was excited and intrigued by Gandhiji's mental attitude towards problems, his deep involvement with the depressed section of society, his positive postures that indicated his personal reaction to situations as they arose and his strong grip on the basic and vital need of the country: freedom, of which he never lost sight. To him all problems radiated from this central focal point. To me they had almost a personal answer as they seemed related to my own internal conflicts over discrimination against women. For Gandhiji believed in women's rightful place in society and public life.

More significant, he was a leader who showed to a growing generation a picture of a new life through a programme of action which was satisfying and made politics real to us.

The righteousness of the world war had been trumpeted throughout the years of conflict. India's contribution had been tremendous. More soldiers had been killed on the battlefields of Europe than the total number recruited from all the British colonies and dominions put together, around 1,200,000. Also a hundred million pounds given outright while in addition 20 to 30 million pounds contributed to war expenses ! The day it ended in victory for the Allies, fresh hope for the subject people had sprouted. In the victory celebration with sports and games, in which I won a prize, I took it as a good omen that the long-awaited freedom was at hand, little dreaming what was in store for us.

The political stirrings generated by the war aims got accelerated demonstratively when the country swung back to *status quo* ! This roused the wrath of the rulers, who, to enforce severe measures, incorporated harsh and repressive clauses in the grim Defence of India Act, historically termed the Rowlatt Act. To my budding imagination this stood out like a death sentence stamped in large black letters. Then followed the convulsions from the unbelievable massacre at Jallianwalla Bagh. Instantly came Gandhiji's call for a day of fast and prayer to prepare for the big plunge : Satyagraha. Self-purification before going into any great venture is an ancient custom. But here the action projected was original and novel. The application of this concept of Satyagraha as a political weapon was startling and exciting. It was like viewing a new instrument, simple yet promising to be powerful in operation. There were detractors who were aghast with fear and felt Gandhiji was letting loose a demonaical weapon which would not only cause destruction but ultimately recoil on the one who had let it loose. Like all youth, I was dead earnest and found myself fighting many wordy battles in its defence. But my real preparedness lay in silent meditation morning and evening in the privacy of my own room. I prayed earnestly that I may someday become a worthy instrument through which Satyagraha could be practised, for I was not sure if a girl not yet sixteen would qualify to join the great battle to be launched, although physically and mentally I felt strong enough.

I heard that Gandhiji was starting a Satyagraha Sabha whose members would pledge to oppose and disobey unjust laws and court imprisonment. Gandhiji was to be in Bombay for it. To me it was a historic occasion, the first important national collective positive action. It would also give me a chance to have a glimpse of him.

This meeting was to enable the would-be Satyagrahis to pledge themselves to not only civil disobedience, but also to adhere to swadeshi, communal unity, above all to observe complete non-violence and truth. I found myself in a small group, so different from the vast concourse of the previous day who had gathered on the Chowpatty sands. I discovered later that not everyone who was ready to fight the British was prepared to strictly adhere to the leader's other conditions. Gandhiji himself, as he read out the pledge, commented on how exciting events drew crowds while for silent constructive work only a few serious people came. He explained the meaning and significance of the pledge and the great responsibility assumed by those who chose to take it. It was the first time that I was hearing him speak. He expressed himself in chaste literary phrases and I was to realise later that he did it with all the languages in which he spoke. There is the famous incident of the Viceroy Lord Irwin who, after a few negotiations with Gandhiji, confessed, "The English he speaks sometimes drives me to consult the dictionary." His words came slowly but emphatically, as though each word was weighed and phrased before it was uttered. The magic of his personality and his grip on the audience was visible; this I was to experience many times in the days to come. As he expounded his philosophy it confounded you by its verys implicity. Though he talked in a gentle tone there was a steely ring in it. His eyes so full of affection and kindliness threw sparks, as it were. 'This is going to be a great struggle with a powerful adversary," he reminded. "If you want to take it up you must be prepared to lose everything and train yourselves to the strictest non-violence and discipline."

I had by now begun to become something of a doubting Thomas on the practicability of maintaining complete non-violence, conscious of the fears and anger which had begun to rage within my own bosom. Moreover, who had ever in history won freedom without violence and struggle ? Such doubts kept plaguing me and I communicated them to a lady who was close to Gandhiji. She evidently warned him against persons like me who hung on the fringe but were not steeped in non-violence. I was surprised one day to receive a card from Gandhiji in which he expressed his apprehension and asked me not to join the movement if I did not have faith in non-violence. Of course, the occasion for it was not to arise for over a decade.

It is now part of history how the big movement that was to be launched was called off by Gandhiji because of the outbreak of violence, in Chauri Chaura. The irony of it is that at this very stage the answer of the government to this was to arrest him for writing what is undoubtedly an exquisite literary piece in English titled 'Shaking the Manes' describing the British lion shaking its mane. There can be few compositions in the English language comparable to this in its sheer beauty of imagery. Alas, it was lost on the prosaic magistrate who admonished him with a jail sentence. When the curtain was rung down on an agitated political scene, an unusual lull descended. So my thoughts went back to the foreign study I had prepared myself for.

3

When I arrived in England it was to pursue the normal academic studies, with also a hope of continuing my piano lessons on the side I had been advised to seek advice from Susan Stebbing, a senior professor at Newman College, Cambridge. She, however, wished to know the object of my study. "You seem to have a definite mind of your own. Do you propose to become an academician?" Startled, I gave a sharp 'No. I want to be educated to serve society'. 'Oh, a social worker, I can fix you up, but for that you do not need a scholastic career,' came a quiet reply. She directed me to get admission in Bedford College, London, for the sociology course which included subjects like social science, psychology, economics, hygiene, theoretical work in the morning and practical training in social work in the afternoon. This sounded like the perfect answer to my need.

The Principal of Bedford College then, one Miss Tuke, a very elderly lady, however thought otherwise. She gave one quick look and abruptly started to turn me out. No, she could not admit me for this course. Crestfallen, I sought an explanation even as she started leading me to the exit. With blazing eyes she broke out : "You realise you will have to work in the East End of London and you simply cannot go there in that weird garb of yours. The alleys are haunted by wild urchins who would soon chase you out. I don't suppose you propose to change your costume, do you ?" I halted my steps and turned to her : "No, I don't. But please remember if I take on this course, those urchins would be seeing me every single day for weeks, months, years.

They are bound to soon become bored staring at my dress or chasing me. They will look for some other novelty for excitement. Let us try it out. If I am prepared for a trial, why don't you let me ?" She looked annoyed but had no ready answer. I siezed the moment and took her nonplussed silence as consent. I got my admission.

The lectures on psychology stand out in my mind as purposefully directed to stimulate the imagination. One intriguing exercise was to make us aware of the lack of concentration in thought. In this we began with our focus on one thing and then let the thoughts run on and then made an abrupt stop and traced the entire sweep of the chain. You realise with a shock that you are at a point that is neither related, nor even relevant to where you started. It gave one a sense of futility. Another interesting exercise was to find the relationship between sound and colour or *vice versa.* For this we were advised to close our eyes to concentrate better. Many protested they could not see the connection—crazy, they protested or sat silent, bewildered. Quite a few entered excitedly into this though they felt it was rather a weird experiment. I was probably amongst the very few to see the reality behind the so-called mystery. This is an ancient truism that we have inherited through the knowledge of vibration, according to which movement, music, colour, all are closely related. Years later, Dr. C.V. Raman displayed this on a screen in his laboratory. The musical sounds generated became dancing lines on the screen and revealed how closely they resembled the kind of movements musicians indulge in when they do their musical exposition. This made me realise that the movements had a pattern determined by the vibrations made by music. I discovered later that the psychology teacher, a lady, who set the exercises was familiar with Indian thought and had been influenced by it. It was however strange that it should be used as a classroom exercise in a London school.

The sociology course proved immensely practical and useful to turn me into an efficient social worker. Luckily sociology had not then become a *discipline* to turn into a bookish affair, as now.

The practicals took me to the old notorious East End of London which World War II has rendered just a sad memory. The afternoon was spent mostly in different institutions, educational and corrective, for adults and children. The evenings were passed in workers' clubs or institutes. England of those days lacked the many educational, social and cultural institutions which were later set up by Labour Unions. I got a good grounding in the approach to the different sections of society that developed in the slums and their varied needs. The study of the special institutions for the handicapped was generally to be taken up for specialisation later, if one wished to. Unlike in India, I had to put in a full days' hard work, starting at 8 in the morning, working all through the evening to attend the workers' evening classes and their recreational pursuits.

My family had been greatly perturbed at my abandoning the normal academic course to get trained in social work which in India was still a leisure hour occupation generated by compassion and goodwill, not academic discipline. My decision would therefore have sounded unfamiliar, so disturbing.

Though the political lull in India continued, I felt the pull to return grow stronger daily, which made me restless and impatient.

On my return trip I visited a few places in Europe and was appalled to see a war-torn and uprooted world : the utter collapse of the fabric of society, the emotional devastation, and particularly the frustrating impact this had on the youth, all served to question the kind of world in which we had lived so smugly. The brutality of violence generated by the greed of power maniacs made a deep mark on me. Though the Russian Revolution created a glimmering of new hope, one wondered how far it could change this vast world. It was however obvious that somewhere sometime a new pattern of living would have to be evolved.

A pleasant break in this gloom was provided by the Moscow Art Theatre which offered me a rare experience in dramatics. It was launched in 1897 as a new venture given the lead by Anton Chekov becoming its very first shareholder, with other luminaries like Constantin Stanislavasky actively participating in the plays. The theatre had won great acclaim all over Europe. Fortunately it was playing in Berlin. I had the good fortune to have Suhrawardy from Calcutta, an authority on European art and a close friend of Germanova. He took time and pains to introduce me to European painting and theatre. We spent hours going through picture galleries, noted private collections. He also briefed me on Italian pictures and persuaded me to visit Florence and Venice, besides Rome, which I did.

The Moscow Art Theatre opened a new dimension to me in the theatre arts. I was enchanted with the 'Cherry Orchard' in particular.

Fortunately Madame Chekov, herself a well known actress, was taking part in it.

"The Three Sisters,' by Anton Chekov moved me the most. Germanova played Olga in it and her acting was stirring. The echoes of her concluding speech, when in the midst of her great agony she cried out, left long echoes in me :

"Time will pass and we shall be gone for ever, but our sufferings will turn into joy for those who will live after us—and they will remember those who live now and will bless them."

There was a refinement about the theatre properties. Years later when I was making a study of the Russian theatre, I realised that the creation and preservation of these properties was an art world of its own and the artists working in this seemed as gifted and important as the actors. The manipulation of lights to me held magical effects, not having seen this kind of lighting before. This in fact induced me to acquire a small set of these lights for use in our productions.

Most exciting and pleasurable was meeting in Berlin Virendranath Chattopadhyay, the eldest of the family who to us had been more a legend than a real being and never in my wildest dreams had I believed I would see him in flesh and blood.

Virendranath Chattopadhyay with whom I spent some time was a vibrant personality. His hearty humour and scintillating repartees flew like flashes of lightening. He had left home at the beginning of the century to study at Oxford, but had in course of time drifted into a group of Indian political revolutionaries. Because of his outstanding brilliance and wide knowledge he was welcome every country he went to, only to be ruthlessly turned out because of the British adversely tarnishing him as a dangerous terrorist. Contact with him brought me new knowledge and political perceptions. Talking with him was highly educative, and enabled me to understand something of the nature of our political and economic problems, and the various components that made for their complexities. He often repeated "before you can fight with your adversary you must know his full nature, for which you must study him. Then you can gauge the type of the battle you have to wage". My political horizon widened steadily, the Indian scene became clearer with different forces emerging as they stood arrayed on either side of the battle lines. The enormity of the problem kept baffling me. For the first time I became widely aware of the Indian economic condition and its place as a colony in the British Empire. The imperialism I now spied was not merely a vast British Army holding our country, but so many other vital forces which were subordinating the Indian people. I began to see India's freedom struggle in a much clearer perspective in all its complexities.

Around Viren were a group of Indian freedom fighters now living in exile abroad. Whatever dreams they may have had and whatever grandiose plans they may have made during the World War to free India, none ever took off the ground. I wondered if they could clearly assess the current situation in India to see if they had any role in it.

Amongst them, Viren stood out the most commanding and also the most tragic figure. His one great longing was to return home. He had a brilliant mind, had mastered many subjects, was a linguist. But his one passion was freedom, over which he became emotional and as he talked, his eyes grew misty. He realised that the real task lay in India and he was denied to be with his people.

Viren's wife, Agnes Smedley, was an American. Because of her great interest in the oriental subject peoples' struggle for freedom, she had become involved with the Indians in California. When the American government began arresting them during World War I, she helped promote "Friends of Freedom for India Society" to win support for India's cause. Americans familiar with events of those days in California, admitted to me that the compliance of the American officials with British manoeuvres to harass Indians, was disgusting. She got more inspired when she came into touch with Lajpat Rai and through him with the Ghadr Party, a revolutionary group of India.

I may mention here that the Ghadr (revolt) Party set up in San Francisco was one of the several stormy petrels composed largely of hundreds of Sikhs from Punjab, settled in California. They had become acutely conscious and sensitive to their status as colonials amidst this vast concourse of free people. They launched a vigorous campaign in support of Indian freedom in the States, inspired and directed by fiery patriots like Har Dayal, an outstanding scholar who distinguished himself in foreign universities. Fired by an ambition to carry the war into the heart of their country by taking advantage of World War I, they launched a ship, Kamagata Maru, to carry arms, ammunition to India to stir up a revolution and drive the foreign rulers out. After an adventurous journey the ship did reach Calcutta port, but was naturally set upon by the authorities and the brave adventurers were subjected to untold sufferings.

When World War I ended Agnes came on to Berlin, and with her strong sympathies for India, it was natural she should be drawn to Viren and try to help him. That is where I met her. We stayed together for sometime and I learnt she came from a struggling family in an obscure village in Missouri, USA. Growing up in a small unprosperous mining town, she got moulded into both an angry proletariat as also a vigorous feminist. Whilst she helped Viren keep the group of Indian revolutionaries together, now pitiably placed and rather lost, she also taught English, history, and Chinese politics as a profession. But as a typical 'do good' social worker, she pioneered in setting up the first birth control clinic in Germany.

The Indian cause she realised, as Viren did, could only be furthered by Indians in India, and it was unreal to think it could be promoted from abroad. In Agnes I sensed a hard core of strength which could not find an outlet in this stagnant Berlin pool.

I was not surprised that she should take up an assignment for the German Frankfurter Zeitung in China. Based in Shanghai she made friends with noted Chinese authors and apart from reporting on the Japanese aggression, she made public the conflict raging between the Kuomintang under Chiang Kai Shek and the Communists, the terror let loose by the Kuomintang Secret Police the "Blue Shirts", and the emergence of the Communist state in Kiangsi.

Agnes conveyed to me through a friend, her adventure at Harbin even as she entered China, when the British maliciously declared she was really a British subject, travelling falsely on an American passport, and charging her as an agent of the Communist Internationale. Luckily she had a friend in the American State Department who directed the American Consul in Canton to rescue her, which he did, but emphatically condemned her support for pro-Asian independence activities as "treasonable". This she confessed sent her into roars of laughter.

Apart from her free and frank reporting, including exposing the presence of German military experts in China to mastermind the war against the Communists instead of against the Japanese, her "do good" habit also got her involved in trying to rescue suspects, particularly women, from Chinese Police clutches. The British however finally succeeded in pressurising the Germans into cancelling her journalist contract.

Agnes however stayed on, joined Madame Sun Yat Sen, working with the China League for Civil Rights, which took her through a series of unusual adventures. Unexpectedly this opened the road for her to Yennen, the Communist headquarters, and to meet all the important personalities there, most of whom hailed from the peasant stock. Her reporting on the long Chinese March by the Communists which Agnes so vividly describes in her epic book "The Red Army Marches." Credibility simply boggles at even the mere description. Picture a 100,000 who started in October 1934, trudged 8000 miles across 12 provinces, touching 62 cities, crossed 18 mountain ranges, negotiated 12 rivers, engaged in a dozen major battles and countless skirmishes, to finally drop anchor in Yennen up in the deep northern province of Shensi, well after a year.

While the anti-Japanese war was in full swing, Agnes remained in the battle zone, tending patients in hospitals, helping distressed families, undeterred by the war risks. She confessed she was appalled to realise how much America had helped build up the Japanese war machine which she watched in operation.

She was one of the most remarkable women I have known, more like a character in an adventure novel. From an obscure twilit hole she strode forward, into some of the stormiest earth shaking events of international history. For posterity she has left substantial records of her startling experiences set in the historical context of the times. She braved wars and shattering turmoil because of her single-minded devotion to the downtrodden, the oppressed. She was basically a humanitarian. To quote her : "I was neither brave nor learned, just historically curious." But the curiosity took her way beyond, with an insatiable thirst to help, to serve. She was a slim delicate woman, with rather a gaunt face, but a tender beautiful smile that lit up her whole personality with an unusual radiance.

The incredible fact is that she never shared her Chinese Comrades' ideology or joined the Party. Her interest was purely human. To quote her "For years I listened to Communists with sympathy, I gave them my active support, but I could never place my mind and life unquestionably at the disposal of the leaders, become a mere instrument in the hands of men who believed that they held the one and only key to truth."

Though we could not correspond directly, Agnes kept sending me some of her writings and books which educated me on China and her revolution.

Agnes's health seems to have finally broken down and she had to return to America. There she met my son from whom she learned of Viren's death. The shock was great and visibly affected her, though she had been parted from him for almost 20 years.

For us in India Viren's death has remained a shrouded mystery. He had moved from Germany to Russia and was working in the Oriental Institute in Leningrad. Then a curtain seems to have fallen. The Indian Government's efforts after Independence to unravel this mystery only draw a blank.

One other legendary figure I met in Europe was Madame Bikhaji Cama, hailing from a Bombay Parsi family, of whom I had long heard of as a young revolutionary, now in exile in Paris. I was thrilled to meet her. Unlike the restless group in Berlin, she was a composed personality though still full of the old fervour and very optimistic about India's freedom. While chatting, I referred to her having devised a national flag at the Stuttgart International Congress. She suddenly burst into hilarious laughter. 'Wonders will never cease', she began in explanation. 'Early in the century when so many of us Indian students were becoming nationally astir, we sorely felt the same need you folks did, for a national flag. So I picked on my little brain and devised a flag which all the Indian students use in Europe. That proves the old saying : Adversity is the mother of invention. Though this meeting was brief, "we are sisters in adversity,' she commented and lovingly she first clasped my hand then clasped me to her bosom and I felt truly blessed.

As she was the most outstanding woman of her time actively in politics and as very little is known of this unique woman I feel I should unfold a few glimpses of her eventful life. She was the only Indian woman revolutionary to attain political maturity, exceptional in that period, with a clear grasp of the true nature of imperialism and its heavy international ramifications. She organised a colourful Fiftieth Anniversary in 1907 of the 1857 war of Independence in London where she first resided and worked. In clear phrases she put this historical record right: that it was not a stray rebellion but a purposeful well organised national war. Inevitably she was forced to move to Paris, for her passionate advocacy of India's cause was stirring interest and their reveberation began to rumble even in the British Parliament.

In Paris Madame Cama continued to wield her powerful pen. She edited a paper called *Bande Mataram* as also contributed to *Talvar* run by the Indian revolutionary exiles in Europe. She stirred up interest in the public on India's struggle for freedom and seemed to have reached out to a fairly large public to whom India had till then been only a fabled name. She built up responsive links with other national revolutionary streams like those of Ireland, Egypt, Turkey, Morocco. She was able to secure an international forum through her close association with the French socialists, and the personal support of the noted leader Jaures. When the Indian patriot Savarkar sought asylum in France, and the French government shamefacedly handed him over to the British, a sizeable French public condemned this immoral act, L'Humanite, the French Socialist organ giving it widest publicity. She then had this case presented before the International Court at the Hague. But while this Tribunal upheld the right of asylum technically, the final verdict became political, favouring the English demand. She carried the Indian cause further at the Second Socialist International Congress at Stuttgart in 1907—Madame Cama's acceptance as an Indian delegate at this world forum was opposed only by the English Labour leader, Macdonald. But the other international socialist leaders like Jaures, Karl Liebknecht, Rosa Luxemburg and one British representative Hyndman, gave her full support. Madame installed India as a political entity in this International Congress by further unfurling an Indian National flag. This had red at the top with eight lotuses for the Indian provinces, Saffron yellow in the middle symbolising sacrifice, with Vande Mataram inscribed in Devanagari, and blue at the bottom with the sun and the moon to represent Hindus and the Muslims. This was based on the flag hoisted in 1906 in Calcutta, first in Green Park, then at the rostrum of the 1906 session of the National Congress under the Presidentship of Dadabhai Naoroji.

As Madame Cama unfurled the flag she exclaimed : "This flag is of Indian independence. Behold it is born. It is already sanctified by the blood of martyred Indian youths. I call upon you to rise and salute this flag of free India. I appeal to lovers of freedom all over the world to cooperate in freeing one-fifth of the human race."

She then moved a resolution calling for support for complete independence for India, which was adopted by the Congress, with only a few English delegates voting against.

It were as though Madame anticipated the Lahore Congress by 22 years !

Madame Cama was fortunate in that she was permitted to return to India around 1936 as she had become very aged and in poor health. Why she died in penury in a Charity Hospital still remains a rankling mystery. For she hailed from a rich family though she had become alienated from it for her involvement first in her working with the slum people of Bombay and later for her radical political activities.

The more I met and saw the various Indian personalities abroad who had sometime been involved in seeking support for India's right to freedom, the more I realised how the British made them into bogey men and women. For however great their patriotism and original competence to strike a blow, their scope and opportunity was too limited to be effective. The result was, the fact of their being condemned and shunted into exile by their adversary, seemed to have clothed them with a shadowy importance. They, no doubt, suffered emotionally and economically, but in their personal make up an illusory glow clung to them but which did not materially help them.

I had hardly been back in India a few days when I received a communication from the Government demanding that I hand back my passport. I declined stating that I was not aware of having violated any provisions covered by the passport and as the period for which it had been issued had not yet runout, I did not mean to return it. To this came a prompt reply that my passport had been cancelled, all travel agencies and shipping companies had been warned not to issue any ticket to me as I was not holding any passport. But as I was keenly intent in involving myself in working in the country, it did not disturb me unduly. It was part of a subject citizen's life.

The political wind in India had dropped, not a leaf moved. But I wanted nevertheless to be within the Gandhian orbit. So I began spinning both on the *charka* as on the *takli* which I could easily carry around with me when I travelled. I took more eagerly to weaving and was fascinated by the complex techniques in weaves.

In my school days I had discovered a definite talent for dramatics which received good support from my teachers. I acted regularly in almost every play the school put on and enjoyed it immensely—of course all in English. Though I enjoyed music and experienced a sense of upliftment, acting proved my real medium. In my childhood I had listened to the legend of how our dramatic theatre came to be. When the Creator was asked to produce something that would please the ears as well as the eyes, the Creator took the element of recitation from the Rig Veda, song from the Sama Veda, the art of mime from the Yajur Veda and the sentiment from the Sama Veda. The Divine Architect was then asked to build a play-house in which the Sage Bharata was to practise the art thus created. This new creation was welcomed with great delight by the gods. Siva contributed to this through the now famous Tandava dance, depicting violent emotion; his spouse, Parvati, gave to it the tender graceful and voluptuous touch of Lasya, while Vishnu gave the four dramatic styles necessary to effect a play. The Sage Bharata then imported to earth this celestial from of enjoyment.

Apart from the wide variety of traditional performances a different theatre had emerged by the turn of the century under the impact of the western stage which came from the foreign influences. Though my home town had none of this to speak of, well known professional troupes from other states travelled to us and camped regularly, providing us a feast of performances. As mother was fond of the theatre, we never missed these shows. The modern theatre had introduced the procinium stage and while we have no firm evidence of professional artists in the classic Sanskrit theatre, such a class had now emerged, who made these rounds of the towns and cities.

The Kannada theatre was presented by Bellary Raghavachar, a towering personality and a moving actor who became memorable as Ramdas, the famous political guru and as king in the play, 'The Fall of Vizianagaram' ; Mysore Varadachar, full of passionate vigour and a name to conjure with, made his mark in Ratnavali and Prahlad Charitram. The Dattreya Natak Mandali provided spectacular productions, and of course, the popular Veeranna in the Gubbi theatre and its contemporary, Ratnavali.

The Marathi theatre troupes also came. The Maharashtra Natak Mandali under Khadilkar presented both mythological and historical plays. There was the Kirloskar and Deval Company who gave us a number of plays, Marathi translations of Sanskrit plays, as also of French and English plays. Bahurao, who played female roles, was equally noted as a good singer ; his place was later taken by Balgandharva, also a prodigious player of female roles, fascinating the audience with the magic of his music. There was Ganpathrao Bhodas, a great actor, especially in plays with social themes. Some plays became noted as allegorical like Khadilkar's *Keechak Wadh* supposed to be a satire on the British rule in India and thus came to be banned. There were social themes like Kolhatkar's Sharada, showing the sad custom of marrying young girls to old men.

The themes were a mixed bag of epic and historical stories, modern social problems of dowry, drinking, gambling, etc. The artists were of good calibre and provided excellent acting. The theatre properties of heavy painted curtains depicting various scenes as backdrops were rather oppressive. Occasionally, the tension of the story was broken by what were simply called 'transformation scenes' when some supernatural being descended from heaven or a stone was turned into a woman or a tree into a statue with a loud bang which made people jump in their seats. The plays of course were so irrationally interspersed with very lengthy songs which were repeated on a shout of "once more" from the audience destroying the dramatic tempo. Notwithstanding these unhappy and irritating features, it nonetheless kept the theatre alive.

Whenever I visited Madras I went to see the shows of the Saguna Vilas Sabha led by Shri Sambandham, which was a well known amateur group consisting of academicians, professionals, lawyers, even members of the judiciary. The famous freedom fighter, S. Satyamurthy, had won fame as a stage actor as Duryodhana in Veni-Sanhara and Maitreyi in Mrichakatika, before he became famous on the political stage. The group performed only prose plays with minimum of singing. They acted in Tamil, Telegu and English and covered epics, historical and social themes. The Sabha certainly elevated drama and acting, endowing them with a kind of respectability.

I had occasion to see the novel performances of the Parsi theatre which was eye-catching, for they had some excellent acting. They were also neater and compact and did not drag like others. The Zorastrian Natak Mandali went back to the eighties. Other Parsi companies followed like Elphistone, Alfred. A repertory was formed in Urdu, Shahanama, that performed colourful shows like Arabian Nights as also Shakespeare, the latter were more crisp and terse than the Shakespearean shows I had seen in other Indian languages. Among actors in my time Baliwalla is best remembered as the most innovative and daringly adventurous. He took his troupe abroad, visited England, played before Queen Victoria and was rewarded by her in token of her appreciation, a fact very few seem to know. Some of these Parsis were resourceful in stage craft besides histrionics. They used for their themes Sanskrit and

Persian mythology, medieval legends, historical events from diverse races and peoples, made adaptations to suit local conditions. They brought women on the stage and the artist Gohar attained much fame. They also did pantomimes. I regret that those who never saw these plays malign them contemptuously. They were a passing phase by their very nature, but nevertheless carried a flavour of their own, which made obviously considerable impact even on seasoned theatre artists of the time.

It was the Parsi Theatre that introduced the Hindi drama to the Calcutta audience. Though matured, the audience seemed to have fallen for it. Even a veteran artist and one of the pioneers of the modern Bengali Theatre, Sisir Bhaduri joined the Bengali Theatre of the Madans who ran the Parsi Theatre, along with several other Bengali artists. Equally interesting is it to realise that Prithviraj Kapoor, the veteren actor of Bombay, had his first innings in the Calcutta Parsi Theatre.

When poet-musician Harindranath and I teamed up it was for sharing of dreams and ambitions to devote ourselves to create a new theatre in India, for much of the existing theatre had degenerated even since my girlhood days. We felt an urge to revitalize this art, for it was potentially a superb creative expression and sensitively a most effective medium for communication, which could portray real life as it confronted men and women, show up the contrasts within society, the strivings and pitfalls of mortals, and realise and experience the ultimate unity of life and shape the integrated man.

And, now at last I was going to taste the fulfilment of my long standing ambition to act on a real stage. I felt almost shaken by a new passion. The plays were in simple prose or blank verse, dialogues light and direct, the themes woven around current life, several on the lives of saints. The last was very much in vogue at the time and which later spilled over into the films in all Indian languages. We did short plays also in English and a few Shakespearan scenes which Harindranath was able to put across by his powerful acting.

To give shape to this we got together a youthful group who shared our aspirations. They were engaged in various professions but would take time off to appear in our shows periodically. They were content to carry on as amateurs, only getting their expenses covered, with some pocket money. We failed however to recruit any women though several were interested. They were obviously discouraged. The two who joined as were the dancer Maneka (Leila Sokhey) and her dancer sister Mira Chatterji. They were glad to have a chance to perform in public, and their dances were included in our shows whenever they wished.

Leila Sokhey—Maneka—the name by which she became known as a dancer, was a leading pioneer in the dance field. She was already trained in European dancing but feeling dissatisfied, she took up Indian dancing very earnestly and enjoyed it. This was at a time when dancing had come under a cloud and public performances by young women were frowned upon. With a natural ease, not displaying any bull-like passion, Maneka ventured into this storm-ridden vocation and won credit.

When she first began her dances on our stage, she did simple lyrical pieces in Kathak. Later she went into it seriously as a life mission, setting up a permanant centre in Lonavala called Nrityalaya, drawing inspiration from Ajanta for the rhythmic significance of forms, and built up a permanent dance ensemble. She built a nucleus, but did not live to see it fully flower. I am however grateful that her early burgeoning was happily intertwined with our brave effort of rejuvenating the performing arts.

The public prejudice against women actresses arose largely because of their association with 'professional' women. In Tamil Nadu there had been a purely professional women's troupe a long time ago, but evidently an *ad hoc* event with no historical continuity.

In this context I should like to describe a short interlude I once went through in Mangalore, my home town. Mrs. Margaret Cousins had come as head of the National Girls' School running in the house my mother had placed at its disposal until its own building was constructed. Mrs. Cousins launched various projects for collecting funds for this; one of them was staging her husband's verse drama, Mira Bai. She enlisted me to play this role. The male roles were to be played by some of the young men of the town interested in acting. I was delighted, for the play was a lovely poem which I knew would unfold itself when acted, like a beautiful lotus. I got busy setting the verses to music and was unaware of the storm this had raised. I could hardly believe that an educated community could generate such active antagonism to a woman playing a dramatic role and for such a commendable cause. We were threatened with boycott of the play, which meant no sale of tickets, thereby frustrating its very purpose. But by now it had become to us *a cause* and to abandon it would mean acknowledging that what we were trying to do was wrong. We had to stand by what we believed was right, specially when we were threatened. In the midst of it all came a letter from no less a person than Mrs. Besant herself to Mrs. Cousins, calling on her to give up the show as it would bring a bad name to the school. Evidently somebody had put this into her head. We felt very let down but it was too late to explain the case to Mrs. Besant.

To save ourselves from a sense of complete defeat Mrs. Cousins decided to have a party at her house and put on this play on the porch with a few personal invitees to witness it. But evidently even this was anathema to these social gangsters. Mother was warned that I would be in danger if I took part, so in panic I was locked up in a room. Later she brought me out to tell me that the man who was to have played the hero had been enticed into a car on some false pretext and abducted. So the play would be off in any case.

I rushed to Mrs. Cousins' feeling humiliated. But she was calm and composed. Gently stroking my fevered head and face, she suggested that we still go through with it, for she would play the hero and I do Mira Bai. That was exactly what we did with a sort of triumph.

And now at last I was going to taste the fulfilment of my ambition to act on a real stage. I felt almost shaken by a new passion. I threw myself wholeheartedly into the theatre vortex. Harindranath wrote simple plays, both on current life as well as on stories from the epics and the lives of the saints. Since he himself composed the music, directed and acted we were able to produce something new and vibrant. We cast away the old stage paraphernalia. Simple properties were created with plain fabric for background, cardboard, brown and coloured paper-cuts which proved marvels in artistic conception and unique in colour effects. The whole look was original and stunning. The popular enthusiasm and the wide response this evoked gave us encouragement and confidence. We were thus preparing a whole new tradition in production and acting. No more the distraction of heavy and costly trappings and costumes which had been the vogue of the day. The stigma that was attached to men and women playing as stage artists was an index of its degeneration. It was not going to be an easy task to cleanse and purify it with simplicity and aesthetic beauty but we did it, undaunted by prejudice and criticism.

I got a lot of pleasure out of designing costumes, experimenting with tie-dying to turn out unexpected patterns, staining fabrics to get magical effects in a variety of colours.

We travelled through the country performing also in small towns. There were no theatres in those days, ordinary public halls had to do duty for them. Often filthy and dilapidated, we had first ourselves to sweep and clean the hall. But it was all very exhilarating and we brushed the many impediments off cheerfully. We were able to attract artists though some could be with us only for short periods. The experience was like a crusade, working tirelessly for the dawn of a new era for the drama and the stage. We did short plays in Hindi, sometimes scenes from Shakespeare which Harindranath was able to successfully put across by his superb acting. We were still a small group of dedicated volunteers moulding into theatre artists. But Harindranath's multifaceted personality made up in variety and quality to provide substance and prestige. As the popularity of the new venture increased we believed that the renaissance of the stage art had taken birth.

In my active involvement with the emerging art world, the inspiration and guidance for me came largely from an extraordinary personality, G. Venkatachalam, one of the several valuable contacts I had won from my association with the Theosophical Society. He possessed a scintillating mind as also a prodigious knowledge of the different Indian cultural expressions and forms; philosophy, literature, music, dance, sculpture, architecture, handicrafts. Above all he was deeply devoted to the promotion of the living artists to ensure their success. He worked tirelessly and selflessly to promote art and artists, seeking nothing for himself. He moved through the country into remote unknown villages to seek out artists, old and young, encourage and help them, collect their pictures, and introduce them to the wider world.

His contribution to the furthering of the flowering renaissance was invaluable. Venkatachalam was much sought after for he was a man of many parts. He assisted as member of the National Art Purchase Committee and as member of the boards of art studies in various universities. As member of the Central Museum Committee he did signal service, for in those days there were very few who knew much of Museology. His unique contribution was in shaping the content and structure of the three National Akademis. An equally valuable service he rendered was in the formation and setting up of Craft Design Centres for the Handicrafts Board in various regions for reorientation of craft objects. For, styles of living change and habits alter, daily functioning calls for transformations in the objects we use and handle. But it needs great sensitivity and creative genius to make alteration without damaging their basic beauty. That is where Venkatachalam's creative genius met the needs.

I felt very fortunate to be befriended and deeply privileged to work with him in several of his varied activities. He often travelled with our theatre outfit, acting some part, and helping in a thousand ways.

In my awakening to new things, handicrafts were becoming meaningful as choice select ones were included in the art exhibitions Venkatachalam and I were organising. Venkatachalam painstakingly revealed to me some of their subtler charms. With my background of an innate preference for the genuine traditional articles of everyday use, I eagerly began to imbibe their history, the nature of the craftsmanship that went into each, and the breathtaking delicacy of the lines, the significance of the designs, the long processes involving tremendous patient labour. Each had a message for us, each was like a new door opening to lead one on into an expanding world that I was later to find limitless. It kept enticing me into a quest that became one of my life's missions.

But it was only after I met Gandhiji that I came to understand the deep relationship of handicrafts with our daily life. How enormously beneficial it was for us "to live with them and make them an integral part of our everyday existence", to quote him. The pleasurable sensation I enjoyed by the mere feel of the object and the tender sensitivity it breathed into the air, were experiences I valued and I still cherish like harmonious tones of music that echo in one's being even after the sound itself has died away, and the sensations that tingle in one's veins at the sight of mingling colours.

In one of my earliest visits to Gandhiji, I found Dr. James Cousins, the noted Irish poet and a theosophist, with him, with a few handicraft objects lying before them. Gandhiji then expounded what was then considered one of his weird philosophies but now proved scientific, the need for using our hands, one of our chief mediums for creative expression. Equally compelling was the need to preserve what we could of this grand heritage and how beneficial it was to live with it. Association is the essence of relationship which endears articles of everyday use to the user. This endearment finds ways of enhancing the aesthetic values in these articles, just as we love to dress up our loved ones, so we love to embellish our homes. Here the Craftsman employs his ingenuity through creative imagination. We are mostly carried away by a finished product, may be excited by watching the process, but remain unmindful of the deep chords within us that are stimulated when we create something with our own hands. Therefore in the Indian tradition, craftsmanship does not mean making novel and exotic articles to please one's fancy, but *endowing* everything we use in our daily life with beauty. Therefore nothing is created without a purpose. Thus did Gandhiji expound his philosophy on handicrafts.

Slowly this kept sinking into me. Later I absorbed more as I read some of our ancient texts on crafts which I later recorded in my book, 'India's Craft Tradition'.

Spinning, which I had already started, led me logically to weaving. Unfortunately, I was not able to practise it long enough (for political events intervened to interrupt) to become proficient in it, but long enough to experience some of its subtler nuances, that I had already begun to experience like my music. Patterns were first formed within me which then found expression in the different designs that I began to weave. Imitation or copying was strictly rejected by our ancient teachers, for each time an artist formulated an image, no matter what the object, it had to be a fresh creation. Even where an existing scene or object was to be depicted, the artist or craftsman had to deeply dwell on it, absorb its essence (rasa), then create.

Venkatachalam attracted my attention to painting, sensitivising me to the subtleties of each painter. He introduced me to architecture in monuments as well as sculptures in temples. I took long stimulating instructive tours with him.

The most pleasurable memories I have are of the cultural events organised by Venkatachalam when exhibitions of paintings by Masters together with those of the younger, up and coming painters were put up. These were combined with music and dance, again by masters and novices, to encourage and project them.

Venkatachalam was also a successful salesman in finding buyers to lift works of art. I acquired a few, one was a set of line illustrations of Tagore's dance drama, Nateer Puja, by Nandalal Bose. They were six different sketches each showing a separate dance pose. After the exhibition closed, I took possession of my treasures, Nandalal's sketches, and arranged them on a table. This was one of the happiest moments of my life. Venkatachalam, standing by me, was also gazing at them. 'Have you spotted anything unusual in any of the sketches ?' he asked with an amused smile. I shook my head. 'No, you won't. You are too blurred by your excitement. Just look at this sketch,' he pointed his finger at one of them. 'Both the feet of this dancer are left feet.' 'Oh, what does it matter, to me it is still a perfect picture,' I retorted with involuntary annoyance. My joy did not diminish because of what may be termed a blemish.

I begged of Venkatachalam to keep this to himself. 'Only an eye like yours would detect it. But how many have your eyes ?' I persuaded myself the episode had ended there.

To my utter discomfiture came a very sweet letter from the artist himself. Someone who had spotted this error alerted the painter who wanted the set back. I wrote a polite reply that I was perfectly happy with the sketches as they were and I valued them greatly. So I must be excused if I refused to send them back. What Nandalal really felt I don't know, but he made no further demand. In fact we had occasion to meet after that but he made no reference to it. I remembered in this context what the famous singer Inayat Khan had once said when he was eulogising Abdul Karim Khan's voice. 'Even if he sang *besoor*, it would still be sweet to the ear.' To me the sketch was precious, one left foot or two.

An important source of this resurgent glow in the country was the cultural complex at Shantiniketan, Poet Rabindranath Tagore's experiment in transforming the ancient Ashram into a current school for a variety of creative expressions.

My first contact with it was during Tagore's visit to Bombay with his dance drama troupe when I first saw his plays, which was an unusually delightful experience. Though originally Tagore used to both produce and act himself, he did not take part any more. He sat at a side on the stage to lend his presence which, for me and the audience, endowed the show with a kind of glory and sanctity. Everybody was literally spell bound. I was deeply moved. Here was a new dramatic force. Never before had we seen any show of such artistic perfection and so vastly different from the usual. Sarojini Naidu who was present, paid a poetic tribute to Tagore, then dramatically placed a garland of flowers at his feet and the hall rang with 'Gurudev ki Jai.'

It was here that Harindranath and I first met Tagore. We told him of our grand design for a new theatre. He became interested and suggested we visit him at Shantiniketan and see him at his work.

I realised how significant was Poet Tagore's contribution to the regeneration of the Indian drama and theatre. Breaking through the old conventional forms, he created new drama forms, bold yet simple. Tagore's dramas were essentially lyrical and his imagery seemed to take wings. Nevertheless through the subtle garb of these poetic metaphysics rang the biting tone of stark reality.

When we talked of his dramas when I was later visiting him, he explained to me how originally these activities had been confined to his traditional home at Jerasanko in Calcutta and mainly his family members. The Poet's grandfather Dwarkanath Tagore germinated a virile seed of the theatre in the family bosom. The senior Tagore ended his association with the English theatre by acquiring the famous Chowringhee Theatre and later helped construct Sans Souce, thus actively helped the growth of the public theatre which to a section of Calcutta was then anathema. The Brahmos I learnt with wonder were stiffly opposed to the public theatre, a trend I had not been made aware of by the Brahmos in the South. According to the Poet, his elder brother Jyotirindranath was the dynamo who kept the theatre activity moving, himself writing plays, directing, acting. His own theatre career, the Poet explained, began in the same vein when he was twenty-five and continued uninterrupted for a full half century.

With the advent of Shantiniketan, dramatics became an integral part of the school activities with the Poet himself taking part.

There had thus come to be built around his superb personality a fine team of choice artists. By their high artistic standard they attracted great attention as the Poet took them to different parts of India. These tours were partly to garner a financial harvest to replenish the depleted chests of Shantiniketan.

When Gandhiji came to know of the Poet's money hunting expeditions, he was both distressed and shocked. 'The great poet cannot be allowed to go around with a begging bowl. It is a national sin !' he exclaimed. He personally met Tagore to stop him from further wanderings. He offered to take on the begging. 'I am a master at that art,' he soothed the bewildered Poet.

What had moved Gandhiji were not only Tagore's writings but

equally a drama performance, Dak Ghar (Post Office) in which the Poet and several of his family members including artist Abanindranath, acted. Gandhiji had once told me of how moved he had been by it to which Kasturba had added her own pleasure in witnessing it.

I was getting more deeply involved in these cultural activities. They opened out my creative channels and at periods I was fully absorbed in a kind of an euphoria. I felt I was an active participant in a glowing Indian renaissance. My concept of renaissance was however not romantic. To me it meant action leading to self discovery, a realisation of one's potential in creativity, in resources, knowledge, aptitude, attuned to a new orientation to flow into the current stream. Its main characteristics had to be all inclusive to bring out the universal quality pregnant in the essence of India's basic message to humanity. For contrary to general belief, the creative principle of the universe in my understanding, is not external, but internal. The past nestles in the present as the future burgeons forth from it. I experienced a sense of both elation and satisfaction to be amongst the carriers as it were, composed of talented people inspired to launch a project bigger than themselves, to enrich the entire nation. "If we are to make progress we must not *repeat* history but make *new* history", said Gandhiji.

In the midst of this euphoria came what then seemed like a little interruption but which was to set me on a very different course from what I was currently treading.

4

There arrived one day two visitors from Hubli, Karnataka, Dr. Hardikar and Umabai Kundapur. The former was a reputed political worker who made history after the Nagpur Flag Satyagraha in 1920. From then on the tri-colour Congress flag became synonymous with a national flag. When a ban was placed on it, a movement was started to assert the right to carry it. Though the response was good, the youth who joined were neither adequately politically informed nor trained to face the hardships the law breakers encountered. The result was a fiasco. Dr. Hardikar, fresh from the United States, after a period of collaboration with the famous political leader Lala Lajpat Rai in political campaigning was deeply distressed by the collapse in Nagpur. He saw the compelling need to give thorough training to political workers, mental and physical, if a political battle was to be successful.

From his early school days he showed intense patriotic fervour, became a devoted follower of Tilak. He founded a youth group Arya Bal Sabha to foster love of freedom through study, group discussion, physical training through a gymnasium. They literally used thrown away packing boxes as improvised platforms from which to harangue market crowds on current political issues. When the police attacked and dispersed them, they carefully saved their box-platforms, moved to another part of the city and began their harangue again. The meetings always began and ended with singing of Vande-Mataram.

Later he worked under Lala Lajpat Rai's direction carrying on intensive pro-Indian publicity and gained considerable initiative in the modalities of work, which equipped him excellently for the very valuable work he performed later in India. The Michigan University in America where he studied was so impressed by his power of organisation, his effective lecturing, it appointed him extension lecturer. His talks were also on Indian history, society, culture. This trained him for excellent public relations as well as keeping India before the American academic community, for he was sent out to places outside of Michigan.

Dr. Hardikar was a most unusual person. Thin, wiry, but full of a hidden robust strength which it was hard to guess where it lay, he worked with a single-minded purpose like a bull in harness, not drawn into sidelines. He was a most excellent organiser. With these basic requisites he was able to build up a superb army of devoted workers in a volunteer body. Thus started the Hindustani Seva Dal, a body that played a very unique role in the freedom struggle, under Dr. Hardikar's driving direction.

Umabai Kundapur was reputed as an enterprising and unusual type of social worker of many parts. She was known to mix dramatics and entertainment in her fare of social work as part of the milieu. She had even written and produced a play 'Swadeshi Vrata'. She was a woman capable of quiet endurance and the robust inner strength that goes with it. She had lost her husband less than a year before I met her, a mate who had also been her companion in her social enterprises. The loss was therefore doubly greater. It meant having to leave her old haunts in Bombay and come to Hubli to start afresh. She had done it, perfectly composed and not making an exhibition of her bruised emotions.

Later as I came to know Umabai, I found in her a unique personality. She had tremendous energy, but it never bubbled and overflowed; though highly disciplined she was never dry or rigid, and though she kept a strict grip over herself to regulate her activities, she looked perfectly relaxed. She had equipped herself to meet the challenges a social worker has to face from the stern school of life itself, for she had not been able to go in for higher specialised training. Her public career in a backward region of Karnataka started when women were still confined to domestic chores. To recruit women volunteers and train them in public camps for physical culture, route marches, etc., was then an outlandish idea. She laid herself open to wild criticism. With great patience and good humour she had to toil and wear down the hard and crusty dykes of conservatism. It was unbelievable but true nevertheless, that streams of women filed into her camp, from girls of seven to old women of forty years. Still youthful at just past thirty, rather frail, of a light frame, soft of speech, she made an odd captain of an army of volunteers training for a national struggle.

Though she attained prominence in politics having been active in the freedom struggle, when offices were offered to her after freedom, she turned them away. She adhered to her pledge of a Desh Sevika and took up instead Kasturba Trust activities. I have seen her well gone in age, still trudge through the stony pathways of our countryside. The early pioneer bodies she promoted, Bhagini Mandals all over Karnataka, Tilak Kanya Shala, girls' schools, have progressed and prospered. Today even at the age of 90 she is still active and proves herself an incredible woman. Her mind is still young and retains the keenness to know and learn, so rare in the old. Above all, I cherish all I learnt from her to be a sepoy and a sevika, which she taught combining it with a delicate sense of humour which lent piquancy and colour to the driest of subjects, the sterñest of occasions.

These two were here on a special mission. They were recruiting volunteers for the coming Belgaum Congress. Umabai had become head of a special women's section newly opened in the Seva Dal. I readily agreed. Umabai however regarded me rather quizzically and with a slight smile said, 'Don't be in a hurry, think it over. A volunteer's life is very hard. You are used to some comfort.' Dr. Hardikar had however a bigger and more serious request to make: ask me to enrol myself in the Seva Dal as a long term volunteer in the new women's section under Umabai. Seva Dal was then only a name to me. Seeing my bewilderment, Umabai intervened: "Let her do one stint, then decide.' I nodded lamely, unable to take it all in. 'Well I will get back to you one day,' was the Doctor's determined retort.

I had no idea what being a volunteer meant. I drew a romantic picture of soldiers of freedom marching with banners. I was equally exhilarated by the picture of Gandhiji heading the vast concourse, for I was given the glad tidings that he was to preside over the Belgaum Congress session. I had never been to a Congress session before and did not realise we would be far from his presence.

I arrived in Belgaum a few weeks earlier than the session to get trained along with a large band of novices like myself, to do the jobs assigned to us. We were quartered in bare thatched huts and being the peak of winter, Belgaum on an elevation was bitterly cold. As I was accustomed to a mild climate this was a trial to start with. The barest of what may be called comfort, was provided. Here was the much lauded austerity with a vengeance. We had to be up at cock-crow, wash in cold water—to me another trial having been used to only warm water. We had to go on long route marches, do vigorous exercises. Walking was easy, having exercised myself to become an indefatigable walker. Keeping vigil at night, shared between two, one watching inside, the other making the rounds of the camp, was novel. Unlike some, I had no fear of the dark and was rather proud of it. But the cold did bite into me.

We had dark blue-black saris with the Congress flag colours for border. While individually this looked smart, *en masse* they made a gloomy picture. Later at the Madras session of the Congress, when I was in charge of the Women Volunteers, I put them into the vivid Indian orange which the girls greatly loved, and the corps came to be known as the 'Orange Brigade', which continued for several years.

Outside of seeing to the needs of the delegates, especially the women and children, in the camp and at the sessions, guarding entrances, keeping order, which included relieving the mothers of rebellious children and pacifying the inconsolable, crying babies, we could not even dream of attending the proceedings, curious though we were, particularly when Gandhiji and his stalwart colleagues were addressing the meet. Once when Sarojini Naidu's daughters wanted to see me, they were solemnly told they would have to get special permission from our Captain. So they literally marched up and saluted Umabai, a perfect picture of feminity and grace, and got her consent. Umabai told me later she was hard put to controlling her mirth watching the two young ladies march single file and solemnly salute. They had even gone to the trouble of wearing black saris for the visit. The girls told me later they had gone to the bazaar and got them for they somehow got the impression that to get entry into the women volunteer's camp, they should also be clad in black! The person who directed them had talked in such solemn whispers as to give the impression that our camp was kind of out of bounds. This comedy apart, the women volunteers were very professional and performed so well, that Gandhiji paid a special tribute to our work and in his opinion, he added, they had contributed greatly to the success of the session. We were highly pleased for we knew that the last thing Gandhiji indulged in was flattery.

This was my first experience of a Congress Session. I had assumed it would be a dull and drab affair as the usual political gatherings were. Here however an original touch had been added by trying to endow the camp with the lost glories of Vijayanager that gave us all a thrill. Noted artists, musicians of the region had been especially invited which to me was like lighting a lamp in the gloom of these otherwise shapeless flapping conglomeration of tents. Veena Seshanna was there, his magical fingers running over the veena strings, the sound glowing like glittering rain drops, and my old friend painter Venkatappa, with a glorious set of pictures on the life of Buddha. There were Kirtankars filling the spaces with Bhajans that echoed far and wide.

Politically it was a momentous session for fears of a split in the organisation were apprehended. Though we volunteers were on duty off and on where the session was going on, we were too engrossed in our very mundane duties to listen to the debates. But delegate friends gave me news sheets or related some of the tense events.

The Belgaum Congress met when the pulls between the pro-Changers led by stalwarts like Motilal Nehru and C.R. Das had reached a critical stage. Gandhiji, who headed the no-Changers, evidently was not happy at the thought of the Congress entering the legislatures under the nomenclature of the Swaraj Party. Gandhiji in his usual simple manner of disarming strong opposition wisely offered to step down to give the Congress an unfettered hand. He assured the Swarajists he had no wish to *weaken* or *embarrass* them, to use his own words.

All is well that ends well was what we all said, our hearts light with relief.

Gandhiji's last act before the Session closed was performing the investiture ceremony of the Seva Dal volunteers which seemed to us like his farewell blessing.

Dr. Hardikar got back to me after the session closed to repeat his request. He wanted my active cooperation, including regular contributions to the Seva Dal Journal, about which I was diffident, never having ventured beyond school compositions. He suggested I begin by recording my experiences of the Belgaum Session, which I did. After this came a longish illness with a prolonged convalescence during which my doctor enjoined complete bed rest. I protested I would feel useless. He suggested continuing with my writing as a follow up of the Seva Dal series I had done. He was very confident my articles would be published. Thus began my career as a writer, the only profession I can lay claim to in the constant turmoil I keep going through. While acting stirred and elated me, writing relaxed and put me at ease. Moments of deepest distress or depression are lightened when I start writing. I am unconcerned whether it finds its way into print or not. The experience gives me ample satisfaction.

Dr. Hardikar claimed some of my time and attention to acquaint myself with the Seva Dal at its headquarters at Hubli. I found that the Seva Dal was building up a composite life of its own. Satyagraha was a unique style of battle and called for an equally original type of training which the Seva Dal had to imaginatively provide. While the main objective was to develop the full personality of each trainee through exercising the fullest potentialities, it called for special use of psychological elements. When attacked the natural reaction is to hit back. Here the victim had to endure untold physical pain as also mental humiliation. Here pain in a manner is invited on oneself, with no scope for relief through retaliation. Similarly in a normal fist fight a result emerges and the matter normally ends. But here the volunteer is arrested after being beaten. Psychologically the struggle drags, offers no immediate satisfaction. This called for prolonged sustained stamina, firm faith in the objective which may not even be realised in the volunteer's life time.

A central training academy for thorough systematic all round training functioned at Bagalkot in the Hubli region, where a band of young men and women were hard at work to carry out the courses carefully prepared towards these objectives. Physical culture was equally important. Included in this were several indigenous exercises handed down through generations, such as lathi, danda, bhala, sword and dagger play, suryanamaskars and various yogasanas. When adapted for mass performance, they appeared almost martial. A whole Hindi vocabulary for giving orders had been worked out.

The Seva Dal gave the Congress flag a national status and with it an emotional respect, as to a national symbol. It originally comprised of two coloured strips, red for the Hindus, green for the Muslims. But when shown to Gandhiji for approval he added white at the top to represent other religious communities, with the Charkha in the centre to symbolise a basic productive activity of the masses. Thus came into being India's first national flag under which millions fought the freedom battles for over two decades, until the current flag was redesigned from it in 1947.

Appropriately the Seva Dal worked out a set ceremonial pattern for the hoisting of this flag to endow it with sanctity and reverence. The hoisting and lowering of the flag on important occasions became a ritual, and for this permanent platforms were built around each flag pole. Every volunteer camp hoisted it in the morning and lowered it in the evening with a fixed ritual carefully worked out, to the accompaniment of the singing of appropriate songs on the pride and glory of the flag. This 'flag-hoisting' ceremony was observed the last Sunday of every month by volunteer units. This ceremony also became an indispensable part of an opening for every political gathering. It soon gained immense popularity through this assiduous observance and whenever a political dignitary visited a place, a flag hoisting ceremony by him or her became a must. Special flag songs were composed and sung at every flag ceremony. The flag songs were taken up and sung all over the country. The most popular was 'Jhanda Ooncha Rahe Hamara, Vijayi Vishwa Tri Ranga Pyara'. Every session of the National Congress opened with the flag hoisting as a prelude performed by the Congress President, although it was only years later, in 1931, that this improvised flag was formally adopted by the Congress as its official emblem with one change, the white strip being put in the centre between the red on the top and the green below.

Having gone through the preliminaries and the required training, I joined the Seva Dal, taking a solemn pledge that I would work as a Seva Dal volunteer wholeheartedly in the freedom struggle until my motherland became free. I took the pledge seriously, determined I would faithfully adhere to it and I did.

As the Seva Dal activities expanded and intensified, its popularity shot up. It seemed the volunteers offered help and service to the public in the most unexpected places and occasions, especially at large festivals, fairs, public meetings, etc. No volunteer was paid, only provided food in the camp or when on duty, and where needed, clothes. Students and those in professions came every evening regularly for their training.

The entire Seva Dal body with its multifarious activities was maintained by public donations. It was unbelievable how people extended cash and gifts, which was a clear proof of the public confidence it had won. All this was but the fruit of the magnificent manner in which Dr. Hardikar and his fast growing dedicated Sevaks and Sevikas had acquitted themselves.

My life in the Seva Dal camp had been a far cry from the art and theatre world in which I had been living for a long time. The effulgence of art objects, the electric throbs I would experience at the shows and the exhibitions, grew shadowy, like a dream. But I drew a different nourishment from the volunteer's career. It filled me with a new sense of robustness, and earthy freshness, an opening out into wider worlds, almost obliterating my little self. On the close of my Seva Dal training I traced my steps back to Mangalore.

It may not be incorrect to say that my public career really started seriously with my meeting Mrs. Margaret Cousins, Gretta as we called her. When I returned to Mangalore she was completing her last year as head of the National Girls' High School. The very first time we met, it was like old friends reuniting again.

Though there was considerable difference in our age, she never made me conscious of it, always treating me as an equal. She had a very powerful face with prominent bones that seemed to hold an inextinguishable strength. The eyes however were kindly, full of soft affection. Her mouth was the most vivacious and the lips had a faint quiver of laughter in them. She was full of energy and worked with great zest, generating her own incentives from within. She could go into ripples of laughter over little things which filled the air around with lightness and joy. Her love for her fellow beings was boundless. She not only gave all of her kind heart and body but also of her entire self. This echoed within me, for we were kindred spirits, for I too have always given myself entirely, and wholeheartedly, not just bits and parts of me.

There were many things that we could share: books, poetry, music, paintings. She had graduated in music with the piano. Many a time on a quiet evening she would play the piano to me, and sometimes I would sing as she played. One day she offered to teach me a song which she had learned from Tagore himself. It was the 'Jana Gana Mana' which was one day to become the national anthem of free India.

Soon I became aware that her entry into my life was of tremendous import. My vague yearnings to serve society, especially women, could now take concrete shape. For she was a seasoned and practical worker who qualified to blaze the trail for Indian womens' freedom. Irish by birth, she had been active in the Suffragist Movement in Ireland and England and was arrested and imprisoned for her activity. But she was not exactly what was called a blue stocking in those days. She was an intellectual, but not dry, with unflinching devotion to the cause she had espoused and the humans she took under her wing. Human freedom and dignity were dear to her and the Indian women drew her sympathy and support. Mrs. Besant backed her and together they set up the Indian Women's Association in Madras through which Gretta and her band of workers laboured to organise the women and educate them on their claims to rights.

The first political move by the Indian women was made when Gretta organised a women's delegation in 1917 to Mr. Montague, the British Secretary of State for India, to press for women's political rights. In the early twenties, after the advent of the new political set up, when the Indian Provincial Legislatures began to grant franchise to women, she was thrilled. Every time any such news appeared in the press she would rush to share her pleasure with me.

Women were beginning to assert themselves in different fields. One day, Gretta, her face all aglow, showed me the picture of a mammoth procession led by Kamalabai Deshpande, daughter of the famous political leader, N.C. Kelkar. The Pune Municipal Council had resolved to make municipal primary education compulsory, but no mention to include girls was made. Within 24 hours the women of Pune almost spontaneously came out into the streets in their strength to show how keenly they felt this discrimination.

There was another unusual event of a teenager, Snehalata, killing herself to save her father from having to provide dowry for her and ruin the family. The whole country was electrified. Young men took pledges not to take dowry, girls swore they would not allow themselves to be sold. It was a little more than a seven days wonder. This was in the late twenties and the social reform movement was gathering momentum and striding ahead.

In 1924 representatives of women's organisations in Madras like the Bharath Sthri Mahamandal, Tamil Ladies' Association, the women's branch of the Brahmo Samaj, etc. led by the Women's Indian Association, appeared before the Governor, Lord Willingdon, to ask that the disqualification which prevented women from membership of the legislatures in India be removed. It was pointed out that this bar did not exist in the new Reforms Act but only in the rules. So it just needed the deletion of the disqualification clause which consisted of three significant words 'Is a female...'. They were a group of gracious charming women 'quite an eyeful', as someone remarked, speaking faultless English. But the only response was Lord Willingdon's unceremonious exit leaving a tantalising void behind.

The frustrated gathering had to be reminded that the demand that 'women be regarded as people' was first made in 1917 when a women's delegation waited on Lord Chelmsford and Mr. Montague. The long awaited Reforms of 1921 had however remained ominously silent on this vital question. This was not strange since the English women themselves at that time did not enjoy the right of franchise.

After this had followed the Southborough Committee to 'gather evidence' to prove that the Indian women *really* desired franchise. Similarly, later in 1924, a Reforms Enquiry Committee started recording evidence and views for the next two years on whether the Indian women *really* desired membership of the Legislatures. Finally with the removal of the ban in 1927, the Madras State Provincial Legislature threw open its membership to women when there were only a few weeks left for a fresh election.

Though a constitutional victory had been scored the question was : who would have the temerity to contest with so little time to prepare. It was bound to be an unequal contest. As the candidates selected by the various parties for the election were already busy in the campaign, it seemed too late and would need a bulldog courage for a woman to venture into the fray.

But Gretta took up the challenge instantly and made a bee-line for me. I could only wobble an answer that since I belonged to no party, I could only venture as an independent. Gretta was undaunted. Like a shaft from the blue she stirred up Mangalore, launching me into a contest for the Madras Legislative Council. We discovered that my name was not even in the voter's list ! For in those days franchise was based on ownership of property and I owned no property. A long term lease of some property was hurriedly arranged to enable me to pay the tax on property and be entitled to vote. So more time was lost, which I could ill afford.

It was Gretta who organised the campaign, publicity, volunteer corps and all the necessary paraphernalia. Music and cultural shows were introduced at election meetings which people thoroughly enjoyed. An entirely different atmosphere was created by Gretta's creative brain and all tension, vulgarity, abuses were scrupulously avoided. The band of volunteers with dark blue badges (this was the first time that badges were introduced), had a sense of purpose, an emotion of romance and chivalry injected into them by the style of the campaign. It was an election that people continued to remember over several years as a great experience. Gretta worked very hard and made everyone else work too.

Time was, however, against us and as is, I presume, common in elections, one group of voters changed sides literally overnight over the Central Assembly candidate, and as the two were kind of tied being simultaneous, I got ditched in the process. I lost by a difference of barely 55 votes. I felt more sorry for Gretta having to meet with defeat inspite of her hard and sincere effort. It had been her plan, on which she had so set her heart. For myself I felt singularly unaffected. It came on me suddenly how little political career meant for me. This seemed to set the key to my future career.

Before the parting, Gretta pressed my shoulders and laughingly made the following enigmatic remark : 'Now that you have pledged yourself as a volunteer, I have a big job for you and these firm shoulders must carry it.'

Gretta now got busy organising a national conference of women to formulate proper educational policies to be recommended to the government in answer to a challenge from the Director of Education of Bengal, asking the women to state what they wanted, instead of merely complaining. She asked me to help her with this meet. Finally began for me the social service career for which I had qualified academically.

It seemed natural that Pune should be the venue for the Conference. Gretta, with her unerring instinct, had selected it, and naturally the seat of the activity was to be the Seva Sadan.

Ramabai Ranade was no more, but her spirit still seemed to linger. Now there were her devoted colleagues, Shrimati Janakibai Bhatt and Shrimati Yamutai Bhatt. They were both venerable elderly ladies who breathed solidity and reliability. Thus the Seva Sadan came to play a pivotal role in this pioneer activity. For it not only provided a physical centre but the necessary energy, hard working disciplined workers, organisers of experience and maturity. Above all an atmosphere of idealism and selflessness. It is no wonder that Gretta after her close contacts with this institution set up a Seva Sadan in Madras.

I worked only as a volunteer specially doing night duty to meet the delegates coming by odd trains, getting them settled, seeing to their needs, etc. I was however dimly aware that this pioneering effort would give birth to something big and worthwhile. The All India Women's Conference that now emerged was to play a key role in the life of the Indian women for almost three decades.

I saw for the first time many of the veteran women leaders of that time. Being far senior they looked rather imposing. Gretta was of course the centre, like a generating dynamo.

As the Conference was about to close, Srimati Sarojini Naidu conveyed to me a request from the Assembly to accept the General Secretaryship of the Conference. I became panicky and quickly declined, for I hardly knew what this meant. Sarojini was quite annoyed. 'Don't be silly now. Did you not want to be a social worker, and here when your services are being sought, you refuse. You better accept it,' she said with finality. 'Gretta will explain what you have to do, so don't start any argument.' The next I knew Sarojini was on her feet to deliver the vote of thanks. I was to discover in course of time that whenever she was present at a conference she was called on to do this, for her magnificent oratory left everybody elated and in a good mood, wiping away the earlier strains and grouses. In the course of her speech she commented on the excellent choice of the new Secretary on whose young shoulders had fallen an onerous task. In her inimitable way she made a slight passing reference to my painful election episode. 'Her spectacular performance blazed a new trail for Indian womanhood. We should however congratulate ourselves on that unhappy result. for the loss of one State now means the gain of the entire country.' On the loud applause that followed I felt as though my fate were sealed. Gretta bubbled with laughter when she looked at my woebegone face. 'You look like someone condemned to the gallows,' she mocked. I was really atremble as I confessed my fears of disgracing myself before these grand women. For I did not even know what exactly a Secretary did. 'I will guide you. I have agreed to be the Chairman of the Standing

Committee and you will work with me,' reassured Gretta. With such faith reposed in me, I had only one desire, to make good and justify it. One thought however baffled me, why did she have to make Sarojini feel it was her choice. Gretta replied softly, 'Some day when you have learnt to handle public affairs, you will see my wisdom.' I left it at that. Unluckily very little of such wisdom seems to have come my way.

The first President of the Conference was Maharani Chimnabai Gaekwad of Baroda. She had been chosen because of the promotion of women's education that she and the Maharaja had done in their State which was also among the earliest to bring in legislation to raise the age of marriage. Her husband Sayaji Rao, the Maharaja was a progressive ruler and the Maharani a fitting mate. She was the first in the royal family which kept strict purdah, to throw it off. The Maharani was a definite personality with very much of a mind of her own. She took interest also in the welfare activities of the State along with her husband. To promote women's education she set up a Trust with a large initial donation from herself, to provide scholarships for girls. As the Maharaja enjoyed the company of creative and intellectual persons, she lived in a stimulating atmosphere of ever widening fruitful horizons, different from the decadence associated with royalties. She travelled constantly with him when he went abroad and saw a good deal of the western world.

I was a bit in awe of her rather forbidding appearance, but when she found me conversing with her in Marathi, she thawed a good deal and we became fairly companionable.

Gretta now became like a Guru to me and as Chairman of the Standing Committee of the Conference we developed a more intimate relationship. She assured me, 'I am always with you. Whatever the problem, however deep the crisis, come to me. I will never let you down.' These words were to me like a premonition. For some critical incidents did overtake me from time to time.

I decided that this conference which had started with some pomp and frills should be moulded into a business body. For this, in the first place, I had to set up an office when I knew next to nothing of running it. For a start I got myself a small typewriter and taught myself typing. While at school I had taken a course in shorthand and did well at the final test. The school encouraged me because of my partiality for writing. I now began to brush it up. In short I myself became the conference office, for there was just nobody else. Apart from doing clerical jobs, I trotted around mailing and distributing letters. To gain maturity in public work even apart from the technique of conducting an efficient office, Pune was an ideal setting. It seemed to buzz with active bodies, enthusiastic workers and above all I had at hand my infallible guardian angels at the Seva Sadan, Janakibai Bhatt and Yamutai Bhatt. The former had now become Treasurer of the Conference and showed her personal interest and concern in the Conference. She was a heavily built lady and seemed to ooze confidence and strength but was surprisingly soft spoken and of few words. I was glad for this, being rather exuberant myself, her quiet, cool disposition held promise of balancing it.

I devoted a part of my time to travel throughout the country, carrying on continuous propaganda among the public for social and legal changes to give women their rights. Judging by the large audiences of all classes of people that attended my meetings, I realised that my efforts were proving effective. Whenever possible conference bodies were being built up to provide structural shape to the movement and inject power into women's demands. I was striving to build up a live and vibrating body which would become dynamic enough to revolutionalise the scene. It never took on what in Western phraseology is called a *Feminist* role, in the narrow sense. As time went on I realised we would have to move and function within a wider parameter. The demand for national freedom had already been sounded as basic for our national well being. Thereupon followed the demand for equal opportunities for all, as obviously women were not the only victims of social and economic disabilities and discriminations, others were equally oppressed socially, and depressed economically. It was dimly growing on me that the women's struggle had therefore to be an indivisible part of the larger political, social and economic struggle.

My stay in Pune brought me into close contact with seasoned social bodies and their mature workers. One was the Servants of India Society. I had heard as a girl from Gopal Krishna Gokhale when he visited my uncle, how he had set up this great organisation which some of the best men in the country joined on a minimum monthly salary of Rs. 100, to devote their lives to the service of the country. It was he who had first given the idea of social service, as our duty, our obligation, that while we lived we should serve our fellow beings, and early in his young life he had given concrete shape to this concept.

With two members of this Society I had built up a very close association. One was Shri G. K. Deodhar who was a big prop behind the Seva Sadan and a vigorous champion of women's rights. He was also active in the cooperative movement in which I had already become interested. As I came to know him I leaned closely on his advice and guidance. The other member for whom I developed a very deep affection and regard was Shri Kodanda Rao. Later when Gandhiji was in Yerrawada jail, Pune, Kodanda Rao was our liaison with him. He was specially permitted to look after Gandhiji's needs, particularly the English paper 'Young India' and the Gujarati 'Navjivan' to keep them going. Kodanda Rao's scintillating mind, his extraordinary sense of humour and his pleasant, lovable disposition made him a most enjoyable companion. He was later reinforced in these qualities by an equally bubbling and bright companion, Mary. I greatly valued their friendship over many years as one of the bright spots in my life. Kodanda Rao however was perhaps better known for his vigorous championship for the retention of the English language.

It was however Srinivas Shastri whom I met first amongst the Society members. He looked an impeccable gentleman, faultlessly dressed without wearing formal clothes, generally in a dhoti and turban, elegant manners, nevertheless with an air of asceticism. He was what is popularly described as a 'finished' speaker. He belonged to a class of speakers that we rarely come across now. I was deeply impressed by his style which had clarity of thought, a hard core of substance which stays back in the mind of the audience as against a flashy, frothy, clever talk which leaves only thin vapours hanging, which evokes power, dwelling on persuasive expression rather than direct hammering. It etched an image of wisdom and moderation of balance. A colleague of Shastri's who attended the negotiations in South Africa was all admiration for this technique that Shastri had perfected in fairly successfully coming out of those long drawn battles unscathed. Mrs. Besant was another speaker of this calibre. Her speech was a work of art, finely chiselled as though coming from an electric needle.

In 1923, Shastri, who had devotedly espoused the cause of Indians abroad, was touring the country describing to Indians the tragic condition of the Indians in South Africa. He was a born teacher cum a social worker, and he could do both public speaking as also work in the community. He was visibly distressed by the South African situation.

He was to address a meeting in Mangalore. He invited me to speak along with him, but I became nervous. I was barely 20 and outside school debates I had never addressed meetings. He however pressed me to sit beside him on the platform, presuming that I would be moved by the sorrowful African scene and his own advocacy to break out into speech.

I felt weak with fright specially to speak on what seemed a far away political scene. Under Shastri's encouraging smile and kindly nod, I got onto my trembling feet and began to speak, my very first time to address a public meeting. I was relieved and happy to realise I had the facility of public speaking. I tried to keep the images of Mrs. Besant and Shastri before me to model on them : keep the voice low, clear enunciation, no emotional bubbles, let the thoughts flow with ease.

In all references to Shastri, his exceptional gift of oratory is emphasised. Earl Balfour, one time English Prime Minister, declared him as one of the foremost world orators. He was also hailed as one of the British Empire's silver tongued speakers. The Master of Balliol College, Oxford, confessed Shastri made English language sweeter. Of course Shastri was lots more than a silver tongued orator. The piquancy in the situation lies in the fact that his eloquence was expended in so many stormy, cantankerous negotiations at Imperial gatherings fighting for the rights of Indians abroad, especially in South Africa. He spoke calmly, in crisp, tight, telling sentences, no ranting, no tearing of humans to tatters. The lawyers of the League of Nations observed : 'His speech has a literary quality that excels anything in our public life, the pervading sincerity and comprehension of his arguments, restraint not distraint is his choice, the restraint of an apostle with brains but under control.'

Though I could not be a Shastri or Besant style speaker, modelling on them helped. When I was actively involved in the freedom movement there were two occasions where my speech carried the day for me against the official stand. Once it was at the All India Congress Committee meeting in Calcutta when I moved an amendment to a resolution on the political atrocities in the then Mysore State, and carried it. The Calcutta

Statesman highlighted this in its leader as a red letter day, for opposing and carrying a modification of the Working Committee resolution was indeed a rarity. The next occasion was at the open session of the Congress on the prevailing Congress policy on Indian States. Dr. Rajendra Prasad moved the main resolution which sought to convey a sense of satisfaction on the success reaped by the Congress through its current policies on Indian States and if the States people gain further strength the Congress may be able to identify itself more closely with the States' people. My amendment wanted this condition of 'waiting' to be replaced by immediate offer of every assistance by the Congress to the States' people in their struggle. Even the demand for a division was itself rare, made worse by its coming up at midnight. But this was accepted luckily with more good humour than anger by the Congress leaders.

But the Calcutta episode upset Gandhiji and the elders, and Pandit Nehru, who was presiding then had to bear the brunt of it for not throwing his weight sufficiently on the side of the Working Committee to see the resolution through.

I had occasion to work with Shri Venkataraman, another member of the Servants of India Society, a silent and diligent worker who had through the Society done pioneering work in the tribal belt in the Nilgiris, and he invited me to join him in this task. When I was Chairman of the Handicrafts Board, we were able to promote some of his projects, especially to preserve the beautiful Toda embroidery after rescuing it from extinction, or rather, distortion. The well meaning missionary women engaged in transferring the rich, heavy embossed embroidery to tiny household linen items, were destroying its native glory.

To me the rescuing of the Toda embroidery was compelling. A special centre was set up in charge of a young Toda lady with formal education. I discovered that the formal schooling, one of the earliest in the community, had unsettled her native taste. She preferred the pale characterless simplified work introduced by the Christian Missions as modern to the gorgeous original. She resented my insistence on keeping to the traditional. But as the women who actually did the stitching were very cooperative, we were able to turn out a large variety of items like garments, curtains, bed spreads, all carrying the dazzling real Toda work yet very current and functional. Years later I met the same rebellious Toda lady of the Centre. She began with an apology for her former evaluation of her native work. She had married a German, travelled in the west and 'seen the world' as she put it, and learned incidentally that the demand was for the 'traditional'. She promised to continue to devote herself to keep it going. She invited me to visit her work centre and assess her work now.

Pune had now become a great educational and progressive social base having travelled a long way from the days when reformers like Karve faced abuses. In Pune I came into touch with academicians belonging to the Deccan Education Society, promoted by Gopal Krishna Gokhale which had attracted some of the most brilliant and distinguished intellectuals of note. Like members of the Servants of India Society, these professors, many of whom had won high academic distinction, were content to accept just a pittance for their services. Dr. Paranjape, popularly known as the 'wrangler' as he had won the title in mathematics in Cambridge, was Principal of the Fergusson College in Pune, the centre of the idealistic youth, set up in 1885. He was a hearty, friendly gentleman and very good company. He talked enthusiastically of the age of idealism, of patriots like Tilak who once taught mathematics in Fergusson, and of his own generation, fired by zeal to serve India, to inspire the youth and build up a new world of knowledge, history, literature.

Shakuntala, his only daughter, was packing to go abroad for studies. Her father probably hoped she too would become an idealistic young intellectual. She turned away from academics to social work and on her return took up Family Planning with the same zeal as her father had teaching. She became an ardent field worker, going into the villages on her mission. In recognition of her services she got nominated to the Rajya Sabha. One may describe her as a picture of the 'liberated' woman. Frank, open, free from the kind of inhibitions that become a convenient cover for falsehood behind which people live a double life, she has the solidity and strength characteristic of the Maharashtrian women. But she seems to retain still a core of the sense of liberalism of the middle class intellectual that replaced the traditional social arrogance.

Shakuntala was a conscious rebel of her age, running to type, proud to be one. A rebel of a sort myself, I never ran to type and laid no claims to intellectualism. Rebellion was to me not a role to play, it propelled me by compulsion. Nevertheless. I admired and valued the

Shakuntala Paranjape types for their courage and readiness to face the consequences of their convictions.

This was my first close contact with the new sophisticated young women. There was an air of ease and freedom about them that we had never sported. We had grown up on a tenor of restraint. We were not expected to be exhuberant, gushing. If one was she got *marked.* Here girls freely took part in public sports and games. Girls cycling was a common sight. One or two rode motorcycles, and I saw one participating in a motor cycle race in the city. Hard to believe that this city had once been the bedrock of a hard crust of conservatism against which social giants like Karve and Pandita Ramabai had to knock and bruise heads.

Along with Shakuntala was Irrawathy, also a senior college student. Our contact was brief but she impressed me as hard headed, solid and practical. I was intrigued and attracted to her for she did not conform to any type; she was quite original in her thinking and objectives. So I never pictured her as a very devoted wife, and once when she confided to me that she loved and valued her husband greatly, 'I miss him terribly when he is away, and nothing can fill that void or compensate for the loneliness I feel,' the remark sounded strange from one who looked so completely self contained, in whom I presumed emotional dependence would have no place. Nevertheless she was deeply emotional but evidently found for it other outlets besides her life mate. As an anthropologist she did intensive studies in remote rural areas. Her writings were exciting, often reflecting her novel experiences with several rural working women especially of several states. She would relate perfectly stirring anecdotes from her talks with women she travelled with in buses and trains. They would have been ordinary no doubt, but she somehow made them sound unusual.

Once when I was her guest we discussed at length her reaction to my support for monogamy. Her partisanship for polygamy for agricultural families was strengthening with time as she spent long periods with them. She explained that it was traditionally accepted and no social ethics entered here to complicate the family harmony. So far as marital life went, they were content. How many couples under monogamy really lived a full satisfied life, she queried ? Here the woman had security, a comfortable home and a happily shared responsibility for care of the children. Children were provided decent homes and family care which few nuclear families could give. What was more, the additional marriage was free from the sordid transactions of dowry. The girls were sought and appreciated for themselves, for they would adorn the homes, not be as burdens. Thus she would plead and argue. She thought the Women's Conference, so demanding on monogamy, should be discriminating, since for her the socio-economic conditions differed between the urban and the rural.

Notwithstanding our differences, my affection for her grew as did my respect. Her views did not stem from orthodoxy. She had a robust and objective mind, her scholarship commanded respect. Her untimely death was a big personal loss. She was so vital, so full of zest for experiences.

These contacts, watching these groups actively at work brought a new and wider dimension to my outlook and ideas, I was particularly impressed by the simplicity, hard work and a determined doggedness of these men and women, and many of these impacts I seem to have carried on through the rest of my life.

Other personalities I got to know rather well were Maharashi Karve and his wife Anandibai but lovingly called Baya, for they lived nearby and we established a free and friendly relationship. Now she was a typical old fashioned looking woman like millions of others in the country. It was hard to believe this quiet, shy retiring couple had to go through such shattering experiences with a long period of persecution and ostracism. Yet through it all she continued to be an unfailing source of inspiration and support to the husband. She helped him at the Widows' Home, an institution for training widows to become independent and self-respecting citizens instead of being thrown on the scrap heap. This had roused the fierce wrath of the Pune orthodoxy. Every morning as Karve walked down the streets to the Widows' Home at Hingne beyond the city limits, the doors of houses he passed would be shut with a loud bang by men and women both, while some would pour vile abuses on him. There was an incident of someone even spitting on him. He had a slim frail frame but he walked silently on holding his head high, a suggestive smile playing about his firm lips. Such wild shafts of anger may have shattered a lesser man but not this gentle soul. Spurred on as it were, he founded the Widow Remarriage Association to resettle young widows in family life and several other socio-educational bodies. He reminded me of the old Maharashtra saints whose lives I never tired of reading in a book titled 'Bhaktivijaya—triumph of devotion', moved by their enthalling lives, for there was an indescribable grandeur in these men and women hailing from the humblest social and economic strata.

In this context one should take note of one significant fact that at certain periods a single individual emerges to draw together like-minded band of idealists to build up a hard core of leadership committed to emancipate those caught in the cruel shackles of blind conservatism. One such was Gopal Krishna Gokhale who through the Servants of India Society and the Deccan Education Society made Pune the centre of great intellectual and social flowering – Maharashi Karve was one out of many who were allured by this hallowed call.

Parvatibai Athavale, Baya's younger sister, was another who stimulated me. She had worked her way doing odd jobs through school and college in America and became a teacher. She had been a pillar of support to the Karve couple in their manifold ventures. Above all she was a shining example to all women, placed as disadvantageously as she was, to pull herself up by the bootstraps, as the English saying goes, and make herself into a personality that left a distinct stamp on the society. The son she brought up, patterned himself on her to continue the tradition. Parvatibai's autobiography vividly pictureses the society of her childhood days and the inhuman customs widows were subjected to.

During my stay in Poona one of the personalities I came in contact with and who left a deep impression and brought a fresh and abiding interest into my life was Verrier Elwin, a young English Missionary who later became a historic figure in the Indian events of the period, and especially for the strategic role he played in the emergence of the Tribal World of India.

Verrier Elwin belonged to a new kind of Christian Mission founded by Father Jack Winslow, who after working for many years in the narrow conventional groove of a Christian Missionary had turned into a true Christian with a vision of world brotherhood. He founded a mission of his own in Pune called the Christa Seva Sangh based on love and compassion for all human beings. But he wanted it to be grounded in the indigenous culture and Indian-orientated. Elwin together with two other young men Algy Robertson from Cambridge and Bernard

Clarke from Oxford joined him in launching his adventure of a re-orientation of the Christian Church. Their intellectual honesty, sincerity and simplicity appealed to me. They had something of the flavour of the ancient hermits of the early Christian Church, images on which I had fed so assiduously in my convent school days.

Elwin remained on my horizon right up to his end. I always looked forward to meeting and talking with him. He told me of his life among the tribals which stirred in me a new interest which grew with time. I followed his studies through his writings hoping someday I would devote myself like him to mingle with the tribals, understand something of their culture, hopefully serve it. His personality in my imagination remained the same. Neither time nor distance could dim the warmth, friendliness and the stimulation he always held for me. He was one of the most lovable persons I had known. He typified what I thought was a Christ-like man.

Years later as Chairman of the Handicrafts Board when I toured NEFA and Nagaland early in 1962 my old ambition to do something for the tribals came near fulfilment. I arranged an exhibition of Tribal Crafts of the North East and he was gracious enough to open it. Later I was able to at last visit Elwin in his home in Shillong. It was a rare treat and privilege to be shown his fabulous collection by himself, to sit in his library and browse over the books and listen to him. By then alas his health had been shattered, and he had become a heart patient. In fact he was then just recovering from a serious attack, and I had been told he was not to be up and moving. I had been shocked and disconcerted to find him up, fully dressed, looking spruce and handsome as ever. I remonstrated with him but he insisted on playing the active host. To us both it was a rare occasion to share our common interest, to compare notes, and above all for me to discuss my tour plans and my own approach to the problem of Tribal Crafts. Before I submitted my report to the Government, I sought his reaction to my assessment and recommendations. I felt a flow of satisfaction when he fully agreed with me. He had his own which he shared with me. That was to prove our last meeting for he died early the following year, leaving a big void in my heart. There are people that you may not meet often, even communication with them may be fitful, but one has a sense of closeness and an identity of interests that lends a fullness to ones own life. Elwin was one such personality. The emptiness left by him cannot be filled for he was the only one of his kind in my life.

Elwin identified himself fully with India's struggle for freedom though he could not obviously participate actively. He was once called upon by Gandhiji to play a strange role. When Abdul Gaffar Khan's Red Shirts began their activity in the frontier province and a strict censorship was clamped on that region and no news could come through, in despair Gandhiji sent Elwin there on a news gathering mission. When he was ready with his report, he was arrested and deported, shorn of all his papers. But he managed to hide some of these precious papers in a breakfast cereal packet called "Force" and thus was able to give to the world almost the first most sensational story of the exploits of the Khudai Khidmatgars band of volunteers and their wizard of a leader who later came to be known as the Frontier Gandhi.

He had made a complete departure from the established approach to the tribals. To him they were not a species to be studied by anthropologists. Their style of life was one they had evolved to suit their needs, conditioned with their own sense of values, norms, codes, patterns of culture, which non tribals should not go riding rough shod over with contempt, flushed with a sense of superiority. To dilate on it he gave an elaborate exposition of it in a book he named 'A Philosophy for NEFA' which reveals the delicate nuances of his sensitive make up. Though I was not putting on full-scale dramatic shows now, people who had seen or been aware of my work in the theatre kept inviting me to present small items in the new style that we had introduced. I did these as I travelled around the country on Conference work and quite enjoyed it. This also provided a channel for the creative elements within me, an outlet for my surging emotions. The shows became doubly rewarding as they provided enjoyment to those who saw them.

In the course of my travels I arrived in Calcutta. My visit to Calcutta was a memorable one, and most fortunately under the affectionate care of Indiradevi Chaudhrani, one of the shining lights of the Tagore family. It seemed that here one met everyone worth meeting. Outside of the Tagore family there were a few other big names, like P.C. Roy, the 'Alchemist', and J.C. Bose, the 'Magician'. I was still young enough to anticipate a visit to J.C. Bose's laboratory with awe and thrill, a kind of a modern Ali Baba's cave. From what I had formed the image of a visionary whose great ambition was to see his country now looked down upon as backward, exalted, not a primitive antique put away on the shelf, but honoured by the world. So he had juggled with plants, tubes, glasses to prove 'Plant Response' as he called his monumental book, recording his series of wonderful discoveries, which evoked in us lay people considerable interest in the emerging new scientific world. My visit however revealed much more. 'The study of responsive reactions in plants must be regarded as of fundamental importance to the elucidation of various phenomena,' he explained to me in his laboratory. He had dedicated 'My heart and soul to discover the existence of similarity of phenomena in various spheres of things on their molecular basis of matter,' he continued, to clarify the wide range of his objective.

What Bose had done was to prove through modern scientific processes with modern equipment the ancient Indian fundamental philosophy that life is one, indivisible, that there is no basic difference between human, animal and vegetable life—that the process of vital actions is identical, the forms of life are on the path of evolution. Thus he showed that all forms of creation are equally responsive to stimulation. Of course what our knowing ancestors wished us to know was that the same inherent divine principle permeated in all manifestations in their bewildering varieties.

Another of his unique triumphs was the invention of a High Magnification Cresograph which magnified the pace of growth of the plants in as short a period as a single second.

What burst in on me as a delightful surprise however, was to discover a sensitive artist in him. No wonder his laboratory had been described as a temple of art. He admitted that he planned and supervised the structure to 'wed art to utility in our old tradition'. Old motifs had been used to raise a modern structure, that research work may be done in a beautiful setting. There was a massive doorway with suggestive carving to symbolise the bringing down of the divine fire (wisdom); the small amalki fruit inevitable in most ancient Indian temple carvings was the chief motif. There was of course the now famous mimosa plant, an important factor in his experiments. A different element was introduced in front of the corridor shaping it after the Karnakudu (horse shoe) seen in the Buddhist Viharas. The most moving was a bronze plaque of a woman carrying a lamp. This I was told symbolised womanhood as the torch bearer of knowledge.

The most striking was a water colour painting on the wall by the great Master Nandalal Bose, called 'The Quest', an allegorical manifestation of an ancient truth: the duality in life, the positive and the negative, man and woman, the creative and the preservative. A startling diversion was caused by the sight of a picture in an adjoining room, a cubistic study of Bose throwing a powerful light on a dark cubistic background, showing subtly the waxing and waning of life.

There was much more to see in this Ali Baba cave, but I could not take it all in. I was so overwhelmed by Bose's personality itself. He was so vibrant with energy and yet soft with dreams lurking in the eyes. With what indomitable will and perseverance he had struggled and toiled in a colonial country, lacking the wherewithal, pierced by prejudices, contempt, for to the rulers he was an upstart, until he had well established the study of basic fundamental physical phenomena. Thus he made his important pioneering contribution in Quantum Mechanics, and the scientific world accepted him. His unfailing source of inspiration and sustenance he confessed was the ancient Indian philosophy which he shared with the world in his first memorable address at the Royal Society in London: 'Those who see but the One in all the changing manifestations of the Universe, unto them belongs eternal truth, unto none else.'

I was exhilarated in Culcutta, meeting personalities and visiting institutions pregnant with rich memories of the days when it had been one of the cradles of the Indian social reform movement from Raja Rammohan Roy down the long aisles of time. I was youthful and unjaded enough to feel the thrill that could still conjure up figures, images, events that seemed almost palpably real.

Calcutta to my theatre hungry soul was like a Mecca of my dreams. As I moved around avidly seeing all I could, meeting and hearing, I came to know that the modern Bengali Theatre as it had emerged, was largely under the impact of the English theatre which had a fairly long tenure starting from the 18th Century. It seemed strange to me that plays in English should have held sway here for almost half a century It was equally disappointing to find that the celebrated Chowringhee Theatre had been *exclusively* English, running Shakespearean plays and the only Indian connected with it was Dwarkanath Tagore, grandfather of Poet Tagore. I also learnt with amazement of the enterprise of Gecasim Lebedoff, a Russian theatre lover, who with the help of his

Bengali teacher Golaknath Das, launched for the first time Bengali dramas. A new feature in it was the induction of women to play minor female roles. It was Madhusudhan Dutt, the noted poet-playwright who felt strongly that women should be brought in and recruited them for all female parts, unmindful of the press criticism and public prejudice. The most disparaging attacks on the advent of women actresses had come from the English language papers then run by the English community, which was not surprising, English society being very conservative at the time. It had taken 64 years after the appearance of the public theatre in England for English women to appear on the stage! Whereas in Bengal it had taken hardly a year.

Bengal seemed to have gone through a whole century of the "Private Theatre" when plays were performed in large private houses particularly encouraged by several of the Rajas of little States some of whom actively participated in the shows. Among these was Jerashanko the traditional Home of the Tagores with the family members. As I listened to dazzling descriptions of these shows I was put very much in mind of the Royal households in Europe, especially in the different states in Germany where the ruler himself directed and acted in plays and patronised artists and musicians.

From current social themes the dramas had moved on to economic themes like Nil Darpan, a ruthless exposure of the oppression of the indigo plantation labour by the English planters.

The story behind Nil Darpan is an important part of India's colonial history and the revolt of this oppressed humanity was one of the earliest in the Gandhian era, and sadly enough, so little known.

Before the advent of the British the rural scene was one of self sufficient communities. The peasants grew their basic needs. The skilled craftsmen provided the communities' other needs.

In Bengal (the Bengal Presidency of the time included Bihar also) in particular with India's defeat at Plassey, the entire scene started getting drastically transformed. The new rulers rushed across the fertile land stripping it of its crop wealth and stamping on the exquisite handicrafts, especially the superb home-woven textiles.

A new era of cash crop was forced on the region through the new plantation system, whereby the unwary peasant was pushed into the trader's money-spinning orbit through plantation cultivation of opium, jute, tea, above all indigo. Indigo ensnared the cultivator into practical slavery, making him victim of a most hateful economic bondage. The peasants were forced into indigo cultivation to sell it to these planters at dictated prices. The planters were themselves imposters, who had got themselves transplanted from the West Indies where they had worked with slave labour, a relationship they tried to maintain here. For peasants used to growing food grains, indigo was not a profitable cultivation. But they were compelled through foul means by the planters seizing their implements, impounding their cattle, sometimes even seizing their lands, to force them into becoming the factory-feeding labour force. Oppression and serfdom grew as indigo became an indispensible dye for Britain's large scale textile industry. The factories in Bengal alone had shot up to 1000 ! After the 1857 war, the racial animosities of the planters increased, their assaults on labour sharpened with the free use of leather thongs known as Shamchands, for flogging. The planters retained their own little armies to terrorise labour. Because of the blatant pro-planter attitude of the law courts, the indigo labour revolted. This finally caught the urban people's attention, later, of all India with Gandhiji himself rushing to their aid.

The deep impression this made on the intellectuals was a moving play in Bengali by Dinabandhu Mitra, an official of the Postal Department, called Nil Darpan. It was later translated by the famous Bengali playwright Madhusudhan Dutt into English. It bared varied outrageous scenes from the lives of the indigo workers, like a life-documentary.

An accidental fall-out of this became a pathetic tragi-comedy. One Reverend James Lang, a newly arrived Christian Missionary was so moved by Nil Darpan that he had the English translation published. The enraged planters brought Lang to trial on the charge of holding his countrymen to ridicule and had him sentenced to a month's imprisonment—all for trying to be a true Christian !

The peasant revolt however assumed enough power to make the Viceroy admit this was the worst period after 1857.

This was followed by the promulgation by the Government of the Dramatic Performances Control Act in 1876 to throttle the rising series of patriotic plays that were having a long run.

Here for the first time I saw the modern drama emerging, all aspects integrated, no one factor overpowering, each element in its rightful place. The old style of loud brusque talk was replaced by natural meaningful delivery, the melodramatic body gestures by subtle suggestive movements. This had been achieved by the introduction of a producer, 'rejesuere' as the Western term went. I met Probodh Chandra Guha who was the prime mover behind the Art Theatre with a body of a serious theatre people with initiative, dedication, practical sense, above all aesthetic sensitivity. I saw *Seeta* with Sisir Bahadur, the powerful actor who had almost become a legend, a totally different presentation from what I was used to. Here was not only powerful acting without any of the melodrama, but also a finely integrated production. Also Karnarjun Shah Suja with Ahindra Chaudhuri, a memorable production, distinguished by a sense of balance to make it a closely knit web.

I was delighted to see a galaxy of women acting and winning laurels like Krishnabhamini, Niharbala and a host of others.

Enveloped in this euphoria I arrived at Shantiniketan to visit Gurudev Tagore. Pratimadevi, his daughter-in-law, a gracious kindly personality, well known as a dance artist, took charge of me. A tiny message was there from Gurudev to ask if I would care to walk with him in the morning. 'Can you manage ? He is out before the sun rises,' Pratimadevi asked. I nodded assent.

I can still see his tall figure with a slight stoop waiting in front of the house, both his arms locked at his back. We moved eastwards watching a million coloured shafts break up as the sun, a ball, rose. The ground was absolutely flat and rolled on and on like a horizonless ocean. 'I like this landscape which stretches unhindered away and beyond. I don't like high rises like hills that obstruct my vision,' he commented. I told him it was exactly the opposite with me for I came from the foot of the ghats and I found elevation uplifting. To me his preference for a flat country was puzzling. I looked into his sparkling eyes, warm and kindly, but they held no answer to my query. He asked me about the theatre activities I had been involved in and as I described them with enthusiasm, his eyes lit up and I felt rewarded. I confessed how his dance dramas had opened out a new world for me, but to me any close association with them seemed beyond my realm. 'Maybe someday you will realise your heart's desire,' he murmered like a blessing and so it proved. Two decades later in Delhi the Poet's dainty dance artist grand-daughter Nandita, a very valued friend and comrade of mine, put on some of his dance dramas, that I could watch and study at close quarters. They revoked for me that old magic and haunting flavour of Tagore's own shows.

I started on what I thought was closest to his heart – Shantiniketan. He laughed lightly : 'I never had any formal education myself, it therefore seemed incongruous that I should start a school.' 'Is it not because your creativity had not been snuffed out by the so called formal schooling. that you could try to save the creative in children that they may flower'? I interrupted. He nodded, then with a faraway look again across the flat plains, he added :

'Yes, the school life which I had experienced in my early days had been most distasteful and I had played truant when I could, and finally I gave it up. This experience had impressed on me the suffering the students endured through suppression of their personality. Out of my restlessness came a clear idea that I should found a school which should be different from my present school, where I could make the children happy by giving them freedom. I never said 'don't do this'. I trusted them and won their trust. The students were encouraged to manage their own affairs. Where an enquiry was called for and action to be taken for some transgression the children were made to elect their own tribunal including the judge, and they would willingly submit to the verdict. I never punished them myself.

'If education was to foster the growth of the personality and cultivate modes of expression, Shantiniketan had to be a fountainhead from which the youth drew inspiration and sustenance. Realising how insipid, gloomy. colourless the usual school environment is, I sought to provide elements of inspiration and stimulation, making creativity the central focus, so that grace, elegance and dignity are lent to what otherwise would prove an experience of abject deadliness.'

After a brief silence he continued : 'But education should be wide open to let in the breezes, sounds, echoes, freely, not be narrow, walled in. Friendship with the wide world can come only through true understanding, which must start early in life. That is why I started Viswa-bharati, a world centre to become the confluence of many streams to enrich us. Gradually I tried to model it on ancient Nalanda, drawing on the cultural and moral resources of the whole country, the students being rooted and grounded in the soil of India. Then it would be easy for them to assimilate a foreign culture, for the East has to know its own mind as the West has, then the two can meet on equal terms. That was how Viswabharati was born', he concluded.

Little did I dream as we kept talking of the flowering of Viswabharati, its ambition to recognise and honour artists and those who had served it, that I would one day be among the recipients of its highest award : Desikottama – the Excellent Preceptor. I have been fortunate to receive other awards in the course of my life-journey, but none has given me the pride and satisfaction that this one did. Pregnant in it was Tagore's great dream of the *World Centre.*

For his institutions he had chosen the spot hallowed by his father Maharashi Debendranath as he came to be known for his ascetic ways, by ending his last days in meditation in an Ashram under the sal trees which had something of the air of the old ashram As I sauntered through the grounds I saw classes largely conducted under the trees. The medium of communication was made alluring through the use of music and dance. The aim was to stimulate the creative faculties and talents in the growing students, and not by cramming their heads with readymade sops or weighing down their tender arms with heavy tomes. The Poet believed that for the growing youth an atmosphere of freedom and love, surcharged with aesthetic symbols like drama, dance, music, were essential ingredients.

Worldly knowledge and physical facts were taught through seasonal and other festivals, wearing gay apparel, decorating oneself and the surroundings from nature's bountiful gifts. Sowing, tending, shearing, garnering the ripened grain or fruit, tending and caressing the cattle, each was intertwined with muted clang of bells, sonorous sounds of drums, cheery sounds of music, dance-dramas, in short, total festive celebrations. Yet, each was a fruitful ritual, a new birth and blossoming, shorn of tedium, for the creative spirit moved not only the emotions but also the muscles.

Kala Bhavan (art school) was the heart throb of the place and historically significant. Here Abanindranath Tagore, the poet's nephew initiated the School of Art. 'This was to reverse a deadly trend of producing cheap western imitations, piteous for a gifted people like Indians,' he explained. Later scorn was poured on the Bengal School as 'alien', 'anaemic', etc. I believe few are aware how this phase called the 'Bengal School' came to be. In Abanindranath's time, Kala Bhavan, the Art School of which he was the head, was the only *living* art centre in India. In fact in all of Asia, only China and Japan had drawn world attention to their classical art works. It is not surprising that Abanindranath should be influenced by this in his experiments, the purity of the Chinese and the delicacy of the Japanese, the Indian image providing the base for which he sought his inspiration from the Ajanta.

Many budding artists sought him as Guru, and Abanbabu was one, in the traditional style. His role was to encourage and guide in principles, but the execution was left to the artist himself. He was emphatic: 'No imitation, only creation.' This is what our ancient texts have always said.

His own brother Ganganendranath himself drifted into Cubism, but his cubist expression was pictorially his own synthetic vision, not a *copy*.

The first batch of artists emerging from Kala Bhavan distinguished themselves in India and abroad. Nandalal—the master Mahashoi: the Preceptor, rose as a great Guru on the fast awakened art horizon through his powerful lines which put one in mind of the painters of the old Buddhist age, entirely new but not conforming to the prevailing conventions.

There was Rahman Chughtai, painting in a world of his own, in his Persian tradition but filtered through his Moghul ancestry, he showed the delicacy and the meticulous finish of the Indo Persian Art, yet with an overall air of 'radiant simplicity', as Venkatachalam described it.

Venkatappa, hailing from Karnataka, was unlike any other artist of Kala Bhavan. He lived alone, a severe ascetic kind of life, regulated by his own individualistic norms and codes, and accepted assignments only on his own terms. He developed a style of his own, blandly termed 'realistic', but transcended the mere ines by revealing an inner spirit. His landscapes were a class by themselves, usually a single canvas showing the many fleeting moods of nature with a superb sense of colour.

I had an intriguing experience with Venkatappa, the great Mysore artist with whom I was closely in touch at the time. Venkatappa liked painting mountain landscapes. As he and I spent several summers in Ootacamund, he would let me watch him at work on remote hill tops. He started out at 4 o'clock in the morning for he loved to catch the delicate hues bursting into gorgeous shades as the sun rose. One morning I found him in an exasperated mood, almost in a temper. The Nilgiris were aglow in an unbelievable blue. I kept rubbing my eyes. 'Oh, this is the real Ananda', I exclaimed meaning the Indian blue. 'This is why the hills are called the Blue Hills !' 'Yes, but you have to do some tapasya (penance) to have it stay that way to let me transfer it to my canvas. See how quickly it vanishes even as you blink your eyes.' He was right. Other shades had come in, pushing out the blue. 'I got some of it finally, but . . .' and he broke off, gazing at his unfinished canvas. Then he laughed and continued. 'I had a similar battle with the famous pink sunrise in Darjeeling. There it was not the time factor; I simply could not get the right shade. After several failures, I emptied the whole bottle of pink colour on my canvas to just destroy it — and lo ! before my unbelieving eyes there was the exact shade I could not get through my brush. Isn't that something?' The sunrise colours in Darjeeling have an enamel tinge that makes them burn like flames. Venkatappa had got its magic — no matter by what unorthodox method.

One can take any of Abanbabu's many distinguished students, and find each distinctly individual, which falsifies the careless lumping together of all of them as 'Bengal School', where even the two brothers' works differed so distantly. These diverse works from Kala Bhavan students and the Masters prove that they inspired every talent to find its own distinct expression, so unlike the art schools set up by the British rulers which worked to set models.

In my talks with Gurudev I once referred to his paintings, creations he conjured up rather late in life. He gazed far off into the horizon-less stretch as usual and said slowly as though lost in some faraway thoughts: 'I made the exciting discovery in the course of my perpetual searches that, in these quick changing millions of forms around us, there is a methodical natural selection in lines and I concluded only those that deserve to survive do so in the realm of the natural law that stands for equilibrium and therefore fulfilment.' I recalled reading earlier his comments on them: 'My pictures are my verifications in lines. If by chance they are entitled to claim recognition, it must be primarily for some rhythmic significance of form which is ultimate, and not for any interpretation or representation of an idea or representation of a fact.'

We drifted into the topic of music one morning. I was keen to hear him talk on Rabindra Sangeet, which had fast gained popularity as a distinctive style of musical expression. Here his eyes lit up, I had may be an illusion, that his body straightened as years fell away in a twinkling. 'The art of vocal music has its own special functions and features,' his words came crisp and firm, 'so the less a song is burdened with words, the better. In the classic style of Hindustani music, words are of little account, and leave the melody to make its appeal in its own way. Vocal music tu me reaches its perfection when the melodic form is allowed to develop freely, and carry our consciousness with it to its own wonderful plane. I often felt this while composing my song, humming my tune as I wrote to its accompaniment. I know that had the tune not been there, I cannot say what shape the poem, the song, might have taken. It is the melody that wafted me and to it were the words addressed.' I was silent and pondered for a while. Maybe he felt he had not made himself explicit, so he added: 'The song being great in its own wealth why should it wait upon words? Rather does it begin where words fail, it tells us what the words cannot.' This was indeed a common experience with me, yet I had never consciously analysed it. How often a significant experience lies deep within, enmeshed and buried under layers of irrelevent scraps until some powerful hand strips them away and a streak of light illumines one's self.

Stressing the unity of the essential thought and feeling of India, Pankaj Mullick, the noted lyricist-musician, offered examples of Tagore's songs where he had drawn on melodies from different languages, and pointed out that his famous song Anandlokay Mangalalokay was set to a melody from a Carnatak bhajan, another to a Sikh-bhajan and so on.

'How did you come to plan Sriniketan and work of rural reconstruction?' I asked as we took our usual morning stroll. Prompt came the answer as though he was almost anticipating the query. 'Even as I was working out my plans in Shantiniketan, another current of thought was flowing through my mind. I am a born city man with a long urban ancestry. So I had no touch with villages until I came to take up my Zamindari work. When I accept a responsibility I get immersed in it, doing my duty with all my heart and soul. I kept my doors wide open, a sign to villagers they could come in freely whenever they felt the need to see me, no matter how odd the hour may seem. It was my first contact with rural India and I got not only a great interest but joy from this. As I penetrated beyond their outer peasant life, travelled through the dim hoary villages, meeting, talking and studying their poverty, the deep core of sorrow that comes of insecurity, became clear. A twinge of guilt started to engulf me as I saw myself as they would see me, their landlord, engrossed in collecting the dues, cherishing my profit. Their joyless monotony of life hit me poignantly. Oppression, even more, indifference to their lot, undermined their self-reliance therefore self respect. I then decided to do something to change this. I was lucky to get a few friends to share my dreams and help me. We realised this would have to be a separate project by itself, not tied up with Shantiniketan. To make this venture truly professional, I sent my son and another of our workers abroad to learn agriculture and allied activities like animal husbandry etc. One truism I have learnt, if we really wish to serve we must first learn ourselves; and if we are to succeed, those we wish to instruct must feel a complete sense of freedom.'

I saw in Sriniketan another dream of Tagore's that had taken shape. Agriculture and dairy development, crafts to cover the daily needs of man, like weaving, pottery, basketry, wood, metal and leather work (the last named attained special distinction and fame). Here work was taken out of its mundane setting and the effort transformed into creative impulses, for they alone can mellow the harsh drabness of physical expenditure. The mere functional became a work of art. Here students realised that no object was too insignificant to lay claim to aesthetics.

I realised more than ever after my visit and talks with him that Tagore was intrinsically a poet, and it was as a poet that he expressed himself in several fields like taking different *avatars*. Rabindranath had brought a new effulgence to Bengali in structure, form and content.

One can fully endorse W.B. Yeat's outpourings after he had been carrying around the Gitanjali manuscript for a few days, reading and digesting the poems. 'So abundant yet simple is this poetry—a renaissance that has been born in his country, full of subtle rhythm, untranslatable delicacies of colour, of metrical invention—Work of a supreme culture, they yet appear as much the growth of the common soil as the grass and the rushes.'

One day he asked me to go over to the house in the evening and he would sing to me. I had longed for this but had never dared to ask.

He talked even as he sang with his typical tilt, his body swaying to the rhythm, and I was amazed at the wide range of his musical knowledge. It was crossing an ocean. He had more than delved, he had seriously tried to grasp the varied tonal waves with all their intricacies. He demonstrated each with equal ease.

He then went on to explain the strong impact Western music had made on him. 'It has an entirely different resonant richness that I am trying to catch and intertwine in a new music,' he explained. Then to illustrate he sang the now famous 'Ami Chinigo Chini', which he explained was inspired by an Italian serenade.

It was my last moment with Gurudev. The morning discourses had enriched and like alchemy, transformed my budding imagination and sensitivised my perceptions. His last words keep ringing in my ears. 'Now as I keep coming to the end of my life, all I am left with are my dreams.' I would like to add to them these lines of his:

> I do not want to die in this beautiful world
> But live in the hearts of men . . .
> I want to build on this earth my eternal home.

Viswabharati had been a controversial idea. Some thought it would disrupt the serenity of Shantiniketan. Even the rise of new structures had irritated some. But the real distortion was yet a long way off.

In the early fifties when I began my work in the Handicrafts Board, Rathindranath, Tagore's son invited the Board to meet in Shantiniketan. Viswabharati had just been converted into a University by a Parliamentary Act. The place had already undergone much change. Its air was listless, no more the idyllic setting, the ashram-like simplicity, informality, warmth. It had become colourless, anaemic, like any other university campus, shorn of creativity. Later I was invited there more than once to help in the development of crafts which had been fast declining. The old experienced master craftsmen had been retired under the government rules as they would be. It is just such regulations that make formal education a dead end. Sriniketan that once hummed, wore a tired look. Rathibabu, Tagore's son, had long left the place, Pratimadevi, his wife, was an invalid. There seemed no one with whom to even evoke the old radiant memories. The institution seemed caught in the deadly straitjacket of a conventional university with not much hope of a real rejuvenation. I however carry two pleasanter memories of the last two visits, once when I received the coveted award and next when I delivered the Viswabharati convocation address. For I was pleased to find Sriniketan astir again with some of my old colleagues working on crafts and a fresh breeze in Kala Bhawan.

Two outstanding, original and basic contributions that Tagore made to India's national flowering stand out in my mind. The education in the current government sponsored schools was edging us away from our tradition. Our vision was fast getting distorted, and we were creating hybrid images. This was causing Tagore agonies. He must have searched for fresh sources of inspiration, for new influences, harmonising impacts. He naturally turned to our age-old neighbours. Shantiniketan and Sriniketan became the Warp and the Weft of a rich fabric to clothe India. After a long lapse he tried once again to tie together the silken cords of culture between India and the Asian peoples. He attracted, then nurtured artists, thinkers in Viswabharati, erecting a Chini Bhavan, a symbol of centuries of close embraces between two harmonising cultures. He made at least our creative youth look at and draw inspiration from our fellow Asians. There crept into our creations, flashes of their tints, flavour of their images. In turn the guest artists carried back some of India's choicest gifts in their bosom to weave subtle links that span spaces, language barriers, personal constrictions.

The other, even more fundamental concept, was providing the basic need for a total rural development as essential to cultural growth. He unearthed and re-established the image of the *totality* of life which the western emphasis on specialisation had so disastrously disrupted.

The next annual session of the Women's Conference drew near. It had been decided to invite the Begam of Bhopal who was then actually the ruler of her state, to preside over it. I was directed to proceed to Bhopal to meet her in person and make the request. I walked into her presence rather naively and informally to make my request and got a big jolt. No one had prepared me for a rock-like personality, sitting in an imposing man-like posture. In an imperial manner she was gracious and kind in her tone when she agreed, but later turned hard and cold. She said she had to make it clear that though she would appear in public while presiding, she would have to wear the burqa. I was stunned but quickly recovered my wits to politely thank her and accept her condition. After this she softened a bit and talked of her keen interest in women's education and the many measures she was adopting to provide the girls in her state opportunities for education. Now she had an air of keen earnestness which made her a little less distant.

Sultan Shah Jehan, Begam of Bhopal, hailed from a dynasty whose history has blazed through three hefty volumes showing us always a woman's benign hand guiding the State's destiny and holding the reins with every succession, starting from 1777 when ruler Faiz Mohamad Khan ruled under the guidance of his mother Mamola, her voice decisive even in political negotiations. After Faiz died childless, his wife, Bahoo Begam carried on. From 1819 starts a continuous succession of women, when Nawab Nazar Mohamad died leaving the throne to his wife Qudsia Begam who established her rule firmly. She got her daughter Sikandar Begam married, it is said, rather reluctantly, and only after she obtained a sealed undertaking that the husband and his adherents would be subordinate to the ruling Begam, which proved most beneficial to the State. In fact Qudsia Begam proved an enlightened and progressive ruler. She kept personally in touch with the common people, visiting them in their homes to check if they had the essentials of life and to see to their general welfare. She paid special attention to the soldiers and their families. Out of her yearly income of seven lakhs, she spent two on charity ! When her son-in-law realised he could not seize the throne except by military action, he attacked her and engaged her in a regular military battle and wrested it brutally.

Nevertheless it was daughter Sikandar Begam who was installed on the throne in 1844. She proved one of the most outstanding women rulers in our country and deserves to be better known. Born and bred in one of the most turbulent periods which saw the decline of the Moghul rule, she weathered disorders and onslaughts of fierce gangs like the Pindaris. Her first 30 years thus were full of clash of arms, when men of muscle rather than of brains seemed to dominate. Her court has been described as a nest of war-like feudatories. To tame them into law abiding citizens was a mighty challenge to face. Equally herculean was the task of welding into a proper integrated army, scattered groups of disorderly retainers. Each of these 'unfeminine' jobs she set herself to resolve.

Her hardest battle was with the British, the Paramount Power, who would not recognise her claim to the throne as she was found too independent for their liking. Thoroughly frustrated she yielded, for the husband died just then leaving her single handed. A man was set up as regent by the India Government. But he mismanaged the State so grieviously that the Begam could get back her throne with ease in 1860.

She resumed her duties by personally going to the people to find out their real condition. She set up agricultural banks to provide credit for farm operations, for she had special concern for the farmers. 'Cultivators are the wealth of the country', she reminded her officers. For the first time *separate* administrative units were set into motion. She paid particular attention to enlarging educational facilities with special care for development of handicrafts. A novel item undertaken was metalling the main roadways leading to the Capital. One personal talent that distinguished her from other Indian women royalties, was a rare ability at navigation. She won laurels when she navigated her ship with extraordinary skills through the perils of a fierce hurricane, when it seemed on the point of sinking.

The present Begam who succeeded her had carried forward administrative improvements such as streamlining regulations for collection of land revenue, codifying criminal laws, clearly demarcating village boundaries. The Begam did most of the inspection work *personally*, realising its significance. Shc also delighted in embellishing the Capital and toning up its appearance.

The Begam proved a very conscientious President at the Women's Conference, listening attentively to the talks and discussions. Only one crisis erupted. The Conference had been keen on promoting creative and cultural forms by getting them incorporated into the school programmes. The lady who was dilating on this referred in particular to the significant role of music and dance in education. When the word dance was mentioned the President interrupted sharply, shaking her hand in protest : 'I can't have dance in any form discussed or approved in this meeting while I preside,' was her emphatic comment. The speaker Zimha Lazarus, Principal of the Women's College in Bangalore, was charming and humorous and very resourceful. With a slight nod she accepted the Chair's ruling and went on with her speech advocating rhythmic movements to music, speaking with speed, I presume, to prevent any further interruption. So the resolution was passed with small changes so as not to hurt the President's confirmed susceptibilities. Any crisis was thus carefully averted.

We had however to face rather a serious crisis on the *eve* of the session. The political tempo in the country was daily increasing and political activities such as demonstrations, meetings, marches, etc were going on daily. This session was being held in Delhi which in those days used to proudly proclaim itself as the 'Imperial City'. It certainly was, for without India there would be no British Empire. This was the time when the Simon Commission was due in Delhi and preparations were afoot by the people to organise protests through mammoth demonstrations.

A word of explanation on the Simon Commission may be called for, not for its intrinsic importance but the terrific havoc it wrought, completely out of proportion to the purpose it was supposed to serve. Ten years after the 1919 Political Reforms a review commission was due, and one was sent in 1928 by the Conservatives in power, presumably to control its findings and recommendations while they were still in office. Sir John Simon described by an English writer as the coldest legal brain across which no unconventional thought would ever flit, was made the Commission's chairman. But before this iceberg even touched the Indian shore, a terrific flood of protest rose from the ground like the summer heat in a desert. Even Jinnah thundered in fury : 'The Jallianwalla Bagh tried to destroy our bodies, the Simon Commission is sent to destroy our souls.'

The Simon Commission was pursued by cries of 'Simon Go Back'. There is a plaintive story of how the Commission members when in Delhi complained of raucous cries disturbing them all night.

They were politely told that they were the crises of jackals which infested Delhi. The sparsely inhabited New Delhi spaces were in those days the free hunting grounds of wild jackals which were harmless as compared to the human ones that now prey upon their fellow victims.

Delhi was witnessing a flood of protests. I was invited to participate in one which happened on the eve of the Conference which Lady Irwin, wife of the Viceroy, was to inaugurate. On the morning of the opening we were informed that the Vicereine could not possibly patronise an organisation whose General Secretary was participating in activities intended to embarrass the Government. Srimati S. R. Das, wife of the Law Member in the Viceroy's Council and Chairman of the Reception Committee who was rather a mild woman, looked utterly helpless. But not Gretta, who took it upon herself to straighten this out and asked us not to be perturbed. She was full of righteous indignation against this threat and felt it should be met. She argued with the senior officials that the Women's Conference was in no way involved in the demonstration. If the Secretary did so, it was in her personal capacity and she had not identified the Conference or her office as Secretary with the demonstration. The Secretary was holding the office in an honorary capacity and therefore no restrictive conditions on what she did outside could be imposed on her, and if that were done no self-respecting person would want to hold the office. This was her firm stand and she won hands down. She said to me 'don't let anyone muscle or bully you, my dear. We stand for freedom all through.' We carried the day, the Vicereine opened the Conference and all went off peacefully. I wondered how many Indians in that high official coterie would have stood up to the officialdom of the Viceregal set up as Gretta did.

A Special Committee on a new constitution for the Conference in view of the expansion of its objectives, was meeting in the Viceregal lodge after the Conference as the Vicereine, Lady Irwin, had expressed a wish to take part in this discussion. As the meeting proceeded it became obvious that it would have to go on into the afternoon. Lady Irwin became restless and went into a hushed conversation with her Social Secretary who in turn whispered to Gretta who looked rather annoyed. Then she drew me aside to explain that the Vicereine would host a lunch for the members and she wondered if I would feel embarrassed to be her guest. I was quite amused and said that I had no objection at all. When the Vicereine heard this she looked genuinely surprised and addressed me: 'You mean *you* will eat with us?' and I said, 'Of course'. Later I asked Gretta what had annoyed her with the Social Secretary. Gretta, said, The lady thought you would never eat with Britishers. It was so silly. I said you certainly would but she still was doubtful, so I ended by asking you directly.' 'Anyway all is well,' I concluded.

5

After the conference I stayed on in Delhi to do some lobbying in the Central Assembly where there were Bills like the Sharda Act to prevent child marriage and Age of Consent, pending. Hence I was a frequent visitor to the Assembly building, now known as Parliament House. Those were the days when the Swaraj Party had its members in the Central Assembly. The Assembly Speaker Shri Vithalbhai Patel had very thoughtfully given me a corner in one of his offices and provided clerical facilities, while Dr. Jayakar, a member of the Assembly, got me a residence in Western Court where the members stayed. I could thus ride to the Assembly and return with one of the members.

One morning after I finished my office work and there was still time for the House to rise for lunch, I decided to go into the gallery to listen to the debate. As I went from the Speaker's office I was able to slip in without the normal admission pass. As I sat down my eyes caught and held for a while right across in the gallery opposite, a striking, handsom man who did not seem interested in the proceedings, but restlessly looked about as though waiting impatiently for something to happen. And it did. There was a big bang, a spurt of smoke that hid everything for a moment, then a big shower of white leaflets flying all over the House. To me the episode was a complete mystery. As I tried to move out of the gallery I realised that all passages were barred by the security men who were asking each visitor to produce the entrance pass before the exit could be opened. I suddenly went cold inside as I confessed I had no pass. I was asked to stand aside and wait for the others to depart. Fortunately I had asked Dr. Jayakdar's river to wait for me so that I could ride back in the car. He informed Dr. Jayakar of my plight and he rescued me after giving what seemed almost like an *affidavit* : that the Honourable Member knew me and would stand guarantee for my good conduct. Only as I drove back with Dr. Jayakar I knew what had happened and I felt small and foolish at my small fears in the context of the grand heroics of Bhagat Singh and his sensational act.

For it was he who had thrown the bomb. I was still rather dazed when my fingers felt the crisp paper I had picked up as it alighted on my lap which I had almost absentmindedly thrust into my hand bag. 'It takes a loud noise to make the deaf hear' said the pamphlet quoting a French anarchist, Matyr Vaillant.

The pamphlet pointed out 'the irony of a Central Legislature, a hollow show, a mischievous make-believe stage which kept enacting repressive measures to enslave the people in the name of the law'. 'There never has been within living memory so manifestly stage-managed an exhibition of India's helpless subjection than this.'

The Simon Commission had become a nightmare because of the merciless baton-beating of the protesting crowds by mounted police. Among the prominent victims were Pandit Nehru, who escaped with a minor but painful injury, Pandit Govind Vallabh Pant on whom the physical effects stayed *permanently*, and Lala Lajpat Rai who died very soon of the blows. The last one led to several sad repercussions. The most spectacular probably being Bhagat Singh's blowing leaflets into the Central Assembly at Delhi with a 'bang', as he called it. This demonstration was repeated again but without the loud bang in 1983, 55 years later, by Bhagat Singh's sister, Bibi Amar Kaur, probably as an expression of her anguish that even after half a century the national scene her brother so tragically protested against remained the same.

When lobbying in the Central Assembly for support to social legislation, Dewan Chamanlal, a young and lively Congress Swaraj Party member of the Assembly invited me to enter the trade union arena. 'Women are not the only sections of society exploited. It is worse in industrial establishments, and there are lots of women among the workers. Why not help them too ?' he pleaded earnestly. 'We need radical but equally responsible elements in the trade union activities.' He invited me to the ensuing session of the Trade Union Congress at Jharia, Bihar, in late 1928. Political extremists had gained success in the Bombay labour front, projected through the Girni Kamgar Union and some Railway Unions and they were helped by the increasingly oppressive government policies, he explained, and wanted national workers to enthuse labour to rally round legitimate trade unions. To me this was a new field, a new experience, yet vital. I took myself to Jharia and the All India Trade Union Congress. The sharp tussle between the old and new forces at times got toned down in view of the increasing aggression of a common opponent, the government. The star visitor there was Pandit Nehru, also present for the first time. Many well wishers wanted to bring the political Congress and the Trade Unions closer especially with the fast rising political tempo, to provide a new leadership. This was sealed by Pandit Nehru being elected President of the Trade Union Congress at the Jharia session.

The situation however worsened as we moved into 1929 with large scale labour trouble. Workers especially in Bombay were clearly becoming sharply class conscious, consequently more militant. The long established union leaders like N. M. Joshi, honest, devoted, had to face a tough labour roused by the Marxist upsurge. The Girni Kamgar (textile workers) Union of Bombay, still a power to contend with, took root and identity in the prolonged agonising strike that erupted when the workers doggedly held out in the face of stark starvation and continued harassment. Government and mill owners seemed helpless. This growing Communist influence was made the provocation for a sudden round up of Union leaders on charges of conspiracy against the government and clamped in Merrut prison. When I was in Meerut visiting Acharya Kripalani and the Gandhi Ashram he was in charge of, I asked and was granted permission to visit these prisoners. I hardly knew them, having briefly glimpsed them at Jharia like Dange, Ghate, Adhikari, etc. My visit was primarily to show my sympathy with them. The 'Conspiracy' I knew was a pure figment and I wanted to give expression to my protest for I knew I would not be able to do anything for them. The one prisoner I was personally interested in was Jhabwalla because of my close friendship with his wife, Mehra, who was going through a world of tribulations because of his indefinite detention. The only offer I could make was to send books for them to read, which I did.

While the title of the charge against them was hilariously comic 'Conspiring the Deprive the King of his Sovreignity of India', the trial proved even more comic. Said the Prosecutor : '*For the purpose of the case, it is unnecessary to prove whether the accused did actually do anything* ; it would suffice if only 'conspiracy' could be proved !' The proof according to him was: creation of workers' and peasants Parties, Unions, Youth Leagues. etc. and encouragement of strikes. In short it was a blatant perversion of a legal trial. Stranger still that this happened when a Labour Government was in power in England, and when the Indian Trade Union Congress appealed to the British Trade Union for intervention, the curt answer was that this was a political offense that did not directly affect the Indian Trade Union movement ! While this was bad enough, what made the incident even worse was when the same British Trade Union Congress, the moment Labour was out of office, declared the same proceedings of this same trial as 'literally indefensible' and a 'Judicial Scandal'. So much for British Labour's sense of justice !

Later, almost on the eve of the Civil Disobedience movement, these Meerut prisoners had another unexpected visitor, no less a person than Gandhiji himself. They could hardly believe it when his visit was announced. Without any preliminaries he told them he was launching a countrywide movement and he had come to solicit their support He was aware this was the Communist High Command who had attacked and torn him to shreds. He was nevertheless big enough to walk into this den and seek their support. Dange, as the spokesman, assured the Party's assistance on condition Chauri Chaura was not to be repeated. Gandhiji accepted it. It may be mentioned here that both in 1930 and 1932 struggles the industrial workers solidly supported him.

As I continued my stint of lobbying in the Central Assembly both at the Simla and Delhi sessions, I naturally kept running into Pandit Motilal Nehru. He invariably pulled my leg over our first encounter. 'This is a dangerous woman,' he would tell those around, pointing to me. 'She once threatened to have me mobbed by a crowd of old women unless I took instructions from her on how to conduct myself in the Legislature especially how to cast my vote.' Inspite of the ragging he proved sympathetic and helpful towards my thorny mission.

This referred to an amusing incident that took place in Simla when I was lobbying for the Prevention of Child Marriage Act, introduced by Shri Harbilas Sharda, a lawyer from Ajmer, Rajasthan I was a novice at what seemed a tricky kind of an assignment. Almost every one I approached nodded politely while a few knowingly smiled indicating 'don't be fooled by their nods, they don't want to be rude to a guideless young woman and hurt her pride' I was advised to win over the party bosses: 'Win over the boss and your job is done,' was the wise counsel.

To me the most important of them was Pandit Motilal Nehru,. Rameshwari Nehru very kindly fixed up the meeting. He surveyed me, it seemed to me with some amusement as he asked me for the purpose of my visit. I told him I wanted him and his party to support the pending bill. I can't explain what made me suddenly stress, 'You will won't you?' He broke out into rather a strident note: 'Are you trying to instruct me and my colleagues how to vote, you chit of a girl?' Far from wilting, I stood up to say 'If your objection is to my age, I will bring a batch of old women to seek your vote'. With that I turned on my heels and almost ran out of the room, as he shook with loud laughter. Far from causing a breach, the incident led to a softening of his encounters with me, notwithstanding his light banters that we both enjoyed.

Motilal Nehru seemed a person apart not just because of his political position but his superb bearing, of absolute self confidence, above all the unusually pleasant rapport he had with his arch opponents in the government who on occasions readily arrested and imprisoned him. Most English members in the Viceroy's Council, confessed they found him delightful even though a formidable adversary in a political battle, and all of them characterised him as a clean fighter who commanded their respect.

Lalaji as Lajpat Rai was popularly called, was another of the party bosses. He was a renowned champion of women's rights. He put me quickly at ease. 'You don't have to waste your time and words on me, I have always been one of you. All success to you', he assured me, warmly pressing both my hands. I felt blessed and controlled a strong impulse I had to rest my head on those powerful hands.

I could not bring myself to approach party boss Jinnah. He seemed distant carrying an icy aura around him. May be I was influenced by memories of Rati his wife. She had once adored him as her 'hero' as she put it, for he had then raised the banner of national revolt in a Bombay hall which still carries his name. Full of him she talked of I (as she stylishly called him) as though he were the oracle. She was dainty, exquisitely sculpted as by a Master artist, something that flashed through our world, something you could never grip or hold. Possessed of an unusually sharp intelligence, she was also intrinsically warm and affectionate and a vivacious talker. How did these two meteors from two different firmaments come to be entangled in a marriage knot, I wondered. As time sped by Rati changed, the vivacious tongue grew tart, giving expression to ideas and phrases poised to shock and hurt. She sometimes posed high sophisticated sentiments like an armour to cover up a deep hurt within. Like how bored she was by her little daughter and had to bring herself to see her once a day. I was not shocked. I saw her tied to a man inordinately ambitious, who made himself the center of his whole existence, with no room for anyone. Rati had filled her entire life with him, created no niche for herself. Obviously she became twisted and warped, broke away and finally passed away. Jinnah's ambitions proliferated until he broke up the entire Indian sub-continent, which is still reeling under those conclusions. I wonder how many are aware of this mini family tragedy, an early prelude as it were to the larger disaster.

When we parted Pandit Motilal Nehru very cordially invited me to visit his family at Allahabad. 'It is one of the backwaters. May be you could stir up the stagnant waters,' he said. Rameshwari Nehru followed this up by fixing up an assignment for me at Allahabad.

The Nehru family then lived in the old Anand Bhavan, a large endless sprawling building. This being my first contact with this family about whom there were so many fairy tales, I was a bit overawed. The person who quickly put me at ease was Kamala Nehru. Swarup Rani, the hostess, was ailing and in bed. Jawaharlal took me to visit her as she wished to meet me. What struck me instantly was that though she looked frail, she could be a dominating person. Kamala on the other hand, though equally slim and frail looking, was gentle and kindly. She was one who could be known only by close association. There was a hard core that hid behind her soft exterior. Though she never seemed to dominate, she could be assertive in her own quiet way. I could not but feel that she had nurtured a mechanism of her own to preserve her entity and not be reduced to a shadow by the menfolk in the family, especially her husband. At close quarters one saw that she was neither an echo nor a pale reflection of him. It was remarkable how she stood out so distinctly beside his overpowering personality. Having to keep up with a demanding life with failing health and feeble body, called forth all one's compassion. As she once said 'it is alright being famous, but is very nerve-racking.'

When Motilal was about he filled the scene, there hardly seemed room for anyone else. He had a bubbling warmth which he seemed to spill all around him, drawing everyone into its glow. He was a hearty man, full of humour, laughter, gaiety. I dare say he had had his dark moods and cold sulks, but to me they were not as obviously tantalising or chilling as in the case of the son. This was my first real association with Jawaharlal Nehru. It was not easy to get a grasp of his personality that seemed almost mercurial, but in reality was not. Once the talk came around to the impending elections under the new political reforms. 'Wouldn't you be participating in the elections?' I asked. 'Me, oh, no. I simply would not have the *patience* to sit in a legislature.' I was at a loss, not knowing how to take it. It seemed so childish unless he was talking for effect, trying to say outrageous things.

What I found most enjoyable and exhilarating were the heated arguments between father and son at the dinner table. They were not only full of sparkle, but also very penetrating and to me, politically most revealing. My one regret is that I did not keep a record of them.

As I watched these two personalities in wordy combats, I saw how the son held his own. A misfortune that at times befalls a worthy child of being eclipsed by a towering father did not happen here. In fact the former, as time went on, carved out a marked place for himself with his own individual stamp. The supercilious assessment that he owed much to the imposing Anand Bhavan setting and his father's colourful personality, adding what I call a sneering epithet, about the Nehru clothes being laundered in Paris, whether it be true or not, could not be counted as attributes. Jawaharlal had surprisingly simple habits, with a minimum of needs. I had particularly remarked on this during our travels, and he nodded with a rare modest smile. 'I try not to be too big a burden on anyone.' he admitted. I once asked his attendant Hari how exactly he served Panditji. 'He is very kind,' was his answer. I can think of a few well publicised 'Gandhians' who are meticulously sensitive about their clothes and irrationally fussy over their food. If Pandit Nehru attained the position he did, it was due to hard work and a severely disciplined routine.

When I was covering the Sind area during one of my Conference tours, I took a trip to Mohenjodaro, the ancient excavated city. It is one thing to read of its being 4500 years old, that it may even have preceded the antique Mesopotamian civilization and therefore is the oldest known to mankind and which flourished on the wide stretches bordering the mighty Indus flowing for 1920 kilometers, nurturing 400 highly urbanised cities whose precise planning put experts in mind of Manhattan. It is quite another experience to actually visit this wondrous site, something never to be forgotten. Moreover it was my very first experience of viewing an excavation of such tremendous magnitude and with such little known history. The little that is constructed is from the rubble.

This was in the late twenties. We were two young women on this adventurous jaunt, my valued colleague from the Women's Conference was Anandi Khemchand, a teacher from Larkhana, Sind. We did the approach on camel back. My only experience of such a ride was on a tourist trudge in Egypt, jogging merrily along on a richly caparisoned camel that snootily sniffed the air. Here within seconds of my mounting, it seemed to leap into the air, taking me completely unawares, and then running as though it had been whipped. While I was trying to catch my breath and trying not to scream, Anandi had simply vanished, leaving a cloud of dust. When I finally landed safely, I rebuked my friend for not alerting me. She opened her wide eyes wider, reminding me I had said I did camel riding in Egypt. I reminded her I was not a maiden of the desert land like her and I had yet to learn the difference beween a tourist camel and the flying ship of the desert.

As I stepped on this very ancient site, time shed its parameters. Here was an urban civilization that acquired spectacular heights in the third millennium B.C. on the Indian Sub-Continent, *supported* by an agricultural economy based on the utilisation of surplus production. Urbanisation of this dimension also presumed large scale trade and commerce for such extensive urban life could only mean a substantial non-agricultural population.

As one surveys the vast miles of ruins, one grows philosophic. Here were buried cities that once must have glowed with pride not only in structures but also achievement of a grid system that showed advanced scientific knowledge. The guide from the Archeological Department who now joined us pointed out the sophisticated town planning and perfect extensive underground drainage and ingenious method of providing amenities like water supply, sanitation, all proofs of considerable technological experience, together with samples of metallurgy, weights, measures, compass, etc. Foreigners have remarked on the resemblance to Troy, built atop and at several levels, which proved what intensive and concerted skill had gone into it. This also meant, according to this expert guide, that the lower levels buried roughly 60 feet below could be much older and may predate anything else we know. I was not only overawed by this, I felt small and humble. Why did the young so often feel superior, that we knew more than those long gone by did ?

The All India Women's Conference which had started seeking educational reforms had soon expanded its objectives, widened its parameters. It was now amongst the early pioneers of many important causes. It took up the problems and welfare of children and drew up a Children's Charter, the first of its kind for India. It also campaigned on the food front for the use of the traditional indigenous foods, specially for children, to counter the doubtful tinned and bottled stuff, which has only now assumed importance, with repeated emphasis on the superiority of breast feeding. It pursued for the supply of adequate and good milk specially during the war years, when expectant mothers and children suffered its lack the most. When National Governments were set up later in the Indian States, the project for supply of milk was pressed upon each of them, starting with Bombay, which was the first to respond, and resulted in the Government taking on milk supply for the public, later followed by other states. Bombay was also the first city to launch family planning on a nation-wide scale. Where there were no special public clinics, private doctors were approached to take up this problem, and vigorous propaganda to limit families was carried out on various fronts.

Promotion of cultural expressions and forms was equally pursued. Folk dances, music and indigenous dramatic forms were encouraged in schools. Similarly handicrafts were actively promoted through small training and production centres by the various branches. At the anuual session of the Conference, each branch was expected to put on cultural shows by its members as also organise exhibitions of crafts by the production centres of the Branches. Other problems like consumer protection, social and moral hygiene, in fact every aspect of the life of the women and family were sought to be covered.

Problems of women labour received special attention. Surveys to study their conditions in various sections at first hand were carried out. I myself covered some of the plantations labour, also labour in mines and similar isolated sectors. This led to getting suitable legislative enactments adopted to benefit women labour and children.

I had felt a certain sense of uneasiness in inviting figure heads to preside over our annual sessions, instead of distinguished *workers* who were also Conference members. It was time, I thought, to honour our own veteran workers by electing them to high offices. This proposal was readily accepted by the Conference and for the next annual session Srimati Sarojini Naidu was elected President.

Countrywide social reform movement initiated at the end of the last century and carried forward by many noted leaders into the 20th century had been organised into a single national body named the Indian Social Reforms Conference. As several of these social workers were also in politics, it used to hold its annual session alongwith the Indian National Congress to achieve maximum attendence and achievement.

At the Madras National Congress I was requested to organise the women volunteers on behalf of the Seva Dal. I thus came into active contact with the social reform workers. Prominent among them was Shri Venkataraman, a member of the Servants of India Society. I found him a most active and devoted worker. He persuaded me to become one of the Secretaries of the Social Reform Conference. The session was presided over by Shri K. Natarajan, an outstanding national figure in the social reform movement at that time. He was also editor of the Indian Social Reformer, a well-known and most respected weekly. I felt fortunate in working as Secretary with Shri Natarajan. He and his colleagues opened up new and more diverse avenues of thought and action. Though not of the agitational kind they could campaign vigorously and powerfully for the causes close to my heart. Their greatest asset was their integrity and sincerity which won them respect and confidence from the public. Even where they did not agree fully, as for instance with Gandhiji's political methods, they seemed understanding or tolerant. 'We could live together as friends without calling each other reactionary and traitors', was veteran Natarajan's philosophy.

Working as a Secretary in the Social Reform Conference I savoured more deeply of the social reform movement and the many benefits it had brought to women through educative propaganda and establishment of fine institutions, I became aware of a close growing kinship. There was a placid but strength-giving quality about this movement which for me added a significant weight to the work I was engaged in.

As time went on and I grew more aware of women's movements in the West, I realised how important the motivation had to be and how appropriate and closely related to the objective, the items of programme. The basic realisation that strengthened within me was that society was indivisible even as one saw the global community shape after weltering through the agonies of two world wars. The main aim of this social reform movement was correcting the dangerous imbalances in our socio-economic organism. The confrontation here was between the blind forces that opposed any compulsive changes and those whose vision, sensitivity and maturing experience pointed to changes. In this forward movement the well-being of the society as a whole was sought, irrespective of sex, creed and social caste. In this India displayed a very important principle. For in the West, instead of a cohesive social current the society had broken into two rigid sex groups, the unhappy results of which time has only served to accentuate. There has continued a harsh confrontation between men and women, this trend getting more and more stratified, distorting the very premises and therefore drawing erroneous conclusions. One unfortunate trend has been for women wanting to *ape* men which often ends in pathetic results leading to no solution. The women have been showing a subtle undercurrent of prejudices against *womanhood* as though they regretted being born women because of several natural functions that went with it. I saw the great tragedy of women isolating themselves from a cohesive society.

Women of those times who adhered to the concept of the totality of society showed tremendous self-confidence and inner strength even though they were suffering from many more disabilities and lacked many of the opportunities available to women today. They never sought reservations for women in any sphere. Nor nominations on bodies as *women* but because they qualified as citizens. They claimed and struggled forcefully for equality but the claim was on merit and not on sex alone wnich they felt cut at the very foundation of the principle of equality and betrayed a lack of self-confidence.

It was therefore not surprising that women made tremendous strides where they could assert themselves and take their stand on their own qualification.

As my involvement with the Indian Social Conference deepened I became conscious of the widening of the parameters of my vision and activities, especially drawing inspiration from their different leaders engaged in a variety of very commendable pursuits.

In my travels I tried to combine the programmes of the Women's Conference and the Social Reform Conference giving my activities a larger dimension and a deeper significance. This enabled me to think and function against a bigger canvas, thus reaping a richer harvest of experience. An ever widening field also gave me access to newer sectors and richer resources, bringing me encouraging rewards.

After 1947, with the adoption of the new Constitution which removed discrimination on grounds of sex and the introduction of related legislation to give effect to this, a complacency seems to have gripped the women and all the old dynamics have melted away. Diffidence has begun to undermine self-confidence and women have since begun to seek the path of the weak and the defeated. Tragically they are beginning to isolate themselves from the community, from the nation at large and have ceased to march with the whole society, with the nation to reach new goals as they once did.

In the latter part of 1929 I decided to go on a foreign trip, partly to attend some International Conference and partly to see something of the 'New Education' of which I had been hearing and reading reports ni practice.

I seem to have been afflicted by a short memory for my previous passport had been cancelled and though no reason had been vouchsafed, I was obviously considered an offender. Therefore when the passport office refused to give me a form to apply, I kind of woke up from my slumber of forgetfulness. Soon after I came on a visit to Delhi, Sir Biren Mitter, who was then in the Viceroy's Council, and his wife had become friends with me. When I told them I had to abandon my trip abroad, they were surprised. Sir Biren exclaimed in a shocked tone there must be some gross mistake. Then I related to him the genesis of the government's displeasure, all because I had spent a few weeks with my brother-in-law, Virendranath whom I met for the first time. I had not done any speaking or indulged in any what may be termed dangerous activities. He assured me the error would be rectified. So my passport was restored to me.

I first attended the Conference organised by the International Alliance of Women in Berlin. My first shock was to find it was a misnomer to call it 'International' as it was composed of, national representatives from the East limited only to Egypt and India. Other colonial countries were represented by their *rulers* and not the country's nationals. Egypt and India, however, between them made a pretty good and spirited showing. For their delegates were led by two dominant leaders : for Egypt, Madame Charaoui Pasha and for India, Sarojini Naidu. Madame Charaoui Pasha was a revolutionary leader who made history by leading the women of her country to throw off their veil and actively participate in their national freedom struggle. When I visited Egypt later as her guest, I found that she had become a legend to her people. She and Sarojini Naidu with their personality and golden eloquence were able to sway the Berlin audiences which came to hear them at special meetings arranged by Sarojini's brother, Virendranath Chattopadhyay, to project the cause of the colonials. In particular, was a mammoth gathering organised by the German Socialist labour unions. This enabled me to talk to the workers and learn of the various activities of their unions such as conducting adult education classes, sports, vacation tours—national and international, leisure hour activities, entertainments, cultural programmes, etc. I was not surprised to learn that the auditorium where this lecture was being held, belonged to a labour union.

In the midst of all this I felt humiliated when in this International Congress hall I saw all the other countries had their own flags fluttering. Only the Indian delegation had none; except notionally, we were supposed to be huddled under the British Union Jack, which to us was a symbol of our slavery. I complained about the absence of the Indian flag to the organisers and they confessed that they did not know that India had a flag of her own, if she had, it should certainly be hoisted. We had only a night before the opening. So the Indian delegates pulled out their saris, cut up pieces to form the colours of the Indian National Congress flag, i.e. red, green and white. No one grudged tearing up their fineries. In fact, we felt free and liberated at the gala opening function watching our flag fluttering proudly amidst others.

The next Conference I attended was in Copenhagen, Denmark, organised by the New Education Movement. The basic theory of New Education was that the child did not come into the world as a blank slate on which its parents and teachers could write what they willed, but it was born with potentialities, gifts, talents, all of which had to be stimulated and drawn out into operation. It was still a pioneering effort, the old ideas having deep roots. To us in India this was not a new concept because Indian tradition believed that a child has all the potential within it which needed stimulation in the early years itself. In the old days there was a ceremony on the sixth day when the future of the child was supposed to be written by fate. Unfortunately English education drew a curtain over that tradition and introduced the same blind system practised in the west, ignoring the burgeoning talent.

The Indian delegation was led by Professor Dondo Keshev Karve who was already recognised as a pioneering educationist and had promoted several new institutions. He was, of course a doyen amongst the social reform leaders. I felt elated and proud to be in his team, and bask in the glow of his fame. I also listened with distress to some of his amazing but painful experiences of the early days, the kind of martyrdom he and many of his colleagues had to go through, the utter vulgarities of those insults which cannot even bear to be recorded.

We were a very small delegation, Maharashi Karve, his young son who looked like a school boy, though a lecturer in a college, and myself. We were knocked over to find we had made the front page of the leading newspaper with the caption, 'The venerable Indian professor and his young wife'. Karve did look a typical patriarch with his long hair and flowing beard. By his side I seemed even younger than I was, in my mid-twenties Thrown into angry confusion, I protested to the Conference Publicity Officer. With a benign smile he explained this was because of the general impression that an Indian women only travelled under the protection of the husband, it was a natural conclusion in our case, no offense meant.

The Conference on New Education proved more exhilarating than expected. It was dominated by young representatives and headed by a lively bright-faced lady, all of which made for a lively session, as many new ideas were generated and worthwhile examples picturised.

The Conference itself was held in the romantic Elsioner Palace where Hamlet, the famous Shakespearean character is said to have lived. For our entertainment Shakespeare's Hamlet was put on in the palace theatre. In the European renaissance period, in some European countries, the ruler built a theatre in his palace where shows were enacted regularly. Some of the princes themselves also took part in the dramas.

The next Conference in Prague, was of the International League for Peace and Freedom. It was entirely different. This was an unexpected event that came through an invitation sent by Miss Molly Carrol, an American social worker, and close colleague of the world famous Jane Adams. The International League for Peace and Freedom, a purely women's body, was founded by Jane Adams. A noted pacifist who had shaken the world by her firm and open opposition to the World War I, an act regarded then as treachery, Jane Adams was basically a humanitarian. Her greatest virtue was her love and compassion for human beings. Spurred by this she had reversed the approach to social work from the correctional to the preventive, from institutional to home care service. At Hull House in Chicago, her main institution, services were basically planned out to preserve the family intact, for it was realised that a weak or broken home led to many social evils. She was a pioneer in the larger concept of community service which is today such a vital factor in social welfare.

It was this deep humaneness which had led Jane Adams to condemn violence and oppose war as an instrument for settling disputes. She was one of a small anti-war group of protesters, facing the verdict of treachery for this. But she remained undaunted.

Now what Molly related to me were scenes of horror as the war had raged and ended, families affected by the loss of loved ones; equally the loss of prized landmarks. Above all the loss of fundamental social values, undermining of faith in human integrity in the face of oppression, unabashed and unashamed. The brutalising of humans complete the tragedy.

She told me the crisis of conscience which resulted in tragedy in her own life. She was engaged to marry a church minister, and planned to jointly do community service. He had been a pacifist like her, but war hysteria unbalanced him. She found him changing and with America entering the war, he enlisted. The chasm between them had become too deep to be corrected by mere arguments or cemented by phrases. So they broke off. Molly never married. The hurt in her was not merely personal. It was a way of life had been distorted and through it were destroyed many other cherished elements. She could not accept violence as a weapon for achieving any kind of liberation.

Though my own association with Jane Adams was comparatively brief, as we kept meeting I came to feel that she was someone I had known a long time and inspite a difference of 50 years between us, she accepted me as a comrade. To her India was the land of Gandhi, a soul after her own heart and she had so much to ask and learn about him. She listened with rapt attention to my paraphrasing Gandhiji's concept of non-violence, that it was not a passive non-cooperation but a positive dynamic weapon which he believed to be more powerful than any metal object. She was moved to silence as my words flowed. So we talked of the past, present and future and she came out vividly as one of the great women of her age, who blazed a new trail and poured out a new sermon. What struck me was her personality: simple, free of tensions or tantrums, with a heart filled with love, there was no bitterness towards those who had assailed her mercilessly. I realised that hers had been a long and lonely battle, so different from our own struggle where millions stood shoulder to shoulder as one. Nevertheless she still seemed ready to carry the cross.

An unusual gathering I attended during this European trip was the International Session of the League Against Imperialism held in Frankfurt, for which the invitation had come through Virendranath Chattopadhyay who was among its prime organisers. What I knew of this congress was that it was an anti-imperialist front, a significant effort to hold together genuine anti-imperialist forces buttressed by European workers bodies. It had been set up with much publicity in 1927 at a conference of representatives from national organisations from colonial countries, and working class organisations along with left groups from western countries. The initiative had come from the communist world.

I was tempted to attend it as we in India were moving to a decisive stage in our struggle against British imperialism. When I arrived I was fascinated by the medieval town, Frankfurt, as it was then, with its archaic cobbled streets.

Delegates had come from several colonial countries like Indo-China, Java, West Asia and North Africa with a sprinkling of American Negroes. Some were from labour unions, others from left political groups. As this was considered only a front against imperialism and not identified with any political party, several intellectuals such as Einstein, Romain Rolland, Madame Sun-yat-sun, etc., had been associated with it. George Lansbury from the Independent British Labour Party had presided over the previous session of this congress. Shri Shiv Prasad Gupta, a veteran congressman from Varanasi, (India) was there on behalf of the Indian National Congress. India had acquired some importance in this body as Pandit Nehru had attended the previous congress as India's representative. As I had no familiarity with any of the political parties represented here, it was hard for me to decipher the different strands in this big concourse of political bodies. Communist inspired, it was obviously endeavouring to maintain a broad front, stressing mostly its anti-colonial character. It was also my first experience of listening to the use of sharp expressions, violent language, loud demonstrative delivery, in striking contrast to a rather orderly assemblage of our own Indian National Congress meetings of those days. This was when I picked up the then famous song 'Internationale' that so impressed me, as full throated thousands sang it at the public gatherings.

Gradually as the discussions proceeded, the confused political strands unravelled revealing the outline of each of the many political patterns. I began to grasp some of the several facets of that complicated monster, imperialism, that had with its insatiable greed, swallowed up most of the world. But without Viren's sharp and descriptive guidance I wonder if I could have learnt even what little I did.

Virendranath was an important figure in this Congress and under his wing I was able to meet many leading personalities collected there. Amongst those who impressed me most were Reginald Bridgeman, the Secretary of the League, who I learned had sacrificed a notable diplomatic career to serve this League; James Maxton with his unusual ascetic looking face, leader of the British Independent Party, and the famous French philosopher, Henri Bergson. His writings, especially his book 'Creative Evolution' propagated the theory that the spirit acts out of its own initiative, issues innumerable forms but being infinite is not itself affected, therefore a real renaissance had to be impregnated with spiritual quality, had stirred the placid surface of European philosophy. He sought talks with me, for he probably presumed that being an Indian, to me his thoughts may not seem so abstruse. Fortunately, attracted by the title, I had thumbed through his 'Creative Evolution'. I was fascinated however by his personal paraphrasing of these thought-expressions, how he had evolved his theory, though at this moment it did seem very distant from the long and at times rather raucous debates in progress.

It was a novel experience for me to be received as a mature political personality whereas in India I had been treated as a youth with condescension by elders. As we were the only two Indians fresh from India which was reportedly in revolt under Gandhiji, we were much sought after and had to explicate on the Indian political developments.

Unfortunately later in the thirties the European split on the issue of a 'United Front', in pursuance of which the Soviet Union showed a willingness for an alliance with England and France, rapidly undermined this anti-imperialist League and it sank into oblivion.

One of the most abiding memories I have of this Congress is seeing Russian films for the first time, particularly a few of Sergei Eisenstein's fabulous creations, among which Battleship Potemkin stands out in my mind. It was for me a most unusual and unforgettable masterpiece where the entire Russian Revolution seems to have been distilled into a single episode. The start is unbelievably simple; the sailors on this battleship reject the maggotty soup as uneatable, and mutiny. Amazingly it runs only an hour, a single explosive *drama* not a sequence of events. It was explained to us that real people from the streets were pressed into the film, not professional artists. According to Eisenstein this clothed the film with a complete sense of reality, threading each selective shot in a crucial link with the whole gamut. I also noticed how the intensity of chaotic *movement* visualised the power of the emotion, which is then suddenly blacked out to show a lone woman weighed down with silent grief carrying her dead son.

Equally powerful was the 'Ten Days that Shook the World', where again ordinary people and simple objects were used, and according to its director, was levelled at depicting a whole series of new experiments with startling effects, which aimed at 'Intellectual Cinema' at making people think.

One other 'Storm over Asia' was stirring. It depicted the poor gatherers of animal skins and furs whose goods were marketed in Western Countries at fabulous prices.

On this trip I had greatly looked forward to having a look at some experimental schools inspired by 'New Education' which was very much in the air.

The first institution I visited in England was the O'Neil School. It had been made famous partly by its founder's pronouncement, 'There are no problem children, only problem parents,' which he paraphrased for me when I met him.

As I watched the school at work, the atmosphere made a profound impact on me. There was a deep sense of freedom which seemed to have become a way of life. The air was not vitiated by any sense of bravado, or heroic poses over breaking established conventions. Everything moved in an unselfconscious freedom. To him the trouble was that parents regarded the child as mindless, the old idea of the blank slate, and it was for them in their wisdom to write on it ideas, sentiments, images, etc. completely ignoring the child's own potential and capacity. This meant continuous conflict between the two resulting in making the children rebellious. He therefore encouraged and pursued continuous dialogue with the parents. These ideas had lead to the growth of the Parent Teacher Association.

I was also stimulated by the experimental schools in Berlin, specially for little children. Among the best known were the Froebel whose beginnings went back almost into the end of 19th century, when pioneers in early education conceived the pattern that came to be known as Kindergarten, the expression in German meaning childgarden; Pestalozzi was another among the promoters of Kindergarten.

Equally noted was the Rudolf Steiner School movement by the then famous artist-educationist and scientist, Rudolf Steiner. He aimed at developing in the pupil a balanced and total personality by increasing its capacity to concentrate and coordinate through exercises and basic positions in standing or walking, which would enable the child to gain a balance between itself and the space around. This was expected to fill the child with a sense of equilibrium therefore harmony which could be maintained if pursued from childhood into adulthood. This principle has been brought into focus again, some modern dances being based on it. Another institution was Salin, on Lake Constance, run by Dr. Hans of which Prince of Baden was a Patron. The basic principle was the same, to stimulate the talents and capabilities within the child to bring them out into fruitful action.

In Geneva I saw an unusual institution conducted by Emil Jacques Dalcroze. The principle here was to co-ordinate the mind and body by music. Dalcroze told me that he was originally a Professor of Harmony at the Geneva Conservatory. Here he was sought by some of his pupils who moaned of their inability to hear, i.e. they could not readily assimilate sound in their ears. He then observed that when a musician played on an instrument, his entire being was called into action, i.e. along with the movement of the finger there was an oscillation of the head and body, coordinating with substantial foot movement. This made him realise that an indepth musical sensational call involves the muscular nervous system of the entire organism, and so he created the Eurythmic method of education, which meant organised physical movement responding to musical stimuli. This also included coordination of brain, nerves and muscles and thus students experienced greater and finer depths along with a total sensitivity and absorption. He stated that this could be practised from the pre-school child to senior citizen with great benefit.

He also told me how this had penetrated into the modern dance and that pioneers such as Ruth St. Danis, Doris Humphry, Mary Wigman, Hanya Holm had incorporated this principle into their art. What is more, when the legendary Russian dancer Nijinsky, staged Stravinsky's *Le Sacre Du Printemps*, a Dalcroze specialist was called in to operate with this score.

I have described this at some length because I found it popular in other countries specially Scandinavia.

A Danish lady called Anna Ornshelt came out to India as a Teacher of Eurythmics through her Theosophical connection. She was called upon by several schools to teach it. Some adults also formed groups to practice with her. I joined one and went through a course, when she was in a school in Trichur in Kerala. No less a person than J.C. Bose, famous scientist, seemed to have been attracted by this and Anna spent several years in his home, acting as his secretary.

I would like to quote here a perfect definition of rhythm by Rabindranath Tagore to understand its great significance:

'The only training which I had from my young days was the

training in rhythm, the rhythm in thought, the rhythm in sound. I had come to know that rhythm gives reality to that which is desultory, which is insignificant in itself. And, therefore, when the scratches in my manuscript cried, like sinners, for salvation, and assailed my eyes with the surliness of their irrelevance, I often took more time in rescuing them into a merciful finality of rhythm than in carrying on what was my obvious task.'

I returned to my post as General Secretary of the Conference full of renewed enthusiasm and ideas, eager to effect improvements in the functioning of the Conference, including office routine. I wanted to give the impending annual session a new image and create a more relevant and energising climate. I was gratified that for the first time we would have as President a known worker amongst the women, like Sarojini Naidu. We would have the usual performing arts by the various branches as also exhibition of crafts by the members. To this I had added a new item : modern kitchen gadgets to help women in their house-hold chores and lighten their burden. In my foreign travel I had seen the use of these mechanical gadgets that would transform much of the drudgery into ease. In the days of joint families the various jobs were shared. In the current living pattern of a single struggling couple, the domestic routine was making heavy demands on the already overburdened housewife. Even small tools could ease the nervous strain and save time. As electricity spread it could be used to manipulate some of them. Thus for the first time the modern tools, hand operated as also power operated were demonstrated in this special exhibition and the effort was received with acclaim. This exhibition was made possible by the ready cooperation and help of Siemens, the well known German firm dealing with electrical goods.

Another factor I had come across in my tour abroad were the Home Science Institutes which incidentally had students of both sexes, a very welcome feature. It obviously was to meet the modern needs of the women who now, absorbed in formal education, failed to get grounding in domestic activities. It therefore became necessary to provide this knowledge through institutional channels.

As the Women's Conference had started with the idea of introducing new elements and strands into our education, it promoted a special Education Fund Association towards this objective. To this body I submitted my plan for a Home Science Institute for Women in India. Lady Irwin, wife of the then Viceroy, showed great interest in this and agreed to act as its Chairman and help in the collection of funds. Hilla Faridoonji became its Secretary and proved a most devoted, hard working executive and made possible its setting up in 1932.

This was indeed a bold adventure for an organisation that was just finding its feet. It was like a leap in the dark for we had no tradition to pattern it upon, nor the necessary ready funds nor the required trained personnel to venture on it. Only one foreign expert from New Zealand was called in at the start to help. Most of the credit for its realisation goes to the staff who earnestly and selflessly contributed funds out of their own salaries. A few were even sent abroad through such contributions, to take special courses to get equipped for teaching these new subjects. While several contributed in the success of this pioneering project, two personalities stand out: Hannah Sen and Tarabai, both of whom became Directors of the College. The latter who served long as Director contributed towards continuously upgrading this college and lent a hand in starting similar institutions elsewhere in the country.

Her most memorable contribution was helping in the setting up of a Home Science Institute in a rural area in Vidyanagar, Gujarat, which was a new experiment. In fact it was fresh adventure for the whole concept of development of current Home Science was a purely urban product geared to urban communities. To fit this into a rural setting Tarabai had to make a complete departure to divert this knowledge, the various processes into a new channel, modify and adjust to an entirely different world with varied demands, new challenges. This opened a new dimension in the old conventional idea of Home Science, more relevent and realistic.

Continuing in the spirit of the early days, Tarabai put in ten long years at this rural institute giving free service without accepting any remuneration and left behind a most memorable record. Both Hannah Sen and Tarabai were active workers in the Women's Conference and also headed it as presidents and obviously drew inspiration and direction from it.

The college continued to function without any recognition or aid from the then government. It was indeed a remarkable achievement to build it up into an outstanding institution and run it successfully until the advent of the national government when it got affiliated to the Delhi University.

It is regrettable however that one or two late comers to the key post of director made a sharp departure from the original objectives of the founders i.e. to mentally train and physically equip young women bring them into the current family and community stream with the aid of modern science and technology through conducting 'practising homes'. It has now been converted into the same dead institution as others where students are forced to mug up bookish subjects, completely divorced from life.

A strange incident that took place immediately on my return from abroad was a demand from the government to surrender my passport, which I declined to do as its validity had not expired, nor had I violated any laws national or international to forfeit it. The answer to this was the cancellation of the passport and a threat that due publicity would be given to it. Accordingly letters had been addressed to the various shipping companies not to issue any passage to me as I had forfeited my passport. There was no explanation as to what was my crime.

While I was on tour organising women, one of the striking women I had come across was Tripurasundari, wife of the scientist Dr. C.V. Raman. A keen mind and lively conversation made her an individual apart. She appeared to me like an ornament to heighten her husband's scintillating personality. Dr. Raman had just received the Nobel Prize, making him the first Asian to get it in Science.

As I greeted him at the Indian Institute of Sciences with congratulations, he gave a faint answering smile and said : 'I wanted to prove Indian scientific research was of the highest order, equal to any in the world.' He related how with the limited requisites as his disposal, he had worked over many years to finally startle the scientific world with the "Raman Effect" as it had now come to be designated. 'You are of course aware that such discoveries do not come out as chance phenomena. One is forever questioning nature which tantalises us, cramful as it is of what seem mysteries, until they are wrested out for public exposure. The answer or solution comes only through sheer dint of hard relentless work, keen perception, analysing, collating every particle. It is an endless moving mission.' As a matter of fact he explained he had recorded for almost a decade his observations made on light and its properties. 'As I was pursuing this I could almost foresee the results the scientific world sees day. To me science is the highest form of creative art. It is my hope to help true science take deep root and we should cease for ever looking to the West for it.'

Then he got up rather brusquely saying 'I think you have been very patient with all my abstruse talk. Let me treat you to some visual sights that may intrigue and even entertain you.' With this he turned on what looked like a small T.V. apparatus. 'I shall start some music and you just watch the varied shapes the tonal sounds take on the screen. As I have already described this episode earlier elsewhere, I shall not repeat it.'

Sometime later when I met him he seemed far from satisfied. 'We still seem to go on as camp followers of the West', was his cryptic comment. May be he would have felt less dejected had he lived to see nearly a thousand researchers the world over working on his findings and admitting its effect on development of laser technology.

A most surprising and unexpected event took place at this stage which was to take me along an entirely new path. I was approached by Yusuf Meherally, a rising youth leader in Bombay, to join his movement. During my travel in Europe I had been stimulated by the Youth Movement, a post-war current that was assuming a special social and political significance. Youth had become after the world war vocal and assertive. Young people felt that elders were making a mess of their lives and they should also have a voice in the moulding of their lives and their destiny. The movement was welcomed and was receiving considerable support, and taking on a marked identity. One of their programmes was to travel and cross political frontiers to build up understanding and friendship with youths in other countries, as a bulwark against further wars. One saw groups of these young men and women with knapsacks on their back trudging along highways. Youth organisations were also making their own demands on society and governments. I had described this movement in the Indian Press and that must have marked me as one interested in the youth. Hence this invitation.

Many young people pressed on me that we were on the eve of a critical situation. The coming session of the Indian National Congress in Lahore, was only a few weeks away, and it was necessary for the youth of India to provide the key note decision in Lahore. Therefore this youth Congress which they wanted organised immediately was of crucial importance. I was needed to preside over this.

The session was held in Ahmedabad on 14th December, 1929, amidst a new spurt of enthusiasm. Thousands crowded in singing *Bande Matharam*. Dr. Sumant Mehta, a well known political leader, was the Chairman of the reception committee.

The main issue facing this youth congress was India's ultimate goal ; dominion status or full independence. In its resolution it appealed to the National Congress leaders to declare 'POORNA SWARAJ', as our goal and not to compromise on this issue. If they did, the youths would carry on the fight inspite of them.

In my speech I widened the concept of freedom to also cover many social evils in our society, particularly the oppression of certain sections socially and economically as also the low status given to women. I condemned the prevalence of double standards in society and called upon the youth to do away with these inequalities.

In conclusion I exhorted the youth to action, not be content with vehement speeches but purposefully launch into speedy action. I stressed the need for *direct action* and readiness for any sacrifices. I reminded them however that the youth organisation should work along with the National Congress under our leaders to prepare and plunge into the liberation struggle.

The history of the declaration for independence however goes back to the Madras Congress of 1927 when Pandit Nehru fresh from his European sojourn, moved for complete Independence as the goal which was readily adopted. A piquant situation arose however at the following annual Congress at Calcutta presided over by Motilal Nehru, when he sponsored the recommendations of the All Parties Conference which did not make independence a condition. To meet this strange contingency, the Calcutta session declared the Constitution envisaged in the Report as a trial of good faith with a year's ultimatum. If the British Government failed to implement it, the Congress would press ahead for Independence. The Lahore Congress decision was a fulfilment of this. Its significance lay in its being the final ultimatum indicating a plunge into direct action.

The Lahore Congress under the Presidentship of Pandit Jawaharlal Nehru declared complete independence as India's goal. It also announced that a public declaration of this was to be made throughout the country on 26th January, 1930. For the youth this was a triumph since it was the youth congress in Ahmedabad that had been the pace setter.

Vast crowds assembled at Azad Maidan in Bombay, on 26th January where we hoisted the National Flag and took the following pledge : *We believe it is the inalienable right of the Indian people as of any other, to have freedom and to enjoy the fruits of their toil, have the necessities of life so that they may have full opportunities of growth. We believe also that if any government deprives a people of these rights and oppresses them, the people have a further right to alter it or to abolish it. The British Government in India has not only deprived the Indian people of these rights and oppressed them, the people have a further right to alter it or to abolish it. The British Government in India has not only deprived the Indian people of their freedom but has based itself on the exploitation of the masses and has ruined India economically, politically, culturally and spiritually. We believe therefore that India must sever the British connection and attain Purna Swaraj—complete independence.*

Flag hoisting was just finished when a small group with a red flag with the familiar sickle hammer symbol on it, suddenly appeared near the flag post to plant the red flag on it. I rushed to the flag post to protect the threatened hoisted flag. As the sun had set and it had got dark, one heard voices more clearly than saw faces. I was, however, conscious that there was a definite effort to pull down the national flag and that I must hang on to it to prevent this disaster. My hands became bruised in the struggle to hold on to the flag and probably drew some blood that kept trickling, but I was not conscious of anything except that I must save the flag from defilement. Suddenly I became aware of a tallish man whose face I could hardly distinguish, standing behind me with two hands raised, excitedly shouting 'BRAVE! GREAT'. Then he wrapped my hands in his handkerchief to stop the bleeding and kept shouting to the crowd standing around us : 'SHE SAVED OUR FLAG FROM DISHONOUR'. The man was Johri who later became a close and dear colleague of mine, first in the youth movement and then in the freedom struggle. Highly imaginative and dramatic, he created a cadre of children named 'Vanara Sena' to train them in purposeful activities rather than that they run wildly around shouting slogans and indulging in destructive escapades. It was one of his several original and dramatic contributions to the freedom movement, unfortunately unsung, unhonoured. Ironically other more pampered and publicised persons have claimed authorship to it.

The declaration of purna swaraj and the oath taking on 26 January electrified the country which now stood on the tip toe of expectant action. Gandhiji in his characteristic manner, made one more appeal to the rulers, 'on bended knees' as he picturesquely described it, but to no avail.

The Congress Working Committee met in Ahmedabad early in 1930 to finalise the blueprint for 'direct action', as millions waited with bated breath for the great call. I was in Ahmedabad where the momentous decisions were being taken. I felt youthful enough to suffer the goosepricks. It was from Pandit Nehru that I heard the plan: launching Salt Satyagraha by breaking the innocuous, little remembered tax on salt. For a moment I felt a chill, then bewilderment surged over me. 'Is that all our Great Leader could device ?' I asked haltingly. He gave a knowing nod, and with a flicker of a smile, said, 'You have yet to learn his ways. We cannot always grasp his ideas in their entirety. But rest assured there is a method in what people think is madness.'

Pandit Nehru confessed Gandhiji put him in mind of the famous Puranic ascetics who by there severe sacrifice and discipline became kind of supermen—even the smaller gods fell to his bid : 'These myths have come to my mind as I have watched the amazing energy and inner power of Gandhiji coming out of some inexhaustable spiritual reservoir.'

That he too was equally bewildered and irritated, unable to equate a national struggle with common salt, I was to learn from him only later. Even more puzzled were his colleagues by Gandhiji's attaching to it his Eleven Points of what was popularly known as the Constructive Programme with its emphasis on Swadeshi Khadi, communal harmony, abolition of untouchability, etc. as an integral part of the revolutionary action. In his crystalline vision the 'India of his dreams' was clear. Its full import struck us as the curtain rose over the mutilated body of India at the hour of freedom. Today half a century later as we find ourselves throttled in the grip of these menacing problems, we realise to our cost the tragedy of our having bypassed them in the crucial hours.

Pandit Nehru explained they had no time to argue, for the fast moving political events were overtaking them and they had to jog along with Gandhiji, as he was the propelling force. An important point on which Gandhiji's clarification was sought, was the threat of calling off the movement on grounds of violence. He seems to have assured that unless violence became *part of the actual satyagraha movement* and was only a sporadic incident, the movement would be allowed to go on.

To meet the exigencies of an abnormal situation the launching of Satyagraha would create when the normal Congress organisation would be forcibly prevented from its normal function, the Working Committee devised a pattern of 'dictatorship' under which the leader in charge or rather a series of leaders—'dictators' would be selected, their names announced in succession as each was arrested. Two significant characteristics of a non-violent struggle are : the leader is publicly known and in the forefront unlike in a violent war; the battle plans would be open, no secrecy to be observed. Thus here the generals and soldiers were in the full glare of the public and publicity media. Ironically it became the prerogative of the authorities to suppress news and developments of the Satyagraha, as this inspired more people to join. But this hardly worked, large numbers flocked and as the prisons filled to overflowing open areas had to be pressed into service by erecting fences around. It was easy enough, for satyagrahis who voluntarily courted arrest were hardly likely to abscond, fence or no fence.

What was this image of *Revolution* that had fired our imagination, we the youth, I asked myself, ruminating over my sinking spirits. Could I possibly heighten my fancy to blow up a picture of us volunteers marching with our lathis as we did in our training camps, when under the Indian Arms Act even large sized knives were banned ? I simply could not conjure up any elevating picture of a revolution. 1857 could not be revived. What then ? The blankness depressed me for a while. We had called for 'Direct Action'. What did we mean ? I thought of the common salt as only a pinch of which could be consumed how could that be converted into an explosive to blow up the mighty British Raj on which the sun never set ? More and more everything got consolidated into the big question mark. Whatever it was, we had now to take the plunge. The British Government would never yield power voluntarily. The cry for independence grew daily compelling.

The voice of youth had first given the call to break the bonds with Britain and sounded the clarion signal to prepare for a great struggle which had thrilled the young hearts and breathed hope into the veins of the country. I became aware my life was taking a new course. True I had been aware rather dimly at the Seva Dal training camp, that we were preparing for a grim long struggle. But it had been vague, and freedom yet seemed distant. I would sometimes ask myself if it would really come in my life time. But now it seemed to be almost knocking at my door.

The Salt Law we had been called on to storm had a stormy history most people were hardly aware of. A Salt Commission had recommended a tax on Indian Salt, make it expensive to enable English salt to be marketed. There was also urgent need to provide keel ballast to British ships trading with India, and nothing could be better than Cheshire Salt ! Seven years earlier to 1939, the Finance Minister in the Viceroy's Council had tried to introduce this to cover the budgetary deficit with the plea it was a tiny item in the household of an Indian workman. The Council nevertheless threw it out *twice*, with some prominent Englishmen also opposing it. It had to be made into law by certification by the Viceroy. Significantly enough this was the first exercise of this extraordinary statutory power—shades of phantoms to come. For this poor man's solitary spice exploded like an explosive shaking the once believed impregnable foundations of the mighty empire.

The impending civil disobedience movement threw me for a while into a whirlpool after the first flush of excitement had waned. Many sober thoughts began to assail me. I began to realise I had come to a turnpike, where I was stepping on an uncut track whose end was yet distant, uncertain—would that goal we longed for be reached in our life time ? If not what then ? But the die had been cast, for I had taken the pledge and for me my course was clear.

I stepped mentally out of the whirlpool, to stop, draw a breath and review the scene. I was leaving behind all that the past decade held for me : the buoyance and glamour of the theatre, music, games, sports; the deep human involvement with women, building intimate channels for love, affection and mutual confidence to flow; above all there would henceforth be precious little of a personal life to envelop one in its warm comfort, soothe the bruises, provide the pillow on which to rest. Each activity had brought me its own wealth of experience. Our theatre group had matured into a happy family. Would we ever perform again and relive the great moments when we let other spirits take us over and generate other emotions.

As I decided to resign my secretaryship of the Conference, hundreds of memories tumbled over me like a shower. They were wonderful days which never did come back again. The backbone of the Women's Conference was made up of women from the small income groups. I lived with them in their modest homes when I travelled, sharing their little rooms. We generally sat in the kitchen as the woman or women of the household cooked, and others helping or sitting around, discussing local problems, making plans. Their formal education was rudimentary, but they were fiercely propelled to be rid of their disabilities and the insults to womanhood. They were clear on their goals and sure of the measures called for. They were powerful speakers, never minced words. They knew when and how to tone down, when to press on the accelerator. Their fund of practical common sense was astounding, their ingenuity in getting round obstacles stunning. I often felt a raw novice beside them. They had battled through tricky currents, faced oppression and exploitation. What they now needed was organised resistence to break down the *status quo*. So they easily rallied round the Women's Conference.

Being in my mid-twenties I was very much younger than most of my colleagues in the Conference executive bodies. In fact many were veteran women leaders who had already sowed and garnered many harvests, while I was raw and still searching. I was overawed by these personalities to begin with. But behind their imposing figures was kindliness, understanding above all patience with my inadequacies. Everyone of them took me under their wing to guide me.

There was Mrs. Huide Kuper, one of those Indianised English women devoted to women's education and an expert on Constitutions, who patiently led me through the knotty intricacies of the Conference Constitution while in the making In a way she was responsible for the birth of this Conference. For her instant repartee to the challenge thrown by the Bengal Director of Education, in the form of two articles that she got published resulted in the women at large taking up the challenge through the convening of the first All India Women's Conference. Hilla Faridoonji, another of my close colleagues, was a regal figure, tall and statuesque, with rather a chilling aristocratic air. She however proved kindly and really took me under her wing. It was she who wholeheartedly took over the launching of the Home Science College, and contended with the million prickly procedures and details, to raise funds for the new construction and see that the improvised college kept going in the meantime, for all of which I was deeply indebted to her. I remember her as a generous soul who mothered me as though I were her own child.

Begam Shareefa Hamid Ali was the most picturesque woman in this group, always trim and spruce, as though she were a bride stepping out for the ceremony. She wore the typical Ismaili dress made up of exquisite decorative material, with a full regalia of appropriate jewellery. The marvel of it was that she looked *just right*, never overdressed or ostentatious. Notwithstanding all the friils, she was the big intellect. She had a scholarly approach to problems, a sharp thrust into the heart of things. All her outstanding qualities came into full play while lobbying in London for the Indian Constitutional Reforms as member of an Indian Women's delegation when the Bill was on the British Parliamentary anvil. The English press described the Indian women delegates as 'firm and resolute, speaking soberly and with extraordinary lucidity.' Once when someone from the public volunteered to offer tips, Begum Hamid Ali vigorously retorted : 'We have come to tell you what we expect, not hear even from friendly English people what *they* want to tell us.' This kind of summed her up.

Dr. Muthulakshmi Reddy, an equally valued colleague was entirely different. Extremely hard working, studious by nature, she put in an incredible amount of solid work, initiated medical and social institutions and succeeded in getting many welfare legislative enactments adopted as member of the Madras Legislative Council. Though she looked staid and down to earth, she showed a great vision, a comprehensive approach to socio-economic problems and a deep concern for human beings. No problem was too small or insignificant for her where human welfare was concerned.

With Rameshwari Nehru I felt a personal kinship from our very first meeting, apart from my high regard for her. Though hailing from an aristocratic family and an exclusive upbringing, she was singularly simple and outgoing. She was specially moved by the lot of the Harijans and under Gandhiji's direction she took charge of the Harijan Sevak Sangh and become immersed in it. After partition she gave herself to refugee rehabilitation. Thus while we had worked closely in the Women's Conference, we came together again in the rehabilitation activities and I found in her a haven of warmth and affection.

Anasuyabai Kale was another life long friend I found in the Conference. One can describe her as a born social worker. At a very early age she met Thakkar Bapa, a lieutenant of Gandhiji devoted wholly to tribal welfare and was drawn into this activity. She founded the Bhagini Mandal in Nagpur for actively pursuing the Women's Conference Work. With her family I found a home and she had a special room built exclusively for my use as a standing invitation. When we proposed her name for nomination to the Provincial Legislative Council, she accepted the membership only after the Government agreed to give her full freedom of vote and not expect her to always vote with the Government, which in those days was quite a triumph for us, thanks to Anasuyabai's standing and record of service. She was nominated as Assistant Commissioner for her Province, on the Whitley Commission enquiring into the Indian labour problems, and proved most helpful to the cause particularly of women labour. From 1930 like several of us she went actively into Satyagraha. In one of the fall outs of the Quit India Movement, was a death sentence against 24 villagers from Ashti and Chimur in Madhya Pradesh. Anasuyabai took the lead in waging a fierce battle for three years and saved them from the gallows. But it shattered her health and though she gallantly tried to carry on with her social and political work, she never regained her health.

I first met Sarladevi Sarabhai at the Delhi Conference. She shared with me her experiments in education and got me to visit their Home School in Ahmedabad. I was met at the station by Mridula, Sarlaben's eldest daughter, grim with stern eyes, a grim face, speaking in monosyllables.

In contrast Sarlaben was all warmth and smiles and welcomed me like a member of the family. In fact from then on she became my home in Ahmedabad during her life time. 'I sent Mridula to meet you and I hope you two will get to know each other. From the moment I met you I had a feeling you two would become friends,' she explained. Too perpelexed for words, I just wondered and waited for time to translate her expectations.

Sarlaben's ideas on education had taken full shape in the Home School which she ran professionally for her progeny, with the best of teachers, aids, equipment, to help each child flower into full blossom, right upto the high school. The success of the experiment was obvious in the band of lively, well informed children, full of a healthy curiosity, outgoing yet restrained.

Mridula did not run to the Sarabhai type, she looked apart, set to live a life of her own which she did. Deeply dedicated to social reform, especially the women's cause, she built at a very early age major institutions like the Jyoti Sangh to aid and help women to become independent through appropriate education, to stand on their own boldly and with self confidence. Then she set up Vikas Griha a special institution to help those women who were abandoned or lost who had to be guided back into the normal social stream. To become an effective propagandist for the women's cause, she even took a course in Journalism.

Mridula built up her association with me delicately, for temperamentally we were far apart. To me she was the symbol of renunciation, for she reduced herself to the simplest style of dress, food, living. We worked closely in the Women's Conference, the Congress, the Satyagraha, finally refugee rehabilitation. She was upright, frank, tremendously courageous and suffered untold miseries for her convictions after independence, including imprisonment and house internment. Through it all we kept in touch. Though saddened, she was never bitter. Something tore within me when she died, yet I could not but feel that for her it was a release.

As I sat beside Sarlaben after the funeral, with a vast sense of emptiness engulfing me, I said: 'So Mridula has left us.' 'Mridula left us, the family, long ago, when she was only fourteen, to tread her own path,' was Sarlaben's quiet comment. I had realised Mridula was one of those who choose their own path and tread it alone.

Of the old Women's Conference colleagues, with two my associa tion has continued; Renuka Ray and Raksha Saran. Renuka, definitely politically orientated, did have a long political career beginning with membership of the Central Assembly in pre-independence days. She then made history when she remained neutral, though a nominated member, on the final budget vote, and let the government get defeated. Her stand was that she was there as representative of the women and as this was not directly a women's issue, she chose to remain neutral.

We worked together in the Women's Conference. We shared some unusual experiences together were when we visited the tea plantations in Bengal. All those we visited were owned by English planters. The war had ended and political changes were already in the air. We had armed ourselves with a labour leader as an expert, Dr. Maitreyi Bose. The Women's Conference had already done an indepth study on Women in Mines and had proposed the ban on women in mines, a measure which decades later became controversial, with some women labour ladies opposing the ban as a measure of sex discrimination. So our expedition was no novelty. The planters were courteous and cooperative, each showing himself as a liberal employer providing many amenities to labour, especially the women. As I have dealt at some length on this in my book on the women's movement, I shan't pursue it further. I found the survey instructive and rewarding. Renuka's participation lending a much needed warmth and liveliness to the trip. Raksha Saran had done a somewhat similar course as myself subject wise, but hers had been more academic and at Oxford. Though she started with an academic career, she turned fully to active worker and still continues as such. But she had a brief political career when at the age of sixteen at Gandhiji's call she abandoned her studies and turned to work in a village. When I met her she had just started her teaching career which was to be interrupted to get married. An old friend of her father's said to me as an aside; 'Marriage has become the bane of an Indian woman's life; look at this young lady about to blossom into a fine career, now the axe will fall and shatter it to smithers', and he ended with a loud snort, obviously to avoid more severe words—Raksha's career flowered in several other ways, with the accent on service, through the many offices she held, or on her own. To me she has been more than a colleague, a friend with real care and concern for me and every such gesture of hers moves me deeply.

Mithan Lam was someone apart in the hurly burly Conference crowd, for most were self educated or semi-trained. Mithan had a meticulously orderly mind, in which each item seemed properly docketed. In fact every thing about her was precise, spruce. We presumed it was because she was legally qualified, a Barrister. She was also a gold medalist in Economics. By some historical coincidence the time Mithan entered the bar in England, the English women who until then had no entry into it had the bar opened to them. Mithan joined Lincoln's Inn. In fact she was amongst the first ten women to take the law examination. She was also the first woman to practise at the Bombay High Court. In India however there had never been any prejudice or restriction in this matter. Her presence however had a restraining effect, for she noticed that when she entered the Common Room there would be dead silence! She also worked as professor in the Bombay Law College. She served effectively on the Board of the Parsi Marriage and Divorce Act of 1935. She then joined the Indian Institute for Social Services, moved actively into the field and finally left the bar for social work. Mithan was thus a most valuable asset to the Conference, not merely because of her legal knowledge, but her utter devotion to the betterment of society and therefore women.

She developed a number of links with international bodies, particularly with U.N. units and became our expert on international affairs. Like many of my senior colleagues, she had taken me under her wing, to initiate and guide me with great pains in the U.N. Affairs to which I was allergic. She was keen I should take over this portfolio from her. I did, as a stop gap but over a long period I could not. I preferred to work in my own backyard and see things I plant grow, reap the fruit, not sit shuffling papers and indulge in endless discussions that seemed to get nowhere. She was understanding and tolerant and we remained close friends.

Shardaben Mehta was distinguished as a pioneer mainly in higher and adult education. Not only her learning but equally her gracious manners held a special appeal for me. There was a radiance in her affection that touched me with its warmth. From her I learnt the modern methods of adult education which won quick popularity. A special institution was devised by her to propagate social reformist ideas aided by her prolific related writing.

There were many others from whom I learnt, whose company I enjoyed. Phulavati Shukla, young and spirited and like me striving at building a new society to replace the old jaded one. She was a pioneer student and the first graduate in the most orthodox Brahmin family she hailed from, as also the first woman president of the University Student's Union, always a tough post. Later she became active in organising women under Gandhiji's inspiration for carrying forward his programme. She shared my excitement as she took me in her car to Ayodhya, Mathura, Brindavan, Gokul, places she made come alive. The thrill of it all lingered long. The folk around talked of Krishna and his pranks in such vivid terms as though they were taking place at this moment if you had the vision to see. I saw the exquisite Ras of Brindavan, today mostly a faded dream. The thrill of it however lingered long like a subtle perfume you breathe into your being.

I had a similar experience in North Bihar, the one time haunt of Buddha, with the village folk pointing out landmarks in vivid phrases where he had walked, sat, slept, as though it happened yesterday. Buddha became so real, I almost believed I could see him, hear him, happy at this reassurance of his having been with us mortals. I recollected this as I watched pictorial scenes from Buddha's life with a group of young Chinese in China, products of the Chinese Cultural Revolution. I noticed the emptiness in their glances, the scenes meant nothing, evoked not even curiosity. 'Buddha was a real person who lived with his people,' I could not help saying in a challenging tone for their blank eyes hurt something deep within me. A cruel fate in the shape of blind leaders had deprived them of a great heritage. 'I have been where he was born and lived', I went on to relate what the simple folk had said to me. For the first time interest flooded their faces. 'Did those folks say that?' they asked, 'Yes, it may have been a long time ago, but he was not only a powerful personality, he loved the simple people and shared his life with them. So his presence is still real to them. He helped and supported the little republics against powerful monarchy. I respect him because he was the greatest revolutionary the world ever produced' I asserted. After I moved on they were gazing at the pictures with a new interest. I saddened even more for the generations who have grown up in India to whom Gandhi means a man on whose death the school got a holiday. This is exactly what a gentleman in his mid-forties, a writer who claims to be an intellectual, replied when I asked him what he knew of Gandhi when he was growing up.

When Mother Earth droops down with the weight of man's waywardness, great spirits take birth to lighten the burden, said the Lord in Song Celestial. Thus are born men overflowing with an all embracing love. 'Let all beings call my name – even trees and grasses can attain enlightenment', said the Compassionate One, as he was rightly called.

One of the attractions this group of women, colleagues of mine had for me was a touch of the old world, each carrying a distinctive flavour of the region, of the community, she hailed from, her dress, mannerism, style of hospitality, each adding a distinctive beauty to a grand bouquet as it were. In these days of standardised dress, ways, talk, steamrolled into a single pattern, life has become all the duller and drabber. Whatever originality is displayed, it is one of high sophistication, an all world fashion culled from hints out of modern magazines, not the expression of a tradition, personalised through a seasoned individual.

Salt suddenly became a magic 'word of power' as Pandit Nehru put it. However inane and formless the Salt Satyagraha may have sounded, the Dandi March, Gandhiji's long journey on foot to the sea opened with a most unexpected bang. It seemed the country hardly slept waiting for the dawn of 14th March when the fateful campaign would start. The strongest army conceivable to demolish the mighty British Raj which encircled the entire globe began its historic march. An old man with a large staff in his hand was accompanied by a struggling group of 71 of varied ages, indifferently clad. Included was a recently released convict sentenced for criminal offence, over whose inclusion there had been protests which the leader overruled. 'He has atoned for what he did. He feels in tune with us and this experience would help him. How can we deny him this?' was Gandhiji's verdict.

As this motley crowd marched in disciplined silence, each foot fall seemed to echo and re-echo through the land. Each day the tempo kept rising. Each evening crowds gathered to hear about the progress of the march. Was Gandhiji arrested ? Would he be allowed to complete this strange mission; fevered speculations kept people guessing. Each who night the marching party stopped at a village and Gandhiji met those had gathered and talked with them. The distance to the seaside where Gandhiji was to break the law was 240 miles, from Sabarmati where he started, and was to be covered by 5th April. As the march progressed it were as though the millions of Indians were marching, keeping pace with him. The whole air became so surcharged, every nerve in the body tingled. I felt elated as part of one of the most spectacular dramas in India's political history, pulsating every moment to its subtlest nuances.

Other hopes and plans were running through my mind. As batches for the first Satyagraha were to be selected I asked that women be included. I was told that Gandhiji did not want them as he had other programmes reserved for them. I was flabbergasted. I had built up a whole edifice of hopes of involving women in this great adventure. This was to be their breakthrough. They simply had to be in it, I told myself in desperation. The only course was to get this clarified by the leader himself.

I rushed to Surat, took a bus to the village near Jambusar where he was expected to halt. Enroute I luckily met a journalist friend headed for the same destination. The heat was burning up all my insides when he handed me a water melon and I revived. Young and energetic, how could I be wilting after this short trip. Here was an old man doing on an average ten miles a day. I quailed within myself—how was I to champion the cause of millions of women ? I watched him as he talked to the gathering in his chaste Gujerati, but simple enough for even the young to follow. It revolved round his present mission, what he expected of the people. 'The secret of freedom is fearlessness. This gives you self-confidence. When you have self-confidence you do not resort to violence,' and so he went on, expounding the need for maintaining non-violence under the greatest provocation.

My conversation with Gandhiji was fairly brief. As I expressed to him the cause of my unhappiness, he cut me short, emphatically disabusing my mind of the suspicion of discrimination. 'The tasks reserved for them are a tribute to the high qualities they possess, such as promotion of Swadeshi through promotion of indigenous production and their exclusive use; picketting of foreign goods; elimination of liquor from our society. The call for them was not for slogan shouting or marches, but utter dedication, which was a natural quality in women,' he explained patiently. But I had to persist. 'Let them do all this and also participate in direct action. The significance of a non-violent struggle is that the weakest can take an equal part with the strongest and share in the triumph as you have yourself said. This struggle is ideally suited for them.' He readily conceded, only he did not want the other sector to be neglected. 'Are you content', he asked as I rose. 'I have one more request to make. I want you to give a call to the women asking them to join the struggle. I would like to carry the message'. His eyes twinkled as he gave a hearty laugh. "You don't know your sisters if you think they need a special message'. 'It is because I have been in their world which is confined to their four walls. This is their one chance to emerge out and to realise their strength.' He was not convinced. But as I was so insistent, he said he would. He held out a paper with a few lines on it. 'All may regard this as the word from me that all are free and those who are ready are expected to start mass Civil Disobedience regarding the Salt Law from April 6th.' I felt I had won the world. But the day was not far off when I was to realise how raw and immature I had been while preening myself on my experience !

Now that the question mark of women's participation in direct Satyagraha action had been resolved, it became easy for the Women's Section of the Seva Dal to issue directions and organise participation of Women Volunteers in all the programmes. One important task remained before I closed this chapter of my life to send in my resignation as Secretary to Gretta. I wondered with a slight apprehension how she would react to this. Would she feel I had let her and the Conference down ? But time was running too fast for lengthy rumination. I wrote a very brief note and moved on to other tasks. By return mail came Gretta's answer. I could not believe my eyes as I ran over the letter. 'I had always believed I would some day hold you to my heart as my daughter. Now you are on the march to prison and to freedom, I can do so. What more can I say except all my love and good wishes will continue to flow to you.' Then came a few lines that the resignation would be accepted and the post filled. My heart swelled up and my eyes grew misty. How little I knew even those I thought I knew.

Taking advantage of the rising political fever, some of us in the Youth League began a vigorous campaign in the labour areas of North Bombay. We addressed real mammoth gatherings, met labour workers in groups enlisting their support, making plans to secure their active participation in the coming battle. As the meetings could be held only after 8.00 p.m. they would last until midnight, and often enthusiasm overflowed even into the early hours of the morning. In those days such activities especially involving young men and women were new and strange. But the people out to shape a new world took them in their stride, especially as they watched the labour areas ablaze with political fever.

6

The launching of the Satyagraha was fixed for 6th April, observed annually in memory of the agonising tragedy at Jallianwalla Bagh in 1919.

The front line unit to formally break the Salt Law in public in Bombay city was to consist of seven, five men and two women, Avantikabai Gokhale, a well known local social worker and myself (neither of us with any political background) with K.F. Nariman, provincial Congress President as leader. Avantikabai, a seasoned public worker was composed and serious. I was yet raw and felt privileged and self-conscious in my spotless khadi, conspicuosly displaying the badge with the national flag colours : orange, white and green, proud to have a place in the first batch of Law-Breakers !

The pearl grey April morning sky was brightening into crimson as I walked down the street. Already crowds were beginning to collect and line the roadside, their faces aglow with a new excitement. It was the 6th of April, the day on which India was launching her revolution. Mahatma Gandhi, the supreme leader, had decided to initiate it by breaking the Salt Law, the law that the British imposed. To him the appropriation of this right was symbolic of the exploitation of the large masses of the country. Salt was about the only luxury the rapidly impoverished Indian peasant had got reduced to, and now even that had been snatched away from him. A tremor of revolt ran through the land. The cry filled the air 'We shall defy the law.'

Although India has a long illustrious tradition of women warriors, this was their first appearance in any modern militant political campaign and I could hardly suppress my excitement at the enormity of the occasion and my own good fortune to be amongst the first. As I attached my name to the pledge to devote myself to my country's freedom battle, my hand shook a little under my tumultuous emotions. It seemed such a stupendous moment in my life, in the life of the women of my country. I felt I was tracing not the letters of my name but recording a historic event.

There was not much time for thought however. The next instant we were filing out, taking the road to the sea, marching with quick steps. Great sky-rending cries of 'Jai' filled the air. Heavy-scented flower-garlands almost smothered us. From the balconies and roofs unseen hands showered rose-petals until the road became a carpet of flowers. Often our march was stopped and bright eyed women sprinkled rose water from silver sprays, tipped our palms with sandlewood paste and perfume and blessed us waving lights round our heads and faces for good omen.

The long narrow strip of sand that borders the city like a white ribbon was transformed this morning into another sea—a sea of human faces that swayed and danced and bobbed about even as did the deep azure waves that rimmed the shore. The city seemed to have disgorgedof almost its entire population onto the sands. It was not the straggling batch of seven that was breaking the Salt Law, but hundreds and thousands now filling the water's edge. And still they kept coming, thousands of women amongst them, striding like proud warriors, gracefully balancing their pitchers of maroon-red earth and shimmering brass that scattered a thousand hues as the sunrays struck them. Even as I lit my little fire to boil the salt water, I saw thousands of fires aflame dancing in the wind. The copper pans sizzled in laughter while their bosoms traced the white grains of salt as the heat lapped up the last drop of water.

The sea of women's faces shot a spasm of shame through me—Gandhiji knew the women and I did not and I had boasted that I knew better. How many more such lessons I was to learn in the days to come.

The police who had looked on at this advancing avalanche of law-breakers seemed almost stupefied and had to shake themselves up as from a trance and enter on the scene. Some of my Youth League friends joined me to form a separate salt pan of our own and formed a circle around to guard it. The police found it hard to break through the circle so deep was it, that they charged with their batons. The human wall was still unyielding. In the meantime police on horse back charged at the general crowd, but they sat silent and immovable. I could hear the dull thud as the blows fell, faint moans as the wounded struck the ground. Still not a cry, not an angry snarl. Men and women, young and old, were all facing the attack with unbelievable composure, their faces alight with a strange composure.

We were still guarding our pans. The blows now rained like a blinding shower. They were directed either at the head or the legs, designed in either case to swiftly and effectively fell the people to the ground, and clear a pathway to the pans. I felt sick as I caught a youngster near me with a cracked skull. A rough boot pushed me aside and I came down with my arm right on the burning coals. For a while I seemed to remember nothing. When I opened my eyes it was to look into a pair of kindly eyes. They belonged to a figure in a police uniform. 'Can I take you to a hospital?' The words sounded genuinely solicitous, 'I have a car here.' I shook my head. 'According to Mahatma Gandhi you should not regard me as an enemy you know' he went on. I could hardly forbear a smile to find this police officer attempting to interpret the Gandhian philosophy to me after perhaps having battered a good few people.

The Bombay sea-side spectacle was but symbolic of the entire country which had become transformed into a battlefield with millions breaking iniquitous laws. A snowballing of law-breaking and repression, the latter leading to more civil disobedience, this in turn sterner reprisals—so it went on.

The news came that Mahatma Gandhi had been arrested in the dead of night. A quiver ran through the entire peninsula. How full of fear the government had been to time it so. Was it its own guilty conscience that made the police steal like thieves in the dark?

The Congress decided on a mammoth procession to mark this. As all activities had come to be banned at the time, every move had to be in defiance of the law. The procession swelled into immense proportions even before it reached the main road. Here the police halted it, columns of uniforms forming a dead wall. Very quietly without a murmur the processionists led by a woman, Hansa Mehta sat down on the road. All traffic on the main road of this vast metropolis was stopped. The early afternoon mellowed into early evening and the marchers were still there, lustily wiping their faces hot with sweat and dust, men, women and children, sitting patiently as though at an elaborate ceremonial. Evening passed into night, the police guards changed with clang and bustle. There was complete silence in the crowd. Babies sank into dreamless slumber as their mothers crooned softly over them. The city people brought nuts and fruits for the besieged, who spontaneously passed some of it across the front line to the siege layers. Like a happy family they shared a common meal, the police and the people. As the night deepened the heavens frowned and soon the trickling stream of rain swelled into a tiny torrent. Mothers sought to shelter the babies under the folds of their garments. But no one stirred. A few warm covers were tossed to them by the people in the neighbourhood. Once more they crossed the barricade and some of them went to cover many a policemen keeping his weary vigil. Fate was casting a strange cord to bind them into a happy union, the rebels and their fierce guards. New history was made that night on a weary road under a dark purple canopy of the heavens. In the early hours of the morning the spell was broken, the siege was raised, the police bowed and passed out. The procession rose and moved on to meet a new dawn, a new life, as silent in its victory as in its adversity.

The procession terminated in an open ground in the middle of which was stuck a pole. The women volunteers corp formed an immediate circle around it while the crowd surged on the outskirts of this circle. The national flag was to be hoisted before the crowd dispersed. Needless to say the flag and the flag-raising ceremony were banned by the police. The function commenced with singing of 'Jhanda uncha rahe (Let our flag fly high)' led by the women volunteers and joined in by the crowd. As the tri-coloured flag rose into the sky, lusty voices rent the air 'Up up with the National Flag'. The police had by now forced their way into the inner circle and they struck the flag post down. But before the flag could reach the ground an old lady had snatched it and almost with her last ounce of strength waved it aloft. 'Up up with the National Flag', the cries resounded again. A dull thud! It almost seemed to echo in my own heart. The old lady had slipped and was down on her face. As I reached out to her, I heard once again as in a faraway dream 'Up up with the National Flag'. No, I was not dreaming, there were the three coloured bands up and flying in the breeze. A little girl of eleven, grand-daughter of the old lady (as she later turned out to be) was waving it, perched high, cosily on the shoulder of a tall hefty man. 'Up up with the National Flag' the echoes kept ringing.

I made tiny packets of the illicit salt we were manufacturing in defiance of the law, began to sell them and found there was nothing I enjoyed better. I sold them at street corners crying out 'We have broken the salt law, we are free. Who will buy the salt of freedom ? Who wants the salt of Liberty ?' The cry never went unheeded. Every passerby slipped a coin into my outstretched palm and proudly bagged his packet of salt. One more recruit won for the army ! Emboldened I began to hunt for richer quarries. I invaded the cotton and cloth and grain markets, even the gold bullion market, and the stock exchange, and auctioned salt for fabulous sums. Higher and higher the bids went as I waved the salt packets temptingly in the air. Once a single packet fetched me Rs. 10,000. Thus were the rich and the poor slowly drawn into the game. One day I had quite a brain wave. I marched into the High Court of Bombay, the solemn citadel of law. I found it easy enough to lure the lawyers into the salt bargains. Then I had my final inspiration. With a beating heart I tiptoed into the judges' sanctuary ! They sat in their imposing wigs and gowns, high symbols of law and order. 'Won't you buy my salt of freedom ? Surely you won't reject these magic grains!' and I held out the packets to them. The air grew tense and I struggled to lend a natural tinge of allurement to my voice. They looked shocked, then grave and finally embarrassed. They shook their heads. I had my first defeat ! I did my best to bear it with good grace.

The individual breaking of the Salt Law on the 6th seemed an incomplete exercise in the midst of a whole city's millions taking it in their stride as though it were a daily chore. I began to plan for a mass Satyagraha by calling on the people to raid the Wadala Salt pans of Bombay.

The War Council, as the group of planners was proudly called, decided to sit through the night previous to the planned raid, sending out directives through messengers to the different ward offices, indicating the routes to be taken by the people to reach the salt pans simultaneously. Thus were the people to be mobilised for direct action.

Side by side were the other offensive programmes launched for intensive boycott of foreign cloth and liquor shops through picketting of such shops. This was to be mainly undertaken by the women. As Commander of the women volunteers I had naturally to finalise the plan the same night working out the tiniest details. I had a hunch my hours were numbered.

The authorities had grown rather desperate by now as I seemed to them to be behind many of the schemes for civil disobedience and whatever plans they had to frustrate me had not succeeded. But no orders for arrest for women had yet gone forth.

The stars were failing as I started to go back to my room in the chill dawn after the all night session. The final plans were with me. I had a premonition and I quickly handed them to one of my colleagues walking beside me, whispering 'for safe custody.'

As I reached the door of my room, a hand shot out from the dark in the corridor lightly touching me on my arm, 'You are under arrest". The long expected words came out of the gloom. When I turned on the lights in the room I saw at the door two Anglo-Indian police officers with an Indian evidently for the purpose of correct identification. My little hand bag had been ready for days. I only delayed to write a short message to carry out the plans just finalised, especially the raid. When I emerged from the room it was to confront a crowd with a deep sullen air about it. If looks could have shrivelled the officers they would have turned to crinkled sheets. I stopped the slogan shouting as I left.

Lock-ups in India are by no means model dwellings. I found myself in a dark gloomy room, full of murky air and putrid smell; bats hanging from the ceiling occasionally startled the room by sudden flights from corner to corner. Women crouched all over the floor and huddled into every nook; young and old, all sizes and shapes, some in dowdy clothes and tinsel, some in rags. They hardly stirred when I entered. They must have become much too accustomed to doors opening all night to land new cargoes. I saw down on my box as the heavy door clanged. So I was a prisoner. It seemed like a weird dream.

The daylight broke at last, the door opened and we filed out. The cell had no human conveniences. Morning, noon and evening we were taken out as for a parade. No light was provided and I had to lie idle or chat with the women through the long evenings. At night the police often beguiled their dull vigil by poking fun or jeering at the women in the room. I was the first political prisoner and the other inmates were rather dubious when they heard for what purpose I had chosen to enter this asylum. They shook their heads rather sadly. It seemed all wrong to them ! Three days of hellish waiting in that room and finally I was produced for a trial. It was brief and sharp, as I put up no defence. I reiterated my belief in civil disobedience much to the disgust of the already exasperated judge. He concluded his very concise judgement with the following illuminating remark : 'I am obliged to treat your case with severity for you have been responsible in making more people break the law than any other single individual.' I was sentenced to one year simple imprisonment which I thought sounded rather light after the ominous pronouncement that preceded it.

When I arrived at Yerwada Women's Prison, Sarojini Naidu was already there. We were lodged in a separate block of one longish room with two small rooms at the two ends for toilet facilities, away from the main prison. We divided the room by a curtain, to give each of us a sense of privacy. The large garden around made the bare block less grim.

My contacts with Sarojini since she welcomed me into the 'Lotus family' (all the Chattopadhyay women had lotus names) ten years ago, had been casual. She had always been kind, showing something of a family proprietorship as its head. Now we were on a different footing as political prisoners, which at least for me made companionship easier.

I always knew she was a women of many parts and that made her a scintillating personality. She had already proved her mettle on the Dharasana sands. Then she led the Salt Satyagraha batch after Gandhiji's arrest. The episode of how they were stopped and how they sat through the day under the open scorching sun in mid April, is now part of history. Unlike us who had been facing the rough and tumble of life for some time, she was more delicately nurtured and never exposed to such rigours. She nevertheless took it in her usual stride as though it were an every day occurrence she was habituated to. Now at close quarters I began to spot and admire her many qualities. Unlike me, she had been used to a sophisticated luxurious living with varied comforts. She loved good company, dainty dishes, fine clothes. For her the prison must have been a real trial. She was used to evenings of entertainment, a weekly film show, drives to feel the zest of breezes caressing the face. All these things she must have missed in this monotonous clockless existence, broken by clanging bells of changing guards, the day ending with the lament of the "Last Bugle", its mournful tones still haunting me. I was amazed at her poise and equanimity, no grumbles, no sulks. She got permission to garden, spent hours pottering around searching for new plants, exotic flowers, fresh seeds. She kept the cycle of regeneration moving so that almost everyday there was a new life sprouting. I learnt much about plant life. I was however only too conscious of my own inadequacies, that I was no proper company for her. For I lacked small spicy talk laced with humour that makes the air thin and light and would have enlivened her.

She was keenly aware of the small creatures around, the mouse, the lizard, the sparrow and endowed each with a human personality naming each after some political leader who she believed it resembled. To me the evenings were full of sparkle for she generally would reminisce, recalling anecdotes about people, known or unknown to me, each with a dash of sparkle. I once asked her if I could record them, she refused. I thought it a pity for several reasons. Some of them were historical, some of social importance revealing deep recesses in human nature; most of all, while Sarojini entertained her close visitors with these sparkles, the public at large had had no taste of any of it since they never went into print. True I refrained from pressing it further lest I would offend her susceptibilities.

The Gandhi-Irwin Pact came into force just as I came out of prison. The reaction was clear. Nobody thought of it as a settlement, that freedom had come and the freedom struggle ended. Yet there was a new element in the air stirring our chests. The Satyagraha had been a wonderful experience. By some extraordinary alchemy Gandhiji had used common salt to galvanise the age old inertia stemming from a sense of hopelessness, into self-confidence. The under current of fear evoked by a mighty weight sitting on our chest had evaporated, leaving us with a spirit of fearlessness. There was now more than hope, there was expectation, that freedom was within our grasp. The enormous mass that is India was now on the move. Everything seemed to have been set into motion by the Dandi March. The March seemed to be still on.

Two pats on the back added zest to this euphoria, provided by the leaders and participants in the movement who were equally pleased with the role of the Seva Dal Volunteers and the women whose performance was overwhelming, especially to the men who had long regarded women as hens in the backyard. It was a new experience for both the participants as well as the public. The women proved extremely good organisers, and where key men were swept away in a single scoop were dictators, organisers, captains, messengers, and a whole lot of things. Their special preserve, the picketting, had been quite successful. There were instances when owners of some shops were moved to shame when customers began to shun them as public antipathy against them sharpened and sympathy for the picketeers deepened. Quite a few who had a change of heart came and apologised and closed their shops. The public held their breath in wonder to see these unbelievable events. Every such experience augmented the newly spurted reservoir of self-confidence and optimism.

The Seva Dal had emerged from this Satyagraha cauldron as a commanding factor in the struggle. 'Volunteers must be our greatest weapon in winning Swaraj', Gandhiji had pronounced at the Belgaum Congress Volunteer camp, when he paid a special tribute to them: 'In my the volunteers at Belgaum reached comparatively the highest water mark in efficiency within my experience of Congresses', which proved a good foundation had already been laid.

To grasp and evaluate the uniqueness of the Indian struggle, the like of which has never been witnessed, people of today must conjure up scenes of thousands of volunteers led by their captains marching as front-rankers. Any Satyagrahi had to face and take on the full scale wrath of the adversary unlike in a military battle, where the top brass normally stays in the background.

Here I may quote Webb Miller, a foreign correspondent's impression of one such scene: 'In 18 years of reporting in 22 countries, witnessing innumerable civil disturbances, riots, street fights and rebellions, I have never witnessed such harrowing scenes as at Dharasana, where the salt satyagraha took place. Sometimes the scenes were so painful that I had to turn away momentarily. One surprising feature was the presence of the volunteers. It seemed they were thoroughly imbued with Gandhi's non-violence creed.' Undoubtedly what substained the unbreakable morale of the vast participating crowds, was the example of the highly disciplined volunteers.

The annual session of the Congress met in Karachi in March 1931. Coming on the heels of the Satyagraha, it promised to be even more popular and important. The big question mark that loomed before us was: What next.

Some new elements had appeared on our political horizon, one was the Red Shirts, the Pathan Volunteers from the North West Frontier, led by Abdul Gaffar Khan, popularly called the 'Frontier Gandhi'. The real name for these volunteers was Khudai Kidmatgars 'Servants of God'. The term 'Red Shirts' was because they wore red uniforms but had no connection with Communism. Attracted and convinced by Gandhiji's instrument of non-violence, Abdul Gaffar Khan adopted it, what is more, tamed his band of fierce followers to practice it in their struggle for freedom. We heard extraordinary reports of how these habitually violent youth had got so perfectly disciplined as to remain completely peaceful even when attacked violently by armed forces with gun fire. An equally rare occurrence was the firm refusal of the Garwali jawans to fire on the Pathans because of their sympathy with the rebels. The Frontier Gandhi and his Red Shirts became glowing symbols of the non-violent movement in the public mind.

The other element was the youth movement. Having burgeoned into a new life on the eve of the Lahore Congress which marked a radical departure in our goal from the past, the youth had lent spice, vigour and weight to the staid political scene. Emboldened by this new sense of strength and confidence the youth came to the Karachi Session keen to play its own hand in the affairs of the National Congress. We in the youth group had long been keen to provide clear and rationalistic content to the vague concept of national freedom. Gandhiji had no doubt drawn a picture of the India of his dreams. Basically it answered our purpose. Nevertheless we felt the need to present to the millions, now roused to jump into the freedom struggle, in precise and terse terms, what life in free India would mean to them. This was perhaps the impact of Marxism exercising our minds The full implications of Gandhiji's phraseology, like Daridranarayan, we could never grasp. Some rejected it as deifying poverty. Trusteeship seemed more wishful thinking than a solid objective. Communal unity, abolition of social evils were essential but once the masses were roused, we assumed the prevailing forces of division would be wiped out. Experience however was to prove otherwise, but that was yet to be.

We had savoured the flavour of freedom however mildly and were confident we had set our course to the right shore. To us now was the time for the Congress to declare what *Swaraj* would mean to the masses. So we discussed the points to be embodied in a special declaration. Fortunately Nalinakshi Sanyal, an active youth worker of Bengal, had a draft which he placed before us as a concrete propositions to debate on.

The core of the draft embodied what became the basis of the Fundamental Rights Resolution of the Congress. Being a member of the All India Congress Committee I was asked to hand it over to Pandit Nehru, the then General Secretary. We also were confident he would both understand and appreciate our initiative. As he went over the draft, I expressed our wish that he should discuss it first with Gandhiji personally to get his acceptance, but avoid mentioning the source of the draft. He agreed. Panditji made only slight verbal changes in the draft. As he concluded, I said this called for a preamble as a lucid pointer to the resolution and to avoid call for further explanations.

The Economic Policy Resolution was however Pandit Nehru's own and had been framed by him in consultation with Gandhiji which I knew he had long been wanting to do. The two, the Fundamental Rights and the Economic Policy Statement, somehow seemed related in the public mind and were assumed to flow from the same source. The entire Resolution with the Economic Policy part became a historic document. It injected fresh rudiments into the body politic of the Congress, furnished it with new tools for taking on added measures to meet the age old cries now risen to a crescendo making compelling demands.

To me the clause 'there shall be no discrimination on grounds of sex', opened the gates to a new world. Vague aspirations like the right to free speech, assembly, were transformed into meaningful functions. Mundane proposals like nationalisation of key industries, terms which today would not stir a blade of grass, then became surcharged with red explosives. I heard that a few in the Working Committee were rather surprised with the draft on economic policy, for on economic matters the Congress had not gone beyond 'swadeshi' and 'khadi.' But some cf the phraseology stuck in the throats of our rulers who saw in it the finger of Moscow. A mysterious person was thought up who had transported these dangerous sentiments across the vast space between the Soviet capital and Karachi, to corrupt the Congress. So the authorship was stuck on M.N. Roy, a recent arrival after decades of absence. But some obvious facts were either not known or ignored in building up this canard; Roy had long broken with Moscow; no confirmed Marxist would ever draft this piece which would be reactionary in terms of his ideology. For the Resolution had categorically declared itself against confiscation of private property or advocacy of class war, basic tenets of Marxism. Pandit Nehru had unambiguously blown up this story. Nevertheless it persists. In recent years at least two foreigners working on Indian political affairs have insisted on this fable, one even asserting he had concrete proof of it.

As we had enjoined on Panditji not to divulge the source of our resolution he could not go beyond firmly denying the authorship to Roy. I understand Nalinakshi Sanyal who later became an important political figure and played a prominent and helpful role in the difficult partition days, has recorded the facts in his autobiography. To me the other important subject before the Congress was the Resolution on Bhagat Singh.

I felt unhappy over its wording which, while commending his patriotism, wished to dissociate itself from violence as a political weapon. The latter assertion to me was redundant for everybody was aware of this and could therefore be conveniently deleted, to me it was also graceless. Since the execution had already taken place, the praise sounded like a left-handed compliment.

I grew even more unhappy when I found that Pandit Nehru was himself moving it. Was this because feelings on Bhagat Singh were running high?

Bhagat Singh had been accused of being involved in the death of the police officer Saunders, who had done Lala Lajpat Rai to death for no other crime except intense patriotism, and for which Lalaji had earlier been transported to a prison in Mandalay in Burma. No charge against him was ever pronounced. A wild story had appeared in the London Daily Express, charging him with plotting with the Amir of Afghanistan to overthrow British rule in India! Some Indian friends had then instructed an Attorney at Law in Bombay, Dikshit Sunder Das, to serve a legal notice on this newspaper and then take legal action for publishing the canard. The lawyer sent a letter to Lalaji in Mandalay prison for his authorisation for this. The letter was withheld from the prisoner and Lalaji had to lie rotting in Mandalay prison. Lalaji's death by a cruel lathi blow had roused the country to fierce rage, leaving a particularly deep wound on Bhagat Singh's emotions.

To me Bhagat Singh was one apart from the normal run of terrorists and I believed he deserved to be treated differently. I therefore gave notice of an amendment to the resolution for the deletion of the 'dissociation' part.

Acharya Kripalani opened a discussion with me on this move of mine. Ever since my visit to Khadi Ashram at Meerut, which he was conducting, we had become close friends.

'Are you very insistent on your proposals?' he asked me and when I replied in the affirmative, he gave a deep sigh. Then he added: I wonder if you are aware that Gandhiji pleaded very hard with the Viceroy to save Bhagat Singh, though it was outside of the purview of the talks. He pressed forward every plea he could think of. He is in deep anguish and your omitting a portion of the resolution on the plea that it is a left handed tribute will only increase his sorrow over what he feels is his failure to save Bhagat Singh. Of course it is for you to decide according to your own conviction.'

All this was new to me. Gandhiji of course never accepted the righteousness of capital punishment. My mind swung into a whirl. I became extremely depressed. If some one like him who abhorred violence had fought for the victim's life and lost, what was the virtue I was trying to uphold? I felt too numb and inarticulate. So when Panditji before mounting the rostrum called out to me to be ready with my amendment, I simply shook my head.

It is not that I shared Bhagat Singh's scepticism about non-violent Satyagraha. We had tasted may be a drop of its immense potentialities. The basis of all patriotic action was however fearlessness. One cannot but admit that where the rebel was unarmed and calculatedly inviting aggression from the opponent, the situation was more menacing which was self-evident. Nevertheless, the terrorists were sceptical of the success of Satyagraha, it seemed to be because they were unmindful of the strength of a million such fighters.

These thoughts led me into a deeper study of the terrorists. With my recent political experience I thought them more emotional, impulsive than realistic. India was too vast a country with too huge a population and unless this human mass moved purposefully, the country could not stand up to the high powered military ruling power, an unshakeable reality that seemed lost on them.

Let me take Bina Das as typical of a terrorist engulfed only by emotion. She tried to assassinate the Bengal Governor. The naivety of her statement is revealing. She confesses that what she attempted did violence to her own nature and she was glad her target survived to be restored to his family, in other words there was no loss of life. Further she plaintively describes how she was enraged by the sight of her sister, a *University graduate* (this is a potent factor, she pointedly mentions) in prison clothes, eating prison food ! Countless of us ate prison food, wore prison clothes, without feeling degraded.

Their emphasis was on the slogan : the individual must die that the nation may live—an idea that has sometimes been used for dubious purposes or uncalled for situations like the demand for a linguistic state.

Bhagat Singh was not of the bomb-pistol cult. His statement revealed him as a student of current politics. He wanted to highlight the futility of the 'legislative politics' of the Swaraj Party days. He was incensed by the advent of the Simon Commission leading to Lala Lajpat Rai's death. Tragedy pursued him even into the prison through prisoner Jatin Das who led the prisoners in a 64 days' fast to improve prison conditions. The authorities finally yielded and the fast was called off but tragically by then Jatin Das was beyond human help.

My study also revealed that patriotic action of this type could rouse very few. At one stage therefore patriotism was sought to be made into a religion, and attempts made to draw in Sadhus to initiate the young into rituals like Sandhya etc. to influence them emotionally.

Very stern codes were laid down by their groups for political prisoners. They were warned to be careful not to show unhappiness or pain, for that would mean the government had won a point. As an example they were told the following story of Emperor Bahadur Shah who when in prison was brought his son's head on a charger by a British Officer and offered as a present. The Emperor gave a quiet smile and declined the gift. His shocked attendent asked him when they were by themselves, how he could smile. The Emperor replied he did not want the British Officer to feel triumphant with this cruel mockery, whose aim was to cause him pain. By smiling he thwarted that aim. Of such stuff should patriots be made.

After Karachi, an invitation from a Youth League in Sri Lanka led to my first visit to that Island. The Youth Congress was in Jaffna, largely organised by the Tamil Youth, were stirred by the Indian Youth movement. My address to the youth led to the first political stir generated in that country and became at the time quite a sensation. I stressed independence as the basic need youth should work for. The visit proved pleasant and rewarding. This was to be my first link with Sri Lanka in the chain that was to follow in the days to come.

Youth Leagues sprang up all over the country. Youth gained initiative and confidence and therefore grew more vocal, more demanding as the young tend to do. People became dispirited over the lull which had replaced the exciting satyagraha. The thinking section became suspicious of the Round Table Conference in London, apprehensive of pitfalls set for Gandhiji in that imperial maze. Some impatient youth kept up attacks as warnings, well meaning but irritating. Sardar Vallabhai, now Congress President reacted very strongly to this and came down with a wholesale condemnation of *all* youth describing them as utterly irresponsible. A deep hurt seized me for this severe sweeping condemnation. I hit back in scathing terms through the press and almost forgot about it.

I became busy with the Seva Dal camp, taking stock, making plans for the future with Umabai and Dr. Hardikar. We all felt a sense of relief and satisfaction, for we had been on trial. I was visiting Pandit Nehru in Allahabad when I learnt Gandhiji had arrived. I went to see him. Lying beside him was a paper with an article marked darkly by a red pencil. Even before he could lift it up, I guessed what it could be. He queried in a low voice : 'Did you write this ?' 'Yes', I replied equally softly. 'Did you really ? When I read it I could hardly believe that.' The only pang I felt was that I had hurt him, which was the last thing I wanted to do. But I had no regret for what I had written and I meant to make that clear. 'Youth is raw, impatient, it may be impulsive at times and lack mellowness that comes with maturity. I don't believe you claim harshness as a virtue. And when an elder, experienced leader maligns all youth labelling it as irresponsible, something within us resents this insult', I replied. He put the paper away. He had a way of closing a topic like locking a box. Five eventful years passed before the repercussions of this hit my path.

We turned to the topic of the day, his impending visit to London. I had by now become familiar with a certain mental process in him : his willingness to meet his opponents and discuss the differences. He had an inexhaustible fund of faith in the basic goodness in men, that there was in everyone a core that can be touched, moved enough to melt down the antagonism, wear down the anger and distrust and win at least good-will. His own forte was the rightness of the cause he espoused.

Just before Gandhiji's departure, the Working Committee met and straight from the meeting Pandit Nehru came to me. When he explained the purpose of his mission, I was struck dumb. The Working Committee had decided to take over the Hindustan Seva Dal, lock, stock and barrel. In the AICC office and Working Committee he would be in charge of it. Dr. Hardikar would be in charge of the men's section and I would take over the women's department. I did not try to hide my annoyance. 'None of you thought you might ask me if I was prepared to take this on ?' was my answer. He looked hurt and surprised. He admitted he frankly never doubted I would accept. I bit my tongue. Of course how could I, a pledged Sevika of the Dal refuse when called on to serve. I must have lost my bearings for a while. Then we discussed a few preliminaries. Before departing, he reminded me that my first job was to meet the Congress President and seek his advice and directives.

Aware of his feelings towards me, I asked Panditji how I could be acceptable to the President. I was assured my name had been unanimously adopted, without any discussion. That included Gandhiji too. He then reminded me we had to be brisk with our plans, as the present respite may be only too short. 'Don't agitate your mind with any preconceived prejudices, we cannot afford to befuddle our thinking by letting cobwebs fill in the vacancies. As for that barbed wire pen of yours I quail to think of the havoc it can do,' with this final shot he left me.

I was equally perturbed at the thought of the Seva Dal being absorbed by the Congress. There were quite a few Congressmen deeply suspicious of the Seva Dal. The reasons were not clear, except for vague references to use of lathis, toy daggers, etc. The latter were used by Sevikas, to practice quick deft movements mainly designed for defense and self protection. What really irritated these unfriendly souls was the Seva Dal functioning independently, getting popular and powerful with the growth and acceleration of political activities. Would this freedom be muzzled now? Dr. Hardikar and I discussed this with some anxiety. But there was no alternative.

When I asked the President for time, he called me immediately. I made sure all the eaves and rafters in my head were cleared before the meeting. I tried to look relaxed and matter of fact. He received me warmly with an unusually friendly smile. He took both my hands saying

'I am glad you are taking over this important assignment. First priority I feel is in training Sevikas in thousands—hundreds of thousands. You are familiar with running of training camps, now they will have to be all over the country. Have you any suggestions ? I nodded, 'We will need an All-India national camp to train instructors who in turn will train the women in their own regions.' 'In future you just go ahead. I want to assure you I will never interfere. And any time you need my help, never hesitate to contact me and rest assured I shall give you all the assistance you need,' he concluded.

For quite a while I puzzled if I had dreamt it all. This was beyond my rational comprehension. Age wise I still fell in the youth category, therefore for him, irresponsible. More so after my scathing attack on his august personality. But soon there was only one thought pressing on me: time for us is running out. Hurry. Hurry, get on with your job, I kept telling myself.

I needed a young companion to assist me, someone enthusiastic, dashing, quick in thought, quicker in action. I found her. She seemed almost tailor-made for me, Sophia.

Sophia Somji from a Khoja family in Bombay, was one of the earliest Muslim woman to join the Civil Disobedience Movement in 1930, when she was only sixteen. Because of her adventurous spirit and courage, she had been made a Dictator in Bombay. Her first dramatic public appearance made a flashy page in Bombay's Satyagraha history: the usual flag hoisting ceremony was arranged in face of the ban, in Bombay Azad Maidan. The surging mass of humanity was there waiting for the lathi charge once the flag appeared. Sophia mounted the platform, hoisting it aloft as in a girlish voice she cried out: 'Bhaiyo Bhaino—Jhanda Ooncha Rahe Hamara'—The crowd took up the refrain. The police demanded the flag from her, she raised it higher and louder grew the refrain. Soon she was overpowered, the flag was wrested from her hands, she was arrested and the crowds dispersed under a rain of lathi blows.

I undertook a whirlwind tour of the country with Sophia recruiting women volunteers, setting up training camps, and selecting candidates for the Bombay All India Camp.

She proved a delightful young companion to collaborate with, refined and with a cultured background. She had no mother and I must have filled a void in her heart, for she soon became deeply attached to me. Sophia had been in purdah and come out only through the Satyagraha movement. For her, all this was a new and exciting world.

I was swept off my feet by the response from the women. An age limit had been put, from the age of 16 to 45, for the recruits. But our efforts to try to adhere to it became a battleground, young kids on one side, and real old women on the other tugged at our recruitment line. Still it gladdened our hearts, that they should be ready to enter a training camp, abandon their families, go out to unknown places, submit to the rigours of a Sevika's life ! A revolution was undoubtedly in the making.

The All India training camp for women volunteers was located in Borivili, a well known suburb of Bombay, in a large bungalow set in a wide open land, ideally suited for outdoor exercises. We regularly took the trainees out on route marches which were novel and spectacular and drew wide attention. The marches of the Orange Brigade soon won popularity. Batches of them were sent to keep order, regulate admissions, provide amenities to spectators at public meetings, conferences, social festivities like melas. They were ubiquitous, offering all manners of services to the assembly. There was always a glass of water for parched throats; willing arms to lull crying babies and relieve harassed mothers; keen eyes looking for the kids that have an itch to dodge the parents and slip away.

But it was the mass drills and the route marches that roused the ire of the authorities. There were angry scenes in the British Parliament: How were revolutionary armies being trained and prepared for battle against the government, without restraint. Did the India Government mean to abdicate as organised revolt was allowed full play? We were daily haunted by threat of imminent closure. By now it was clear the authorities were not to wait for Gandhiji's return.

We had not pinned any hopes on the London Round Table still we watched in dismay the sudden unexpected wild lawlessness let loose in the name of Law and Order that surpassed all imagination. Ordinance after ordinance was promulgated in state after state to unleash reigns of terror. This offensive was obviously preplanned to throw the country into confusion and hopefully submission, and to give no quarter to Gandhiji's mischievous ingenuity to devise some fresh spurt of revolt on his return. A blanket ban was flung over *every* non-governmental body from the National Congress, educational institutions, hospitals, libraries, social welfare bodies, the list ran into countless figures. This of course included the Seva Dal and a sweep on our Borivili camp was imminent. Several important leaders were already arrested. I had may be only minutes left for whatever I needed to do.

After a brief visit to Pune I took an overnight train back to Bombay. From Borivili station I started jogging in an ancient Victoria towards the camp when the first glimmer of dawn seeped across the horizon. Within minutes I was under arrest. At the station prominent posters had announced arrests of Gandhiji and Vallabhai. That had been the Viceroy's rebuff to Gandhiji's request for a talk.

In the lock up I met the Seva Dal Sevikas from the Borivili camp which had been subjected to a pre-dawn raid and a round up of the inmates. We were put up for a make believe trial. One incident made mine significant. I was asked for my Bombay residence address. I naturally named the Borivili camp. 'That does not exist', replied the magistrate impatiently as though I was wasting his precious time. 'Where were you arrested'? came the next question. 'On the road', was my factual reply. 'So you have no residence, you were picked up on the road, you are a vagrant.' So when I was sentenced, I was evidently brought under the Vagrants' Act (S. 109 Criminal Procedure Code) as a person who was 'without any ostensible means of livelihood and a source of danger to Society' and therefore logically placed in C class in prison! I later recalled that the Satyagrahis in the Nagpur Flag Satyagraha too were arrested under the Vagrants' Act.

The Arthur Road women's quarters where I was now lodged was a long way from the Yerrawada private barrack consisting of only two rooms. They were already over crowded. Large crowds of Satyagrahis poured in all the time. We were physically crowded in with the ordinary criminals, some of whom were obviously far from healthy. This ill-assorted mingling was not an ethical issue but one of health hazards. Our repeated requests for segregation were ignored. Perin Captain, a prominent political worker of Bombay, was both vocal and very determined. Though she was among the exceptional few in class 'B', here we were all huddled together. She took charge and decided that we refuse to go in at lock up time. So we stood on the verandah as though our feet were caught in the cement floor, and challenged the women warders to use force. They were physically unequal to the task as we could overwhelm them by sheer numbers. So we won our point.

As convicts we had to wear prison clothes which consisted of very thick, rough, heavy sarees. To those of us who had become accustomed to heavy Khadi, this was not too much of hardship. The large majority, newcomers to politics, were still in the delicate Bombay mill sarees. They were horrified at the very sight of the prison uniform. They absolutely revolted when they were forbidden underwear. True this would mean permitting use of their own garments, not allowed under the jail rules, for there was no provision for underwear in the prison manual. A battle ensued.

With the whole country aflame, the authorities were in no mood for concessions. For them, the movement had to be crushed at any cost. Fresh arrivals elated us with exciting tales of the big struggle on. We remained unyielding.

In the midst of this the Prison Visitors' Committee arrived. We submitted a list of our legitimate grievances, top priority being given to the underwear apparel. It was known that I had drafted the memorandum. Next day the jail superintendent asked me if I was the spokeswoman for the political prisoners. 'If you mean did I draft the memo, Yes', I replied. 'What all of you did is wrong. You cannot do this', was his emphatic comment. 'What is the Jail Visitors' Committee for, if we can not submit our problems for its consideration,' I queried. 'It can only function within the jail manual, it cannot go beyond, and you know that you are only fanning a revolt which must end in regret for you, I warn you,' stating this with an angry snort he walked away. He was a very angry Irishman.

A little later, the jail matron asked me to pick up my belongings and go with her. Being work hour there was no one around. I was asked not to go to the work room and take leave of the others. The black prison van took a quick round and within minutes I was in a barrack at the back of where I had left. I now entered a quiet and what seemed like an empty barrack, when on the threshold stood a tall white figure, holding out both hands and a warm smile on the face saying: 'So it is you, I could not guess though when I was asked to share the barrack'. I really rubbed my eyes. It was Miraben, her eyes as gentle as ever, as she warmly folded me in her arms. I felt like a storm-wrecked boat being docked in a secure cove. I explained I was there really because I was in disgrace. 'What, more disgrace?' she exclaimed and we both laughed.

I realised she would be a state prisoner like Gandhiji. She described her daily rote. She cooked her own food which I was welcome to share with her. I gladly agreed. She let me share her books, her *charka*, join in her prayers. What unbelievable good luck. I rejoiced though I was only too well aware this was a swift transitory stage. However I decided to make the best of it while it lasted. We enjoyed each other's company. We had so much to say to each other, we read together, sang bhajans. And then it all ended abruptly. I was to be moved to Belgaum. I arranged for my son to see me off at the train. For the first time I saw him look very forlorn and depressed. No doubt he was one of thousands of his age going through this trauma. Unlike the earlier Satyagraha jail going, this was grim, bleak. Quite a crowd was at the station with loads of food, flowers, assorted gifts hurriedly put together. All along the route, at many stops, people came anxiously looking for us, with food, flowers, gifts. It was not possible to sleep. We would have to be callous not to respond to them. It was their way of expressing their identification with the national cause.

Hindalga Women's jail at Belgaum was spacious by normal standards but much too small for our contingent. The single barrack, though large, got jam packed. Two small barracks were for the 'B' class.

Belgaum was rather cold for me, for winter was at its height. We had two *Kamblis* (thick rough blankets) supposed to be standard for shepherds. We slept on one and covered our body with the other. It did not fortify me and I shivered all night. A young Sevika, Vidya, who had shared several training periods with me in the camps, became concerned. She slept beside me and when temperature dropped she crept closer, pulling her blanket over me too.

To make matters worse within days of my arrival I developed acute jaundice. All I could now get was sago conji, thrice a day, streaked with milk. The worse my condition grew, the angrier the jail doctor became. He convinced himself I had thought this up to harass him. 'Those with delicate digestive organs should stay at home, not come to jail and harass us', he was never tired of admonishing me.

I had been ill a long time, almost endlessly it seemed until I was losing all count of time. The days flitted past like grey shadows that formed a kind of a monotonous moving curtain. It was as though everything was receding further and further behind this shadowy curtain. Even people around me became unreal figures moving over a screen. The only consciousness was the throbbing pain which dulled in the morning and sharpened from afternoon onwards. Nobody knew for quite a while what exactly was the matter with me, the authorities whose business it was to find out, were indifferent. It was all in the day's work for them.

Having always enjoyed good health, I am very impatient of ill health. I hate the sense of helplessness with its compelling dependence on others, and now more than ever. As sympathetic souls kept coming to me I felt terribly exposed, like a body laid out on view. All the defenses I had with such effort built up were shattered. Even familiar faces became strange as they peered down at me. I could not shut them out, like a house which without the sheltering roof lies exposed in the glare of the sun. I would close my eyes and feign sleep whenever approaching footsteps sounded. Inwardly I shrank and curled up inside myself every time a hand was laid on my forehead. I often felt the need to be taken out of myself. I needed work that would be strenuous, keep me busy where my physical self would have to labour. My entire upbringing had been to make me soft but the life I had adopted was one of enduring toughness. It was familiarity with the rough and tumble that I felt was needed to round my life off.

The thing that did get me down was my diet, a fact that enraged the jail authorities. Sago Conji (porridge) with an invisible streak of milk was my sustenance morning, noon and evening for months, with no sign of recovery in sight.

News of my deteriorating health went out. The daughter of Shri Kamaksha Natarajan, Editor of the Social Reformer and a valued colleague of mine in the Social Reform Movement, Kamakoti, was with us but in 'B' class. When he learnt of my condition through her, he was enraged and pressed the higher officials to depute a senior doctor to report on me. I was by then in my third month of jaundice and naturally very weak. The doctor found out what my diet was. 'What would you like to eat?' he asked. His visit somehow annoyed me, for just at that moment a young sevika had just been admitted into the prison and on seeing me she began to sob. She thought I was on my death bed. So I replied rather abruptly to the doctor that no useful purpose could be served by indulging in polite conversation, that I had been a prisoner long enough to know prison rules. He seemed undaunted. 'I am going to prescribe a few items outside the jail manual. I would like to know your preference.' I said I would like some fruit, even the minimum I felt would correct my digestion. 'That is insufficient. Instead of sago, I am suggesting two slices of bread with butter.' He seemed to have calmed the agitated Natarajan by telling him that all I needed was feeding up.

My prolonged sojourn in bed made me realise with a shock the complete absence of even an elementary clinic for the inmates. While I was recovering I began to collect a few pre-requisites for setting up a hospital. Mridula Sarabhai, who happened to be one of the inmates, assured me she would donate for my hospital some of the more expensive items, once she was released, which she did. As a brief description of my adventures with this hospital has been recorded earlier, I refrain from further dilation on it.

Running the hospital meant a lot of physical labour. I took on the maximum until it wore me out. I revelled in it. At last I got the chance to wade through the rough and tumble my life had hitherto lacked. I was being moulded into a tough fighter. My richest and most abiding experience in Hindalga jail, came through the close relationship I cultivated with the women from the remote corners of Karnataka, mostly Sirsri-Siddhapur and Ankola of Uttar Kannada district where a powerful no-tax campaign had led to severe repression and large scale arrests. These were the poorest women I had occasion to live in close contact with and get glimpses of their everyday life of want and hunger. My knowledge of rural living was of Mangalore, in Dakshina Kannada. Though the two districts were single once, almost half century earlier, a spontaneous no-tax campaign which almost frustrated the administrators, had led to the extreme step of tearing the district into two slices, attaching the northern piece to the then Bombay Presidency, the southern to the Madras Presidency. Bombay city rapidly blew up into a modern metropolis, this prosperity touching little of the tail end of the presidency, i.e. Uttar Kannada. On the other hand in the Madras Presidency all parts developed, educationally, industrially, socially. My own district of Mangalore never had the dynastic landlords owning vast tracts, fields or plantations. There was a much fairer distribution, with small landowners, modest coffee plantations and small industries. We never knew the abject poverty which large concentration of possessions in few hands breeds, as did in Uttar Kannada.

My prison mates hailing from there were an eye opener to me. Their description of their life made my hair stand on end. A full meal was a rare luxury, they simply had to make do with what they could get. They covered their bodies with pieces of cloth. On a rare occasion like a marriage they got a full sari. Their horizon seemed non-existent. Did they ever dream of a different life? The question held no meaning. According to them for generations it had been so. There were no schools in their region, whereas I was used to at least one school in every village. Illiteracy was unknown to us. Their life was a far cry from what I had been familiar with.

How and why were these women here? I was overpowered by a million questions struggling to spill out of me. Quietly over the long evenings they told me stories. Since Gandhiji's call reached them, they had become aware of their own inadequacies, that they did not live as humans, in dignity, in self-respect. Their concepts of what they wanted was not just mere food, better houses, proper clothes, etc. Yes, they needed these but it was more than that, they explained. They wanted freedom, not only for them, but all who were today in bondage like themselves. As the great leader had called upon everyone of them to get free they must refuse to be in bondage. The heavy dues they were called upon to pay now seemed to them like the wages of slavery. They worked hard, they did not shirk but were not treated as humans. They repeated in a kind of anguish: 'No one should be in bondage.' Now they felt they were free for did they not prefer going to jail rather than be content to be slaves? 'Had they seen the Mahatma?' I asked. No, but they brushed that aside—never mind—his call had reached them. It needed much more *punya* (merit) to have his Darshan. He too was in prison to bring freedom for all. He too suffered like them, did not only ask others to suffer. He was a true leader—'Were you not afraid of the consequences when you broke the law?', I asked. Came an emphatic reply: 'No! We understand now that it is fear that makes us slaves. Our life circle was set that way from the moment of our birth. Our dharma, we were made to believe, was to drudge and live on the leavings. The Mahatma has made us free so we are not afraid. His care for us gives us respect. We are asked to serve, not slave.'

Such intimate communication was largely facilitated through my familiarity with their language Kannada But it had limitations. Their words and phrases sketched but the outline. The intensity of their passion and the depth of their sincerity which was the core and had stirred my inmost being seemed to elude my vocabulary to give appropriate shape to it in concrete phrases.

To me it was like listening to a new gospel. Freedom meant different things to different people, but it meant *something*. Would freedom bring this 'something' to everyone? Would life be really transformed by political change? Was it not for this that Gandhiji laid equal stress on several other factors as integral part of our objectives, and which irked some in the Congress as unnecessary appendages? Was it not this very difference that had first attracted me to Gandhiji—gave something within me in a satisfaction, that others failed to?

Uttar Kannada district of Karnataka had a long history of Satyagraha, even before Gandhiji's arrival on the scene. Unlike my own district of Dakshina Kannada, it was a predominently agricultural and forest area, with a large poor, landless population, many living mainly on forest produce, grazing the cattle they tried to breed. Their demands had been for cultivable land, improved breed of cattle, adequate grazing area, remission of grazing fees and the like. From 1904 sporadic agitations had been going on. Early in 1914 a Vana Dukha Navarana Sabha (forest relief committee) was set up for better organised action. The workers were politically moved by every freedom breeze. Thus when Gandhiji launched his Civil Disobedience, every programme he advocated found an echo here, each adding a new vigour to face the resulting tribulations.

In 1932 this movement became a full scale No Tax Satyagraha and an integral part of the national political stuggle drawing in participants from other sectors, especially the arecanut plantation workers, classed as amongst the most backward and poorest. It was reminiscent of Bardoli Satyagraha and though the Karnataka epic remains little known, nevertheless it was wide spread, involving thousands from all social and economic levels, the leadership however staying with agriculturists.

The movement was led by Venkataramiah who showed outstanding qualities of leadership. The Karnataka Satyagraha can be rated as one of the high water marks of the 1932-33 movement. Its unique success won its leader the title of 'Sardar' after the Bardoli fashion. One can claim with pride, Venkataramiah was the finest product of the Seva Dal. He rightly headed the Seva Dal Training Academy at Bagalkot, Karnataka, which turned out thousands of workers of high calibre and the ultimate success of the freedom struggle was in no measure due to the splendid performance of the well trained, highly disciplined Seva

Dal Volunteers under a very humble, almost self-effacing leader like Venkataramiah.

The dimension of this can be gauged by the fact that a thousand peasant families lost their all in this struggle.

It was inevitable in this context for the women not to jump into the fray, especially as each day a new repressive measure was unleashed. Household goods, movable property, apart from land, cattle were seized and sought to be auctioned in lieu of the tax that was withheld. Household goods were being ripped apart looking for hidden gold. In addition auctions had now to be picketted and frustrated. The women naturally became deeply involved. The slogan went: Each day brings a new hour of trial and every trial an ever new symbol of national force.

At first they had a dreaded thought they would all be molested by the police. How could they survive such shame? A few knowledgeable women were not daunted. They stoutly scorned such fears which they affirmed arose from the age old superstition that women were weak. 'Are we weak? Look at all the doughty jobs that we tackle. In Satyagraha women are equally strong, nay stronger. For we are imbued with patience, perseverance, steadfast devotion, the qualities this task calls for.' One of them quoted Gandhiji. 'To call woman the weaker sex, is a libel.' In the forefront were Gauramma, Venkataramiah's wife, with a frail pale frame and Mahadevitai, even younger, hailing from a rich landed gentry. Eagerly a hundred women entered the arena. They did a million jobs as it were. They took long solitary journeys through the hoary forests, carrying messages, doing propaganda to rouse women in other villages, organised 'Prabhat Pheris', pre-dawn singing processions, calling out women to action. The whole atmosphere became surcharged and all life in the reigon seemed to become enveloped in a conflagration.

The spark of revolt seems to have continued to linger in the breasts of the Uttara Kannadigas. It is not surprising that they were amongst the earliest to react to the rising ecological imbalances in their environment, caused by the destruction of forests. Inspired by the Himalayan Chipko movement, these descendents of the old freedom fighters, spontaneously hugged trees marked for felling, and thus stopped the senseless destruction. What is more they were able to demonstrate to the forest officials and the public, including experts, the damage that was being wrought. So was initiated the Appiko movement in the very setting where once the No-Tax battle had raged.

Suddenly a serious crisis was created by the British government deciding to introduce special electorates for Harijans in the new constitution under preparation. Gandhiji's threat to fast unto death averted this, reinforced by his winning Dr. Ambedkar's support to the rejection.

To this internal danger was added the growing threat from Jinnah and the Muslim League which he insisted could alone speak for the Muslims. Abolition of Untouchability and Hindu-Muslim unity, the two factors which Gandhiji had pressed as of highest priority now began to loom large.

Gandhiji now decided to give immediate practical shape to the socio-economic ideas through his items of the constructive programme and bring them into the body politic of the country. To promote these he set up an elaborate village industries complex in Wardha for training in and demonstration of Khadi and Village Industries. Shri J.C. Kumarappa presided over this and made it a stimulating centre. His several experiments and dedicated work drew considerable attention of economists, sociologists, technicians, even from abroad. Here was initiated the use of solar energy and biogas which mark the beginnings of what is today termed alternative energy, though at that time these attempts were ridiculed as the rantings of a primitive mind. Literature was put out to explain and propagate both the ethics and the pragmatic value of these experiments. There thus arose a new theory of socio-economics which dealt with the total man. For that was Gandhiji's idea of human development, which in the elitist language is described as 'Quality of Life'. He indicated guidelines to meet the essential human wants, from dietary needs to preventives and correctives to maintaining good health. He also emphasised certain nutritional values in food through consumption of hand-pounded cereals and pulses, and hand-extracted oils, and cultivation of foods through use of natural manure instead of chemical fertilisers. Communities in the highly industrialised regions of the world have in fact over the last few decades been seeking food sprouted and nourished by natural manure, while so many of us have fallen back on promoting artificial fertilisers. Out of Gandhiji's deep concern for women the first smokeless *choola* was devised as also the solar cooker.

In his way of life were included exercises for physical relaxation and mental concentration through craftsmanship, with emphasis on spinning which everyone could practise. In this context he put full emphasis on basic education for the all round development of the growing child through the free functioning of all its organs and faculties. This was to be through handling of familiar functional objects of everyday use, instead of introducing strange new objects unrelated to its daily existence.

The simple traditional machines in current use in crafts and small industries were sought to be improved both to accelerate the speed and make operations less burdensome. This also extended to items like cart wheels to both mitigate the silent suffering of the draught animal as to save energy, an item that is now receiving a fresh look since an improved wheel consumes less energy.

Gandhiji also tried to lay the ground work for a national link language which he called Hindustani. By this he meant a new language: something fresh to be evolved, not blindly tied to old archaic strings of words and phrases. For he believed that language was made by people using words and phrases which gave life to the medium of communication. He saw that where a nation is in the making, language grows with the people. He suggested the national link language could use both scripts, Sanskrit and Persian Arabic, words which had got naturalised already. Thus more expressive terms could be imbibed from other languages including foreign words adopted to express new scientific forms or processes. Thus according to him would a language be enriched.

We realise the significance of this today when we hear an Indian elaborate on any subject in his native language. He invariably uses English phrases and terms profusely, for the old set form or vocabulary is found inadequate to convey new ideas, images, processes. To get round this the conservative rigidists invent some high flown artificial vocabulary that makes little sense like Doorbhasha, Doordarshan.

Under Gandhiji's inspiration, Hindustani Prachar Sabhas sprang up throughout India. The South took most avidly to this language programme, particularly women, who felt great pride in passing the various examinations in Hindustani. In fact they proved an exemplary lesson to the rest of India. When Gandhiji toured the South, they were most active in organising his programmes which gave him added pleasure. Today we have strayed so far away from his language formula. People now are not even aware of its origin and thus attach no importance to it.

More than half a century has rolled by and so much of what then were ridiculed as "fads" have become compelling scientific facts. In the international world under alternative energy, solar heat and biogas have assumed crucial importance. During a recent tour in China I saw these two items making newspaper headlines. The President of North Korea after visiting centres to watch these at work, was evidently impressed and declared his intention to introduce them on a large scale in his own country.

Gandhiji's basic plan was the conversion of agro-waste like straw, husk, cane, etc. into fuel which according to current planners could easily meet almost 70% of the rural needs. Next, to locate agro-industries in rural parts to be fed by local energy instead of in the urban areas to draw on the limited supplies of fossil energy there. Experiments then had also pointed out that energy can be saved if wood is converted into coal for domestic use. Tree cultivation on a large scale on wastelands was advocated for this purpose. All this however was either ignored or scoffed at as out of step in a modern world. The wheel has however made a complete circle and today we have to fall back on what we once rejected.

Gandhiji's principle can still be maintained even in the industrial urbanised areas of today where the waste consists of tin, scrap metal, plastics and the like. Modern technology has been able to convert these by gassification to be used as coal or oil and become a money earning item.

It is most ironical that India which is blessed with such gorgeous sunlight, makes so little use of it. In fact our modern structures are so contrived as to keep out sun light and depend on artificial illumination. We are thus condemned to long hours of gloom, real 'Darkness at Noon' because of constant power failures.

The most spectacular activity however was his whirl-wind tour throughout the country for a powerful drive against untouchability, a cause that had become almost a passion with him. These tours provided picturesque romantic tales. People in hundreds of thousands rushed for a glimpse of this little man in his loin cloth. He was greedily collecting money for his cause. Drama was provided when women stripped off their jewels to place in his hands, even little girls did the same.

As part of this campaign he encouraged temple entry for the Harijans and where opposition was encountered active Satyagraha was launched, and though Gandhiji himself was not a temple goer, he insisted on the right of every human being to have access to all public places, including temples.

Though no defiance of law was even conceived by me, I found the police eye constantly on me. In my travels the police shadowed me. I had become a confirmed suspect. They saw ghosts where there was not even a thick column of smoke. Those around me were continuously questioned on my plans. Every time I took a journey, there was someone at the ticket office to find out my destination, there being no advance booking in those days.

I suddenly got a call from Gandhiji. My heart gave a flutter as I faced him. What had I done now? His face showed only a serious concern. I was shaken by bewildered surprise when he shot a question at me. 'What do you propose to do with your son? I presume you know that I saw him and had a talk with him in Mangalore.' In the course of one of his tours Gandhiji, when he touched Mangalore, had called my son who was then with my mother, and evidently tried to find out the kind of life he lived. I was then in prison. I had never discussed with Gandhiji my personal problems, as so many did. In fact my visits to Sevagram were very brief, limited to whatever the purpose of my visit was. I had made no reference to my son any time. He obviously had tried to check and find out for himself through a personal talk with the boy. I had been surprised by this also deeply touched by his solicitude especially after my last unhappy encounter with him. But I had given no further thought to it. 'Either you take control of the situation, set a proper course for him or decide to abandon him to an existence of disruption and drift and feel you don't care what happens to him ultimately. I want you to realise that if you can't have a grip on your own life and shape it, how do you think you can break our country's bondage? We have ourselves to become mentally and emotionally free to become soldiers of freedom. It is not my intention to advise you or offer a recipe for your solution. It is for you to work it out.' I was bewildered for a while for this was all so unexpected. Finally I replied I would apply myself to it. 'If so, you must keep yourself clear of arrest and imprisonment to have time to do whatever you decide to do. Is that understood?', he added in a stern voice. I nodded mutely. I was in a bit of a turmoil, then unable to restrain myself, I asked why did he feel this concern. 'There is another one who asks me the same question', and he passed on to me a letter from one of his colleagues, a woman. 'Maybe it is not surprising it should be a woman,' he remarked as I glanced through the letter. 'I am concerned about all those who are in the struggle. I have had occasion to be concerned about this very lady who is advising me today not to concern myself about others like you,' he explained. I was becoming rather perturbed by all this and wanted to conclude the dialogue. 'You once entertained suspicions about my sense of discipline and I had then said only the future can prove to you what I am. Until then you have to take me on trust and I hope you have.' I could not bring myself to say anything more.

At Wardha Station boarding the train for Madras along with me was Shri Kaleswarrao, a prominent Congressman of Andhra. He invited me to travel with him. As we chatted I mentioned that my destination was Mangalore. 'You are not going to do that in one leap, a three days' journey,' he protested. 'You are going to break journey at Vijaywada, stay with me for a day or two, get refreshed and then proceed.' Kaleswarrao and I had become close friends through a niece of his, a rare social worker whom I occasionally visited. On these occasions I was Kaleswarrao's guest. The social worker had thrown open her own house to unmarried girls or widows who became pregnant. She cared for those who came to her and saw them through the delivery, all in great secrecy, and found foster parents for these unwanted children. I know of only one other lady who offered this service, Savitribai Phule of Poona, years ago, who has since been honoured like many others, long after her death.

After breakfast Kaleswarrao invited me to accompany him to his village a few miles off. He was going on some private work. He had informed his village friends I was accompanying him. As was usual in the villages those days, the people assembled as we got down from the car, ladies with garlands, rosewater, kum-kum. Then the inevitable followed, 'Wouldn't I say a few words to the assembled?' I explained I was on an informal friendly visit, not a political mission. Before I could proceed further, a few policemen materialised as though they had sprung out of the earth and arrested Kaleswarrao and me and marched us to a police van that seemed to have dropped out of the sky. We were produced in a court after a few days in the lock up. Kaleswarrao was a reputed lawyer. He was on his feet challenging the magistrate with some pertinent questions. What was the charge against us? The trying authority seemed as lost as us. He asked the police, the answer was : attempt to create disaffection and break the peace. How, what is the proof was Kaleswarrao's next question. The answer was: Kaleswarrao organised a public meeting and took me there and I spoke. He asked prosecution to produce a copy of my speech. There was no record, but, the police officer asserted, the lady generally made fiery speeches. Exasperated Kaleswarrao turned to the presiding authority and asked 'On what evidence are you going to sentence us?' 'No evidence, the case is dismissed,' the magistrate shouted, 'and clear the court'. For it had become jam packed.

We came out. But the police were not to be so easily thwarted. We were re-arrested and were back in the lock up, and later moved up to Nuzvid, a Taluka headquarters. We went through the same motions like a repeat performance. Again the case was dismissed, but this time the authorities were determined to punish us. We were re-arrested under a detention law and interned. We were told that we could get our release the moment we bound ourselves to 'good behavior.' By implication this meant we had been guilty of bad behavior, to which we could not plead. So for the present the incarceration seemed indefinite. I could hardly picture how the deadlock could ever break.

As the arrest had been made in the Madras Presidency, I was lodged in the women's jail in Vellore. The building was very new, located in an open land completely bereft of any vegetation. The new plants were young shoots that had yet to come up. We seemed however to be surrounded by rows and of rows of black rocks. Vellore is exceptionally hot and dry and as summer progressed the heat kept boiling up. All day the sun beat down and at night the day's heat absorbed by the rocks oozed out, penetrating into my very bones. The nights became pretty nightmarish. I sought permission to sleep outside the cell as once the cell door closed, it became suffocating, as all that the breeze brought was heat from the rocks. But I met with a firm refusal. There is no rationale about the operation of prison rules. The only answer you receive is *'rules are meant to be obeyed'*.

There were no political prisoners in this women's prison, for there was no active political movement on. I was strictly isolated from the ordinary prisoners. Apart from the women who did the locking-unlocking and the one who fetched me my food, I saw no one to hold communication with. It was complete solitary confinement. For these women who entered my cell were strictly forbidden to hold any communication with me. I refrained from breaking this rule as it would have exposed them to reprisals and I would be helpless to save them.

I have been asked what solitary confinement was like. I read, I wrote, I tried to study and analyse myself and record the analysis. When one is free from outside influences, pressures, impositions, one has deep, unhampered communion with oneself. There is no reason to hide anything from one's own gaze, it is like pulling down a curtain that has been hanging for a long time. Gradually I felt I was drawing on myself for motivation, power, on whatever energy I possessed. After a time I thought the propellers were slowing down like a battery clock when the battery is giving out. Mine was a situation that held out no expectations for there was no release date to look forward to. So to count time, hours, dates, months seemed an exercise of futility. Each day was like any other day, with the monotony stretching like a long, long track beyond the horizon.

We were nearing the end of the year but no rains were in sight. Occasional light showers seemed to leave the ground panting even more for breath. I kept gasping through the night. One morning when the door opened I was found on the floor. I had simply passed out. A doctor arrived. I told him there was nothing whatever the matter with me. I came from a wet damp region, I needed getting used to this intense dry heat. The district collector paid a visit to see what ailed me. He was surprised to find me a solitary prisoner. He admitted he had no idea of this, he was a new arrival and rather recoiled at this situation. He told his wife he would not visit the jail if I was there.

One morning after I had gasped through the night and was found in the morning on the floor again in a dead faint, I was told I had been released on medical grounds.

When I had been arrested and sentenced I had wondered how Gandhiji had taken it in view of his advise to me just before this incident. I presumed he would understand. I had told him I had to be taken on trust.

7

I came out late 1933 just when the Congress was assembling in Bombay. There were only two events that I considered of note at that session: Gandhiji's dramatic announcement that he was going to resign from the Congress membership and he was leaving Sabarmati Ashram vowing to return there only after Swaraj came. Though Swaraj did come, to him it was a shattered one, and he never did go back again. The other was a resolution to demand a Constituent Assembly for framing the future National Constitution for India.

At this period Marxism was in the air. Some practical reality to it had been provided by the triumphant rise of Soviet Russia overcoming the combined onslaughts of the capitalist countries. This had been capped by Pandit Nehru's account of his trip to the new Workers' Republic. Communism was yet a ripple in the vast mass of India. One also felt the need for a more precise objective of freedom in clearer pragmatic terms. True Gandhiji had outlined the Swaraj of his dreams, which was however far from our practising goals, nor was our immediate path marked by such typical land marks as he indicated.

In this context Marxism seemed to provide the precise and clear-cut economic and social analysis, the idea of an integrated classless society, to a feudal-stricken, caste-ridden country. To the youth it held keen allure.

When I came out of prison the Socialist Party had already been formed. It is said to have emerged in the prison cells with Jayaprakash, Minoo Masani, Yusuf Mehrally, etc. Later Narendra Dev, Purshoottam

Tricumdas and other intellectuals joined, as also large numbers of young people who were excited by Marxism, and eager for action. Before the first Socialist Conference, Minoo Masani as Party Secretary, discussed the proposed move with Pandit Nehru who recorded in a letter his pleasure that a Socialist group would function in the Congress and influence the ideology of that body and the country. Nehru's reaction was sought as in his political writings Nehru depicted the Indian struggle in a world perspective, stressing the clash of class interests as part of a global phenomenon. But at no stage did he instigate, encourage or support the Party as such nor did the Party seek his patronage.

The Socialist Party declared its ideology as Marxist which would determine its programme so as to fulfill its task. At the same time it made it clear that the Party as such did not represent any *single* class. On the contrary it would unite on its platform all anti-imperialist elements to overthrow it and establish real Swaraj. It acknowledged the National Congress as the rightful vehicle of the Indian people's freedom struggle and therefore to stay within it. Its task within the Congress would be to help prepare the Congress for mass struggle. To ensure this, Membership of the Congress was made obligatory for anyone who wished to join the Party, which was now appropriately titled the Congress Socialist Party. The members were also enjoined to show respect to the national leaders and maintain good relations with them.

Unexpectedly enough Gandhiji welcomed the Party within the Congress wanting to bring various streams of thought into the broad national movement. He however expressed that class war was not the right path. I could assume that this was an expression of his acceptance of our bona-fides whatever the ideological differences may be with his habitual liberalism.

With the elder leaders who called themselves 'Gandhi-ites' it was a different story. They took the formation of the Socialist Party as a challenge to Gandhiji's leadership and therefore his ideas. They passed a resolution in two successive Working Committee meetings, dissociating the Congress from class war, appropriation of private property and the like, as these posed a threat to non-violence.

I joined the Party and settled down in Mangalore where in the rural areas I could create a base for sound grass-root work and organise social and economic groups for full participation in community service. The Seva Dal was still under a ban, so its activities were at a standstill, and I could give undivided attention to this.

Labour and peasant unions were unknown in my region at the time. I could concentrate more effectively on the former though industrial and processing establishments were small. A number of unions were soon humming throughout the district.

The Workers' Unions lent a piquancy to the situation, particularly the women-labour unions. The district had large concentrations of woman labour in cashewnut and coffee curing. Very soon a crisis rose in the cashewnut factories. The products were all for export and greatest emphasis was on the neat, clean look of each nut. For this, the thin skin clinging to the nut used to be scraped out by the workers with their nails. This naturally bruised the fingers. Repeated requests for extra sharp knives were ignored. So a strike was called. It was quite an event and stirred up the entire district, especially women, whose sympathies were roused. This was my first taste of conducting a labour strike and proved quite an experience We had however a resounding victory.

The Socialist party grew rapidly, attracting the younger elements from all walks of life, also some maturer ones. A fresh spirit seemed injected into our otherwise humdrum life, since Satyagraha had been called off by Gandhiji after his release in 1933, after which the ban on the Congress had been lifted. The political tempo had therefore been in a low key.

In 1936 Pandit Nehru took over as Congress President. This created great expectations among the youth. It was also hoped that the working relations between the Congress and the Congress Socialist Party would become congenial. This hope was accentuated when Pandit Nehru took three members of the Socialist Party into his Working Committee, which seemed like a break through, a concrete sign that socialists were acceptable, not just tolerated. They were Shri Jayaprakash Narayan, Acharya Narendra Dev and Achyuth Patwardhan. Apart from this gesture, Panditji had not indicated any further leanings towards, or visible sympathy with the Socialist Party.

As Congress President, Pandit Nehru wanted a 'Mass Contact' programme to be launched. A phase of this was holding the annual sessions of the Congress in rural areas. The first one was in Faizpur,

Maharashtra, followed by Haripura in Gujarat, then Tripura. The setting in the open clear environment was free from the garish, oppressive urban surroundings with the air filled with discordent sounds, and strained humanity with tension charged faces. Here one felt fresh, light in body and mind, closer to the Earth which our ancients taught us to respect and warned that man's evil deeds when they pile up lie as heavy burdens on Her bosom.

Congress meetings in quiet village areas garnered many benefits. To identify and associate ourselves with our life-givers, the cultivaters, even if it be once a year, was of some significance. The food supplies were in accordance with the manual compiled by the Village Industries Association. With the advent of independence many such innovations have been discarded.

At the Faizpur Session the 'Mass Contact' programme was launched with some emotional fanfare as the first step towards transforming the Congress into a mass organisation. The core of this transformation was 'land to the tiller.' It was not to be a class struggle, but through legislation, persuasion, liberation of the exploited. A Board was formed with J.C. Kumarappa as head, to work out a full scale programme for this.

Spearheaded by Socialists and other activists the mass organisations spurted up. For the first time peasants began to be organised into Kisan Sabhas to enable them to voice their grievances; Professor Ranga, a noted Congressman, along with others taking the lead. The first All India Kisan Sabha Conference took place in 1936, attended by 20,000 peasants, several of whom trudged many miles to attend it.

Their demand was for a Kisan Mazdoor Raj. Soon workers and peasants of all denominations as also professionals began to form mass organisations. Even the Muslim Divines formed a unit. All rallied round the Congress as the appropriate vehicle for attaining their goal.

The bona-fides of Socialists as patriots it seemed to me, were not in question with the Elders at any time, though there may have been personal equations, suspicious, clashes. We supposed Sardar Vallabhai to be the hardest against us. Yet when a Congress candidate had to be selected for the Mayoratly of Bombay city, he readily called on Yusuf Mehrally to accept the office. Moreover many of the Socialists were known freedom fighters and publicly respected as such, and could not have been cursorily ignored or eliminated.

In course of time I realised that while there were frictions and tensions periodically, there remained an abiding reservoir of goodwill between our elders and the Socialists.

The root of the hiatus between the average Congressmen and Socialists to me lay in the fact that any idea or vocabulary outside their own was 'foreign'. What the Socialists propagated were to their thinking new fangled foreign ideas for which they had an innate contempt. I do not believe this was due to any deep chasm with Socialism but rather to lack of clear ideas of their own either on modern politics or socio-economics. To them, all the ills in India were due to foreign rule, once that was removed all would be well. They indulged in a high-charged emotional image of India's past glories. To them there was nothing that we had to learn from anyone. Some took pride in boasting they had never stepped outside the Indian shores. Their simple minds did not know the dimension or complexity of the imperialist mechanism our rulers operated to keep us in bondage.

Perhaps the origin of the Indian National Congress itself holds the clue to the constraints of its political philosophy and the programme that flowed from it. The real picture has so long been painted up in such benign colours, it is not easy to strip off the pseudo-history and reveal the truth.

Inspired by the Indian war of independence of 1856, an Indian Association was organised with the big ambition to mould it into the Indian Parliament, a real national forum, under the famous Surendranath Bannerji's initiative at a National Conference under the presidentship of a noted educationist, Anand Mohan Bose. All around were seething revolts among most sections of the people due to continued police repression of every patriotic demonstration, with continuous oppressive legislation to curb and suppress manifestations of patriotism.

Allan Octavian Hume, a shrewd seasoned bureaucrat viewing the threatening scene, instigated the setting up of a national body to meet annually to discuss national problems and pass (pious) resolutions. Thus Hume earned the grandiose title of 'Father of the Indian National Congress'. This certainly served to draw the intellectual and thinking sections into its fold, blunting the emerging revolutionary thrust.

Whenever we had differences with Gandhiji we freely gave expression to them as also tried to thrash them out, for he seemed ready to hear our point of view. He claimed to be a Socialist, but this concept was his own, delineated in his own phraseology, while we stuck to the Marxian, which then seemed simpler and more terse. While to us the class war was an existing reality, we did realise it was unreal to emphasise violence as the only means as our weapon. On the whole Gandhiji's fundamental objectives and ours had common meeting ground.

Gandhiji was a being apart. He was patriotic but not sentimental. I quote a few of his phrases: 'Swaraj for me means freedom for the meanest of our people. I am not interested in freeing India merely from the English yoke, I am for freeing it from any yoke. Real Swaraj will come not by the acquisition of authority by a few but by the acquisition of capacity by all to resist authority when it is abused.' In other words to him Swaraj was to be attained by educating the masses to a high sense of their capacities to regulate and control authority. Gandhiji's exhortation for adult education as advocated in his constructive programme was inculcating of basic political truisms, not mere literacy as superficially interpreted.

The Congress decided to work the Dyarchy system under the new political reforms. After the elections, Congress ministries were established in some of the provinces, though everybody was not really happy about them. Perhaps one positive benefit reaped from this were the elections in which, notwithstanding the restricted franchise, the Congress candidates swept the polls.

An amusing upshot of this spectacular event was that the heavyweight British Oracle the London Times, which on election had described the Congress as an 'insignificant body' had to swallow the phrase and admit that its 'Record of success has been impressive.'

The British government while announcing the new reforms exhorted that 'they should be worked in the manner expected by its framers'. In retort Gandhiji wrote in his inimitable fashion: "The Congress has entered upon office not to work the Act *in the manner expected by the framers* but to hasten the day of substituting it by a genuine Act of India's own making.'

The Ministries were able to do a few things, to measure up to their *own maximum limit* which was pitifully little to meet the high expectations roused in the people. Political prisoners were released; bans on various bodies lifted; restrictions placed on citizens removed: freedom of the press restored; a few measures to relieve rural indebtedness were adopted, tenants given protection; limited facilities were created for free education, rural water supply, and medical services. Real worthwhile action was strangled due to limitation of powers.

There were however stresses and strains around activities of workers' and peasants' bodies. It was the officials and politicians on the spot who were the deciding factors in such situations and it was their stand that was upheld of those who championed the organisations a large number inevitably were Socialists. At one stage in 1938 when Jayaprakash was directly supporting the peasants, the Congress opposed the struggle and Jayaprakash resigned his membership of the Congress Working Committee. The struggles persisted. Finally at the Haripura Congress the issue was sought to be diffused through a resolution which accepted the right of the peasantry to form Kisan Sabhas. But the Congress would support only those that refrained from opposing the Congress which circumscribed the orbit and threatened to stagger the forward march of the mass contact programme.

Many of us chafed over what appeared a stalemate. Impatiently we looked to Gandhiji for a sign, but none seemed visible. We had not yet grasped his uncanny capacity to gauge a situation accurately, and the ability to act at the proper psychological hour, turning the right key at the right time. Commenting on this rare insight Pandit Nehru remarked that he was not of the ordinary coinage, but made of a rarer metal, and could not be assessed by our normal weights and measures. Though we fretted and fumed we knew that when the hour came, he would strike and strike hard and one day it would be the final stroke.

Then a light was suddenly thrown on this seeming lull. While Gandhiji was on tour I joined a small group he was meeting for a chat. 'Why have you stopped the Satyagraha movement?', was the first question, to which Gandhiji's prompt answer was: 'It is completely wrong to say Satyagraha has been stopped. Our goal remains unchanged, only the nature of our work towards it has changed. There is greater need for gathering more strength and support to reinforce and keep it going. Implementation of the constructive programme is part of this march.'

There were varied reactions to this reply. For me it reinforced my own conviction which has gained strength as I have moved down the long trail of experiences in diverse fields. A firm foundation and a steady practical framework are indispensible to achieve lasting results, and can only result from dedicated constructive work. I watch with dismay the overpowering growth of paper work and endless round-table talks delivered in enticing phrases and linguistic cracks but with no follow up action.

I watched the old time genuine Gandhi followers, who had dedicated their lives to implementing items of the constructive programme through Ashrams. The ashram drew workers who propagated khadi, village industries, worked amongst Harijans, tribals, and other oppressed social elements. Whenever direct action was called for or launched they joined in, courted imprisonment. The Ashramites were respected and enjoyed credibility. They stayed away from everyday politics, for Gandhiji strictly enjoined this on them. With him it was an article of faith that no constructive worker should normally become active in politics. He knew what the results would be otherwise.

I had occasion to accompany Pandit Nehru on a few tours largely to popularise the activities of the Seva Dal. I had found these tours both stimulating as also educative. He was well organised as a person, could concentrate to write a memo, draft a resolution, anything serious that needed urgent attention even in the midst of the hurricane travels. He could for instance sit down no matter how late the hour before he retired for the night to accomplish whatever he felt had to be done. I marvelled at this capacity of his to concentrate.

On his election tours in one of which I accompained him, he seemed to be playing a highly dramatic role for the occasion. For instance there would be occasional bursts of temper that created turmoil, throwing people into a whirlpool of fear and mental confusion. These took different 'action' forms. He would snatch something at hand and throw it to the ground; if there was nothing at hand, pull out his own kerchief, roll it and shoot, or stride forward with few quick steps, almost giving one the creeps as if he would jump off the platform. The anger was of course against the government or the immediate opponents. After watching him a few times, it dawned on me that it was something of a put on drama. It certainly proved effective for he was not exactly a flamboyant orator as many politicians are, and little dramatic scenes added zest and spice to the scene once it became a super drama. It was in a room where the president of the Pradesh Congress Committee rather a doddering old man—boastfully declared he would ignore even were the Viceroy to ask something of him, a blatantly silly remark. Came a sharp retort from Pandit Nehru sitting beside him 'Who is a Viceroy anyway?' and with it he hurled a cushion across the room. While the group around looked solemn and guilty I could not suppress a smile. Later Nehru asked what amused me. Reluctantly I gave expression to my surmises which obviously annoyed him and he showed it. I had in fact come to realise that his demeanour could be quite misleading. His normal air of aloofness, the challenging manner, put one ill at ease at the first encounter. When he raised his head throwing it back, it created a haughty air, making one feel small, and therefore occasionally resentful. Before long however, these unpalatable reactions would melt away. A brilliant smile suffusing his whole face would disarm you. He could speak in a soft caressing voice, and fill the air with an unexpected touch of gentleness.

I was in Sevagram for a small intimate discussion organised by Nai Talim (Basic Education). This new orientation had made a convincing appeal to me. The New Education System in Europe I had surveyed had the same basic approach as Nai Talim or Basic Education as it was popularly known. Our ancient belief was that a child's psyche is alive, absorbant, active, from the moment it draws its first breath. If education is the total flowering of a growing personality, there has to be a harmonious coordination of all the human-faculties, and their adjustment with the outer world. This had to include the manual, involving skill and labour with materials.

Gandhiji valued children, so was deeply concerned about their education, particularly in the early years. For him the basis of education should ensure the cultivation of the hearts of the young. 'What would it matter if they learnt everything but did not know how to live in brotherliness with their fellow beings?' he queried.

He decried strongly 'stuffing children's minds with all kinds of information instead of stimulating and developing them. I would develop in the child his hands, his brains, his soul. Now the hands have almost atrophied and the soul has been ignored.'

Madame Montessori met this need for the child to touch, feel, construct but through use of modern objects especially contrived. While Gandhiji wanted the child to employ articles that were in use in its immediate home life, in the field or any other sector in which the family was involved. Through these experiences the growing entity explored, discovered the why and wherefore of many operations and came to understand and adjust itself to the world it has to live in. He believed this process stimulated the creative spirit in the child, and made it productive materially and aesthetically. Gandhiji's basic education aimed at : 'Work experience through the early school stage and vocationalisation in the senior secondary', to equip them adequately. Most parents and administrators scoffed at this as perpetuating the *varnas*—the caste system, and rejected it. What we see today is a child of four or five carrying a bookload heavier than itself. Since we can't go back to the old ashram system we had to find a current alternative. Nai Talim was one such.

As I look around today I see the education of the young lacks substance. Looking back I realise that the old style teaching, the village schoolmaster way, may have been too simple yet it was direct and intimately touched the child's life. For instance he would start geography with your own neighbourhood fields, arithmetic with counting your little possessions, calculations measuring your own walls, history round your monuments, religious thoughts through the lives of local saints. In this context the child both *sees* and *feels*, for these factors are part of its life, not read in cold print. These give reality to the child through *experience*. What is close and familiar to it, it easily relates to itself. Lessons that are dry, abstract, are only a mockery. Even a cast or a mould becomes meaningful only through an experience. What is therefore visible in its own horizon it then extends beyond it to the country, to the world beyond. These thoughts kept running like a chain in mind. How vital Nai Talim had been and how fruitful a revolution could have been wrought, had India adopted it.

As the meetings ended I became indisposed. Someone arrived at the guest house where I usually lodged, with a message. I was to shift to Gandhiji's cottage. I became uneasy. It was a slight passing trouble and there was no need to disturb them, especially Kasturba, I explained. The messenger was adamant. 'Ba says if you don't come, she will have to come herself. She can be even more difficult than Bapu, so you better come,' he decided with finality.

Gandhiji had on his delightful smile that lit up the air around. 'I wanted to keep you under my eye. I arrogate to be also a doctor and

Ba will minister to your needs', he gave his infectious laugh. There was devastating charm about him and when he turned it on full, those around fell easy victims. Though loaded with problems and responsibilities, he was so jocular and hearty, many of the jokes being against himself. He thus radiated a light-heartedness, as though he had not a care in the world. None of his close colleagues had that gift, nay not many Indians. Describing this Pandit Nehru said, 'When he enters a room he brings a breath of fresh air with him which lightens the atmosphere'. He had a way of driving people who came with long sombre faces for serious talks into roars of laughter. Yes he was exceptional ! There is the incident of a foreign lady insisting on an immediate visit with him. In a perfectly serious voice he replied, 'My schedule for the day I am afraid, is full up. If you are prepared to come at midnight I am willing to receive you.'

My visits to Sevagram had been few and brief and invariably to meet Gandhiji. So my contacts with Kasturba slight, though friendly, I had always been conscious of her presence, and we had established an easy relationship between us, but unlike some wives of important personages, who make themselves scarce or fade into pale shadows, she was very much there and one was conscious of a *presence* though she never intruded. Now living with her and sharing her daily routine, I could study her deeply.

They were up before the Ashram stirred. I was under orders to keep in bed and rest. I watched however, the speed and deftness with which she got through her chores, showing a long experienced hand at them. It was a pleasant sight to see them busy together, an intimacy that is woven like a web, intricate yet simple, delicate but strong, pregnated with a personal warmth, like two halves of a single whole. The nights were truly romantic. Though they were out of my sight, they were within easy hearing. At first I tried to read as usual, nevertheless their words came in distinctly though I had no desire to eavesdrop. I knew she was gently rubbing his feet. I was not sure whether she did it for her own comfort or his. It was obviously one of those intimacies they had adopted. From the words and phrases that penetrated my reading, I learnt she was recounting to him some of the events of the day to which he made some replies. The nights were their own, they were simple husband and wife like any other couple in the world.

I had in my talks with her tried to find out just how she felt about him, what determined her attitudes, overcame their conflicts. As we talked in bits and pieces, I realised how ill equipped I was to describe the great saga of her life. She alone could have done it but did not and would not. She never thought it important. All I can sum up is like a highly diluted rich dish. The course of their life must have been like a turbulent waterway rushing down a precipice. She tumbled along with him, yet why was she never overpowered by him, he who could shake the British empire? Basically she believed in his objectives, though she could not accept all of his convolutions. It is a well known fact that she joined the Satyagraha movement both in South Africa as in India of her own choice. It was also known that they had had sharp differences. But somewhere down their arduous pilgrimage had been dawning on her slowly but forcefully a conviction not only of his bonafides but also that he was a man of great destiny, he belonged to the world, to the larger humanity, her role was to strengthen and fortify him for this noble mission. What will remain an enigma to me is how she could be such an intimate part of this force and yet retain her individuality, stand upto him when she felt she should not bend. When she gave in, it was not in weakness. She had her own measures and scales in which she weighed his actions and satisfied herself. One may well echo what she had ultimately realised, as she rather reluctantly allowed herself to say : one may not always agree with a course he takes but one does finally find that it was the right one, in any event it was a *straight* one. His wide range of experiments in diet, in medical treatment, a whole host of others, how did she take it all in ? I asked her. Here she gave a hearty laugh. It was a silly question to pose. What I would have liked to ask was how did she live through his several long fasts ? I held myself. It would be treading on very sensitive ground, like trying to break open a sacred door.

What stuff was she made of ? I watched her as she attended on me, unhurried, restrained. That is how I saw her, the last time I was to, August 1942, when the police came to stop her addressing the meeting meant to have been addressed by her husband. That scene and her usual quiet assertion have been recorded and need no repetition. When I had seen her earlier in the Congress meeting, she had seemed rather low, unlike her usual self. But here at what was to be her last act of marching beside her lifemate, she was radiant, with a light in her eyes, as she took leave of us, indulging in some dry humour. It was to be the final farewell.

A diversion was provided for me at this stage by a request from the Sri Lanka Sama Samaj Party to the Socialist Party of India, that I be deputed to Sri Lanka to do some public propaganda to strengthen and give the Party a build up. The Sri Lanka Party was described as a Socialist Party, assumed to be a co-relative of the Indian Party. Naturally our Party agreed and asked me to proceed to our neighbouring Island.

I spent a couple of weeks travelling throughout the country, propagating the Socialist principles and why nationalist ideas had to be clear cut in socio-economic terms. I found the leadership of the Sri Lanka Party of good intellectual calibre, but deeply steeped in Marxism. There were no other political or economic ideologies to influence the Group as in India. Nor any constructive programmes for immediate relief as we had. The Party was trying to establish mass contact, and I had fairly large gatherings to address. Maybe there my visit helped. A woman rebel who had participated in India's freedom struggle could stir public curiosity. The invitation had referred to my previous visit and how politically helpful it had been, hence I had been named.

It was only later that we discovered that the Lanka Sama Samaj Party was a Trotskyite group. May be they had to suppress this to avoid a ban on their party by the British regime.

I had my first contact with Indian labour in Sri Lanka. It was also my initiation into the vicissitudes of Indian labour in British colonies more of which I was to later learn in my travels to farflung lands in several continents over which the Union Jack had once fluttered.

My next visit to Sri Lanka was after independence during Mrs. Bandaranaike's regime on an invitation from her routed through the national women's organisation. I had met Mrs. Bandaranaike a few times during her Indian visits, when she had shown keen interest in development of handicrafts and sought our help for Sri Lanka Crafts. She was keen I should study the craft situation in Sri Lanka and make suggestions for their development.

Then she headed a coalition cabinet with the Lanka Sama Samaj Party. I was intrigued. What had once seemed like a little almost bedraggled party had got somewhere, though tragically that was their undoing though they little realised it then. The Indian High Commissioner conveyed to me their wish to meet me. They were of course in very buoyant spirits and expressed their deep appreciation of the Indian Socialist Party's ready response to loan me at the start of their career.

The next election which brought down the Bandaranayaka government saw also the rout of the Lanka Samaj Party, as it had been an active partner in the discarded regime. The anger against this party seemed the greater as it had originally projected itself as a Leftist radical party creating high hopes.

I visited Sri Lanka again, on a purely cultural mission on behalf of the Indian Council for Cultural Relations and the World Crafts Council. This time I met mainly academicians, performing artists and craftsmen. From the academicians I learnt that my earlier political missions had found their way into the Sri Lanka archives, that the then colonial government had been very surprised and perturbed to find me espousing the cause of the Trotskyites. My speeches had been carefully recorded, to watch if I preached disaffection towards the regime when I could be nabbed. But I evidently provided no occasion for it.

This visit was made exhilarating by my being able to renew my old ties with artists I had long known like Chitrasena, the dancer, and Manjushri, the painter, both of whom had studied in Shantiniketan. One bitter drop fell into my cup of honey the last day, when I conveyed my desire to strengthen our cultural ties to the Sri Lanka Minister for culture, whom I had met in India earlier when he had come to fetch some Buddha relics Sri Lanka was borrowing from us. In a sarcastic tone the Minister said: 'So you aspire to strengthen cultural ties between our countries. You must have heard how hundreds of thousands of our people rushed to view them. We asked your government to let us have a few of these relics as monuments. But we were refused. Was anyone in India aware of these precious relics, until we asked for them? Only then were they resurrected. They obviously mean little to you. We were told that if any relics were given to us, other Asian Buddhist countries might ask for their share. We approached these countries for their cooperation. They offered to give a written declaration they would refrain from such moves. But all to no purpose, 'he concluded on a bitter note. By some lucky chance I was spared by a reference to an old historic incident when relics of Lord Buddha found in one of the stupas of Taxila in a gold casket, were presented in 1917 by Lord

Chelmsford, the then Viceroy of India to the Tooth Relic Temple of Kandy. Otherwise my cup of humiliation would have been full.

The advent of the Congress Ministries had brought me an unusual run of uninterrupted time. Taking advantage of it, I ventured on a trek to Kashmir with my son, to the Kolhai Glacier. Occasional trekking had once been a favourite pastime of mine. Having grown up under the steep shadows of the Western Ghats, mountains held a never ending lure for me. Even in the midst of my busy tours, I used to steal time to breathe the rare mountain air, mostly in my native ghats and the lovely Nilgiris *that were*. But scouring the land of the snows was a new adventure especially stepping on a glacier as the guide book invitingly beckoned. With a tent, a-cook, a guide and of course the lovable ponies to carry our bags, we began what promised to be a long journey. I have made subsequent trips but the wonder and magic of that first venture is still fresh.

There were a few initial hurdles to cross, for in all the Indian States I was marked Red—danger. So I had to slip in avoiding the vigilant security. Not too difficult here for I was unknown to the Kashmir security people.

As we moved higher, the changing scene become more bewitching. First unending pastures dotted with myriads of multicoloured flowers of every hue as the Himalayan region alone have. It is unbelievable how the upper gaunt mountain sides that frown forbiddingly on you when the sun beats down on them, take on different colours, from a golden glow merging into miraculous tints as though by alchemy, as the sunlight wanes and the sky turns a vivid blue. And then there descended on our world a rare unforgettable violent twilight. The day ended. When a fresh day begins, the sunlight seems to give a new meaning to the landscape, for as our ancients said: today rises on the death of yesterday. Notwithstanding the inexorable natural phenomenon of day and night, in this landscape *time* assumes a slower and slower rhythm, and gets less and less compelling, more an accident than a necessity.

How different from a prison where although you are deprived of the mechanism of a clock that traps one tyrannically in its grip, time nevertheless rules rigidly through the hourly clanging of a bell.

The adventure across the glacier had however to be cut short, for all of a sudden it began to snow and nobody could predict whether it would turn into a snow storm. But we had had our fill.

Our guide, to assuage our disappointment, kindly suggested a visit to a blue lagoon in the mountains, not too far from where we were. We gladly trudged to its banks and gazed wonderingly into a blue green sheet that almost shivered like a large peacock feather when the bird was dancing.

For the return journey we adopted a novel mode. We both sat on a galicha which was given a push down and it simply kept sliding until we reached the flat ground. On my return to Srinagar I met K.F. Nariman, the Bombay Congress leader, who persuaded me to visit Peshawar, where he had just been. He promptly telegraphed Khan Saheb, brother of Abdul Gaffar Khan, then Chief Minister of North West Frontier Province to alert him. I was thrilled to take a trip I had never even dreamt of. In those days the North West Province had been to us a spot on another planet, until the Frontier Gandhi, as he was so lovingly called by all in India, arrived on the scene. The first inkling we had of strange events taking place there was through the bamboo phone as the unpublicised political communication channel was then called. The news was that two platoons of the Royal Gharwalis in the Indian Army had refused to fire on the Frontier people as they were perfectly non-violent and, according to them, even by the military code, it would be manslaughter if they did. We just held our breath. The whole episode was unbelievable. Over the centuries the only picture we had of that region was as peopled by fierce and turbulent Pathans. This story was like a myth.

Abdul Gaffar Khan had seemed of rather a retiring disposition, so unlike most of our outgoing political leaders. My contact with him had been casual. I now looked forward to a marvellous chance to get to know him.

To us the introduction to him had come through Gandhiji who described him as 'The man of God'. I knew that in Gandhiji's parlance God was far from the conventional concept. 'God' he said 'is truth.' So a man of God was a man of truth, honesty. In the few days I was with him, Gaffar Khan looked simple, straight forward, gentle, of loving disposition, with all the prerequisites which qualified him for this title Gandhiji bestowed on him.

I asked Gaffar Khan the veracity of the incident of the Royal Gharwalis. 'Yes, our Khuda-Khidmatgars remained so completely non-violent and non-provocative, that the hearts of the hill-jawans, could not but melt.' 'Do they really believe in non-violence, it is not expediency?' I persisted. I saw that the Khan was trying to be very patient, then said very firmly: 'Non-violence has become a matter of faith with us—I believed in Gandhiji's ahimsa much earlier. But the unparalleled success of the experiment in my province, has made me a confirmed champion of non-violence. God willing I hope never to see my province take to violence. We know only too well the bitter results of violence. Moreover the Pathan is seemingly dangerous because of his sharp quick temper rather than violent. We shall prove to be the best disciples of Bapu.' His faith was reinforced almost a decade later when communal riots spurted over some parts of India in 1946 and a few flames burst forth in Hazara district in the Frontier. But his 10,000 Khidmatgars stood steadfastly by their commitment, so as to become a source of considerable succour to the non-Muslims.

As he talked I watched this new Messiah who had wrought this incredible transformation in his hot-blooded, high tensioned Pathans. I had heard how he had been treated by the British, insulted, abused, subjected to violence, fettered in chains. Not many leaders in India had been subjected to such tribulations. There was no bitterness or rancour as he related some of his experiences when I asked for confirmation of these tales. It was the lot of all who were struggling for freedom, was his concluding comment.

A decade later I witnessed his greatest agony on the eve of Partition. He was a shattered man, looked bent under the blow. He said to Gandhiji: 'To think we shall become aliens in Hindustan, to be away from you, from all of you.' Gandhiji, as torn as he, but unshaken, replied: 'Non-violence knows no despair.' Then as though he were blessing him he said: 'It is no doubt the hour of your trial. But what fear can there be for those who are pledged To Do or Die.' To Gaffar Khan it was not the hour of trial but of crucifixion. The agony within Gandhiji came out finally as he said: 'Independence may come, but the brave Pathan will lose his—the sight of Badshah Khan's grief wrings my heart. But he is a man of God, for such a man there can be no defeat.' Today only Gaffar Khan can comment on this!

During this visit Abdul Gaffar Khan had suggested I take a trip along the Khyber Pass. 'That is where you will meet the real Afridis and see what type of people they are, the kind of life they lead.' I had never imagined such a prospect. Khan Saheb made all the necessary arrangements. He warned my son not to wear any headdress that would even remotely resemble a hat.' That would instantly become the target for a bullet,' he warned in a grim tone. He had to offer us other details on these people. 'An Afridi grows up to mistrust everyone, to be on his guard, and to believe that if he has to survive he should strike first. For there are long but strong memories of aggressive marching feet of armies and marauders trooping down the Pass, experiences that have not been recorded.' 'I suppose the earliest record is that of Alexander followed by those of Ghazni, Genghis Khan, Timurlane, Babar, Nadir Shah.' I broke off my wandering narration. 'Ah! but you are not aware that more invaders entered the Pass, also that those who used it once would never enter it again. That is where our Afridis come in, for those who came through probably paid heavily for their adventure. But the lure of the lush plains of Hindustan could not be easily abandoned. But don't forget that every shadow is thrown by a light. If you are kind and trustworthy, the Afridi will prove your best friend, none can touch him in his loyal steadfastness. Unfortunately they have been treated mostly to acts of aggression, betrayal, so they keep showing their teeth first.'

Our car trip through the Khyber Pass is one of my most memorable experiences. When we came into Jamrud, which seems like a suburb of Peshawar, only 15 kilometers away, we were in an entirely different world. Everybody was armed, even little boys, though the arms were obviously country made. I am told that now they carry several foreign made arms, like automatic pistols, even machine guns.

A small group approached us as our car stopped, greeted us, asked us to alight and offered us refreshments. We were treated to saffron rice and sweets. They told us they had great regard for their Badshah Khan, so any friends of his were their friends and welcome. Londi Kotel was our destination. The drive was bleak and grim, through unsmiling country, along frowning rocky corridors. The only mental diversion was recalling pictures of the several armies which had marched down and created the series of upheavals of history, some like Babar to pass permanently into our history.

At our destination food was laid out. Some of the Afridis joined us and we had a long dialogue. Most of the talk revolved round their current opponents, the English. They regarded them with a sort of patronising contempt. 'They are to us like *bachas*', they explained. It is not even a hundred years since they came and we Afridis have been guarding the Pass for more years than we can count and we shall continue to.' Then the oldest amongst them gave a loud laugh. 'Do you know the Angreez call us lawless? Isn't that a joke? When they march their well armed armies, make attacks on unarmed people, loot them and occupy countries, it is *lawful* ! When we make our own native arms to protect ourselves, that is lawless !' They all laughed heartily.

'Where do you get your arms,' I asked. 'We make our own. Would you like to see our factory ? We only show it to our good friends. Badshah Khan tells us you are one of us for you are fighting against our common enemy.' They took us down the hillside into a kind of a cave where some smelting and hammering was going on. No doubt a primitive affair but for them sufficiently serviceable. 'If we are not self reliant in our strategic needs, we can never be free', an old man remarked wisely, nodding his head.

On my return journey I visited Taxila, which I had long yearned to, as it lay within the North West region. It was like a hazy glimpse of a vanished era. It ranked high not only as a hallowed seat of learning with Buddha's immediate presence but also as a cradle of Gandhara or Greco-Buddhist art as it was known, but even more as the renowned university of medicine and surgery, whose ghost image is still recognisable in the burnt study cells and prayer halls, irremovable scars of the relentless fire with which the White Huns devastated a priceless altar of learning. These tell the tale of senseless destruction, that man continues to indulge in throughout human history. I also understood it was at this spot that the famous doctrine of *Tatvamase* was composed. I used to recite it as a girl with some pride, as though it were a magic formula. I realised how *ancient* Taxila was only when I learnt here that among the several distinguished scholars of Taxila were King Paenadi of Kosala and Jivaka, the illustrious physician to King Bimbisara, all contemporaries of Lord Buddha. What bewilders one is why such an important institution was set in such a high menaced route along which waves of fierce invaders kept coming over the centuries. True the large Buddhist monastry itself was ensconced in a spot sheltered by hills.

The most noted is the chapel where a gold casket was discovered, containing minute pieces of bones along with a silver scroll carrying the inscription that these were the relics of Lord Buddha, giving the exact date when they were enshrined.

The Museum held Buddha statues in an incredible variety of poses, while each of them carries its own narrative in the Kharoshti script.

As the guide led me through what was once the Taxila city, I tried to picture the vast medley of people from Greece, Rome, Egypt, Iran and a host of other countries, who once foregathered here to exchange commodities of both the mind and the body.

A constant impediment that came in my work, particularly my travels, was the growing antagonism from the regimes in Indian States and the obstacles they put in my way. It started with the then Mysore State which borders on Mangalore district, and which I had to inevitably cross to travel to most places. Through these trips I had come to know that in this state there was no real people's political body to voice their aspirations. I encouraged those politically interested to strengthen a nebulous existing committee in Mysore city by enrolling members. Whenever I passed through I would meet the group and discuss programmes. The Maharaja was a benevolent father-image, traditionally respected. The Dewan, then Sir Mirza Ismail was an efficient administrator. In fact the State had had a series of honest capable Dewans and it was way better than most States of the day. One like Sir Visweswarayya became a national figure as a technocrat and left valuable legacy behind. I had had friendly relations with the families of some of these personalities like Sir Mirza Ismail, Sir Thambu Chetty, Principal Secretary to the Maharaja, because of my social activities. Lady Ismail, whom I recruited into the Women's Conference, became the Chairman of the State Committee. Her mouthing what she was supposed to have learnt from the Conference in her wrangles with her husband added to Sir Ismail's are against me. To him I was doubly guilty. He railed against me to his colleagues and officials that I was fostering trouble not only against his government but raising a revolt in the private precincts of his home. From then on he declared a regular war. He refused to accept that the Indian freedom movement was not directed against personalities but to bring the State's people into the fold of the rest of India and enable them to participate in the country's freedom. Every time I entered the State I would be chased by the police who tried to drive me out. In these battles there were some comic encounters too. One such took place in Sir Thambu Chetty's house.

He was of a very different disposition, saw no reason to take alarm, and behave like a savage. He was an image of politeness and kindliness. I had become friendly with his wife and daughter Philomena, a violin player of great merit in western music, and was one of the few Indians to be taught by renowned artists of Europe and win laurels in several European capitals, an exceptional experience for a young Indian woman in the twenties. I was pleased by the family's unaffected nature, the simple manner in which they lived in a modest bungalow with a 'native' decor.

Once when I was passing through, I went to tea at Sir Thambu Chetty's. We had hardly begun when an attendant came in to whisper in my hostess's ear. She conveyed to me that a police car was outside and the officer wished to see me. She said to the attendant, 'Tell the police they have no business to enter our house, they should wait outside. They cannot possibly expect me to turn my honoured guest out before she has had a bite and a cup of tea. Don't come to disturb us again'. Years later when she invited me to a dinner at Dorchester Hotel in London, she recalled this amusing incident. 'Here we can eat in peace. No Mysore police here. We only have our old cook and bearer, as my husband must have his *Thilisaru and Kosambri*', typical Mysore soup and salad.

The pressures from the Indian States kept increasing as I got deeper into the State peoples struggle against the age old feudal administration. To us, the younger line of workers, the States were one of the bulwarks of imperialism, an unholy alliance between these Indian rulers and our British masters which to me needed to be broken.

Then came rather a spectacular incident completely uncalled for. I got an invitation from the Travancore State Youth body to open the State Youth Conference, which I accepted. The State had come to acquire a certain amount of notoriety for high powered centralised rule. I had first visited it as Secretary of the Women's Conference when I had been warmly received by the then ruler Lakshmibai as also Setu Parvatibai who later strode that State's political stage. C.P. Ramaswamy Iyer, the current Dewan had been an old friend of my family and had always been gracious and considerate when we had occasion to come together.

Today however the scene has changed. Preceding this trip I planned to spend a couple of days at Courtallum waterfalls situated on the border of Travancore State to get relief from some small ailment. The day I was due to take the journey, the morning paper carried an announcement: The Travancore Government had banned my entry into the State and if I ignored it I would have to face the consequences. A brief note that followed explained that the said government had not been able to locate me at any of the known places, so this paper announcement was meant to serve as a warning to me. This meant the Madras police, now under a Congress Ministry had not revealed my whereabouts. I was however most surprised to meet a few of them headed by a police officer at the Courtallum railway station. The officer approached me before I could board the train to say he had come under the direct instructions of Shri Rajagopalachari, Chief Minister of Madras State, to request me not to proceed. The officer made a lengthy explanation. His advice was not on any political ethics, for as a freedom fighter I had every right to assert my right against irrational interference. The Madras Chief Minister and his State police were however disturbed by the news coming out of the State I was entering which was most disquieting and filled them with apprehension, hence this request. I thanked the officer and expressed my decision to proceed. The police party travelled with me up to the Travancore border as instructed, making one final attempt to dissuade me, then left. The officer had explained to me that I would not be touched as long as I was in the train or in the railway premises as it belonged to the *Indian government*. I sat wondering what would happen, would any strange adventure befall me.

Within a short time it became obvious that the news of my being on the train had spread. At every station there were crowds, soon even along the railway line. It only meant the people were unusually stirred.

At Trivandrum station, there was a huge throng. The organisers had thoughtfully engaged one of the retiring rooms in the Station where I could stay until the next evening when I would proceed to the meeting.

Annie Mascarenhas, an active local political worker, kept me company and I practically spent the night listening to her narrations of the state politics. Next day as I came out of the station I was arrested and taken to a court. I was about to sit down, as we did in the Indian courts, when the presiding officer barked: 'You cannot sit down, you are a prisoner.' The prosecutor began his case but was sharply interrupted by the presiding officer, 'I order an adjournment and that she be kept in the lock-up pending the trial.' A couple of days went quietly by as though everyone had forgotten I was there. Food came from outside sent by nameless well-wishers. On the third day a gentleman came with a uniformed officer. The gentleman said he had come from the Dewan who is most distressed over this. There has been so much lawlessness and grievous incidents since my arrival. The Dewan feels you should have informed him and been his guest. 'I *am* a guest of his', I interrupted, I was getting sick in the pit of my stomach. 'The lawlessness is of your own making not my visit. I came on an invitation from a youth body that has been functioning lawfully. I would have delivered my speech and quietly departed if you had not made a drama of it. My speech I have purposely recorded and given a copy to the organisers. I challenge you to pick out a single idea, a phrase, intended to incite anyone to lawlessness or destruction. We are by instinct and culture law abiding citizens, unless the law goes beyond its bounds to come in the way of our normal functioning or subjects us to lowering of our human dignity. All I can say is that I feel you used my visit to launch a political movement that had probably been bottled up. It will find its own course, and no 'armed law' will be able to stop it.' That was just what happened.

I was put into a train in a third class compartment by my escort, with a silly comment: 'Since you follow your leader's ways and travel third class, we provide you the same.' In truth if he had not made a point of it, I would not have even been conscious of it. Most of us in the political movement travelled third class.

A new scene opened on the Indian horizon. The well known Emelka studios of Munich, the second largest German film producing company, entered into partnership with Himansu Rai who played a great pioneering role in Indian film development through his Bombay Talkies, along with his wife Devika Rani. Himansu wanted, through German collaboration, to improve the general standard of Indian films and to stimulate Indians into producing better quality pictures under German direction. Incidentally he expected these would also open markets abroad for Indian films.

The first film was Light of Asia showing the life of Buddha. A few young Indian women were recruited for small roles in this and the services of Mrinalini Chattopadhyay were obtained to look after them. Thus I came into contact with this venture.

The German director was Franz Osten who along with two German cameramen made three most successful films, Light of Asia, Shiraz and A Throw of Dice. Osten then joined Bombay Talkies and directed several successful Hindi films.

The ushering in of this new era by Himansu Rai and his foreign collaborator was followed by an equally innovative film personality Mohan Bhavnani, also fresh from Germany where he had worked with Ulfa Studios, then the leading film makers.

The prevailing Indian films had simply taken over from the established rather melodramatic Indian stage. Bhavnani's great ambition was to mould a totally different cast for the Indian film.

He decided on Vasantsena or Mrichakatika as the classical Sanskrit title by which the play is generally known. When he began to select the cast, he ran into the problem of finding suitable women for the female roles, for this was still frowned upon by society. Even where liberal parents were willing they were daunted by others.

While Bhavnani was on the hunt, he heard of my adventure into the Theatre world. Venkatachalam, who needless to say was there to assist him, explained I could not be expected to play any serious role as I was too preoccupied otherwise. Bhavnani hoped that if it were known I was participating, it would be easier for the willing aspirants to join up. I agreed.

Bhavnani was lucky to get Enakshi who had made a name in Himansu Rai's Shiraz, to play Vasantsena. Enakshi was a college graduate which seemed to endow her with a status. Equally fortunate was the acquisition of Nalini Turkhad to play Madanika, hailing from an upper middle class Maharashtrian family, also a college product, young and eager to meet a challenge. Interestingly enough, Enakshi married Bhavnani and continued to play in Bhavnani's pictures but later took to dancing and finally ended as a noted writer. Nalini married Keshav Rao Daiberg, one of the founders of the famous Pune based Prabhat Films. The rest of the cast was quite exciting: Shakuntala Tampi, a social worker, T.P. Kailasam, a famed Kannada playwright, Bharadwaj, a Sanskrit scholar and teacher, Jaikishen Nanda, who later became a reputed director. The rest were amateur theatre artists, a professor from the University and so on. The film was to be in English as it was for the international market and the script was based on Ryders play The Little Toy Cart.

My own part was very small and innocuous. According to Bhavnani and Venkatachalam, my participation had served the purpose. As a pioneering debut, it did make a splash—for this was still the late twenties!

Personally the association proved for me most rewarding, for in Bhavnani and Enakshi I found rare lifelong friends who brought genuine love and happiness into my life.

My tribute also goes to those courageous women who deserve to be remembered who braved social displeasure and at a time when there were no compensations such as film awards or front page publicity.

Much later I did a small role in a film called 'Bikhare Moti', produced by a Socialist colleague. I decided I would donate my fee to the local Party work. By some queer irony, I never got to see either of these films as I continued to be in prison when they were released. Film acting failed to attract me, while the drama theatre filled me with a passionate fervour; acting in a studio seemed like performing in a void without the warm sensitive communion with a responsive audience.

In Bhavnani's film production there were new innovations. Some, of the shooting was done in natural locations which interested me. From a technical point of view the film did without artificial sets and the elaborate studio techniques that had been developed in Germany and become its hall mark. This factor must have accounted for some of the success of that film, apart from some of the new shooting techniques which Bhavnani said he tried out.

The entire episode of Subhas Chandra Bose's sudden emergence on the national political scene and an equally abrupt exit is too well known to be repeated, except where it touched and left me with sad and depressing memories that haunted me for quite a while.

My own personal acquaintance with him was both brief and fleeting. I never had the opportunity of getting to know him well which I always regretted. Before he came as Congress President I had a cursory meeting with him at the Calcutta Congress, in his impressive role as the G.O.C. of the Volunteers a whole decade earlier.

Subhasbabu's first election as President of the Congress had been uneventful notwithstanding vague rumours that the elders including Gandhiji had not been happy about it, but that Panditji had pulled his weight. But I had to presume Gandhiji must have acquiesced for it to come off so smoothly.

The Haripura session of the Congress where he presided had passed off smoothly. The organisation too ran *uneventfully*, much to the unhappiness of Subhasbabu's supporters, particularly the youth who had looked forward to exciting times of action. Where differences arose in the States with Congress Ministries between the Party and the Government, it was said that Subhasbabu found himself in a minority. The writing on the wall was clear. Notwithstanding the large support the Congress President had from ordinary members and rank and file, at the decision making level he failed to get effective support. So no worthwhile changes could be wrought in the political scene.

The next Congress in Tripura, however, met under a heavy cloud as Subhasbabu had won the presidentship in the face of a concerted opposition of the veterans known then as the Old Guard, and Gandhiji's final devastating verdict on it as his own defeat. This more or less set the trend for what followed.

To my mind there was something un-Gandhian about Gandhiji's pronouncement. It seemed to have a tinge of petulance. It filled the air with unnamed fears, reckless speculations. To top it all, the President arrived running high temperature, insisting nevertheless he would preside over at least some sessions. He made a most tantalising figure on the dais, with wet packs on the head, all of which seemed to intensify the strained tempo of the session.

As the air was thick with rumours of the Congress willingness to compromise with the British under the threat of a world war, it seemed appropriate for the President to want the organisation to clear its position. What Subhasbabu wished at this stage was an ultimatum to the British government for a timebound transfer of power. Out of the blue came a bolt, Gandhiji's emphatic pronouncement as a retort to this, that he was always willing for an honourable compromise. The metaphor was familiar, for he had always shown this willingness, once had even declared his readiness for negotiation, 'on bended knees!' Here in this context however it looked to me like a gauntlet flung at a bruised helpless creature in a cage, unworthy of the Gandhi the country revered.

The situation kept deteriorating further. As floor whip for the Socialist Party for this session, I could assess the varying trends and leanings of different groups. I would convey my assessments to Sarat Bose, Subhasbabu's brother, regularly to spare the sick man. Subhasbabu still carried a large measure of support, now tinged by sympathy after Gandhiji's stern rebukes, until the final crisis came in the shape of a resolution that made it obligatory for the President to compose his

Working Committee in consultation with Gandhiji. In the present context it meant a call to the delegates to decide between the two: Gandhiji or Subhasbabu.

The crisis was further deepened by the members of the Working Committee resigning in a body, barring Pandit Nehru who said he was not prepared to split the organisation. Obviously Gandhiji had developed deep suspicions of Subhasbabu, had probably heard that he could not be trusted, and decided he could not be expected to act with responsibility, even as he had once decided about me. He was evidently angry with the Congress for rejecting his candidate. So it had to be made to realise the enormity of its defiance of a long accepted leader, though no supporter of Subhasbabu could have imagined this would be taken as a personal affront by Gandhiji.

I watched the piquant scene with utter dismay. Gandhiji seemed invisible. I wished I could meet him, repeat what I had said when he condemned me, that the young expect of the seniors deep sympathetic understanding, large heartedness, not short temper, carping criticism and severe punishment. But that was not to be.

There was some uneasiness in the Socialist Party over the official Resolution and the decision to remain neutral seemed to come from a certain amount of uncertainty, confusion. I know there were some who shared my dejection over it. In my opinion the delineation of the Party stand only made matters worse, by conveying that when we voted for Subhasbabu we made it clear it did not mean also helping settle issues between the rightists and the leftists. I was and still am firmly of the opinion that the official Congress Resolution was not inspired by the Right or the Left and had no political bearings on any ideology. To me the issue was whether a President had any voice or preferences in the selection of his executive or was he to be just an innocuous rubberstamp, whether the President was Subhasbabu or anybody else. For in substance in this context it certainly amounted to a lack of confidence in the President. Is that really what we felt, notwithstanding whatever irritants the Party may have experienced in this session?

Deeply within me I felt hurt, more so because even in those brief meetings I had had with Subhasbabu during the session, I had been moved by feelings of sympathy though I never made them explicit, strictly refraining from expressing my own views, confining myself to objectively reporting what came within my purview.

Even through this detached association I could sense in him a passionate patriot. I never doubted his sincerity. He was full of dare devilry and courage which could make him unpredictable and put him outside the pale of a safe manageable leader such as our veterans wanted. He won my deepest respect which made my anguish over the turn of events, keener.

I bade farewell to Subhasbabu as he lay in the railway bogey that stood at a station siding. He looked so wan and tired but there was no dejection in his eyes, or faintness in the timbre of his voice. I expressed my disappointment at not being of any help to him which he rejected with a jerk of his hand. 'Sarat has told me of all you did. I expect we shall work together in the days to come.'

Little did I dream when I left him we were never to meet again.

Sometime later I was astonished to receive a letter from him. He wrote he had learnt with surprise and distress that I was planning to go out of India – how could I, he queried, do that when the country would soon be facing critical challenges with the rapid international developments. He was right in his estimate of the impending threats. But I had other problems to face and solve.

Netaji's (as he has since come to be called) historic exploits after his daring escape from India, command more than admiration. They amply proved the qualities I had sensed in him. His incredible achievements that won him a hero's acclaim, alas came too late, for Subhasbabu never came back to his country for whose freedom he performed such extraordinary feats. I can still recall Pandit Nehru recounting his impressions of Netaji's work in South East Asia, after his visit there at the close of the war, his face aglow, his eyes lit with emotion as the words came tumbling out like sparks: 'Netaji did very great things, extraordinary things, the successful way he organised the military, the Azad Hind Fauz and the civilians alike. There he was like a god', and so he went on. I was not only happy I felt also vindicated, but equally sad that when he was with us we failed to accept him at his true worth, and let little specks of dust cloud our vision.

Netaji's tragic end drew from Gandhiji a moving tribute. I hoped it was wrung out of his heart and wiped away the dark spots that had blurred his vision. But what was done could not be undone, for Netaji was no more.

To the Tripura Congress session had come a delegation from Egypt, bringing greetings from the Wafd Party which under Saad Zaghlal Pasha and his comrades Aly Sharawai and Abdel Aziz Fahni, had been fighting a vigorous battle for national revolution, which had rallied all classes of people, from government officials to illiterate masses, workers, peasants, students, women, children. The Congress Session extended a public welcome to the delegation through a formal Resolution.

The Wafd Delegation came in to meet Gandhiji when I was with him. He restrained me from leaving and introduced me to the visitors saying : 'You should meet this lady, she is interested in your freedom struggle and has been relating the story to the Indian people.' I had been publishing a series of articles on the anti-imperialist struggles, particularly highlighting the Egyptian Saga. For a special interest had been roused in me for the Egyptian struggle by Madame Charaoui Pasha, a staunch Egyptian nationalist whom I had come to know at the Berlin Women's Congress. When they took leave after a chat, they graciously extended an invitation to me to visit Egypt.

One day I was informed Madame Halide Adib of Turkey was to visit India. To me this seemed like one of those rare dreams coming true. To me she was the 'Rani of Jhansi' of the Turkish revolution. She had learnt to handle war weapons and was the only woman soldier to fight in the trenches, and came to be known as Corporal Halide Edib. I gave to the Indian press a welcome tribute to this rare personality which was spectacularly flashed.

I was very thrilled to meet this unusual woman, and spent several exciting hours listening to hair-raising tales of her part in her country's battles. She was a small-made, wiry figure, with dark eloquent eyes, soft spoken. As she had excellent command over English, conversation became easy yet gripping. It was my first personal intimacy with a living battle-scarred woman soldier and I was rather overwhelmed.

Ten years later on my first visit to Turkey I met her again along with her husband Dr. Adnan Abdulhuk, a noted physician and Vice-President of the First Turkish National Assembly, and also a revolutionary. They had for a time gone into self-exile as a protest against the one party system of Ataturk and had returned after a change of regime.

I had however by now been saddened to read Halide's impressions of India particularly her reaction to the Hindu-Muslim situation. She seemed to have accepted the version of Muslim Communalists. There is something to be said for the social and religious prejudices the

Hindus may show towards them. But these were not the issues she dwelt on. Hers were purely political and there I felt she had become biased. It was tragically ironical that one who had revolted so boldly against a theocratic State and fought for a secular democracy, should be influenced by religious communal politics in India.

The war clouds were gathering in the West, thick and fast, with the menace of Nazism getting sharper each day. The call for the liberal democratic forces to stand together against this threat got stronger under the slogan of a United Front.

The United Front strategy projected by the Comintern goes back to 1935 when the Communist International adopted this thesis. The slogan that now caught on in the face of the Nazi threat was to bring into one Party all groups and individuals who were opposed to Nazism. To Palme Dutt and Bradly who were the Communist Pandits shaping their Party in India, the formation of the Congress Socialist Party was an unexpected gift. For it provided a convenient entry into the Congress to build up their inevitable cells.

The Communists who had consistently opposed the Socialist Party from its very inception as reactionary and certainly not Marxist now performed a volte face under the new London directive. Jayaprakash facilitated this under his own concept of 'Socialists Unity' which to him meant clubbing together all who accepted Marxism. Therefore Communists were to be admitted as individuals, not as CPI members.

I had been uneasy over this development for I had been gaining some experience of the Communist style of functioning. The Communist Party was a tightly closed body ruled by severe discipline and to whom the Party was supreme, everything else being subordinate to it. Their overall effort was to capture the entire organisation by seizing key positions and undermining the body then enter to manipulate it for their own party end. This objective was a long way from Jayaprakash's objective of Socialist Unity. The die had however been cast.

At the Meerut Socialist Party Conference in 1936, the Party took the fatal decision to admit Communists into the Party, with a provision 'with the approval of the Party Executive' which in practice was completely ignored. It had been forcefully opposed by many party stalwarts. I was particularly unhappy since I was chairing the session. Purshottam Tricumdas and I had an exclusive discussion with Jayaprakash on this as he had moved the proposal. But he was adamant and we submitted, for the alternative was the fear of his resignation.

The Royists had already joined the Party. A new euphoria rose to float around as the Party watched those very Communists who had earlier condemned it, now smilingly enter it, never questioning why this volte face. The Party's perception seems to have been mugged by a sense of triumph, for they were immediately given important positions in the Party.

The Communists employed their usual techniques of functioning and secretly built a complete party framework of their own within the Socialist Party, obviously to take over the latter at an appropriate time. Then through the advantageous position it occupied, began to burrow into the Congress from within. In the Congress some of these 'unknown faceless' members managed to get into key offices. E.M.S. Namboodripad, reigned as President of the Kerala Provincial Congress Committee, with whom I worked very closely, never sensing he was an ardent CPI Member, one of the 'Trojan horses' as Jayaprakash termed them later, alas too, too late. Several of the Socialists became aware of this by which time a couple of years had gone by. The dangerous situation was discussed in the Executive more than once. It was fully realised that a drastic step such as expulsion of the key workers who were known as Communists. was the only course to prevent a disastrous disruption of the Party. Tragically it was one of the several occasions when the Party failed to take firm action. It stood like a moth that gets immobilised as the lizard approaches to swallow it up. Some old workers like Minoo Masani, Yusuf Mehrally, Rammanohar Lohia etc. resigned from the Party Executive, demanding dissolution of the so-called United Front, for in this murky atmosphere work had become impossible. I was out of India at the time but was in agreement with the break. The result ultimately was total disaster, for when Russia was attacked and pushed into the Allied side, in the eyes of the Indian Government the long despised and hated Communists suddenly became reputable and were given all support.

Now the Communists struck. They came out into the open, and those entrenched in the Socialist Party also threw off their disguise and stepped out. As a consequence the Party broke up as under a sudden explosion. It could not have happened at a worse time, for most of the active Party workers were incarcerated under the Defence of India

Rules as a War time measure. This disaster proved more than a Party affair, it became a national tragedy. The Socialist Party would have been the natural and appropriate opposition to the party in power when freedom came.

The Socialist Party was never able to re-form itself. The new elements who had jumped into the 1942 movement and naturally drifted into the Socialist Party, lacked political background, education, experience all of which make for maturity. They were what are called 'activists', with all the native aggressiveness, impatience, impetuousity, 'Village Idiots' as one of the senior Socialists cynically called them. They were far from idiots. As products of the '42' movement, they had been propelled by a fiery passion evoked by the call of 'Do or Die'. They were gruelled only in patterns of disruption and destruction. They needed time to be mellowed into new moulds, to shoulder new duties and functions. But time was not on their side. For 1947 overwhelmed the country with new challenges, made a million-fold burdens under the disastrous tragedy of the partition of the country.

When the Party took the inevitable step of breaking away from the Congress after 1947 as it could not tag itself to a 'Ruling Party' that did not have the same commitments, it lacked the core, the stamina and the structure to become a well-equipped opposition. Under the circumstances the decision to boycott the Constituent Assembly, one of our own original demands, and to imagine we could win public attention trying to pose ourselves as an alternative Assembly was unreal and showed a dismal failure to grasp the spirit of the times. The country had at last won its freedom, an incredible victory under the leadership of the Congress. It was its supreme hour of triumph. To offer a frontal alternative to it in the framing of the Constitution was a psychological blunder. The alternatives could have been offered by collaboration from *within* instead of leaving the crucial constitution making to non politicals, moderate professionals like lawyers, doctors, and even some conservative elements that the Congress collected to broad-base the Constituent Assembly, ending in several unhappy results. The humiliating defeat of the Socialists in the very first elections to the new Parliament was an inevitable corollary to this. The original Party could hardly hold itself. Several of the prominent Socialists strayed away one by one. My own connection had ended much earlier in 1948 though for other reasons.

The Tripura Congress Session had left me rather dispirited. There was no indication of any purposeful activity in sight. I was equally perturbed that my son's studies could not be saved from constant interruptions. Moreover Gandhiji's very earnest talk on this topic had convinced me that I should do something about it. For his part he desired to qualify in Communication Engineering for which there was no scope in India, so I decided to take him abroad. He could thus get the facility he needed as also be able to carry on without interruptions.

The All India Women's Conference, taking advantage of my intended trip, requested me to represent it at the international session of the Alliance of Women due to meet in Copenhagen.

Once again I was refused a passport, something I had not bargained for. Maybe I was lulled into a sense of well being by the Congress ministries in function. Unexpectedly Rajagopalachari who was the Chief Minister of Madras came to Mangalore on a visit just at this point. I ragged him, calling his ministry a 'Shadow Cabinet'. He was pricked and asked what was shadowy about it ? I related to him this rebuff. He looked startled and annoyed. He advised me to apply again making no mention of this refusal. Within a week the passport was in my hands.

8

Enroute I decided to take advantage of the invitation from Egypt and break journey. I looked forward to meeting its leaders and the rank and file freedom fighters. In the anti-imperialist vortex, India had attained a notable position. In addition to our civil disobedience movement which won laurels, Pandit Nehru's recent trip to Europe and his avowed stand against colonial and the rising Nazi forces and identification with subject people, our support to China against Japanese aggression and India's boycott of Japanese goods, had served to build India up as a powerful manifestation of subject people's champion.

Gandhiji's avowal of the close identity of the Indian freedom struggle with the world colonial struggle had added a universal dimension to our objectives and actions. Gandhiji had touched the global nerve centre when he proclaimed that India's freedom would mean the liberation of British colonies and by chain reaction, of other subject people. That the Indian struggle was crucial in a larger context, he never tired of reminding us and the world.

It was late night as our boat approached the dock at Port Said when I saw a number of small boats with sparkling lights crowding up to it. Our Arab hosts got us off within minutes and I found myself right in the midst of the twinkling boats, the air shaken by vibrant slogans from young throats. Our hosts explained they were the youth wing of the Wafd party, very excited over a fraternal visit of a freedom fighter from India. They had hit on this novel reception since the boat was docking late at night.

Madame Charaoui Pasha had arranged with the Wafd leaders to let me stay with her even though I had come on their invitation.

I was worn out after the stormy crossing across the Arabian Sea in the early South-West monsoon. So when I landed I was allowed immediately to tumble into bed. When I woke up and looked around I was sure I was dreaming, so closed my eyes and dozed off again. Bright sun was pouring in when I got out of bed. No I was not dreaming, I was wide awake but in an Arabian Nights Palace, so it seemed to me. An exquisite breakfast of sweet melon, russet red grapes, crisp melting toast, fresh dates that put me in mind of palm jaggery at home, was spread out before me. The only object that seemed real and not part of the hazy dream was my hostess sitting opposite me, solid, down to earth, inspite of her exquisitely chiselled face and statuesque figure, Madame Charaoui Pasha. With her keen sensitive nature, she had modelled her house on the traditional Arab architecture. The furniture was Syrian, with the fine lacy carved patterns. The tiniest, the most innocuous item was delicately chosen. But there was much more to learn that looking at a fancy mansion.

She was, as has already been noted, a renowned pioneer who had led the women to throw off their veil and assert their rights to equality in every sphere. She was also a staunch nationalist who actively participated in the national political activities. She was able to intelligently brief me on the current situation. This is the picture she drew for me:

With the passing away of Zaghlul Pasha and his associates, the Wafd had lost its teeth for lack of dynamic leadership. When an organisation attains a reputation, then loosens its muscles, standards get lower, its dynamics grow limp, all and sundry slip in like way farers, and try to manipulate the rudder.

I had several meetings with Abdel el Nahas Pasha who headed the Wafd Party, and his colleagues, with far too much time taken up with parties and feasting. I found genuine pleasure in getting to know the women, who generously parted the curtain of formality and revealed deeper scenes. The most enticing adventures were around the Museums. They laid out an endless panorama of exotic scenes of ancient Egypt, like the fabulous Tutenkhamen treasures.

Though the Wafd leaders indulged in many brave words, there seemed very little fight about them. They were what one might urbanely name the typical bourgeois politicians. Patriotic no doubt but too firmly set in a smooth life of ease. It was therefore not surprising that they could not rise to meet the menacing war situation nor the heavy complexities the war presented. Once again the same treacherous wire pulling of the 1918 post-war days was repeated from 1945 onwards. Nahas Pasha and the Wafd Party failed again especially when the critical situation called for a strong leadership to replace the collapsing monarchy and build a new Egypt. It was a young military leader that stepped in to take over the reins.

I left Cairo however on an inspiring note for I met one legendary person I was keen to talk with: Emir Abd El Krim, the hero of the Moroccan, rather North African battle for freedom, now an exile in Cairo. Though I was warned he generally refuses to meet outsiders, I was sure a freedom fighter from India would be welcome. So we met.

The man who extended a hand and said welcome with a most genial smile was short, solidly built, with the kindliest round bead-like eyes which as we talked began to get shot through by sharp glints like sparks of steel. There was however an air of benevolence about him accentuated by his long cream gown which seasoned warriors from the rugged mountains of the Riff, whose valiant battles and curving fortunes had made world history. His skin still so fair and untanned, shining in its delicacy, like a flower-like sheen, seemed to belie his warrior role.

As he unfolded his life story it got even more difficult to keep a tag on his rebel image. He had risen to be the Chief Justice after a distinguished legal career. I literally sat up to find out how a man administering law at the highest level turned a national rebel and went truly into wilderness and now alas into exile. 'The Spanish pretended to sign an agreement to respect Morocco's autonomy which was only a ruse to grab more and more territory. So I gave a call to throw them out. It was a long, hard struggle for we were a small army, ill-equipped, nevertheless our spirit triumphed. We literally drove them into the sea. The treacherous French, though they don't love the Spanish, flung themselves into the fray, superior in numbers and arms, and beat us back. The imperialists will hold together to preserve their illgotten gains. This was just as the Paris Peace Conference closed, blatantly spilling lies all over the globe of how they had fought the 'Great War to make the world safe for freedom. We lost when victory was within our grasp after several years of hard fighting, it was too tragic, too ironical'. His voice that had been so quiet and prepossessed, quivered then regained its composure. 'Along with many patriots I was exiled to the Reunion Island in the Indian Ocean for 20 years, where we shared our lives with several great patriots like the King of Annam, a queen from Madagascar and other noted freedom fighters, all condemned for the crime of loving their country.' 'Were the conditions very harsh?' I ventured to interrupt. 'The first ten years were the hardest. We were completely cut off from the world. We were allowed only religious books, no newspapers or journals. That was the condition on which the war in Morocco was called off and the price I had to pay to save my people from well nigh annihilation. Preparations for World War II brought some excitement into the Island to break the monotony—more ironies of life.' 'How did the exile end?' I asked. 'Egypt took the initiative in negotiating for my release. Egypt will occupy a key position in the coming world conflict. So the Western powers, especially France which had exiled me, desired to win Egypt's good will. So I got my release, on condition I settled in Cairo and did not return to Morocco, I agreed for I have still to fulfill my life's dream—a free Morocco. The North African Liberation Committee has its head quarters here and we are pursuing our struggle. Our movement is strong—the days of colonialism are numbered. The coming war will end it, I have no doubt.' 'You know of the Indian struggle,' I asked. 'Yes. You have the advantage of the inspiration and guidance of the greatest leader in the world today. I know of his sympathy and support for all the freedom fighters everywhere and we are grateful. Take my good wishes to your people and your great leader.' He then took both my hands and bowed low over them. I looked back at him as my car moved away, a silent rock-like figure that had weathered several fierce storms, so confident he would go back to a free Morocco. 'Of course' he had said, when I asked him, with a light laugh which sat naturally on his face. As my car sped on the picture faded like an epoch crowded with many stirring events.

Today not only the Arab world but all international life is beset by the evil effects of 1945-46 global decisions. The scenes get even clearer if we look further back to 1918 and the disastrous peace treaty of Versailles and the deep wounds it cut that continued to bleed until we were inexorably led into World War II:

'We glibly keep reciting 'history repeats itself' because history is a nitwit incapable of learning from past history, and if history is to be our hope, the good Lord save us', wrote the noted English writer Douglas Reed when Ethiopia was betrayed and the League of Nations died. Many years later when I was sitting in one of the marble halls of the League buildings in Geneva, serving on one of those ghostly U.N. commissions, an old press man said to me: 'Today this hall is a tomb filled only with despondent echoes.'

It is hardly known today, may even seem improbable it could have happened, that Balgangadhar Tilak was deputed by Indian nationalists to the Peace Conference at Paris in 1918. The Government of India, needless to say, refused him a passport. He addressed a letter to Clemenceau one of the 'big men' in the Peace Conference, to impress on him the importance of India and the Indian case. Clemenceau like most politicians and arbiters of the World's fate, was a petty provincial minded men, soaked in bitter hatred of Germans over their seizure of Alsace-Lorraine, a French province he came from, and annexed by Germany after inflicting a crushing defeat on France in *1870*! All he thirsted for now was a vendetta for that. It is the wrong memories that seem to remain green forever.

The disastrous decisions of the Paris Peace Conference after World War I left indelible bitterness that continued to rage. For not only were President Wilson's Fourteen Points promising everything to everybody massacred, fresh perversions were inducted into the global body politic, that continued to plague the world.

The role of the British in all crucial situations was ignominous. Having lured subject people into supporting them on promises of freedom after World War II, the Allies as victorsly ruthlessly countered every freedom struggle whether it be in the Russian upheaval, the Arab cauldron or the Turkish revolution, though these struggles were against decadence, corruption or imperialist rule, and in every case against their own oppressors and not against any of these Western powers. Their struggles won world wide people's sympathy. But the Arabs had unitedly struggled against Turkish rule, now their land was fragmented into artificial irrational units for distribution amongst the victors. Their aspiration for their consolidation into a powerful unit was shattered. The entire West Asian region still continues to suffer from the aftermath of this, just like the fragmentation of the Indian subcontinent, of Ireland, so down the ages leaving behind long trails of misery.

The world is more familiar with the Czarist Russian scene due to Communist propaganda, but the pre-war Ottoman setting is rather obscure. I shall only expose here a tiny fragment of that situation *vis-a-vis* the big Western Powers. When the Ottoman Empire was in its last gasps, Sultan Mohmed, the *Sick Man* as he was notoriously designated, was unmindful of this crisis, involved in one of his usual passionate obsessions, this time with the daughter of his palace gardener, already engaged to a man of her choice. The Sultan long past seventy, forcibly married and bundled her up to go off into exile in Italy. That was typically illustrative of the Ottoman empire, now a mere debris. One happy fall out of this was this captive bride's return to liberty and her glad reunion with her rightful fiancee, patiently waiting for her!

The Paris Peace Conference is a standing example of an astounding event that repeats itself over and over again, how three or four men divide up the globe as though it were a ripe melon, national frontiers wiped out and redrawn and the fate of millions determined by their idiosyncracies, petty personal fancies, and irrational prejudices, above all an insatiable greed. The result, a most unsavoury mess. A seasoned American diplomat adviser to President Wilson related to him one of Nasruddin Hoca's pithy tales as illustrative of these goings on at the Paris Conference. Hoca was the Turkish Birbal and had endless stories overtly against himself but covertly at others who could not be publicly named. This is how the story went: one full moon night Nasruddin happened to look down a well and was distressed to see his beloved moon at the bottom. 'I must save the moon', he decided. So he went on drawing out buckets of water, but the moon still continued to lie at the bottom. In desperation he made one big tug, lost his balance and fell on his back. And when he looked there was his beautiful moon coolly glowing in the sky. He gave a gentle pat on his back, saying 'Never mind, never mind, though it was a tough job, *I have* at last saved the moon'. 'Mr. Wilson this story faithfully represents your peace efforts at this Conference' concluded the diplomat. A veteran pressman who vividly acted the story for me in Istanbul, said Wilson laughed ruefully and agreed, and became an ardent admirer of Nasruddin. Turkey has raised a monument to this popular story teller!

It had not struck me that during a purely personal visit I may be called upon to play a political role in England. I was coming there after over eighteen years. Never having treasured any sentimental memories of that country I continued as detatched as ever. But Krishna Menon and the India League had other ideas. So when I arrived I was confronted with a ready made schedule laid out to meet a number of people. Several that I met as by rote, meant little or not at all. Some I valued and still treasure their memory.

I met several Labour Party personalities, especially those who I knew through their writings or their avowed sympathy for the Indian struggle. Amongst the most lovable I would rank Fenner Brockway, who apart from his being friendly to India was of outstanding character who stood for his principles and suffered to uphold them. He was the first Member to move a Resolution in Parliament to grant independence to India at a time when the English public took India as its backyard possession. He was an active pacifist and was kept in prison for his anti-war propaganda during the World War and subjected to severe persecution, denied even reading and writing materials. Referring to this he explained: 'I think what sustained me all through is the depth of my convictions. I am not religious in the usual sense. To seek, to work for freedom of peoples, for peace, social justice, these have been my way of reaching towards a fuller life.' He talked very feelingly of his long association with India, going back to 1911 when he first met Pandit Nehru as a student and was impressed by his power of political analysis, his continued highlighting of the Indian problems in the 'Labour Leader', the then organ of the Independent Labour Party. His most abiding memory was of Gandhiji's extraordinary magnetic, spiritual power (as he termed it) that came from a rare experience he had when Gandhiji visited him as he lay ill in an Indian hospital. As Gandhiji held his tired hand, he began to feel soothed and revived as though a power had passed to him.

His unique service in my opinion was the report of the Prison Enquiry Committee which he promoted through the Labour Party research department. So many of us political figures and workers have suffered in prison, gone through inane prison routine, experienced its dehumanising rules and regulations. All this though once strongly registered on our minds, was brushed off from the memory slate after we were released. Not so to Brockway, who doggedly pursued the problems of the prison through this enquiry. Four hundred witnesses gave evidence, of whom 300 were ex-prisoners. Some distinguished personalities such as Lord Olivier, Mr. & Mrs. Sydney Webb, Margory Fry, the

Principal of Somerville College, Oxford, the Director of BBC, George Bernard Shaw unofficially assisted in this. An indifferent ex-prisoner my conscience pricked me and I became very avid to at least glance through this bulky report of 30,000 words. Even at a cursory glance I saw it was very exhaustive, thorough and so telling. It became a standard work and stirred the public into a conviction that reforms had to be introduced.

One of Brockway's several ventures on behalf of India that occurred just before the launching of the Quit India movement, was a motion for release of political prisoners in India, and the Labour Party's recognition of India's right to independence to be followed by a Round Table Conference in which the real representatives of people, not Viceroy's nominees, would participate. Wedgewood Benn who had been introduced to me as a genuine friend of India, garbled rather than enumerated Labour's stand on this motion. He began by declaring he knew little of India, that a government's resolve could only be announced through the Viceroy of India, that release of political prisoners would be determined on merit, not politics.

Brockway raised the India issue again after the Quit India movement pointing to the ironical picture of India's prisons seething with prisoners seeking freedom for their country, and demanded a discussion on it. The Speaker refused and ordered him to sit down. When he refused and persisted with his demand, he was named by an angry Prime Minister, led out by a security man and released. A colleague of Brockway's who related this incident to me added that there was a little sequel to it which touched me. When he remonstrated with Brockway the futility of his battling with a set of blind insensitive rulers, prompt came his reply 'At least India will know she has one friend here,' and he had to concede reluctantly.

Brockway had also direct cultural interests. He created the Masses Stage and the Film Guild for the common people, of which Miles Mallesan, a noted playwright became the director. Plays never attempted before, delving deep into the people's lives, revealing sights generally curtained off from audiences were put on. A special feature was the attempt to attract amateur talent into this alcove. I was delighted to find a galaxy of noted artists like Sybil Thorndyke, Lewis Carson, Elsa Lancaster, Milton Rosmer and a host of others at the Strand every Sunday. Bernard Shaw, John Galsworthy, Laurence Houseman offered the group Special One Act Plays. The plays were reinforced by appropriate films.

Amongst the other Labour Party leaders was James Maxton whom I had first met at the Frankfurt Congress of the League against Imperialism. In a medley of varied personalities, he stood out, the picture of the old time conventional English artist, long unkept hair falling all over his face, and a practised act of brushing it aside, loosely hanging clothes, but most typical of all, flashing eyes and fierce gestures. He was reputedly the strong man of the Independent Labour Party and now international Chairman of the League. He had then expressed great regret over the miserable let down of the Indian cause by even the Labour Party and was in fact advising the Independent Labour Party to break away from it.

When I met him in London he was Chairman of the Independent Labour Party. I saw that he had built himself up as a courageous man of deep convictions. It was therefore a terrible shock to find him support the Munich Pact and even congratulate the Prime Minister on it ! Of course this speech of his also contained powerful indictment of war-making imperialism, which to me made the whole speech even more hollow.

With Sir Stafford Cripps, leader of the Socialist League, my relations began on a personal note and continued so, as we met through a mutual friend. He treated me warmly and informally as though we were old acquaintances. He was cast in a delicate frame, was palpably sensitive. He struck me more as a humanitarian, filled with good intentions, who could argue his case with the earnestness of a crusader, but I could not see him marching in a crusade. His keenness to bring about an *entente* between the Independent Labour Party, the Communist Party and his Socialist League (a body he had fostered) showed up his lack of grasp of the basic politics of each of these vastly differing bodies.

I found in him a sincere friend with a personal concern for me. He helped me to make my impending trip to Scandinavia pleasant and fruitful. He wrote personally to the Socialist and Labour Cooperative leaders, literary and art personalities to introduce me. He also advised me to stay in the hotels or hostels run by the labour unions to enable me to mingle closely with them, all of which made my trip more rewarding.

I had already learnt of the varied educational, recreational, cultural activities conducted by labour unions for the worker's benefit, in the West European countries. In fact it was in a fine theatre hall owned by a German Labour Union that I attended an important public gathering. There were regular schools for labour workers, especially for higher education.

Now I was told of the Special Vacation trips and Holiday Homes, with special rates, to encourage workers to take their holiday with ease, particularly foreign trips, and meet with their counterparts in other lands, sponsored by the labour unions.

Sir Stafford and I did not meet during his Mission to India in 1942, we just exchanged letters of courtesy. As a long-time advocate of India's freedom, his present role was disheartening. Gandhiji's description of his offer as a post-dated cheque on a falling bank seemed apt. I had in my last letter that must have reached Delhi as the talks broke down, told him I was involved in running a women's training camp to prepare them for the coming struggle. In his farewell letter he welcomed my preoccupation to train the Indian women 'For future eventualities and I wish you every success in your present work.'

It was Krishna Menon who had suggested my meeting Palme Dutt, the Secretary General of the Communist Party, 'I think you should' he decided positively. So we met. I had heard of Dutt being lightly called the 'Ascetic politician' or a 'Buddhist Monk'. I disagreed with both. He looked too cold for a spiritual man whose usual temper is warm. He talked in rather a pontifical manner, which to me was too impersonal to carry any conviction. Someone who had the same reaction as I, described it as reciting one of Moscow's creeds. I would not go as far as that, for I knew of him as one of the top Communist theoriticians, who had attained important standing in the International Communist World. The cut of his face had faint suggestions of his Indian ancestry. But the smooth polish of his demeanour, the mesmeric gestures were pronouncedly European.

He talked in a soft, polite tone. As I had anticipated, his remarks revolved round the much discussed *United Front* and its corallary the Socialist Unity. 'I believe amongst Indian Socialist leaders, Jayaprakash Narayan had advocated it.' I assented. 'It was on that principle that Communists were admitted into the Socialist Party', I replied. 'Good', he said in the some pontifical voice, 'that was very wise. Now the need has become even more crucial with the rising menace of Nazism.' And so he went on until he took leave in the same smooth polite way.

At this time the Western World was torn by this pressure of the need for a United Front, boosted by the emergence of such a government in France, as the war fever kept rising. There were endless wrangles on loyalty to one's country versus loyalty to Socialism, anti-war struggle and socialist unity, in which the biggest brains seemed caught up. These discussions were serious and many seemed confused over the implications. I hardly realised then how deadly earnest the dilemma was until I learnt later that just as war was being declared the desperate Socialists were smuggling messages across the frontiers declaring their solidarity with their comrades, and their stand against war.

Bernard Shaw, after a ruthless exposure of British imperialism, concluded: 'Since the German policies are equally infamous, and as England is now involved in a war with Germany, they must fight it out.' While I watched these emotional turmoils in which the Western World was caught, I witnessed another anguish, even more stricken, of those who had been through World War I, which covered a wide range of individuals and organisations. I recall a vivid picture of a distinguished army general holding his head, saying in a voice of despair. 'I never thought it would happen again—never'. It brought home to me what a short span 20 years was in the march of history. How prophetic Lenin's verdict was when he declared: 'Any peace treaty arrived at by imperialist governments only sows the seeds of future wars.'

I had not quite realised until my London visit that Sir Oswald Mosley and John Becket who took the lead in forming the Union of Fascists, had been active Labour Party members. Later they changed the name into the National Socialist Pary, modelled on Hitler's demagogy. Equally traumatic was it to see P.J. Dollan who suffered as a conscientious objecter in World War I, now knighted for his efforts in supporting World War II !

The genuine political elite in my opinion, like Brockway and his mates, expressed their unhappiness over the downward slide among several of their parliament members. 'Unless they set hard consistent tasks for themselves, they tend to fill in their idle hours in club rooms' they bemoaned over the rapid demoralisation. Keir Hardie the founder of the Labour Party, when in parliament, sensing this, had forbidden club rooms to his partymen as this was where those at a loose-end congregated to sip drinks and indulge in desultory gossip. Particularly as young members were glamourised when they could rub shoulders with 'important personalities', and tended sometimes to stray away from their moorings.

Quite apart and away in a class by herself was Agatha Harrison, who grew grey in her earnest devotion to India. Ostensibly she held no high ranking office, nevertheless she had easy access to the highest in the land. Her good deeds for India alone would fill a fat volume. I think her sheer unadulterated *goodness* gave her a status and position, above all a rank which could not be measured by any known yardstick. She sought nothing for herself, to her the good deed was an end in itself which made her a very rare person. True she had become a Quaker, but that itself was no answer. Why was she vouchsafed to us? How and where did this devotion ignite? Though she lived in England and made occasional trips to India, it were as though her one eye was always on India, a part of her heart beat here. For when we needed aid from outside she was sure to be there. It was almost uncanny. For instance Pandit Nehru's sudden release from prison in 1936 to be at his wife's bedside in Switzerland was by her thoughtful intervention, when all efforts in India had failed. She helped me too during my English visit as she did so many others. Gandhiji had infinite trust in her. When he asked her to work for achieving mutual understanding between India and Britain, she told me, she wondered how she could do it. She asked him who would guide her and he simply said: God will direct your steps. She felt he knew that she was ready for such a mission. At the start she had wondered if she would know which way to turn at a given situation, but now she seemed to know just what she should do. 'That is why I agreed', she explained to me. Now she rests as an abiding figure in my consciousness for her passing away simply would not register on me. We had all taken her so much for granted. I cannot bring myself to accept she is not lurking just beyond the threshold, with one ear to the door, listening intently in case we need her.

Amongst writers in this political group was Zilliacus whom I got to know. Though physically short in stature, Zilliacus seemed to tower like a giant. He wrote powerfully with great sincerity on the inadequacies, and weaknesses of both his party and the rulers. Bernard Shaw described him as the only international minded politician of note then. His single passion was peace on which he dilated at length and which was under grave threat when we met. 'We solemnly sign covenants, charters to keep the peace but cynically continue to juggle with the balance for power and indulge in a reckless arms race. There is obviously no serious desire for peace, for it cuts at the very foundation of mutual aid and inter-defence,' he explained why peace eluded the world. When Labour was in power after World War II ended, he fearlessly arraigned its foreign policy, accusing the Labour Party of betryaing its principles.

A few interludes lent a little comedy to our visit. My son, keen on Communications, was eager to visit the BBC Station but he was refused as he was 'under age'. He was only fifteen. I appealed to Lionel Fielden who had just retired after a commendable stint in India as Director-General of the All India Radio. He had not only a commendable professional career, but was one of the few English officers who was for a National Government and propagated India's cause in England. Fielden readily intervened with the BBC and got permission for the young man to accompany me. In fact he came personally to escort us around.

Another amusing incident was a summons from the Scotland Yard to my son to present himself. They put the usual questions: why he was in London, duration of stay, programme, etc. The impression he got was that they had not expected a teenager, and were definitely taken by surprise. They had only been perturbed by the arrival of a Chattopadhyay—shades of the uncle Virendranath.

The International Women's Conference in Copenhagen proved a source of aggravation. While righteous wrath was directed against Nazism, a tight curtain was drawn over imperialism, as colonial problems were treated as 'internal matters of the ruling country.' In other words the ruling country possessed a legal right to rule its colonies. Madame Charaouni Pasha and I were again the only rightful representatives of our people. Utterly frustrated by our failure, we walked out of the Conference. I straightway sent a strongly worded directive to the Indian Women's Conference to promptly disaffiliate itself from this international body, which it did.

My son, who had accompanied me, and I were lodged with a Danish family who I discovered were real fisherfolk; I first took them as traders in fish. But they explained they actually caught fish. The young son gallantly offered to take us on one of the boats going fishing. It was our first experience on a foreign fishing expedition right out into the sea, in what was to me a huge fishing boat. As children we used to sometimes take a short lift in the little boats in Mangalore, then a biggish fishing town.

Farming was still the most respected vocation. Special facilities provided for imparting general education to farmers in special short term courses, were of great interest. I wondered how such a pattern could be worked out in our country.

Cooperatives were of special interest for a study of their organisation in Sweden which I covered through short trips for detailed studies. A substantial portion of production and marketing was in the cooperative section which opened up for me new vistas for cooperative work in India, which stood me in good stead after the 1947 debacle.

We rode to Oslo in what was called the 'Iron train', for it carried nothing but iron ore. The young fisherman had fixed this up as an adventure. We had to perch on a small seat just behind the engine meant for helpers, and we rattled on as though on a novel merry-go-round.

I saw here for the first time one of the highly mechanised factories where enormous machines rattled on all sides, yet you rarely saw a workman.

The biggest thrill here was of course the midnight sun, something I had dreamed of when I read of Lapland and this novelty. Lapland was wide stretches in those days, dotted by groups of shepherds in their picturesque costumes, grazing sheep. I came across town people on hiking trips going up to Geldepiggen, the highest peak there. We too began the trek. There were rest houses at convenient distances, very welcome, for the nights were bitterly cold. At the very first stop we found the sun lingering on and on and we wandered in the open late at night drinking in this unusual scene. At midnight my son took out his camera and easily got snaps of the setting, the surrounding countryside bathed beautifully in this unusual light.

We just managed to get back to London as the war broke out. Overnight I had to make alternative plans. I fell back on our friend, philosopher and guide Krishna Menon. Though he remained a controversial figure all through his life, he was an unforgettable personality. The India League which he headed and ran from the late Twenties, was more than a mini Indian Embassy, for the prestige it enjoyed and the confidence it won. It kept India before the British with clarity, force and insistence, reflecting Krishna Menon's own devotion and sincere adherence to the cause of India's freedom. His fearless advocacy often carried the day for India. There was also a soft and kindly side to his nature though he brusquely tried to cover it up.

Krishna Menon with his unfailing optimistic manner helped me decide to shift speedily to America, and get my son settled in a Communication Course there. He was sure I would have plenty of opportunity to strike a few blows for India, in fact he was sure, there they would be effective.

In the meantime, while waiting for passages, we lived through a weird existence. We were enjoined to carry a gas mask with us always, and whenever the siren sounded to bolt into the nearest air-raid shelter. Something within me revolted at this exercise. Psychologically I felt a grave sense of humiliation and defeat. There was a sense of pride when we flew into the sky, higher and higher as though we would soon touch the stars. Now we were scrambling into scooped out holes like frightened rats.

The political atmosphere too got murkier as the general public woke up to the fact that these very countries now arrayed against Hitler and Nazism had helped in building up the war machinery by steadily supplying armaments to Germany.

Into this depressing gloom came a sudden ray of sunshine, an invitation from the Elmhirsts to visit them at the famed Dartington Hall. They had been told of me by Uday Shanker, the famous dancer. Mr. Leonard Elmhirst had long been deeply interested in India, and like most India devotees had had a long sojourn at Shantiniketan with Tagore. Mrs. Dorothy Elmhirst was to take me down personally to Dartington.

Like to most outsiders Dartington Hall was associated for me with progressive education and arts and crafts. But when I arrived there I was stunned by the vast complex with an infinite variety of activities. It was one of the largest medieval houses built in the 14th Century. Though it went through a period of dilapidation, the new architect had with great concern adapted the old structures to new purposes boldly but with the minimum of distortions to the original pattern. What is even more astounding, every part of this mansion has been in use for

600 years without a break. The magnificent hall was memorable as having been one of the haunts of Richard the Lionheart with his Crusader knights who sat here and made merry. The open-air theatre, now in correct use was in days of yore the 'tiltyard'—tournament arena—where medieval knights held their jousts. It brought that romantic (to me rather unreal) age closer.

The landscaping of the 35 acres alone called for a laborious study. Its general elegance here was heightened by a careful layout of trees, shrubs, lawn, to show off the natural contours of the land. Then the vistas were so designed that when you strolled towards the house it seemed the medieval building were beckoning to invite you in. The garden had another remarkable feature to provide a different blaze of colours at different times of the year. Similarly were colours employed in painting the structure, so that even the stone surface blended with its border softly. There was a sensitive and meticulous approach to the smallest detail that filled one with a pleasurable warmth. I understood Dorothy had directed this entire operation. She explained, 'it is like acquiring an antique jewel ravaged by age, to gently coax its intrinsic beauty to reveal itself. That is all I did.'

The many sided activities of Dartington were even more important. The Elmhirsts wanted to show how security of employment and economic vitality might be maintained in a rural area—more, they wanted to create a working community that provided opportunity for stimulation and functioning of individual talent and development that brings a sense of inner satisfaction.

Leonard and Dorothy related to me how they went about it. 'It meant a venture without compartments, without a cultural divide, without social or economic class confrontation, and of course none of what may be called generation gap, avoid the fragmentation of the existing cohesive rural communities that inevitably results from too much specialisation. We want those in residence working here to experience a wider sense of parameter to their duties, wider purpose and relationship with one another, than we feel there commonly is. None is allowed to feel isolated, each touches a good many others at different points. We did not mean this to be an adventure in ideas. It has been our sincere wish to provide ample scope for a full life for everyone who shares in this enterprise'. They also told me that Leonard's four years with Tagore in rural development evolving Sriniketan, which was to combine the best of the East and the West, had been an enriching experience.

'Arts have always been regarded as Central to the Dartington, and as an indispensible element in the growth of both the individual and Society. It is Central to the College of Arts which provides courses in theatre, music, art and design. The evaluation is determined by the benefit derived from it by the whole Community'.

There is also a summer school of Music which lays emphasis on community singing and a definite effort is made to popularize such music sessions. The Beaford center has a photographic archive and organises programmes of music, theatre, dance and film run by the Arts Council, a pioneer in cultural animation in a rural setting. Equally have Dartington's industrial and commercial enterprises expressed its basic commitment to the economic viability of rural areas, and the creation of employment. The tweed mill, the glass works, joinery, cider press are all parts of Dartington Hall Corporation. The joinery is a big complex making furniture and even boats, called Honnor Marine.

I visited Dartington Hall again in 1976 and found it had maintained the same integrated personality, activities had however expanded.

Once again I ran into the old political hurdle. The U.S. Consulate declined to give me a visa on the advice of the British. I explained that in view of the war, I was now forced to return to India. As the Atlantic route was hazardous, especially as I had my son with me, I had to go via the States to cross the Pacific. Agatha as usual pulled strings and I got a transit visa with two months stop over, as passages were not easily available.

We got berths on a Dutch boat. I was shocked to experience even worse colour discrimination here than on an English boat. By 1939 the English conduct towards Indians had begun to tone down. Here it was raw, crude, iniquitous, hit one like a physical blow. It is not surprising that the Dutch kept a grip on their colonies, even long after the British began to '*unburden*' themselves. This is one of the ugliest memories I have of racial antipathy.

When I stepped on the American soil, I did enter a new world, also then still a younger world. There rose the tall skyscrapers challenging the skies, that put me in mind of high structures raised by adventurous children with wooden playing blocks. Pandita Ramabai has recorded that America made one lively for there seemed to be an electric current in the soil. The people seem restless, such an enormous blending of diverse people and cultures could hardly have produced subdued temperaments. In the dim morning light stood the Statue of Liberty holding aloft the torch to guide the wanderer seeking shelter. I wondered how many Americans themselves remember the appeal in the inscription at its base:

> Give me your tired, your poor
> The huddled masses yearning to breathe free,
> The wretched refuge of your teeming shore,
> Send these, the tempest.tost to me,
> I lit my lamp beside the golden door.

It was found necessary to apply the axe to this at some stage. The worst sufferers in this had been the Indians who were not only debarred from entry while others got quotas but also deprived of citizenship, even though a number of Asians from various countries could enjoy them. Batches long settled were harshly shipped back. This pointed discrimination was obviously the result of British pressure. For many of these Indians were politically astir. Even the Supreme Court of the day had made a ridiculous interpretation of this by stating that to a man in the street Indians would not appear as belonging to the Caucasian race, and only they were permitted entry. This was the main problem in which the Indian community was enmasked.

I was plunged into almost a round-the-clock programmes. I had invitations through some personalities. Others came through bodies like the League of Womens Voters, Civil Liberties Union, League for Peace and Freedom and a whole host of them.

The course the women's movement had taken in the New World was to me a tremendous surprise. For one had pictured only the Pioneer women, of their battling along with men the wild inhospitable land in unedifying conditions and winning fierce battles with nature, and naturally endowed with equal rights. That the premier body should be the League of Women voters seemed inevitable for every State had denied the women this fundamental right. They had no legal rights either. Even more surprising they could not testify in a court which could convict them with ease! They were debarred from colleges and an attempt to enter a law college at Harvard was withdrawn after it led to mob protesters raising a riot, as a female attorney would be against common law and the 'Delicacy of the Female Sex would be endangered,' and their influence on 'administration of justice would be *questionable*'. Even the Supreme Court decried women straying into other callings as a gross violation of the laws of nature. The pioneer women doctors met with worse fate. The medical societies forbade its members consulting women doctors, nor could these doctors get a druggist to fill their prescription.

The battle for citizenship rights for women is a grand saga starting with Susan B. Anthony casting a vote in 1872 without the Constitutional right and therefore being convicted, ending in the adoption of the Constitutional amendment to grant women citizenship rights in 1918. Through those years the women were subjected to ruthless physical attacks, abuses, prison terms, dubbed as *Cannibals*.

True I had been aware of the traumatic experiences of Suffragists in England. I had not expected this in the States, especially under President Wilson. Though women had progressed considerably they still continued to suffer under various discriminatory laws in the different states on inheritance, property ownership, rights over children, etc. One still detected a double moral code maintained by law. I was told a spicy incident that occurred in 1840, at an International Anti-Slavery Congress in London. Three women delegates from America were rejected on grounds of sex. A compromise was offered by the male organisers under which the three women would be allowed to sit but hidden behind a screen, in complete silence. Why call keeping women behind a screen a purely Oriental Custom?

But in the New World which I was now entering women had come a long way. There were for instance special courses for fathers with diplomas under the title of 'Prepared Parent', to enable both the parents to share the domestic and family duties.

I found the country stimulating, and I could learn both from the positive as well as the destructive characteristic. Under the former a formidable social awakening had led to purposeful socio-economic activities to combat relentlessly the volcanic power of the billion dollar firms like giant corporations, combines, sweat shops and the like.

An assuring feature, to me new and gratifying, was the coagulating of social sciences as a permanent lever to direct human affairs and become an integral part of the nation's daily life. The vague 'Social Work' was no more a leisure hour diversion of the rich or haphazard experiments of the amateurs. Social work was directed by experts and executed by trained workers.

The New Deal initiated under President Roosevelt had activised several progressive measures, though not radical, devised out of the broken strands of a crisis more as a temporary bridge to cross a flood. It certainly was proving a break like the first streak of light peeping out of inky blue sky.

The wide all pervasive activities under *Home Science*; the Americans prefer the term *Home Economics*, impressed me, especially the rural extension work which included even construction of houses with modern amenities, remodelling old ones, full instructions on the use of modern appliances that made life less burdensome for the housewife, etc.

As Roosevelt himself answered his critics in typical American phraseology: 'We may not know where we are going but we are on our way'. The carrying of the benefits of modern science and technology to the rural households to transform the lives of those women by-passed by the rushing mainstream, stirred new hopes in me. I did not realise then they were vain hopes. Over 40 decades have rolled by since, and what we are gasping for here is still drinking water for our village women. Equally encouraging was it to see almost as many boys as girls in Home Economics institutions.

I kept meeting political leaders who were interested in India. I got many calls to address gatherings. I had an aversion to talking to light 'club groups', so I declined to take on any lecture contracts, decided to be selective. I was aware it was politically a crucial period. Whatever antiwar tradition America might have tried to build up, it seemed inevitable that this country would sooner than later get embroiled in the conflagration.

Individuals and organisations were pressing me to prolong my stay and try to pose the Indian question before the public more graphically and purposefully in the war context. Was it really worth it, was the big question posed before me. Suddenly it seemed to get solved by itself by a strange quirk of fate. An invitation arrived from Mrs. Roosevelt to meet her and her husband over a tea. The Roosevelts were championed by those I became friendly with loosely known as *liberals*. They functioned with unusual informality. Of course the New Deal was a real asset to strengthen this phase. Mrs. Eleanor Roosevelt to them was the magnet that made the wheels go round. 'The woman in all American history has played the biggest part in public affairs,' was their verdict. She obviously indulged in some unconventional doings and carried them in her long and rapid strides. It was whispered in hushed tones that one had to literally run to keep up with her when she walked. Many other tales, like how when she was knocked down by a car in a New York street, people running to help her had to wave their hands in thin air, for she had already tramped off on her errands.

Her daily column 'My Day' was as avidly seized upon as What the Stars Foretell. Some of it at least to me was of doubtful value. Most unusual for me was her selling commodities like soap, facial cream, through the radio media or answering questions in the Ladies Home Journal. Any such parallel by our Vicerine would have sent shivers through the Empire!

Against this background, meeting her was to me quite an event. Mr. Roosevelt was for America understandably, still a controversial figure, but to me, vaguely rumoured as sympathetic to India's freedom. Mrs. Roosevelt was a big-made woman, with rather a gaunt face, a personality breathing solidity, power, with an air of informality, and kindly manners. I was relieved to find we were by ourselves, except for a couple of secretaries, remote in the background.

Her first question was on the shortness of my visit. I explained the circumstances. She looked rather cross. 'I am not shocked for we do face such discomfiture sometimes. Please do not take this country as inhospitable. Feel free to stay as long as you need or wish to. The visa matter can be easily fixed up. We have a lady minister whom we would like you to meet and if you explain to her your needs, she will have them attended to. We would be most unhappy if you were to pack off as though we turned you out.'

'Your Immigration Department has probably been alerted to beware of me. In war time, patriotism is at a high premium. But in a subject country it is treachery', I commented. I explained how I had originally been point blank denied a visa to the States on the ground that I was an undesirable, likely to cause breach of peace. 'Just visualise the picture of a totally unknown single woman like me able to set a vast country like this on fire. It is obviously their own guilty conscience that distorts their vision and they see a dagger lurking in the bosom of every self-respecting Indian,' I concluded.

Roosevelt who until then had been making a few desultory queries now chimed in in his deep sonorous voice. 'You may be aware that I feel strongly on India's right to freedom. It is one of the questions on which Churchill and I have clashed. The war in my opinion has accelerated the urgency of its solution. He gets impatient over what he feels is our inability to see how vital India is to their successful conduct of the war; and irritated over interfering in their affairs as he calls it. On this, at one point, I had to rather jocularly but appropriately remind him this was natural as at one stage we were in the same position as India now is. In his habitual obstinate note he asked me not to press it least our serious rift get known and undermine our unity, so essential for our success.' I now realised that what was a rumour had reality behind it, as more evidence has since come to light to prove that Roosevelt had nonetheless pursued it by addressing Gandhiji on the eve of Quit India. The letter was suppressed at the Delhi end. Instead the Viceroy directed London to stop American sentimentalists from trying to visit India and leave us to mind our own business. Earlier it was Roosevelt's as well as Chiang Kai Shek's pressure to reconcile India and get her cooperation that is said to have resulted in Sir Stafford Cripps Mission to India. This further convinced me that India would have to fight her own battle and singly, unlike America, to win her freedom.

I sought from Mrs. Roosevelt some details on her work with the youth. She visibly brightened up. 'This I think is the sorest point against me, that I encourage and make common cause with these turbulent elements. What most people forget is that we too are responsible for aggravating this turbulence in them and our earnest efforts should be to contain it.' Hesitatingly I referred to the ire caused by her having some of the youth invited as house guests to the White House. They both laughed, then she replied, 'It was not inviting them so much as letting them sleep in the beds hallowed by Washington, Lincoln and the like.' She broke off rather abruptly and suddenly suggested that I visit her again with ample time in hand, as she would like to take me over the White House. 'You would like to see the House, would you not?' she added. I nodded, 'Especially the hallowed beds.'

I did the tour and Mrs. Roosevelt pointed out the great beds, disturbed by the young people. 'Strangely enough they had mixed feelings. Some thoroughly enjoyed it, some felt out of sorts, one found it so big he felt lost in its vast dimension.' In the period of war hysteria, she probably stood out as the Right Thinker with objectivity, poise, above all a fund of courage, to play her own part in American public affairs.

Over a period we kept meeting and each contact was enlivened afresh, and threw light on her.

I saw that the afflicted human beings moved her to instant aid. Once when she heard of the woes of the miners' families in West Virginia, she drove herself down, sitting incognito at the wheel. As she moved round the hovels, she chatted with the miners' wives who had no clue to her identity. Instant relief to the needy followed, while long term rehabilitation was set afoot for the community.

When I referred to this episode she remarked: 'A country is a collection of human beings. It is this element we have to touch if we desire to serve the country, for it is the most important.'

I once asked her how rewarding were her activities with the youth. 'I try to make them feel they are *necessary*, to stimulate them into involvement with community activities or they will be lost to the country.' Thus under the New Deal was the National Youth Administration got going humming with a wide variety of opportunities for the young to use their talents.

As the war went apace, she grew visibly concerned for the future. 'We must make a better world when this ends, unlike in 1918, or......' and she would throw up her hands. That is why, she explained, she was most keen to see that no encroachments were made on the socio-economic facets of the New Deal.

As I received an invitation to the Presidential inauguration in Washington I attended it. Being mid-January it was a bitter cold day, but keen to see it, I braved the weather, for the Oath-taking ceremony is public. The President delivered his inaugural address starting by underscoring the themes that dominated his previous period, then going on largely to stress the need for strengthening the Nation's defence capabilities in the grim realities of a global war.

The other national public function I witnessed in San Francisco was a Republican Party Congress. It was noisy beyond description, garish, chaotic, people dressed up in weird costumes, more like a typical vaudeville show. I wondered how any serious could be conducted with bands striking up unexpectedly at all odd times, groups marching to their beats, shouting slogans. Evidently all went to schedule, for candidates for Presidency, Vice-Presidency were elected with the whole assembly triumphantly filling the skies with the announcement.

My visa was extended. Now many doors seemed to open out to enable me to travel and see whatever I wished to.

There were what seemed to me several freaks and anomalies in this New World. I had read over the years of the fierce battles of labour to unionise, which was a curious *phenomenon* for a highly industrialised prosperous country. There was the notorious case of a Federal Court imposing a fine of $22,000 on 200 workers for the sole crime of forming themselves into a Union! The scene that met my eye was even queerer. Unions were not only strong, with added power under the New Deal, but equally prosperous. Heads of Unions drew what to me seemed fabulous salaries, not to speak of the other substantial perks they enjoyed, all of which was to me worlds remote from our straggling pitiful workers' unions. I could see how officering unions could become attractive, lucrative careers for the ambitious; as any other business or trade. I kept hearing the popular saying: 'Unions are big business !'

An intriguing experience was a visit to the famous Sing Sing Prison. Warden Lewis Lawes himself met and escorted me round. He had by now attained a great reputation as a rare jail official who had tried to humanise the grim prison life. There was an air of benign refinement about him. I wanted to visit the women's section first. He asked me to take my own time and chat freely with as many inmates as I wished to. I first looked round the cells. Each had newspaper clippings obviously with her own picture prominently pasted over her bed. They were loud and highly coloured descriptions of the accused, the crime, the trial, playing up the interview given on the crime by her, all of which rather shook me up. As I introduced myself as an 'Old Timer', they crowded round me, chummy, free and frank. I asked them about the 'Pin ups'. They narrated their stories with a sense of pride and satisfaction that thoroughly disturbed me. This evidently was roused by the wide publicity the press provided as though they were heroines talking of their successful careers which an avid public lapped up with relish. Naturally they were proud of their pictures, some seemed to flaunt their vanity, giving vent to their tales in boastful tones. Some were deemed big shots! It meant a terrific effort for me to adjust myself to this world of crime as sport and fun.

Warden Lewis led me to his office, placed refreshments and a cup of steaming coffee before me. 'I am sure you need it after that visit,' he said with a smile. 'It was rather an unsettling experience. I was totally unprepared for it,' I admitted. He then asked me about Indian prison life. 'By the way it may amuse you to know that in the official communication I received on your visit, you were described as a 'distinguished prisoner from India', so I presumed you had seen the inside of a jail'. I explained I had a few bouts of imprisonment for political activities. I described briefly the Indian political struggle for freedom. 'I salute you Madam, privileged to be an associate of that great man Gandhi. He inspires all of us.'

I then asked him to tell me about Sing Sing, its strange name that sounds like a lullaby, what distinguishes it as an institution apart. He explained. 'Sing Sing is an American-Indian word Sint Sinks, the name of a local tribe that originally lived here. It may sound strange but this place has a dark distressing history. One of those 'well meaning' reform societies decided to isolate the prisoners as a puritanical measure to make this a Reformist show piece. Each was confined solitarily, which led to a real outbreak of insanity, for even conversation was punished by beating with leather thongs. There was no communication with the outside, no books, papers—most crucial, no laughter. They only looked at the officers faces. '*Unbroken Silence*' was the motto.

'They were ill fed, enjoyed the luxury of eggs twice in a year. The cell was lit high up by slits. The education routine consisted of a teacher coming for two hours after lock up. He went from cell to cell with a lamp. This was considered a great privilege.

'Then the reforms came, slowly but positively. There was a time when a wife could see her husband only on producing her marriage certificate. The efforts are difficult but rewarding for the responses are touching. You know of course that they do not favour preaching morals with pontifical airs, prefer straight talk. Guide rather than try to lead. A warden is burdened with a heavy load of responsibility for in a way he is the arbiter of so many lives, the direct influencing factor. He needs to have not only a deep knowledge of the nature and problems of each, but also assess them accurately so that distortions can be rectified, obstructions that cloud the vision dispersed, and to decide on the right action.'

I recalled Bernard Shaw's stringent comment in the U.K. Jail Enquiry Report, on the qualities the Warden should be endowed with: 'What you look for is a God and no warden today can be expected to be that.' When I repeated this to Warden Lewis he solemnly nodded assent.

The Warden concluded with a confession: 'One added disturbing factor is the large number of visitors we get. As the Tourist Agencies say: Sing Sing is more sought after than the Statue of Liberty.'

An exhilerating trip was to the Southwest. At Phoenix, Arizona, I spent a few days with Margaret Sanger, then called the Mother of Family Planning. Magnificently handsome, always with a radiant smile, soft spoken, gentle, she looked anything but a battle scarred soldier. Nevertheless hers had been a relentless fight against the blind laws of bigotted conservatism, and she had even courted imprisonment for the right of the mother to decide on the size of her family. Sunk in a luxurious padded chair in the fabulous Sanger mansion on the edge of a desert, I listened to Margaret's hair raising tales of her fierce battles. Even sending literature by *mail* was illegal, leave alone vocally advocating birth control. Looking regal on a high-backed chair, her exploits to frustrate the ignominy of the law, sounded incongrous, like bad fairytales. I told her of my learning birth control clinical work in one of her clinics in New York under her deputy, Florence. It was almost a decade later that Margaret and Florence both came out to India and the Family Planning Association of India was inaugurated, the first nation-wide effort to launch this crucial movement in which Dhanwanti Ramarao took the major lead.

I moved West into New Mexico to visit the Amer-Indians. For here they lived in their old style in their honeycomb terraced community dwellings, rising up to a kind of a pyramid, made of *adobe,* brick-clay mixed with straw and water moulded in rectangular forms and sun-dried. With some changes that machines had wrought, life still looked like of their ancient ancestors. They looked so pronouncedly Asian, that the theory they had shifted continents, crossing the Behring Straits seemed more than credible. Their tribal pattern was not much different from that of our tribals. Their arts like dance, crafts also bore strong similarities. They too had been through the same kind of traumatic experience as ours, of being dispossessed, isolated, but a new era had dawned for them now, with the advent of the New Deal. Amongst the thinking section I had been coming across individuals who proudly claimed a tribal heritage. I was also told that when the Constitution of a free America was being framed, the raw men of today sought counsel of these wise men of yesterday, realising they had much to give and to teach.

A most memorable event for me was visiting the Sree Coomaraswamy at Bostom Museum, heading the oriental section. Ananda Coomaraswamy had meant to us something special as a unique interpreter of our cultural tradition because of the totality of his vision that never blurred. So much like Gandhiji he treated culture as a significant index to the social organism. Though I had conjured up an image of him as an established Oriental Scholar, his dress and demeanour was typically western.

He first showed me round the Indian section of the Museum. He felt it would make our talk later more relevant. As he moved amidst the exhibits, he seemed a part of the set up, a strong kinship bound them together. 'I presume you notice in India a reassertion of your very early assessment and warning of what a highly industrial society does to the individual, with a call for a different socio-economic pattern. This is being particularly emphasised by Gandhiji and those of his way of thinking, who advocate it as a way of life for free India,' I remarked. He nodded but confessed he was too far away to grasp its totality. I continued, 'The strength of this lies in its upholding the same values which according to you a society should practice.' 'When I started, and it is so long ago, I had to literally break new ground, like deep digging to excavate and reveal to the world the essential significance, not the mere surface beauty of Indian art, and its being meaningful. Nothing was created that was not without a purpose. No craftsman would turn out an object that was not functional. The so-called students of Indian art also miss its totality, its relationship with every aspect of life. Ideas like art for art's sake are meaningless to me. A high quality aesthetic external expression can only be a reflection of an inner harmony,' he said in a vigorous voice.

'It must have meant tremendous effort for you to put this across the Western Art World,' I recalled for him the scene way back in 1908 when he stood a solitary figure before an awesome audience of 400 Western Orientalists assembled in Copenhagen, to convince them that the Indian Buddha figure was truly indigenous and not a copy of a Hellenistic statue. He gave a gentle laugh when I asked him whether the scholars were convinced. 'I think I did a fairly good job. That is where my study of Western art and scientific training comes to my aid. I had over the years talked and written so much on the differentiation of Western art from the Indian, that I could marshal irrefutable arguments. I had however to prove not only its distinctive identity but focus it in the setting of a unique civilization that flourished until India became a colony and its multifaceted character got clouded over. I think I had the advantage of being able to give expression to our interpretation with the Western scientific tenets. As I always say use one tradition to illuminate another. There are however wide gaps yet for art in the West was still an isolated activity then, whereas with us it had been an integral part of our entire existence'. 'So much of what you endeavoured to put across then, has become self-evident today. Art is now beginning to be recognised as part of the totality of humanity's basic culture. That must be a matter of great satisfaction to you,' I commented. There was a lurking smile on his face but a dim shadow over his eyes. 'My new fear however is that when this war ends we will be flooded by high mechanism, all that has insidiously gone into perfecting the deadly weapons. So what was let loose to destroy only the bodies, will now be turned on to destroy our inner selves. I talk not of metal weapons, but equally the mental. A body is after all only a tool of the mind. The carnage that has gone on unabated over the centuries, is conceived and directed by the mind. I wish I could hope the Orient would try to be a bulwark against the modern monster of destructive technology. My greatest sorrow is the threat of the individual being wiped out as a human force. To me the man, not as an artist or professional, but the mere man is special, each in his own way,' he said with a firm emphasis.

I remembered how he shunned any personal write ups. Later when Durai Singam of Sri Lanka began to collect biographical material on him and approached us, I felt very hesitant for I could clearly remember his withering comments on the 'growing passion of artists to have their biographical details spilled all over to feed the vulgar curiosity of an idle public. So far as a creative person is concerned it is his *work* that should count and all evaluation done on it alone.'

To me his most memorable pronouncement was at the celebration of India's Independence, August 1947. 'India's culture is of value not so much because it is *Indian* but because it is *culture*.'

As the war in Europe grew more menacing and American aid to the Allies more pronounced, war became a burning topic in the States. As the ties with England were the closest as the book 'Blood is thicker than water' blazoned forth, the largest focus was on that country.

I had come to have close links with Harry Bridges, Secretary of the Civil Liberties Union who strove to keep the issue of the colonial struggles before the American public. He would often call on me to meet liberal groups or address meetings of bodies interested in India. So though I was averse to doing the usual 'Lecturing', I spoke to small audiences which I was assured were genuinely concerned.

So it happened that some of the *active* anti-colonialists invited me to a meeting to be addressed by Mr. Duff Cooper, the British Foreign Minister. I was given a seat prominently in the front row.

Duff Cooper lacked physical stature and obviously debating talent. He assumed a pontifical air, that he and his allies were the custodians of all the virtues, most of all the British and the countless blessings they had generously bestowed on the world and this was endangered by the reckless adventures of a man intoxicated by his ambitions . . . and so he went on.

After this peroration had gone on for some time, my companions alerted me. 'This messiah should be challenged. You are a colonial from his empire, you are hundred per cent authentic,' they whispered. One of them addressed the chair as the speaker began to wind up, and conveyed that an Indian, a British subject would like to comment on the British Minister's address and she should be given the floor. 'Let's hear the Indian', said some. Within seconds I was on my feet and challenging several of his statements. 'India is no paradise under British rule,' I began and was soon pouring out facts and figures to paint a true picture. I sat down to let the Minister reply. He had gone red in the face. Obviously it was a bomb-shell for which he was totally unprepared. He could only fumble a few inaudible phrases. Tempers began to rise and continuous demands came from all parts of the hall. 'Reply to the lady—Answer the lady', became insistent cries. By now more and more were on their feet, angrily asking for answers. 'We want the truth – don't try to bamboozle us. Answer the lady.' Very soon half the hall was on its feet, gesticulating excitedly. Then we found the speaker was not there any more—he seemed to have vanished. He had been hustled out by the back door

One of the trips I undertook during my sojourn in America was to Western Canada. I was flying from Seattle to British Colombia. The Immigration Officer at the airport who looked at my passport asked me how I could go without a Canadian visa and I pointed to my British Indian passport. But he shook his head with some concern. 'I think you are in for trouble Ma'am and if I were you I would not take this trip'. I shrugged it off saying I was used to these risks and hazards and could take them in my stride.

But what I actually ran into was a totally unexpected and novel situation. As I handed in my passport to the Immigration Officer he quietly put it aside and asked me to wait. When all the passengers had gone through, I was led into an office and given a chair. The officer there explained to me that he had instructions not to allow me to enter Canadian territory. He pleaded his inability to give any further explanation, he confessed he simply did not know. He was only carrying out instructions. I was completely nonplussed. He further advised me to take the same plane back to Seattle, due to leave in the next 15 minutes. I refused—I made it clear I had no intention of going back as I was not a criminal, was not aware of having broken any Canadian laws and was perfectly within my rights to claim entry into the territory. The plane left—several planes in fact arrived and left but I continued to sit on a bench. The sun rose high then dipped. I had arrived about 8 in the morning. Every time a service to U.S.A. was about to take off the officer would come and prod me and I would refuse. Finally it was time for the office to close. The last flight for the day was leaving. The airport would be closed until next morning and I could not possibly sit there alone through the night. But I remained firm. The only alternative would have been to use force. They seemed to falter. Instead they telephoned for instructions. In the meantime the last plane had taken off. Finally I was told I would be allowed to go into the city but I would have to get a transit visa even though I was on a British Indian passport and normally needed no visa for travel within the British empire. I wanted to telephone those who who had been expecting me and who had probably been sent back in the morning on being told I was flown back to Seattle. By now the airport was completely deserted except for one man to keep guard on me. Suddenly a group of Canadians and Indians arrived to take me. As I drove into the city I was rather surprised to find the Mayor amongst them.

A couple of people who had come in the morning had gone back disappointed when told I was not there. They tried for a while to unravel the mystery, then decided to go to the immigration authorities but they drew a complete blank there. Finally they were told the lady had flown back and there was no point in any further discussion. Nobody could explain why. Towards evening one of the leaders of the Indian Community and a Canadian lady friend of mine were told I was to be picked up. They had earlier conveyed this mysterious incident to the Mayor who was friendly to India, and expressed their deep suspicion that all was not right. He had been deeply shocked and had already been in contact with the immigration authorities. He came personally to apologise that a freedom fighter from India should have been insulted in his city. He had given assurance on my behalf to the authorities for my 'good behaviour' until my entry could be officially regularised. He had already fixed up an informal lunch for the following day, which the Mayor successfully persuaded the Chief of Immigration to join. He came and brought his wife, who confessed she was dying to see the woman who was out to set the mighty British empire on fire. The Immigration Chief was placed next to me at lunch and I watched his constraint gradually wear away. Before we parted I asked him what led to this weird episode. He said the warning had come from Scotland Yard, London. I said an accused under British Justice was entitled to know what the charge was. He frankly confessed he had no dossier on me. Vaguely the charge was that I was in the habit of creating trouble for the British. I said 'would not you if they continued to rule over you?' He had not thought of that. I explained I had no quarrel with the Canadian government, why would I come half round the globe to create trouble here and if anything antagonise an otherwise friendly government instead of winning its sympathy. Were we in India such bums? I asked him. Very politely he apologised for the incident, I was welcome to stay as long as I wished. I explained that however pleasant this visit, I had to leave, as I was now returning to India, back to the struggle with the alien rulers, to get India free.

He seems to have confessed in some bewilderment to the Mayor later that I seemed quite a reasonable person, with nothing 'wild' about me, for the city to be put on guard! The Mayor asked me what I would have done if I had not been allowed to come into the city. 'I would have just continued to sit there', I said and gave him several instances of Satyagraha where individuals, groups, even thousands in a procession, would squat where they were stopped on the road to assert that the moral right was with them and not with such laws, and an uncalled for obstruction was unlawful in the real sense of the term.

An outstanding figure among friends I made in Washington was Ambassador Hu Shih of China. He was rated very high in the diplomatic world as an intellectual giant—the Wise Man of the Orient. What endeared him to me was his genial warm personality which put me at ease notwithstanding the legends of how he had mastered Chinese by the age of ten, all those countless picturesque characters of the Mandarin. Now he was famous as the father of the modern simplified Chinese, Pai Hua, to replace the ancient Mandarin. 'I was overpowered by the burden and multiplicity of the alphabets. I felt compelled to promote a simplified media, easy to learn and facilitate quick communication.' 'I heard it was compared to the Chaucer's historic reformation of English,' I interrupted. 'Oh that was child's play. Still I succeeded in confounding my critics by producing appealing Chinese verse in the new jargon—and it was warmly accepted—I am now a happy man.'

'You do not strike me as an orthodox Buddhist'. 'You are right for I am not a conventional Buddha worshipper. But I am attracted to the Master's teachings. I am drawn to the ideal of non-violence and I am deeply moved by Gandhi's efforts to turn it into a political instrument to win freedom.' 'I suppose there was no possibility of an attempt in China where Buddhism seemed to have taken deep roots,' I asked. He laughed: 'I fear I am unable to measure the impact of Buddhism on my country. To me it seems that it was only selectively accepted, like vegetarianism but only to be confined to the priests! Man's agile brain fashions an adaptive brain that rationalises and stills doubts.' Then with a far away look he resumed. 'Anyway to come back to combating the Japanese forces non-violently, it cannot be attributed to failure of Buddhism. For we had neither the leader, the opportunity, above all the time to practise your method. You are lucky, you have all of it and my heartfelt good wishes for your success'.

One day a most unexpected thing happened as I kept meeting people. Someone brought me an informal invitation from Robert Oppenheimer, a noted physicist, rather a hero at the moment, for having 'split the atom,' considered a most remarkable feat. Rather bewildered I sought the genesis of this. The scientist was greatly interested in Indian philosophy, culture, had even tried to learn Sanskrit; he was also curious to meet someone active in the Indian freedom struggle.

Oppenheimer's physical personality was a surprise. Very lean and extraordinarily young, for his achievement, he was just approaching forty. The most striking were his eyes, kind of piercing grey blue in contrast to the sickly pallor of his face. He proved easy and friendly to chat with. I was curious to know what led him to delve into Indian philosophy. 'There is much ancient wisdom in it and I was specially keen to unravel the relationship between science and the future of man,' he explained. 'Have you unravelled it?' I asked. 'I think I have only a glimmer of the answer.' He then meandered for a while, but what he said was rather hazy and no answer at all. 'What led you to the atom adventure?' was my next question. 'Just what you say, the adventure, daring to venture into new areas, probe our atmospherics—to see what is the source and nature of the energy released when the uranium nucleus is split. For it was soon apparent that this nuclear energy will leave behind the prevailing sources of energy, for every atom undergoing fission liberates millions and millions of volts.'

'Since you are familiar with our old texts I presume you are aware that our ancients knew of the atom. They must also have been aware of its enormous potential power as they knew of the nature of most of the elements that comprise our atmospherics. But they reckoned man as the most powerful, with almost limitless potentialities yet to be attained. For we are still caught up in our primeval shell that we have to break away from to reach our inmost depths. Then man could do or acquire anything he desired. But to what purpose, was it something that would elevate, ennoble him, liberate him from the dross and muck that drives him down or is it mere curiosity?'

'The Orient is not mysterious or airy-fairy as the West assumes. Deep study as also strong intuition must have guided the knowledge seekers for they did not possess your sophisticated laboratories. To grasp the ultimate knowledge they touched life at various points to gain the wide range of experiences, acutely aware of the complexity of the universe that you are now discovering.'

Oppenheimer responded in a serious tone: 'Though I cannot pretend to know all the wisdom of the East, I entertain feelings of respect for the vast dimensions of its knowledge.'

'I would like to go back to the problem of the role of the scientist in society which you say led you to the Indian studies. Can you define it?' I asked.

After a brief silence he began: 'It is not only a knotty but bewildering proposition. Because for me scientific discoveries with their new knowledge are hardly communicable, a widening chasm divides the two.' 'Then does it mean the scientist can play no vital role in society', I asked. His answer was: 'Like the artist, both live in a world of their own like on a tricky edge of what to the average man is a mysterious world. What the scientist, even as the artist, strives to do, is build contact points, bridges so to say, for a meeting of the new with the familiar.' 'What next', I asked. After a thoughtful silence he said: 'Why, hit on some new ideas—try to accomplish something exceptional.' I did not realise at that stage and I wonder if he did, what this 'exceptional' was to be though he had already assiduously laid the ground work for it. To me his answers sounded vague, like indulging in diffuse generalities. It left me with a sense of emptiness. Was he devoid of conviction or commitment? How much of the Indian philosophy had he assimilated.

The answer came four years later. The scene was in a desert, Alamagordo in New Mexico in mid-July 1945. The first atom bomb—the first nuclear explosion took place and a weird thing happened simultaneously. When the explosion lit up the sky with an unnatural light, two lines from the Bhagvata Gita flashed through Oppenheimer's mind, so he says, as he clung to one of the uprights in the control room:

> 'If the radiance of a thousand suns were to burst into the sky
> That would be like the splendour of the Mighty one'.

Then as the sinister and devastating cloud of destruction filled the scene around, Krishna's sonorous voice sounded reassurance to Oppenheimer:

> 'I am become death
> the Shatterer of Worlds.'

To him the atom bomb was the god incarnate himself! Will the pious Hindus who recite the Gita heed this and await Krishna's coming with a Sudarshan Chakra transformed by modern *bhaktas*, the nuclear scientists, into a nuclear weapon, to bring about the long predicted global *pralaya*?

What was the driving motive behind pursuing the use of this bomb at this stage? Today many of the once secrets, are laid bare for history to record the truth.

Hitler was dead, Germany was occupied. Japanese military representatives had put out feelers for terms of surrender even as early as April in Switzerland, followed in July by the Mikado himself, through his Ambassador in Moscow trying to initiate negotiations for cessation of hostilities, giving plenary powers to the Prince for this purpose. As the U.S. was determined to go through with the bombing, this initiative got no response. There were besides repeated appeals by top scientists numbering sixty-seven, to stop it, which were peremptorily ignored. America it is said, wanted to go it alone, before Russia came in to share the spoils in the East; as also believing or rather hoping that Russia's ambitions would be deterred by this. How vain this hope was, was proved by Russia devising a thermonuclear bomb impregnated with a power 2500 times greater, in October 1961 ! The pettiness of the human mind and its blind passion to devastate, has not changed since the jungle warfare of the primitives.

As my son settled down to his long term studies I got ready to return home. Dimly at the back of my mind was a vague hope I may visit Chungking. With nervous hesitation I conveyed my desire to Ambassador Hu Shih. He nearly jumped out of his chair exclaiming 'By Jove that would be great—the most wonderful thing to do.' Then he walked round a few paces, a troubled frown streaking his taut brow. 'You should think it over. I wonder if you realise it would be rather an adventure with the bombings Chungking is subjected to.' I assured him that did not worry me and he in turn assured me he would fix it up. In course of time he forwarded to me a formal invitation from Generalissmo and Mrs. Chiang Kai Shek welcoming my visit and to be their guest. The Ambassador supplied me all the details I needed to get there.

As I made plans for my return journey I decided to go through what is called the American deep South where discrimination based on colour was still almost like an article of faith. So I fixed up the tour so that I would only stay with the coloured, share their life and experiences.

In New York and the Northern region though the colour consciousness was there, it was not crudely brought into one's consciousness, except by gentle hints, like in certain households the blacks were not welcome, so I met them elsewhere.

But in the South it was a different story. It was blatant and crude. It was soon after the train started moving through Louisiana that the ticket checking man addressed me very peremptorily: 'You have to move out from here to the reserved section'. I asked him politely why. 'That is the rule and you better obey it or you will regret it.' I explained this seat had been given to me when I got the ticket and I did not have any intention of moving from here', and I went back to my book. I heard him give a snort and angrily stride away. He returned a little later in rather a subdued air. Where do you come from was the next question. 'New York,' I said. 'I mean which land do you hail from.' 'It makes no difference', I answered. 'I am a coloured woman obviously and it is unnecessary for you to further disturb me for I have no intention of moving from here.' 'You are an Asian' he muttered and went off.

At Charlston I stayed with a delightful couple, highly cultured, well informed. I felt a pang at parting. When we reached the railway station, they escorted me to a point, then stopped, pointed out my train then bade farewell. Seeing my discomfiture, the lady said gently, 'it is best you are not seen in our company when you board the train.' Before I could protest they swiftly vanished in the moving crowd. My long happy stay in this land was beginning to go sour.

In San Francisco where I was to take a ship, I stayed with one of the old Indian families and learnt for the first time some hidden chapters in the *known* travails of the Indian community, during the World War I when it was campaigning for support of the Indian cause and to expose that an empire built on exploitation can't fight for democracy.

The British government in India notified that these agitators would not be permitted to return back home. Thereupon some of the long-time Indians applied for American citizenship. This resulted in a tragi-comic incident which defies intelligent reasoning: The Supreme Court when called upon to decide if citizenship could be given to these applicants, gave the following bizarre opinion: though an Indian may belong to the Caucasian Race, the man in the street in this country would never take him for a *white* man, therefore he cannot be given American citizenship.

When the Indian agitation for Free India began to pepper up, the local authorities began to make large arrests. At times someone in the Establishment would hint that secret information had come from someone in the Indian Community itself. The whispers grew into angry growls, veiled skirmishes, open fights, alas finally murders! My hostess, a frail gentle lady related to me her own tragedy, how her young husband had been one such victim, and she had been left forlorn with little kids to bring up. To her, like to so many others, it had been a nightmarish period. I was terribly shaken by this narrative.

One of the Indians drove me down to the Imperial Valley which was a large Oasis in a Californian desert, where lived a sizeable Indian Community, who corroborated the lady's tragic tale.

Amongst my several bewildering experiences was a most unexpected one: an encounter with 'Black Power.' I had close associations with the Negro Communities in various walks of life and I kept hearing repeatedly of 'Black Power'. When I arrived at one of its main centres, seeking more knowledge of it, some familiar figures came forward and embraced me most affectionately. I could hardly believe my eyes for I was gazing happily at Atiya Begam, her artist husband and her sister Begam of Janjira—my dear old friends, the famed hosts from Bombay. Obviously they were no casual tourists in this land. I listened to their most surprising explanation for their involvement in the 'Black Power' as it was called.

I was aware of the deep anguish of the Negro community over its continued rejection by the White compatriots. After decades of futile struggles it had come to the conclusion that its identity within this country as people could be satisfactorily affirmed only through an assertion of its own original roots as *black people* with a genuine pride, and to believe that in this role it had a special contribution to make rather than go on attempting to get absorbed in a multi-racial community. Thus a current to help Negro culture to flower had been ignited. The formulation of and stress on Negro culture as a distinct entity was the main element. This had thrown up several what were termed as *Prophets, Saviours, Messengers*, etc. One Father Divine had struck the keynote when he declared with fervour: 'I am a Negro and God dwells in me. Every Negro is like unto me, we are therefore superior to the 'White'.'

Early in this century an American, Noble Drew, was inspired by the Islamic faith which rejected racial differences and accepted all who embraced Islam as brothers. Drew's successor proclaimed himself as Elijah Mahmad Ali, established the Temple and the University of Islam for training Muslim youth. The Muslim Negroes now came to be known as *Nation of Islam* and gained a sense of pride in their own heritage.

Apart from the sense of identity, this worked in infusing self confidence and fostering incentives for self improvement as also proved an added inducement to join the Nation of Islam. In this significant mission this Nation sought the aid of the Indian Muslims, who to these Negroes seemed ideally suited for the task. Thus some Muslim Indian leaders had been recruited to carry the new message into the Negro fold and regenerate this long depressed community. As I got to see more of them, I saw one obvious result of this new impact in the flowing garbs the Negroes had begun to proudly sport. It was strange how India seemed totally unaware of this delicate mission some Indians were being called upon to shoulder!

I made a short halt at Honolulu as I finally flew out of the American continent. My first discovery was of the original natives and something of their culture. For instance the well known Hula Hula dance is not indigenous, just improvised to excite tourists. Then what is the real Hawaiian dance, I asked. So I was taken to the home of a noted dancer. She was an elderly lady, well built with a dignified gait. She welcomed me warmly as though meeting an old friend—a young niece of hers did the Nritya while she did Abhinaya. Both had such resemblance to the Indian, involuntarily I broke into exclamations. She beamed happily and admitted the resemblance. She had seen some Indian dancers, Balasaraswati in particular, she recollected with warm affection and admiration. 'According to our tradition we hail originally from your part. The similarity of the Mudras prove it,' she explained. I next asked why was this dance kept in purdah, and not exposed to the public. Because of a strict adherence to an old custom. The guru was always a woman and she could only teach a girl who was closely related to her, no one else. I was simply appalled at a custom that must result in destroying a fine art form.

As I was leaving the United States I pondered on the 18 months I had passed there. No other country outside of India had touched life at so many points as America. The Federal Government at Washington and the several State Governments gave me the fullest facilities for this purpose. I got equal help and co-operation from the different organisations and institutions. I saw the day to day working of those Federal Departments and their sections that I was interested in, not only at their headquarters, but also in the various activities carried out in the urban and rural areas. I travelled in the little-known South, living in Negro homes and sharing in their community life, disintegrated bits of a society which had crashed like a piece of china. I rode across the long desert country in the South-West to wander over the Indian Reserves, and see those ancient people in their own setting, hear their brave sagas, listen to their songs, see their arts and crafts and trace the pattern of their social life. I did a round of colleges and universities, living in the campuses with the students, watching their daily life.

I attended the special classes run by social agencies like the Maternity Association, Home Economics Association and the like, observed the daily running of clinics and for the purpose of gaining practical experience, even donned the uniform and became one of the workers on occasion. For a closer study I went behind the big stores to see the manifold administrative tasks which are curtained off from the public eye. I tried to understand the mysteries of vast libraries—undoubtedly one of the most complicated institutions. I went into prisons, lock-ups and the police courts. I worked with social agencies conducting investigations into the daily lives of the common people, kept close contacts with workers, labour organisers and leaders, as with industrialists, legislators and administrators. I saw the inside of posh hostels and the pre-war dark East-side slums of New York, breathing in the perfume in one and the stench in the other, rubbing shoulders with the scintillating and the shadowy alike. I was a guest in the streamlined mansions of Long Island and the tumble-down shacks of Negro Share-Croppers in the South. These unique experiences that I seized, the diversities and contrasts, the thrills and the shocks, the hopes and the despairs I savoured in this New World to me are memorable.

India is sometimes given to looking at the United States with almost envy for the fascination of the New World can be gripping. But it is as well to remember that it is not all glamour and glory. It may have proudly soared into the air and sped along sparkling highways.

Still its basic problems remain as unsolved as our own. They are as much tied up in knots and caught up in the weeds as those of us of the Old World. We have as much to absorb from this New World or the 'American way of life' as the Americans proudly claim, as to discard. Where distance lends enchantment, a close-up serves to bring discernment and clarity.

9

My first destination was Japan. To the Asian Colonials Japan had become a sort of a Mecca. Its sensational drive into the modern international current after the Meiji Restoration, had arrested our attention. Emotionally however, it was Lafcadio Hearn, who probably is a stranger to modern readers, with his fascinating pictures of Japanese culture that had captured our being.

Impressive and captivating were the craftsmen and women whose imagination, skill and utter devotion to their vocation, not only drew my admiration but even more my homage. The Japanese crafts world still followed faithfully our ancient guru-shishya relation pattern. The pupil lived with the master in the family, sharing as much in the daily domestic chores as in the workshop lessons. I became friendly with the Kenzai family of potters renowned for the lovely colours in their creations and who maintained the old tradition. Ogata Kenzen who generously introduced me to several of the complexities of manufacture of Japanese crafts, was a pioneer to launch a movement for promotion and preservation of handicrafts.

I may say my foundation for the development of crafts in India after independence was in truth laid in Japan. I saw that even in this highly industrialised country, handicrafts continued as an integral part of the overall industrial sector. In the annual National Plan, handicrafts had a distinct place of its own, with efforts made to avoid competition between the big industries and handicrafts. Later I kept contact with Dr. Soyetsu Yaganagi, founder of the Japanese Craft Society and

Director of the National Craft Museum. In the post-war years, Japanese pottery gripped the American crafts devotees. Noted potter Shafi Hamada conducted regular pottery classes all over the States. I attended one of them and learnt a great deal. I was impressed by the Master's concept of a class, the role of a teacher and of the pupils. No one can really *teach* a craft, pronounced the teacher. Students can be advised on quality of clay, point out different *processes* and *techniques* like firing. Sensitivity to aesthetics, finesse in workmanship have to be cultivated by the students themselves. These parameters could be widened by their own volition, by thought, study, discussions. This was Hamada's philosophy.

The Japanese approach to crafts, according to him, drew inspiration from Zen. It was a way of life. Thus had developed Ikebana as well as the aesthetic cult of the Tea Ceremony.

'Quality pots are those that flow out of the creative urge, not *copies* of masterpieces. Therefore education was *bringing* out from the learner, not *putting* in by the teacher which was deadening', was his motto. A student asked him: 'When you want to make a new object, how do you go about it? Do you visualise the images first or do you shape it as you go along?' Hamada answered: 'Every time I make an object it is *new*.' The dialogue closed. To me it was an echo of what our ancients had recorded in their treatises. Wisdom is universal. *The hearts of the oppressed millions of the Orient had stirred with the hope this would herald freedom. This however had begun to shatter with Japan's assault on China. Nevertheless its current position as one of the leading countries after centuries of a feudal hibernation, was intriguing.*

What struck me first was to see women involved in every kind of job. One saw them everywhere, from pearl-diving and gymnastics to heads of business and universities. This had probably been accelerated by a prolonged war heavily drawing on manpower. What was impressive was the extraordinary speed with which women, tightly ensnared in feudalism, could take on with such ease a million new roles, yet look dainty, not a hair out of place or a crease disturbing the neat folds of the Kimono. They had an air of formalism, yet unlike the rigidity with which it sits on the men, it sat lightly on the women, just as they managed to combine their briskness with an inexplicable grace. No doubt they still adhered to several of their traditions, one to give meticulous attention to their appearance. 'A woman should always look her best,' they explained. Hence the patronage given to beauty salons which were considered a necessity. They puzzled at my reluctance to have sittings in them.

It almost seemed as though each little detail in every day life was traditionally fixed; how to enter a room, how to sit, receive a guest, how to handle objects, to hand out and receive things. Everything was bound in etiquette, spelt in the largest capital letters. It found its highest expression in the flower arrangements and the Tea Ceremony. In fact the entertaining of guests also had fixed guidelines: the scroll to be hung on the wall and the flower or flowers to adorn the room being determined by the character of the guest—What he or she meant or stood for. The core of the Japanese genius seemed to lie in achieving the richest effects with the minimum of details. The smallness of the country with limited space was probably responsible for this. A single flower vase, even a solitary blossom or scroll, a tiny picture may be, was expected to express the mood of the occasion or the personality of the guest. A tiny garden was designed to convey the fulfilment of a large layout. In the same line were the miniature plants they so devotedly developed.

Unique and intriguing were some of their modes of entertaining guests. Kakayachi or painting or glazing of pottery: It was thrilling for me to hold in my hand unbaked dull and drab clay, draw designs on it, splash it with colour and see its transformation under my excited fingers as though it were charged with an element of magic. It then went into an electric oven, and when it came out perfectly, it was presented to me with a ceremonial bow. That is how it ends, I was explained. Equally exciting was it for me when an easel, a rice paper pinned on it was placed before me and I was asked to make strokes with a brush. Soon the paper had a motley bunch of strokes of various shapes, some even criss-crossing. Then the artist whose presence our host had taken care to provide, tried his final hand on it with his brush that worked like a magic wand and turned the splashes and strokes into a pleasant recogniseable picture. I could also hold a lump of clay in the hand and let a sculptor press my fingers almost imperceptibly and guide them into making a purposeful form. Such were some of the rare and most pleasurable experiences I was enticed into. I realised I had strayed into a very special and to me an exciting world.

It was with the artists that I really found my haven. Theirs was a world apart, outside the putrified atmosphere of a war-swept country and the pall of militarism. Here I found warmth and friendliness without any formalism. I could just be my natural self. The Japanese artists were highly honoured and those judged meritorious, given the title of 'National Treasure.'

What really bewildered me was the deluge of letters of welcome. I sought the aid of a young man to read them to me. They were very polite, often in flowery, even flattering phrases that made me blush, like for instance, 'We hope you will become the queen when India is free.' Newspapers were regularly read to me and above all, the radio news interpreted, in exciting tones if there was any reference to India.

Most touching but more intriguing and innovative was the custom to perpetuate the name of an outstanding actor, artist, in case the son had no real talent or the actor no progeny. A gifted, qualified actor took on the distinguished actor's name so that it went on from generation to generation with no break! The one who succeeded to the illustrious title was expected not only to maintain the senior artists' standard but enrich it by adding to its quality through better performance—so different from the custom of transferring the Senior's possession to the legal heir, irrespective of whether he qualified or not.

Refreshingly delightful were their festivals, both for their content and their titles. The Festival of Fresh Green, of Peach Blossom also known as the Girl's Day and Dolls Festival, when girls got dressed up and decorated dolls were set up which friends visited. The Festival of Sweet Flag also known as the Boys' Day, when boys got dressed up; Festival of Stars, of Chrysanthemums—and so they went on throughout the year.

It was gracious for the guest to begin the meal by saying 'Itamakai Masu'—permit me, and end up with 'Gochiso Sama Deskita'—it was a nice meal. Japanese life is strewn with many such exquisite touches.

Since very little is known to Indians of the Japanese theatre I will state a few important facts. Like in India and in Greece, drama has a divine origin. The Sun Goddess once hid herself in a cavern and instantly the world was plunged into darkness. To entice her out the gods performed a dance-drama, so goes the story.

The real significant thing about their theatre is the fact it was the women who gave the lead and built up the theatre which obviously indicates the prevalence of matriarchy in the early days. Specifically the Kabuki was started by a woman, O'Kein, who along with her gifted actor husband elaborated the form. At one stage when they were driven off the stage, the theatre was banished as criminal. Nevertheless, that it not only survived but grew to the heights it has attained in the world's eye, is a tribute to the vitality and dedication of the artists to their art, but above all the ardent love of the common people for the drama. The artists too are well aware that to retain that devotion the plays must have excellent quality.

When the women returned to the stage after their emancipation from feudalism, they quickly formed their own feminine groups. Though mixed troupes are common, the women's groups still carry on under catchy names like Cherry Blossom, Moon troupe.

Though very modern in its use of equipment, there was no trace of any hybridness. I have since seen stages all over the world, for sheer aesthetic beauty the Japanese has few equals. The theatres were not merely elaborate, they were thoughtfully planned to provide a degree of privacy unknown in this country.

The various types of Japanese drama are now fairly well known. The famed Japanese No drama is so very unique that I am tempted to share at least a few of its unusual characteristics. It can have no parallel for comparison. It is heavily symbolic but the symbol itself is more suggestive than positive. For the imagery is subtle and profoundly imaginative rather than illusive. This does not in any way mean the text is negligible. On the contrary the text is highly poetic and a perfect delight even to read, for the word imagery is startlingly original, refreshingly exquisite, and deeply moving, though set half a dozen centuries ago.

A basic quality of No is the untrammelled freedom allowed to the dramat st both in language and structure even in relation to time and space. The last named is true of our classical Sanskrit drama where a few steps can make do for a long journey. But the time element is striking, for timing of the play is inextricably related to a particular season. For the atmosphere of autumn or spring is emphasised not merely by the setting but in the entire mood, imagery, the musical tones and the whole gamut.

Equally a single day, a month or even a year can begin and end in a few seconds, for an actor goes up to the audience and says 'The final day has drawn to a close', as simple as that!

Characters are not etched in the way we normally do. Each seems rather to signify some emotion, but *intensely distilled* so to say. The audience has got accustomed to accepting this with satisfaction. The texts seem to serve in emphasising the inner tensions rather than delineate the different characteristics in each actor or explain the actor's actions. Above all the No is completely unrealistic—any properties used are merely suggestive—on occasions even these are missing, when the setting is briefly described by an actor.

The word-imagery is unanalysable, so each is a word-painting. The writer Zeami who raised the No to a great classic, for instance, describes Profoundity as follows: Snow has Covered the Thousand Mountains, One lonely peak remains unwhitened. Why. Stillness and purity is picturised as Snow in a silver bowl ! and so it goes on.

Japanese puppets were large and openly manipulated by the manipulator, not behind the curtain. They perform in a special puppet-theatre as is still done in some temple complexes in India where the tradition persists.

Outside of the euphoria of the charmed art circle, the world was very grim. The people were given to understand Japan was working for a New Order in the Asia, a co-prosperity sphere, as it was called, for the Asian continent. It was simplified in a breath-taking manner. The picture drawn of all Asians coming together as a single family, Nippon as the father figure deciding their destiny—all love and good will. I kept asking why war with China? The answer was because the Generalissimo has been induced by the Anglo-Saxon powers and the poor Chinese had to be saved. In pursuance of this policy Chinese language was introduced into Japanese schools and societies promoted for popularising Chinese culture. This was quite stunning.

A complete totalitarian pall lay tightly over the entire country and inane social modalities of human relations were being enforced. So much of the original creative vigour and the native constructive energy had become limp. The economic depression was fast deepening, with acute shortages of essentials growing like a menacing cloud.

As with Germany, the Western Democracies had felt no compunction in arming Japan while the going was good. I had witnessed myself sentimental American women generously packing lint and cotton bandages for the Chinese while I was too well aware that the men of profits were equally busy shipping death-dealing weapons to Japan. It was obvious Japan was poised for an Asian Blitz but alas it was to be no harbinger of peace and freedom for the Asian millions in bondage.

Though I did not deliberately provoke confrontation with the 'committed' Japanese, I did not attempt to hide my true feelings towards the political situation, in particular towards the war with China. When I arrived, the Japanese Government made a fairly elaborate tour that extended to beyond Korea and Manchuria. But by the time I was ready to leave, the atmosphere had completely changed. An elderly Japanese lady who had been especially friendly to India and to me came on a Mission on behalf of the authorities. She explained they had learnt of my proposed visit to China, which obviously was a good-will one and they had to deduce where my sympathies lay. Under the circumstance it would be impossible for them to take me to Manchuria and Korea as planned. They had deputed the lady to sound me if I was willing to forego my China trip and prefer to do the tour they had planned. Quietly but firmly I declined, asked her to convey my thanks for their courtesy and apologies for declining.

Thus petered out a trip I had rather looked forward to. As I sailed away came the stunning news of the German invasion of Russia, an event that was to turn the whole fate of this Blitz War.

When I arrived in Shanghai I started hearing disturbing reports about the Chiang Kai Shek regime, the exploitation of the peasantry, the concentration and growth of wealth and consequently power in the hands of a group, above all the Generalissimo's preoccupation with countering the communists rather than full attention in combating the Japanese, and lots more of adverse criticism. I was considerably shaken. Here was I all worked up to fly off to be his guest. But then the Generalissimo was not China and from all accounts, the Chinese people were resisting the invaders with all the resources at their command, a fact that had deeply stirred and drawn me.

Friends around me here were sceptical about my trip. What good was it to India, China or myself? From recent accounts bombing in the Chungking area had been greatly stepped up. The verdict was that I was going to my doom for no worthwhile purpose.

The Chungking trip which had seemed feasible in Washington became elusive in Shanghai. I was stalled from informing the Generalissimo and his government my arrival date in Hong Kong. Communications with Chungking, never easy, were made even more arduous by the

British who had endorsed or rather scratched my passport to force me to make a bee-line straight back to India, with no lingering by the wayside. To fill in the indefinite waiting period till the call from Chungking would come, I hit on a visit to Nanking, seat of Wang Ching Wei's regime, when I happened to meet one of the Ministers of the Wang Cabinet through their representative in Shanghai. When I expressed my desire, he seemed pleased. I explained I was in a difficult position because of the obstacles being put in my way by the British. I, an Indian wishing to visit China which we look upon as a friendly Asian land, and why should I be prevented from doing so. His eyes softened as I showed my sense of humiliation. 'You will come to Nanking and you will be welcomed as a guest from India should be' was the Minister's assurance. 'I shall make all the arrangements. When do you wish to go?' Prompt was my answer: 'The day after tomorrow'. He seemed confident it could be done. He was able to contact Nanking on the phone and finalise the visit.

Friends around were furious. 'Sheer madness', they protested 'you need to travel by train which is walking deliberately into an abyss. For the Red guerillas attack these trains regularly. What is more they pull out the rails and bury them to prevent their future use. What fate is meted out to the passengers is anybody's guess—it is too awful to dwell on the possibilities.'

Armed with all the necessary letters, documents I arrived at the railway station. I was perplexed to see lots of people lined up in a lengthy queue at the entrance. All the approaches were fenced in long rows and the crowd moved between them very, very slowly. How could one ever take the train at this rate, I wondered. Then I discovered to my relief that one passage was reserved for the non-Chinese, through which I could enter. At the gate I was stopped. All baggage had to be examined. This was the explanation for these enclosures and the queue hold-ups.

A few minutes later I realised how futile were all these precautions. At the ticket counter I was given the astounding news that there were no trains running to Nanking at the moment. The scheduled trains had been suspended, since a train on that route had been blown up by the Chinese guerillas earlier in the week. These were normal occurrences. Nobody could say when the service would be resumed. I felt frustrated.

But I decided simply to wait around until some train got up steam for Nanking.

Late in the afternoon a slow train moved out although normally trains do not run after nightfall in these 'Guerilla' areas. A friend who had travelled on that route once, had told me he had sat with a revolver in his hands, throughout the trip.

So I would sit literally with my life in my hands.

Half of every compartment was occupied by the military. Soldiers with guns moved up and down the central passage which ran through these trains. These carriages looked obviously Japanese in design. My neighbour whispered confirmation into my ear, adding 'the Chinese took away or destroyed most of these carriages'. Armed guards stood with pointed guns all along the platform.

I passed through destroyed suburbs after the train moved out. The ravages were great, the attempts at rebuilding negligible. The reason was obvious. No foreign power probably ever held a conquered country so unrealistically as Japan held what was known as 'occupied China'.

All along the line, every few yards stood a soldier with a pointed gun. There was a tense heaviness and strain in the atmosphere. The passengers were silent and only indulged in occasional whispers. Every time the train moved after a stop, uniformed men came along and searched the person of every passenger. Yet at every station were the same long lines of men and women waiting for the train.

Evening was creeping over the world bringing with it the twilight hush. The sharp angles of the landscape were being softened by the greying light. It was as though some kindly hand were trying to cover up even the gaping wounds in this torn countryside.

We were now nearing Nanking. Suddenly I gave a gasp of thrill. There before me stood the Great Wall of China, even as it had stood through the centuries, a silent and gaunt witness to so many scenes and events gone by. How childish and futile would seem today the effort to build a wall to shut out the world! Yet while the Maginot Line and the Stalin Line have cracked and collapsed, here stands this superb structure, ageless through the ages, immovable through swift moving events, almost a challenge to the ravages of time. It has withstood not merely the ruthless hand of time, it has defied the weapons of modern warfare. The Japanese brought their artillery to hammer on it again and again, and repeatedly hurled against it only to be broken into pieces, like delicate china dashed to the floor. In desperation the Japanese Command ordered the soldiers to scale this unbreakable wall. The suicide squads went forward, and as each soldier reached the top became an easy target for the Chinese guns within the walls. One by one they fell like dry leaves softly slipping to the ground. Slowly the dead mounted up. The China Wall consists really of two walls running parallel to each other with a corridor between and this filled up slowly with the falling dead and on this bridge of corpses, the Japanese army secured a footing to pour into the city. Not only the Chinese but today even the Japanese have a superstition about a wall that even modern batteries cannot pierce.

There was nobody to meet me at the station as my arrival could not be intimated due to the uncertainties of the train. No taxis were available. I took a bus to the hotel where I knew a room had been reserved for me. A few yards ahead at the City Gates, we were made to alight, and our bags gone through once again.

The place seemed oppressive as I strolled out into the night. Here was a ghost city. Even babies seemed to hush their cries. Long afterwards in Chungking I recalled this experience. What a contrast the two were: one was dead even in the midst of quiet, the other alive while death reigned around.

In the morning I tried to contact Wang Chiang Wei's Secretariat. Nobody at the hotel knew its location. I tried the travel bureau with no success; nor could any of the offices around give me the information. Of the former offices of Chiang's days, many had been destroyed. Those which were intact were occupied by the Japanese military. Japanese soldiers were in evidence everywhere. In fact Nanking was like a Military Camp, although it was now supposed to have an independent Chinese Government! Of the original million and a half population of Nanking, barely two hundred thousand remained with an additional hundred thousand Japanese troops for the protection of Nanking, an astounding situation!

After two hours of fruitless search I decided to abandon the hunt for the new Government Headquarters. It seemed incredible that the people should not know, but it was true nevertheless. I decided to do some sightseeing of my own, until luck should come my way. The first thing I naturally thought of was the Sun Yat Sen Memorial. Here again I met with continued disappointment. 'We never heard of this gentleman' came the simple answer to my persistent query. 'The father of the Chinese people' I tried, with no better result. This seemed terrible and then it dawned on me that he must be known by his Chinese name, something I had entirely omitted to acquaint myself with. The whole trip was taking on a nightmarishness when my taxi driver gave the welcome news that he had secured the services of a man who knew the Secretariat.

I met Wang along with the members of the Wang Chiang Wei's Government. Wang was the only impressive person in that group. Undoubtedly one of the ablest and cleverest, he had been the right hand man of Dr. Sun, with General Chiang running a close race with him. In fact so commendable were Wang's interpretations of Dr. Sun's principles and teachings that his books came to be prescribed as texts in schools. Ten years ago, Wang indulged in one of his usual coups to unseat Chiang and failed. The rivalry had persisted however.

Wang Chiang Wei welcomed me warmly saying 'you come from a great country, who has been amongst our oldest friends.' I assured him India still cherished genuine friendship for his country, reminded him of our medical mission, then added; 'We even started with boycott of Japanese goods on your account. I am however bewildered by your collaboration with the invaders. May be you can explain.'

He went back to the 1911 revolution. 'I was amongst the earliest rebels to gather round the great leader Dr. Sun, go into exile with him as the party organiser. When we rose against the monarchy I was captured and would certainly have been beheaded had I not come under the Empress Dowager's eye. She was moved by my tender age and only kept me a prisoner. The collapse of the Monarchy freed me. I rejoined Dr. Sun as his chief assistant. We lived through hazardous times but I faithfully stayed beside Dr. Sun to be of unfailing succour to him. In fact it was his wish that I should be his successor. That is how I came to write his will and last testament. Chiang however manouvered to snatch the leadership. I went into exile but rushed to join Chiang when the Japanese invaded our country. I soon discovered I had become a suspect in the faction-ridden situation. I moved off only to rush back to Chiang's side when the Sian crisis occurred—humbly agreeing to be No. 2 under Chiang. For the situation was so serious.

'Then I saw a bunch of hot heads bent on scorch earth adventurism. They were raw, with no sense of discrimination. So they burnt down a great big city like Chiangsha, acting on a worthless rumour that the Japs were at its gates. Horrible—Horrible. I could not tolerate such horrors as patriotic acts. I therefore decided to turn to peace. That is how I came to sign an agreement with the Japanese. Not that the Great Chiang fights them wholeheartedly. He does not want to down the Japs—oh no—That would not suit him. You see he wants to keep the Communists tied up. So he plays his game—this way—that way.'

He narrated this dramatically like a seasoned actor. He had laid bare the tragedy of their great country. The precious freedom that Dr. Sun had won was now being squandered by two of his closest lieutenants. Wang may be sharper intellectually but he obviously lacked Chiang's purposeful organisation and drive—above all an uncanny shrewdness. Gossip in Shanghai had it that when Wang was to set up the puppet-government, Chiang quickly saw that his own men ingratiate themselves into Wang's bosom and be included in his cabinet !

I left completely dispirited. I had no heart to go through the programme prepared for me. I made a few brief rounds, begging excuses as I was tired.

Word of my impending visit finally reached Chungking. The boat immediately available for Hongkong was English. As this boat with me on board neared Hongkong and I stood on the deck watching the rocky city come into view, I realised the boat had suddenly stopped moving and a small steam boat had approached us. Before I quite knew what was happening, a group of English police boarded the boat and surrounded me. One of them asked me to proceed to my cabin which I declined to do as they had no right to direct my movement. I was then told I was under arrest and would not be allowed to land. I asked them what my offense was but they declined to explain. By now several of the passengers had gathered around. I felt strangely insulted. They must be taking me for a common criminal perhaps a dangerous criminal, for such precipitous action. The ship had by now come alongside the quay. I saw a group standing together, a number of Indians and some Chinese who I felt sure were there to meet me. For my intended trip to Chungking had become a bit of a sensation. After some delay I was told I would be allowed to land. When I entered my cabin to collect my bags, I found a police officer on duty.

He asked me to sit down for according to him some formalities had to be first gone through. Soon another English officer arrived with some paper which he said was a Police Order he was formally serving on me. When I glanced at it I recognised the very familiar parole order which we had already become accustomed to in India. The purport of it was that while I was in the Hongkong Territory I would be allowed to stay in a hotel but I would not be permitted to leave it; I would be expected however to present myself twice a day at a nearby police station to sign my presence. When he asked me to sign it, I replied I was quite familiar with this in my country under the British regime, and this is how we dealt with it, and with that I tore it up and threw the pieces into the wastebin. May be to him it was a relief. I heard later he anticipated me to attack him. My reaction must have however confirmed their worst apprehension that I was unpredictable.

I was then allowed to go with an Indian family to a hotel. I was now told that the original plan of the Hongkong authorities had been to prevent me from landing and to let the ship carry me on to Singapore which was its destination, and there to transfer me to another ship bound for an Indian port, and thus keep me interned on the ship. The exigencies of the war intervened however, for this ship was suddenly commandeered by the British Navy and had to be immediately cleared. And plans to transfer me directly to another British ship going east could not materialise. So I had to be allowed to land. At this stage Madame Sun Yat Sen who at the time lived in Hong Kong helping the Chinese war refugees pouring in from the mainland, and her brother Mr. Soong who was an influential man in the Hong Kong business and banking world, intervened and a compromise was worked out to enable me to be comfortably lodged until Chungking could be contacted to officially intervene. Under this agreement I was to be permitted to stay in a hotel as the guest of the Indian Community, subject to some surveillance. Before the day ended arrangements were afoot to fly me off at the earliest to Chungking, which had been appraised of the developments here. The Chinese Government had contacted the British Ambassador in Chungking who in the course of the day managed to reach the Hong Kong Governor to tell him I was travelling to Chungking as a guest of the Generalissimo and Madame Chiang and to let me board the very first plane to Chungking.

The day had been quite uneventful. To test how free I was, I had wandered down the arcade around the hotel sauntering into shops, lingering around counters doing an eyeful of shopping. It was rather fun keeping the guard guessing, and hopefully, apprehensive. The demand for my reporting for parole had been unobstrusively passed over.

To meet me as I came off the boat from Shanghai, in the group awaiting, was a petite figure who held out a slender hand of welcome to me saying 'I am Soong Chingling. For a moment I was thrown into confusion. Before me stood a pale dainty woman, looking remarkably young with beautiful chiselled features, looking anything but a revolutionary, more like an elegant society belle. I had by now seen enough of Chinese women in Shanghai to know you can never guess their age. But I had not assumed a partner of Dr. Sun Yat Sen, who shared his hardships, dangers, went through a revolution, to still look like an 'Exquisite piece of humanity,' as an American writer described her.

With her was her brother, T.V. Soong, who I later discovered had helped work out the transit arrangement for my stay in Hong Kong. One main condition was that I would not be permitted to meet anybody or step out without the special permission of the concerned local authority. In fact a police guard would be posted at my hotel room. I begged of the Indians not to visit me lest they become suspects. My only visitor was Madame Sun Yat Sen.

Probably to put me at ease she talked mostly of her current work among the Chinese war refugees and welfare projects for children. I was a stranger to her and I had to hold back a million questions that came bubbling to my tongue. My situation laid a heavy pall on me as it were. I was sadly aware of my causing a lot of problems to these good friends. There was the uncertainty of flights to Chungking, the unearthly hours when the plane had to take off in utmost secrecy at dead of night. I felt caught in a net of suspense.

Chungking balances itself on the hill tops, steep and severe like a fortress. The plane as it approached the city, heaved over peaks, curves dangerously and bent in and out of hills and suddenly slipped on to a narrow stony strip of land along the Yangtse river. The usual generous open airport was not to be seen, nor the hospitable rest rooms. All round was bleak and barren, with sheer mountains rising on all sides. Two large cloth umbrellas sheltered the few immigration and customs officials, while people stood around, indifferent to the drizzle or the sun.

Where was the city and how did one get there, I puzzled. 'You cross the river in a Sampan (a Chinese craft) and then get carried up in a sedan chair', some one informed. In Chungking you were either ascending or descending. Everything about Chungking was strenuous.

This world famed war-torn capital was not the legendary home of the Ming Vase of delicate lines and lustrous colours or of the exquisite intricate scrolls with rich tracings of mountains and streams. The China I now gazed upon was stark, gaunt, superbly undaunted, unbendable in the face of this dark hour of peril. I was eager to see this new spirit in action. The very air service on which I had come was a daring venture which spoke volumes for a dogged determination. I had to actually see the waiting list of the intended Chinese travellers to Chungking to believe it—as though it were a pilgrimage.

From my hotel window I gazed on the Yangtse that my school book described as the longest river, today the only unfailing land line which linked this mountain hide with the rest of the country. Along it moved an endless line of barges, heavily loaded with goods from the invaded areas, pulled by strong hands. I was told the cargo included anything from factories to laboratories, lorries to museum treasures. This startling panoramic scene had been there for years since the war began to transplant the salvaged on a new soil.

I had been told Chungking is hot and steaming. After shivering in the plane, I shivered a little more when I landed. The cold ate into my bones as I journeyed to the hotel. Later, by afternoon I was sweating. I retired to bed lightly clad, fanning myself. By midnight I had slipped under two blankets; by morning I was crying for more. Chungking weather makes the notorious English weather seem sober.

According to all reports the ravages in Chungking were far greater than in London, except that the former did not get the same publicity. I landed myself in one of the worst raids of the season, continuous for the next few days and nights with short respites, no longer than a couple of hours.

The first severe raids on Chungking transformed the midtown section of the city into a mad inferno of flames. Seven huge conflagrations were counted at nightfall, roaring through the heart of the city like a flaming path. By the time night fell the red glow of the flames illuminated the countryside for miles around.

The conflagration razed a good part of Chungking's once busy down-town district, Streets, lanes, and in between them stood a forest of ghostly walls bearing testimony to the structures that once were.

Forces of reconstruction began to work immediately, as though moved by an instant mechanism. Soon Chungking city was given a new facade. Once the all clear was given, a walk along Chungking's main thoroughfares found every shop busy and the streets thronged with pedestrians and vehicles. Life was carried on in hastily improvised structures built out of light material, retrieved from the ruins. Buses began to ply, crowded to capacity.

Inspite of continuous raids, life went on as best as possible. Offices started work before seven and put in two to three hours of work until the bombers arrived. After the all clear was given, work resumed again. But of course it was not quite so simple as all that. The experience was pretty shattering. Sometimes even a hundred planes came in a day in four waves, sometimes even over 60 planes at a time and on an average each plane was said to have dropped six to eight bombs depending on the weight of the missiles.

All doors seemed open to me to see what I liked. meet whom I wished to. I met Rewi Alley to learn of the Induscos; the minister for war who described rather picturesquely what to me was a sombre grey situation. I was moved to my depths, inspired by the many different hard-to-believe facets of this scene, people with serene faces in the midst of turbulence. Faced with the destruction of 80% of its industries, China hit on industrialisation through small cooperatives. These became world famous as Induscos identified by a red triangle embodying two Chinese characters Kung Ho: Work together, under the imaginative leadership of Rewi Alley, a New Zealander Missionary. He confessed to me that he realised pretty soon that what China needed was not a new religion but a new technology. By now there were 3000 working co-ops employing 50,000 workers, trained in both techniques as in principles of cooperation. Wages were as level as possible. Startingly novel were the guerilla Induscos described as 'hit and run' workshops, operating behind the enemy positions, where the workers crossed back and forth through fighting lines to get in raw materials and push out finished goods. I was told of heroes and martyrs like a weaver woman who dismantled several looms and buried them even as the enemy marched on them. A rickety bamboo shack hugging a hill precariously, I saw to my amazement, was a real machine shop with belts whirring inside, turning out precision metal works !

'It is the deliberate policy of war time China to pursue education at all costs and not let the lamp of thirty centuries of scholarship go out,' said the President of the Chungking University situated on the outskirts of the city, as we made our way through some pitiable shambles, stepping over strewn plaster, shattered glass, broken roofing and a whole heap of indescribable mess.

Even as we were doing the rounds, the siren sounded again and we rushed into the cellar. 'This is our treasure trough,' explained the President as he showed me the precious treasures, such as rare books, lab equipment, etc. A sudden concussion threw some of us off our seats, which meant a bomb nearby. When we came out, few hours later, we saw it had landed in a corner of the garden, damaging a part of the main hall as also part of the dining hall. Soon some of the treasures were brought out, classes began, the lab in the cellar hummed. It were as though the disastrous interruption were a normal feature of the day. Work was never to stop, except forcibly. At the usual after raid roll call, one man was missed. Later a workman was found in the debris. 'He may have dozed off and missed hearing the siren', was the explanation. 'All in the day's work'.

Several of the Universities still struggled to teach thousands of students, working in clusters, so they could share equipment, books, above all academic personnel, experts. Adult education was imparted through evening classes as through full day schools.

In this unusual setting my hotel was full of bustle, with visitors coming and going, businessmen, bankers, traders, politicians, statesmen from all parts of the world it seemed, as though this battered capital were in the midst of a flourishing country. I dare say some were only trying to fish in troubled waters.

The setting changed like the transformation scenes in our old dramas, when I arrived at the mountain hide-out of the Generalissimo and Madame Chiang. Tucked away in a well-guarded secret spot, this couple were going through some momentous times.

The Generalissimo was a tall thin man and in his private apartment he was seen only in his Chinese garb and therefore informal, so different from his pictures in the full military uniform. This also seemed to endow him with an air of austerity and calmness, the latter was however only a facade. For he could get quite animated and almost brusque over a conversation. Little of this however came through the translation by the Madame. It left me rather disquieted. I wondered if I were missing something especially when delicate topics were raised like comments on the Sino-Japanese war, the state of collaboration between the Kuomintang and Communists now that the two had combined in a joint front against the invaders. The answers seemed to me to skirt around the point and become bland or oblique or get deflected. Were they subtly circumvented in the interpretation? I could never know.

Madame Chiang by herself was a different proposition. She was a vivacious personality, a fascinating talker, made the air hum. She gave most of her time and made every effort to render my visit memorable. She was gracious and charming, repeatedly reminding what a pleasure and satisfaction it was to have an Asian sister and friend to whom she could pour out her heart and confide in, above all be able to freely discuss some of her problems and affairs of her country.

Before I left she put a fat envelope in my hands. It bulged with Chinese currency. A tiny note explained: As I had come as their guest, the airfare, Hongkong-Chungking should be covered by them. I handed over the envelope to the Superintendent of an orphanage in Chungking.

Back in Chungking I continued my explorations. I met women leaders, learnt of the systematic training given to women to send them out into different parts in batches of four, to help families, particularly women, and in general to face rationally the heavy challenges of a continuing war. I was told of their active participation in war effort. I saw them like Amazons in khaki uniforms and steel helmets. They accompanied the troops everywhere, carrying small weapons for defense, hand grenades when they ventured as gendarmes on guerilla work. They guarded strategic supplies as also military lines when troops had to be rushed to the active front. They figured in every government department. There were a fair number in the People's Political Council, the national policy making body. Nearly half the reporters at my Press Conference were women and told me there were over 50 women's journals in the country ! The Chinese women were obviously playing a significant role in the defense as well as the reconstruction of their country, from building of highways to harassing activities in the enemy lines. Quick in accepting revolutionary ideas, equally swift in carrying them out in action, these women in their restricted domain had however learnt to adapt their talents to ever changing conditions.

China's activities in the cultural field were just as impressive especially in the face of the enemy's concerted drive to destroy theatres, libraries, museums, cultural institutions. All literary and art forms were being encouraged, and such activities were now sought to be linked with the people by involving them.

By Madame Chiang's special request I met her sister Madame Kung for whom the former had high praise as a very practical and successful high-business woman. I had come across a few Chinese women of that type in Shanghai. I don't believe we have any such corresponding model in India.

The friendliest person I had for company was Sir Archiebald Clarke, the British Ambassador to China, whose intervention had got me to Chungking. A sociable, pleasant, soft-spoken man, liberal in his political outlook and human in his approach to national problems, and though fairly elderly, he seemed young in spirit, with easy rapport with youth. I felt I had a genuine friend in him. I was touched that he took me on trust and befriended me in the face of the stern warnings of Scotland Yard, painting me as a wild unbridled trouble maker. He was concerned for me as at times there were incessant air raids. He pressed me to use his own shelter in his house. Jokingly he reminded me that as the British were still the overlords of India, he felt responsible for His Majesty's Indian subject when she had strayed into this perilous land. 'I will never be able to forgive myself if you were hit'. I bowed polite acceptance but never did seek his shelter, though his was a luxurious one in comparison to the rough and ready improvised damp public ones. He met me as often as was possible in these heaving, uncertain times, to advise me on what to see, whom to meet. He also revealed to me some of the hard core problems behind the public facade of the present situation in this country. In this context he talked to me of the Communist leaders giving me a general picture of their situation and current role. He felt strongly that I should meet at least one important leader from the group. 'Your Chungking visit would be incomplete without it,' was his final verdict. Before I could ask how, he had assured me he would fix it up himself. 'I will try to get Chou En-Lai', and so it turned out to be.

Chou-en-Lai was lightly built, aristocratic looking yet with a military bearing becoming the Commander of the East Front Red Army, as he then was, definitely handsome with a pronounced air of self-confidence and as he talked this became infectious.

Foreign educated, he could express himself lucidly in English. Son of a Mandarin he had gone through the traditional scholarship before going to Europe. I surveyed him with keen curiosity—here was a gentleman on whose head there had once been an incredible price of 80.000 Chinese dollars ! He wanted me to understand the basic tenets of the Chinese Communists He was delicate of speech, fastidious in the choice of words, with a neatness in his explanations. There was a lurking alertness in his eyes, the result probably of a long hunted life. 'It is important for you to know that we Chinese Communists are not the same as the Russian or European reds—You know I was actively involved in Communist activities in Europe. The immediate task before us is our national freedom as I expect it is with you. That is why we are whole heartedly working in a United anti-Japanese war. We are confident of a total nation-wide mobilisation against the invaders. Though the Japanese have won victories by throwing in more divisions, barring a few areas they control only points and lines. For it is an indissolubly people's army created out of them, that is fighting for their freedom. Yet the conventional eye would be outraged at the sight of many of our people's army personnel in their cotton uniforms, donning a straw hat and wearing straw sandals. Yet they operate as guerillas even behind the enemy lines and sometimes even attack the well equipped enemy army. The new science of war evolved by our guerillas has won world wide acclaim.

'Great stress is laid on the political education of the army, impressing on them that they are fighting for the preservation of justice and freedom against tyranny and oppression. Even their children are taught to be useful war-time citizens.'

I had already heard of the ingenuious exploits of the guerillas and their almost uncanny knowledge of every kind of terrain without which such matchless resistance could never have been maintained.

'At the moment there is a Chinese government functioning in a kind of a Chinese island of 4000 sq. miles with 7 million in Hopei, inside the Japanese occupied territory, a fact that stuns one's imagination', continued Chou. 'We are equally confident this resistance will aid our national revolution. The peasantry has always been for a revolution, for they are the most oppressed and exploited.' His eyes flushed with fervour as he ended. He asked about India and I described the situation. 'I think our countries are soon going to be free. May be we shall meet again then,' he concluded. I expressed my hope he would visit us.

A decade later he came. Pandit Nehru remembering my China visit, invited me to an informal tea he was having for the guest, with a few people to meet him. We met as strangers meeting for the first time. No reference was made to the earlier visit, whatever reason he may have had. He conversed in Chinese through an interpreter, in a formal tone. One of the photographers sent me a largish photo of us drinking tea with our host. I had no desire to preserve it—it was meaningless to me now. This meeting seemed phony to me. I would rather cherish the Chungking one under those grey skies rent by the siren and clouded by the bomb explosions.

My trip out was even more exciting than my trip into Chungking. The air service had no fixed schedules. If you wished to leave on a particular day, you needed to start making attempts well ahead. The timings were entirely determined by raids. Having to fly over 'Occupied' territory necessarily confined the trip to night time, usually after midnight. I had already made one fruitless attempt. The next night after a long wait the outgoing plane arrived towards dawn. Almost simultaneously sounded the all clear siren and we took off immediately, and flew for hours, unaware where we were headed. All we knew was that we were flying for safety. But we had to sit tight as though it were a most normal trip. After four hours we landed in a field, to wait there without shelter, no food served until the generous darkness should descend to give us safe passage over the enemy occupied country. Each of us had brought snacks and water bottles.

Looking like an illuminated carpet Hong Kong was already asleep when we came in. We had been on the road almost 24 hours, to cover a distance that normally takes less than five hours. Still I felt it was worth every single moment of it. In fact looking back it seemed brief, so much had been crowded into just a few days.

The stay in Hong Kong this time was comparatively uneventful though some restrictions on movement were there. Now Mme Sun Yat Sen took charge of my programme. She or her brother usually accompanied me. She was at this time deeply involved in aiding the Chinese refugees from the mainland through a Refugee Welfare Organisation. Until then she had been to me the wife of a revolutionary who liberated China— But now I saw her as an entity with a personality and mind of her own. She seemed to embody something of the tenacity, the perseverance, willingness to toil of the Chinese. She lived very simply almost austerely. She had a mature type of beauty that spoke of suffering, endurance, experience. She was of a kindly and friendly disposition. We had long deep conversations, but she was one you could speak to even through silence.

Then she related her story. At a very youthful age she had to try to be a companion and comrade to a much older, intellectual and exhilarating mind, that of her illustrious husband.

Here was a fascinating adventure. Deeply moved by Dr. Sen, at the age of twenty she had fled from her home, jumping out of her window in the dead of night, to became his Secretary. 'It was no romance', she explained. 'I simply wanted to serve the people and I was convinced he was the perfect vehicle through which I could fulfill my desires.' Though she was twenty years junior to him, he was apprehensive if they were to be together closely, she may be regarded as his concubine, so he proposed marriage. 'For my part I was delighted, as this was more than a social convenience, for he was my wondrous hero and I had never ever dreamed of such an intimate relationship. An unexpected tragedy however threw a shadow across this happy event, for it enraged my father to the extent of his disowning us, for he had been until then a staunch supporter of Dr. Sen What is more, the entire Christian community turned against us. To crown it all came my sister Meiling's marriage to Chiang Kai Shek which was loudly applauded by the same devout Christians. So much for our Christian principles,' she exclaimed with a sigh.

'In the political sphere not one of the good Christian Western European countries nor America even, cared to acknowledge any communication from Dr. Sen on behalf of the new Chinese Republic. They had evidently been happy to exploit the emasculated rump of a country. The only meaningful gesture came from Soviet Russia which apart from giving ready recongition, gave up its concessions, its extra-territoriality, and signed a treaty as between two equal nations.'

According to Madame Sen, Dr. Sen's continuing disillusionment with the Christian community and the hardening prejudice of the

Christian countries towards struggling China, was responsible for his turning towards the Communists. After Dr. Sen's untimely death when Chiang Kai Shek took over the reins and split the Kuomintang, driving out the Communists, she stayed with the Left for she wanted to adhere faithfully to Dr. Sen's line. 'When Chiang got more busy waging wars on the Communists, soft peddling the resistance towards the Japanese, I moved to Hong Kong to devote myself largely to welfare activities.' She had kept up her association with politics through the National Salvation Group comprised of the Leftists. She had also promoted the China Defence League to wage an all out drive to throw out the Japanese.

I was glad to meet her brother T.V. Soong and talk with him, for I had learnt he had, as Finance Minister made the Induscos in China possible, and even more, to flourish. I learnt he was a Harvard economics graduate, understood the crucial need to promote production and economic service of a suitable pattern that could operate in a war-torn country. 'I believed in making profits out of *production*, not juggling with currency in international banking, for I am familiar with those tricks', he explained as we talked of his patronage of the Induscos. Even in murky Shanghai he was respected as a clean man. Strongly anti-Japanese and a staunch supporter of the United Front, he had clashed with Chiang who also resented Soong's grip on the national purpose, until Soong resigned.

My heart went out to Madame Sun uniformly gentle, kind, poised though she lived under volcanic conditions, her country being cruelly torn apart by the Japanese, worse by a man whom her beloved husband had nurtured and shaped as one of his successors.

At Hong Kong, for my onward journey I was happy to get back to the American President Line. I looked forward to some relaxation after the past few hectic weeks.

By some coincidence I discovered that the governor of Hong Kong was on the boat. When I saw him alone one morning on the deck I pulled up a deck chair and sat down unceremoniously, gave him my name and identified myself as the person whom he got arrested even before I landed in his territory, which was outrageous for it was without provocation. His curt answer was that he had received a communication from Scotland Yard warning him against my visit. 'Did Scotland Yard describe me as a desperate criminal armed to my teeth, that made you send a whole posse of polioo to take me into custody?' He hesitated a while, then said 'not exactly, but that you were a dangerous rebel.' 'True I am a rebel in my own country, fighting for its freedom. Aren't there armies engaged today for this avowed purpose. That does not however make me a lawless marauder, travelling round to disrupt places I visit. In this case I came to Hong Kong by an unfortunate compulsion, not choice, for it was the only route to Chungking. You were aware of that. Would the Chiang Kai Shek invite a disruptive person into a highly sensitive area as their capital is? I am a total stranger to Hong Kong with no links with any underground rebels at work, unarmed, what upheaval could I have brought about within the few hours I would be forced to linger in Hong Kong, waiting for the Chungking flight to pick me up. This whole drama is beyond any rationale. It is an empty melodrama devised to humiliate a perfectly law abiding individual. You provoked me in every way, serving a parole notice as though I were a stray hardened criminal that has to be kept under watch round the clock. By all decent English canons this whole thing is an outrage.' With that I got up and left. Some weight was lifted off my chest.

Manila was our next port where we were to halt for three days. I excitedly waited to glimpse this land of 7000 islands. I found myself amongst generous, lively friends. I could go where I liked including an air trip. So I chose Baguio up in the mountains, one my favourites. That is where I saw some of the old Filipino crafts. I balanced this by a sail in the picturesque *Vina*—an elaborate dugout canoe with outriggers of the Moros—the Moslem Filipinos, and even the Sea Gypsy which collected attractive shells and corals.

The most memorable event was being received by President Manuel Quezon and his wife and Vice-President Sergio Osmeno, of the Philippines. They were simple friendly people who chatted informally. Talking of old times he related his hazardous life as a boy insurrector against the Spanish, who had to finally give himself up to General McArthur's father, who had come to drive out the Spaniards. The President and Vice-President who were trying to be the architects of their country's independence, were confident their day of full liberation was very near. I learnt from them of their tradition in learning, that their first University was founded in 1611!

They in turn showed keen interest in India's struggle for freedom. 'We sympathise, we are with you. God will help you as he is helping us', said the President in a warm friendly tone. I felt sad when I read in 1944 that Manuel Quezon had passed away in exile, his cherished dream unfulfilled.

As the boat came alongside the quay at Singapore I waited eagerly to disembark. Before I knew what was happening a uniformed officer strode up and flashed a paper before me saying 'You cannot land, here is the prohibitary order.' Another officer followed almost ordering about. 'I suggest you rest in your cabin until this bustle of departures subsides.' I turned on him questioning his right to order me about, more so as I was on an American boat. In the midst of this turmoil suddenly the ship's Captain materialised and asked if he could be of assistance. One of the police officers explained I was prohibited from going ashore at Singapore. 'The lady seems enraged', he added with a supercilious smile. The Captain stopped further talk by firmly asking the officers to take leave, and then turned to me apologetically to express his inability to help: 'I shall do what I can to lighten your disagreeable hours. I have already asked the Purser to put fresh magazines and papers at your disposal. Our chief chef is keen to prepare a special surprise lunch, so you don't feel too badly over the shore meals you have to miss. In the meantime I would be delighted to have you join me for a cup of coffee.' He wanted to be excused for a few minutes. A group comprising the President of the Indian Association with some Chinese friends who had come to pick me up were waiting and he wanted to explain to them the situation. I asked him to request them to take an Indian lady, a student on the boat who was to have gone ashore with me and was stranded. This done, we both sat down to our coffee. I gave the Captain a brief background to the bizarre situation. 'It is a bad business', was his final comment. As we parted he invited me to join him at his table. 'You won't feel so lonesome.'

The episode was repeated at Sri Lanka. With so many friends there, I had somehow hoped otherwise. The Indian lady student had friends there and was going ashore. To her I gave names of people she could speak to for me. She returned dejected in the evening. Several had tried, to no avail. The order had been issued by the Governor General himself and when his office was contacted his Secretary explained the instructions had come from London, so pleaded helplessness. The Captain looked graver than ever and shook his head.

Our boat came into Bombay harbour and as I collected my belongings to quit my cabin, I was surprised to see the Captain at the door, looking very worried. 'Is there any delay in our disembarking?' I asked. He shook his head. 'I am seriously wondering what I will do if the authorities don't let you land.' I burst out laughing to see his woebegone face. 'Very simple', I said in an exaggerated consoling tone. 'Your ship will keep on carrying me round the world, the kind purser will keep me busy with fresh supplies of magazines, papers, and the inexhaustible chef provide me with ever fresh dishes.' He walked me down the ladder, up the barrier, watched me cross it. I looked back and waved a happy farewell.

I realised how relieved the authorities in India must have been to see me back, right in their clutches instead of chasing me over the globe. I was truly amazed how quickly I passed through, especially customs. I was asked politely if I could leave behind my box of books and papers for a day to avoid waiting. I did. The very next day I was asked to pick it. Everything was intact, nothing missing.

10

Soon after my return I got a call from Sardar Vallabhai. He wanted to welcome me after some of my exploits abroad. I gave him a brief resume of my trip. He advised me to visit Gandhiji immediately. On this he was firm and so I went. Gandhiji usually greets old faces with an all embracing smile. I missed the glow. Instead a shadow brushed across his face. This had happened so rarely that I felt a slight twinge of apprehension. I had yet to get a total picture of our national affairs of today, in place of the disjointed snippets that had been blowing around my ears.

I sought Prabhavati, Jayaprakash's wife. She was her usual placid self. She is the only person I have known who never could be perturbed, nor had I ever seen her without her gentle smile. Frowns and sulks were foreign to her. She was the busiest bee in the Sevagram Ashram. One saw her with Kasturba in the kitchen, attending on guests, bringing food to Gandhiji and a whole host of odd jobs. Always frail looking, today she looked tired, more, weary.

This was one time when I saw a bluish shadow on her face, dark circles round the eyes. I waited until she began to open up herself. Jayaprakash with over 200 other fellow prisoners had gone on hunger strike in protest against the inhuman conditions in the Deoli Camp in Rajasthan, a notorious detention prison for hardened terrorists. The system of punishment was atrocious. There was also a complete lack of medical facilities. Senseless solitary confinement had driven prisoners to mental instability and one to complete lunacy. When repeated demands for rectifying were summarily rejected and the hunger strike notice scorned, the fasts began as a last resort.

Just preceding this had taken place the highly publicised story of Jayaprakash attempting to send a written message out to his colleagues through his wife, where in he had advocated all means to end this barbarous alien rule. This was an occasion where to me Gandhiji rose to one of his superb heights. He was sceptical of the authenticity of the document publicised as Jayaprakash's. This is what he publicly recorded. 'If the motive was to discredit the organisation of which he is a distinguished member, it must fail. Frankly, all nationalist forces are now at war with the government. Assuming the correctness of the charge, according to the accepted canons of war, Jayaprakash's method is perfectly legitimate. To practice deception, even to plot murder are all honourable and turn the perpetrators into heroes like Clive and Warren Hastings. The sensation with which the event has been publicised is ill-conceived—the annotations unwarranted, and when it is borne in mind that Jayaprakash is an untried detenue, they look very like hitting below the belt.' I was thrilled on reading this.

The Deoli prisoners' fast was in its third week when I reached Sevagram. Very early the next morning Gandhiji sent for me. I was stunned to see his face ashen grey obviously the sign of a night of agony. I had never seen him a victim of such suffering. There was an unusually deep emotion in his voice as he talked: 'You are aware of the hunger strike by the prisoners at Deoli Camp. The demand is for the dispersal of the detenus by sending each back to his own province.'

So far the authorities have been adamant. N.M. Joshi, the labour leader, visited the camp. The Communists agreed to give up the fast. But Jayaprakash and others refused and Jayaprakash was being punished for his 'intransigence' by solitary confinement. J. Chatterji who was in a serious condition was removed to the hospital. There was a long pause, surprising, for he never failed for words. 'I want you to help. Rajaji is staying here. I'd like you to meet him, persuade him to intervene, use his influence to bring this fast to an end. I know you have friendly relations with him.' I was dumbfounded. Why was he deputing me? Where he had obviously failed, who was I that I could succeed? My mind was in complete turmoil, I did not know what to say. Silence meant consent and he proceeded to send Rajaji a message as from me. Instantly my very nervousness made me burst forth. Oh no, no. He did not seem to hear me, he had left the room and I rose as in a daze. In a few minutes the young messenger deputed to Rajaji arrived to escort me.

I had genuine cold feet as I sat facing Rajaji. After a few preliminaries about my foreign trip, I made the request as Gandhiji had suggested. Immediately the friendly smile vanished, a stern look flooded his eyes. 'I did not think you were one of the admirers of this irresponsible bunch who in the name of patriotism create melodramas.' This fast cannot be called a melodrama' I ventured nervously to interrupt. 'What else is it. I believe that when hunger strikers undertakes a fast it should be allowed to run its full course to its logical end. Only then will individuals or groups not rush in, fortified by a kind of built in confidence that someone will intervene and rescue them.'

I could not bring myself to repeat this to Gandhiji. He must have guessed failure from my face. He merely heaved a deep sigh. I only whispered to Prabhavati my failure, She gave her usual smile, patted me comfortingly. 'Don't take it too badly—I was sure it was not going to work.' Poor Prabhavati's agony was to continue, until Jayaprakash finally broke the fast—after 31 days. But a long time had to pass before she could really join him and be with him. Jayaprakash's dramatic escape from Hazaribagh prison and his wanderings in the jungles, across mountains on foot, his final arrest and release on the eve of the Interim Government are now part of the story of the Indian struggle for freedom.

Prabhavati's role in Jayaprakash's life is little known and not recognised. She was, I would say an embodiment of love, full of a rare, selfless affection. She was deeply attached to him and intensely proud of him. I had often watched her looking at him when her eyes held almost an adoration. Nevertheless she was conscious of his weaknesses and foibles, when her reaction was one of amused, restrained indulgence. There was the eternal clamour over his contrary demands. He would sternly ask to travel light, which she had learnt after some bitter experience to ignore. 'You see all what he calls the *extras* that I am asked *not* to carry are the *essentials* he cannot dispense with. So I have to carry the 'unwanted' even at the cost of his irritation. He becomes like a child on such occasions. I could not possibly humiliate him by exposing these contradictions to him. He is too big, too great a man. I am conscious how precious he is to our country, our people. I do all I can to spare him the little irritations of life. He has exposed himself to too many wounds. Those who love and value him need to ease his burdens.' This is how she explained to me their life pattern after they settled down in Patna where I visited to them occasionally. I came to realise she was the person closest to him, who enjoyed his confidence the most, to whom he could open out his heart freely. Above all she was happy, truly happy. Deeply imbued with principles drawn from her long Gandhian association, she knew that as a man, he cherished the same virtues, for he was a man of steadfast principles.

At this juncture I should like to reflect on my relationship with Rajaji. I had first met Rajaji—as he was popularly known---when I was just a young girl, at a marriage, rather unusual for those times, in Mangalore, of a Brahmin bride and a non-Brahmin groom. My social reformer uncle was largely responsible for the marriage. Rajaji was playing the role of the groom's father. The liberal elements in the town were full of praise for him for this unusual role, himself being a Brahmin. My mother was most eloquent. She attributed this largely to the high education which the bride had received and according to her won her the patronage of two personalities like Rajagopalachari and my uncle. Above all she had not been 'led like a meek goat to the marriage haven,' was her final verdict.

When my Uncle introduced me to Rajaji, I warmly gave expression to a sense of pride. He was amused and Uncle explained the cause of my elation. 'What are you going to do when you grow up, little lady,' he asked with a broad friendly smile. Prompt came my answer, 'I am going to change society, especially for women.' 'That is a big ambition.' 'But I am not afraid,' was my firm answer, trying to stretch my chest. This brought a gentle pat on my head as a blessing.

This relationship that started so auspiciously was resumed nearly two decades later when I became active in the Congress. I continued to admire and respect him though I had political differences and even impatience with policies he advocated. But I valued his honesty, his open differences with Gandhiji and the Congress in a world where such courage and sincerity were rare. I never got the feeling he had an axe to grind, never doubted his patriotism. That is why our friendly relations had remained. Never had he occasion to shoot one of his typical sharp barbs at me, for they were never called for. I also admired him for his austere style of living even when he was Chief Minister of the then Madras State, how he had not even drawn the full amount allocated under the budget for his use. Alas such types are unknown now. In fact the demand today is for more and more funds.

When I was leaving Gandhiji suddenly asked me if I would come to Bardoli for a few days. He would be there and we would both be Vallabhai's guests. 'I want you to see him in his natural setting and savour other sides of his personality that I am sure would touch your interests at some point.' To this I gave a quick assent.

Vallabhai's abode had the look of a farm house but was provided with all modern conveniences. Almost everything seemed home grown or home made. Maniben with whom I had grown friendly in prison, proved a most helpful companion, familiarising me with her inner domain. A sizeable flower garden extended into a well kept orchard which made a most pleasing setting.

Sarder seemed a different man here. He, whose domain was normally distant, I found quite accessible, and in spite of his dour. exterior, he could be quite human, with a genuine concern for people. He invited me to sit with him and his visitors, 'to be one of us' as he tersely put it with a ghost of a smile on his thick lips and a little twinkle in his heavy eyes. My old conviction that he was bitterly prejudiced towards those who were not of his way of thought began to somewhat diminish. When a heavy frown darkened his forehead and a growl crept into his voice, one expected thunder and lightening to follow, instead he would be intently listening to his dissenter, and the cloud would gradually disappear.

He graciously walked me round his well-kept garden and the orchard in which he showed special interest and a fund of knowledge that comes of long experience. I realised as he pottered about and around plants and trees, here was a personality other than the renowned Iron Man, as he was popularly known, handing seedlings with incredible sensitivity, and with a rare soft light in his usual stern eyes. They were fleeting experiences but opened little slits in a grey curtain that seemed to hang over his personality. I could not forget that he had been uniformly kind and thoughtful in all our dealings after my harsh attack on him. Here I was now, a privileged, personal guest of his. He had never referred to that attack, nor had I shown any inclination to apologise for it. Both Gandhiji and he either had had second thoughts or presumed I had mellowed down into a disciplined worker. How else could they have been party to putting me in charge of the political training of thousands of women, such a delicate and responsible office.

One other incident in this context stands out in my mind. A heavy strain was threatening to mar the relationship between the Socialists and the Congress high command during a session of the All India Congress Committee in Bombay. Suddenly I was called by Vallabhai. In a very friendly and persuasive tone he asked me if I would bring about a compromise between the two. I expressed my inability. His face suddenly fell and showed keen dissappointment. He heaved a deep sigh saying 'Why don't you try?' I was completely perplexed and shook my head. Years later when the Sardar was no more, reviewing the Sardar in retrospect, Jayaprakash confessed to our being too involved in ideological theorising on occasions and putting off his friendly gestures.

In the running of his establishment and directing its many activities, he showed the same attention to details, getting a thorough grasp of a problem, turning it over with intense concentration as though he were getting his teeth into every problem posed before him by those around him or by a constant stream of visitors that kept calling on his advice and help. In later years I was to see many other sides of him both with admiration as also with dismay, and I hurt him again for what he felt was rank indiscipline on my part.

Gandhiji for his part was happy to watch an easy cordiality warming up between the Sardar and myself. I was deeply touched as also wondered at his taking the trouble to bring about better understanding between us. I then recollected my attack on him which evidently Gandhiji continued to feel was uncalled for. He probably hoped my seeing the softer and more human side of Vallabhai might result in modifying my earlier assessment.

For my part I was glad I saw the more veiled sides of the man more objectively and glimpsed trends in his viewing problems and his assessments of situations where I differed from him. I hoped like Gandhiji that we would have an easier meeting ground in the future. But I could not bring myself to justify his earlier sweeping and wholesale censuring the entire youth of the country.

However for today it was warmth and peace and I left in a lighter mood.

The annual session of the All India Women's Conference was on and after a longish break I attended it. I was only too conscious that we would soon be plunged into another active political struggle. Having tasted the exhilaration of revolutionary action, spread out their chests in self-confidence and pride, the people were in no mood to continue in slavery. Since the Seva Dal was banned, I decided to use the Conference Organisation to resume my old project to train women for better citizenship with the growing need to equip them with initiative and leadership. The Conference welcomed my proposal for women for purposeful training in community service and national service. The women responded most enthusiastically. Mridula Sarabhai, a great enthusiastic for field work, organised the camp in Abrama Village in Gujarat. The training was aimed at broad basing the Conference's activities through programmes reaching out to the larger masses of the women. Besides the Conference's own recruits, 33 other women's institutions sent candidates. The trainees came from all communities, including tribals who brought their traditional crafts.

The studies were general : to open up new vistas of knowledge and special classes for the actual training for implementation. Aesthetics were provided through music, dance, drama, handicrafts. A pioneering subject was mankind and environment, and of course physical culture. The site was chosen for its proximity to the village, and every effort made to involve the village folk in the activities of the camp. Unfortunately the camp had to close after 3 months as the political air was heating up. In winding up the trainees recorded their impressions thus:

> 'Our feeling is that we have come into a new world. We came ignorant of many things. The weeks we spent here gave us the feeling that we leapt from darkness into bright light. We have learned much that had remained a closed book to us. We can now better appreciate life's many problems and its many struggles in their proper perspective.'

By now Japan was on India's door step. Indian refugees from the regions conquered by it kept rushing in, defenseless and abandoned by the British. India felt helpless, herself exposed to invasion. For Gandhiji the time for sounding the final bugle had arrived.

On 8th August, 1942 he called on the British to 'Quit India'.

For the first time there crept into his voice fire and bitterness as he said to the nation : 'This is open rebellion.' Gandhiji's speech on this occasion is a perfect classic, every word, phrase to be cherished. 'I want freedom immediately, this very night before dawn. Freedom now cannot wait . . . Let every man and woman live every moment of his or her life hereafter in the consciousness that he or she eats or lives for achieving freedom and will die if need be, to attain that goal. Take a pledge that you will no longer rest till freedom is won, and will be prepared to lay down your lives in the attempt. He who loses his life will gain it, he who will seek to save it shall lose it. Freedom is not for the coward or the faint heart.' He thus went like an inspired messiah.

'Here is a mantra, a short one that I give you : You may imprint it on your hearts and let every breath of yours give expression to it. The mantra is: Do or die. We shall either free India or die in the attempt.' He outlined detailed instructions to the various classes of the people, from the princes to the hamlet dwellers. The crux of his call was that each was free, untrammelled to act—each to be his or her own leader. In his usual dramatic manner he said 'From today we are free. Paralyse the government.' This was indeed a magical moment, never to be repeated, only to be cherished as a precious experience. For India the bell of freedom had begun to toll. The Socialists met at Yusuf Meherally's house to chalk out our plan of action. 'This night is momentous', declared Meherally in his usual dramatic tone. 'Whatever needs to be done, has to be done this moment.' The National Executive had already decided to support the mass struggle under Gandhiji's leadership.

I slipped out of Bombay for Bangalore as the news of the round up of Congress workers began early 9th morning even as the Quit India movement burst upon the country. I wanted to be in this big metropolis in the South where I had been preparing the ground over the years, to launch a campaign. The friend who met me as I arrived, threw up his hands exclaiming 'a revolution is on here, men, women, even children are participating'. I had barely time to hold confabulations with the available colleagues before I found myself under arrest.

I was relieved to find myself in the local jail. But this was an illusion. Within hours I found myself being transferred to Vellore. Several non-political public men rushed to avert this but in vain.

I was back in Vellore. This term in Vellore proved even more difficult than the previous, for my body began to act adversely even from the early days. As mid-summer approached, my system began to deteriorate rapidly. But time ticked on, slowly, agonisingly.

As I entered the 1944 summer and my condition worsened, an outside doctor was called in who evidently advised early release. So I was released. Releases of some political prisoners had already started after Gandhiji was released on medical grounds soon after I was.

As I sat in the Katpadi Railway Station waiting for the Mangalore train to take me home, a special messenger sent by a friend from Madras arrived with an urgent letter. It was from Dr. Cousins to tell me that Gretta had had a paralytic stroke and her brain had become weak. This made a poor homecoming for me, more so as I could not be with her very long.

I immediately rushed to her. She recognised and clung to me almost like a child, something that was new. But her memory was unstable and tended to get blurred. She would laugh and talk excitedly then suddenly get silent, dispirited. The Gretta that I leaned on was no more, but love and devotion held. I got a foreign friend, specialist in curative exercises and massage, to be with her until I could come to her again.

I had hardly time to lean back and take a deep breath, when I got an urgent call from the Bombay branch of the Women's Conference. Although I had been elected Conference president early 1942, no session could be held for me to take over due to my incarceration and that of many others as so many of our active workers had plunged into the Quit India revolution. The coming session was to be in Bombay. The organisers decided on an immediate meet and I was alerted. Hardly were the dates announced, when a prominent announcement appeared in all the papers to proclaim that a prohibitary order had been issued by the Bombay police authorities to prevent me from entering Bombay city.

The general reaction was one of shock and disgust. It was obviously most uncalled for. I conveyed to the Conference organisers that the Conference should be held and I would positively be there. A few days before the Conference date I slipped into Bombay at night by car and took residence with a newcomer to the city, a young woman journalist from Kerala, unconnected with politics. On the day of the Conference I arrived at Victoria Station by a slow local at mid-day which in those days meant an almost empty train. I was formally received by the Reception Committee and I became Premlila Thackersay's guest. The first thing I did was to telephone H.V.R. Iyenger, then the State Home Secretary, to inform him I had broken the prohibitory order. 'Now what do you propose to do. I shall preside over the session tomorrow as arranged. No one but you know where I am. In the evening there is a Reception for me by the Mayor where I shall make my first appearance. You know better than me, today the Bombay Corporation is richer and politically more powerful than your government. You may convey your decision to Premlilaben, Chairman of the Reception Committee.' I had known H.V.R. over quite a few years, for he had been one of Pithaji's proteges and we had often come together. He rang back, and told my hostess, the ban order had been issued by the Police Commissioner without his knowledge as a police routine. Then he talked directly with me. 'When the Conference dates were announced and you were expected, I presumed you would contact me and I would then withdraw the order. I grant it was a stupid thing to have done for the police chief. But unless the impending situation arose I could do nothing. You are free to stay as long as you wish. In a way this is your city, where you unfurled the flag and the success of the first Salt Satyagraha was in no mean measure due to your ingenuity and drive. I would be the last person to debar you from your capital. We are to meet very soon. A mutual friend is going to invite us both to dinner. Till then wish you all the best.' Thus was averted an ugly situation by a sagacious man. For the women had decided if I was touched, they would offer Satyagaraha and get arrested. Minoo Masani as the Mayor, was delighted to get up his Mayoral reception 'by a jail bird to a jail bird' as he publicly announced.

In my address to the Women's Conference I wanted the focus on women to shift from sex to a social gene. I had never been in tune with feminism as advocated in the West where men and women were lined up in confrontation, as though they were irreconcilable elements. In India the women's problems had been treated as *social*, part of a malaise in the body of our social constitution. Men and women had been struggling to rectify this for half a century or more, a joint battle to better the whole society, wipe off caste distinctions, the concept of untouchability and the like. I wished to carry this further to its logical conclusion by altering the aims and objects of the Conference to bring them within a wider social parameter.

A new note I tried to strike was affirming the human value of a housewife in economic and social terms. Her contribution as the basic cohesive element in the family and therefore in the society and the nation needed recognition, whether she held a job and contributed monetarily or not. She was entitled to an equal status with the husband. The point has been debated off and on but has never got into the normal national stream.

I saw to it that for the first time the Conference had a permanent headquarter with a Central Office with separate departments, a library, publication of small books, pamphlets for education and propaganda. Later, as the World War ended, a small employment section was set up to meet the needs of large numbers of women who got thrown out of employment. The Central Office began to actively collaborate with other women's organisations in the city, so that a real woman-power bloc emerged.

I had realised with considerable shock that while Bombay possessed sleek hospitals, beyond its immediate suburbs, medical service was nil. The Conference planned a medical van to service those neglected areas. A friendly English organisation donated an uptodate vehicle called Skippo. Dhanwanti Ramarow in her grand embracing manner took it to her bosom. Soon it spread like a bracing wind and several branches of the Conference were operating similar vans under the breezy slogan 'Keep the Vans moving.'

During the Conference itself I had sensed that attempts had been made to politicise the Conference for the first time during these intervening years when we were imprisoned. Till then though women with different political affiliations worked in this organisation, their ideologies or tenets of political faith were never projected for the acceptance of the Conference. That situation had undergone a change during the Quit India movement when most of the old conference workers were absent from the active scene. With the entry of Russia on the Allied side and the removal of restrictions on the Left groups, in particular the Communists, they had had the field to themselves and they made the best use of the opportunity. Now this was being done in several subtle ways which only the politically aware could sense. But others could not grasp it. Therein lay the danger. While I did not object to the Left or Marxian ideology as a political faith, I did not want non-believers or those innocent of its implications to get involved in resolutions, either garbled or subtly disguised or be committed to actions not fully grasping the consequences. Corruption had set in through bogus membership. The Membership of a single district outran the membership of the entire country!

Most members were unaware of what was happening and got irritated with those of us who tried to alert them. Some of our senior members like Sarojini were irritated by our caution and condemned us as partisan, narrow minded and the like, so opposition came from various quarters. Those like Mridula Sarabhai who had been elected one of the secretaries and refused to wear kid gloves in dealing with the dye-in-the-wool political elements, came in for severe criticism as disrupters, and I got caught between these crossfires.

My most effective and dependable helper was Mehra Jhabwalla who as the wife of an active and dedicated trade unionist, was deeply versed in these political machinations of practised manipulators.

At the annual sessions of the Conference, special programmes were organised by these political elements after dinner, in the form of singing, recitals, dances, interspersed with alluring talks on the themes under discussion, what to support, and finally how to vote. I watched these multipronged approaches to brainwash delegates, most of whom were a political.

For the two years I held office, there was a determined drive to capture the organisation by these groups. This struggle came to a head at the session when a new general secretary was to be elected. A young lady, an associate member of the Servants of India Society, under this august label, was put up by them against one of the old workers. It put me in mind of the Do or Die situation of 1942, for the entire future of the Conference hung on this crucial election. We won by just a few votes. It was obvious that the majority of the voters were blissfully unaware of what was at stake.

I laid down the presidential office with some satisfaction. The old framework that had disintegrated during the political movement and reduced to a mere skeleton had been restored and restructured, in fact invigorated by the revolutionary glow sweeping the country and setting many more women astir I could relinquish my post with a deep breath of relief, for the crisis had passed. The retreat of those forches was final, the attempt was never repeated again in the Conference. What is more the senior amongst them became friendly and cooperative and with some my friendship has remained.

The evil effects of the war had however created new problems. Famine for instance made care of children compelling. A special body Save The Children was created and Homes for Children set up. While I was touring Orissa on this mission, I literally ran into the Mahanadi floods, walking through rushing waters on a rescue mission to get at stranded children. Later a Children's Home was set up there. I saw some farmers' families watching the devastation. I tried to get their reaction for they seemed more quiet in striking contrast to our agitation. I was accompanied by Urmila Mehta, one of our seasoned workers and a close friend who had volunteered to venture out on this tough expedition, even though she was not in robust health. The peasants told us the flood was an annual occurrence which they had learnt to accept. 'Even though it causes so much destruction?' I asked in amazement, for it meant starting anew every year. 'Surely there must be other lands where you would not get uprooted every year. Why don't you move?' They looked hurt. One old man picked up a little earth in his hand and let it drop slowly to the ground, his eyes intently on it. 'Do you see this?' he addressed me. 'It is not mud, it is gold. When the water recedes this will feed us again. as it has me and my ancestors over the ages. No we belong to this earth. She is cruel at times but kind too. I can never abandon her'. There was a light in his eyes and a tender lilt in his voice. This memory has stayed with me and I trumbles when I hear from some of the older people in the villages that young people alas have no more that attachment to the land.

I began to give considerable time to reorganising and strengthening the Socialist Party. To me as to several others, further struggle was inevitable to complete the unfinished revolution.

As 1945 was going over into 1946, several things began to happen in quick succession as the World War came to an end. The Indian National Army nurtured and fortified by Subash Bose was now, after the Japanese collapse, in British hands, and some of its personnel, in particular its three arch leaders, were lodged in the Red Fort. Eventually their trial was planned as a military Court Martial. Though sought to be kept a close secret, the Indian National leaders got scent and the news burst like a gigantic bubble throughout the country.

No army exploits since the 1857 war of independence had electrified the country as the establishment of the Azad Hind Government of Free India and the march of the Azad Hind Fauj—the Indian National Army, as it popularly became known, with its slogans 'Delhi Chalo and Jai Hind!'

New developments, unsual, unorthodox started to move rapidly. Gandhiji and Sardar Patel paid a couple of vists to the prisoners lodged in the Red Fort. Gandhiji, a man of surprises, identified himself with the prisoners, took the matter up with Viceroy Wavell and with the Commander-in-Chief, personally. The Congress Working Committee passed a resolution expressing sympathy with the prisoners. It also set up a powerful committee to organise defense of these prisoners. A whole galaxy of the best legal brains in the country offered its services free of charge. The country showed its sympathy through demonstrations, public meetings, etc. Several women vied with each other to patronise these precious prisoners as 'our proud responsibility' sending them food and gifts.

The most spectacular reprisal at this time was the Mutiny of the Indian Navy in Bombay. I was deeply stirred by this as the Chief Naval Officer and some of his close associates were my friends.

The Red Fort Trial drew world wide attention for it injected an element of ethics into prevailing military legalities pushing the latter into the background. The legal world in particular watched its strange course and ultimate outcome. It also touched me personally when Lakshmi of the Rani Janshi Brigade reached Delhi. Her mother Ammu Swaminathan was a family friend, a close colleague in the Conference, latterly a prisonmate. She confided to me that Lakshmi was engaged to Captain Sehgal and they both naturally were in a most anxious frame of mind. Lakshmi was a qualified doctor practising in Singapore when she joined the INA and finally became a Captain. Her exciting exploits in the INA would fill a volume. The story of the Azad Hind government and the Indian National Army is as incredible and scintillating as an Arabian Nights tale.

But at this point my mind was mulling over the deeper issues involved behind a seemingly common place court martial. Though the charge against them was the age old waging war against the king—for so many of us the first alphabet in the Indian Penal Code under which thousands had over the years been found 'guilty' and sentenced. I saw not three men under threat and a death sentence but the picture of India with a new mien confronting England. It was freedom *versus* bondage that was really on trial. All the brilliant arguments of the ablest legal brains dissolved into the 'Do or Die' will of the Indian people in a desperate bid to break off their shackles.

Those at the helm of affairs in Britain were aware of it, emerging out of a catastrophe of near destruction themselves. For those sitting in Westminister had finally come to see that the centuries old ignominous grip on vast territories over the globe had to be relaxed. This was the first test of a dawning wisdom, when the English Commander-in-Chief in India passed the final verdict acquitting the accused! It was also the first political break India had had since the struggle started in the Twenties.

My mind fled eighty-eight years back to another historic trial that took place in the same Red Fort when Bahadur Shah, the last king of Delhi, was found guilty of the same crime, steadfast love of his country, and sentenced to banishment for life! It were as though this trial had to be held and end in the acquittal to compensate for the cruel injustice meted out to a great patriot in 1858.

Most of 1946 was crisscrossed by negotiations between different people at various levels all of which is recent history and needs no re-recording. Gandhiji's persistent demand for Jayaprakash's release, in particular his final pronouncement in this connection is memorable, when he pointed out the incongruity of pursuing political negotiations while keeping patriots of Jayaprakash's calibre in jail. Thereupon he and Dr. Lohia were both released. I was truly aghast to learn from them for the first time, of the utterly barbarous torture they were subjected to in the Lahore Fort. We had been made to believe that such inhuman behaviour belonged to the fascist world. This revealed however how bestial human beings can become if they even smell a threat to their ill-gotten power.

The political air continued to grow murky. A shadow kept creeping over the country and was reflected on Gandhiji's face. I was still preoccupied with Party work and to get a Kannada Weekly called Jagrati going as a party organ for purposeful socialist education.

As the Cabinet Mission's plans for India got finalised, Pandit Nehru took over as Congress President from Maulana Azad. I had a surprise visit from Dr. Keskar the new Congress General Secretary, with an invitation from Pandit Nehru to join the Working Committee he was forming I expressed my inability. I explained I was ill at ease with the current developments and did not feel I could play any responsible role in this milieu. Within hours Jayaprakash arrived to convince me I should agree. He had himself been asked but could not be involved in the Congress affairs at this juncture as the developing situation placed other compulsions on him. I thereupon reminded him of the letter he had addressed to Party members. Was I excluded from its operation, I asked. 'The Congress is facing the most serious crisis. Nehru carries a heavy load. He has sought our active cooperation. He wanted Lohia to be General Secretary of the Congress and me to be by his side in the Working Committee, both of which we declined. He naturally feels we don't wish to associate ourselves with him. I certainly don't wish him to feel that because it is not true, so one of us should enter his Executive at this momentous hour. He hoped you would agree to be there. I therefore plead with you to respond to his wish and I add my own.'

When Jayaprakash pleaded one had to be made of cast iron not to melt. I could not however but feel like the Socialist Party's sacrificial goat offered to stifle Pandit Nehru's discomfiture. I felt I should meet Nehru before giving a final answer. When we met I conveyed to him very explicitly my adverse reactions to the current negotiations and the mood in the Congress. I felt it was but right that he should know how I felt. 'I would not be representing the Socialist Party, and I am not an important enough political entity to add weight to your Executive which is in national terms a weighty body. What exactly is to be my role?' I asked. Nehru was silent for a while then said: 'The situation warrants the maximum of collaborations from all sections. In my opinion a non-partisan individual that you claim to be, is all the more desirable. May I remind you of that popular allegory of an unostentatious squirrel contributing to the final success of an engineering feat that enabled Rama to cross over to Lanka? So you see none is insignificant. Need I say more?' He looked silently at me. Nothing was at stake for me personally, except that the hawks in the Party, would be critical—a futile particle in my dish not worth hurting two colleagues whom I valued and respected. So I nodded my assent adding 'I wanted to be frank and let you know my disposition.' Then I asked who were the other members. The usual list came out with one new, strange name, *Kairon*. 'Who and why is he here?' I asked quite involuntarily. 'We had to have one Sikh and he seemed to be non-controversial.' How ironical that proved considering the gusts of controversy he was to raise in the coming years.

I learnt Gandhiji wanted me. He looked sombre and thoughtful. He said he had heard I had been unwilling to join the Congress Working Committee. 'Is it because of the attitude of the Socialist Party?' he asked. I explained it was in truth very personal. 'Quite apart from my feeling fully out of depth with the negotiations, maybe I am too old to experience any thrill to figure in the prestigious Congress Working Committee'. He gave a hearty laugh. 'Would you have got a thrill ten years earlier? You would have been one of the members if I had not prevented it. You are not likely to know it for Jawaharlal is not likely to tell you that.' I looked at him in puzzled enquiry, then recollected. 'Because you decided I was irresponsible, not qualified for membership of the national executive. Anyway I have now agreed because I could not say no to Jayaprakash. He is my weak spot.' 'He is mine too', he added and laughed again.

Life as a member of the Working Committee proved more of an ordeal than I had bargained for. At times the discussions seemed almost stultifying. Maybe I had pictured a very different pathway leading to independence, free of the grime and gravel over which we were forced to pick our way, to where? At the All India Congress Committee meeting in Bombay, the first after Nehru became president, where the Cabinet Mission proposals were put up for approval, strong attacks came from Jayaprakash and Lohia. While I was equally apprehensive of the Plan, I could not give expression to it, being a member of the Executive.

Relief from political involvement seemed within sight when Nehru joined the Interim Government and Acharya Kripalani became the President. Unfortunately for me the new President took my retirement as a personal affront to him! He was more than hurt, he felt insulted. 'Your running off suggests you reject my Presidentship', he reprimanded in hurt tones. Kripalani had over the years been a good friend to me, one I could look to for advice and help. I was truly aghast at the Acharya's interpretation of my decision and agreed to continue. I was however glad that I stayed on for the Acharya was not to have an easy time. The air grew murkier with time and fresh problems. The Interim Government had proved a sorry farce with the Muslim League's intransigence or rather disruptive functioning, aggravated by the Viceroy's partisanship attitude. The Congress did succeed in getting Wavell recalled. But for us it was from frying pan into the fire.

For a while Wavell had been blunt, openly antagonistic. Lord Mountbatten who succeeded him was subtle, uncannily sleek and his one weapon to master the tangled scene was to convince everyone he was a sincere friend of India. He built up a phony facade with his handsome exterior and studied polished manners, aided cannily, with furtive subtlety by his socialite wife Edwina, of a sincere supporter of India's freedom. True he realised as did the British Cabinet of the day and a substantial section of the politically aware public, that the old time colonial rule had come to an end. The British could not claim the loyalty of either the civil service or the armed forces personnel any more. But the hard core rulers were however relieved to leave the country emasculated by partition, weak aud helpless. Mountbatten's clever role was to get India to accept it as an inevitable, nevertheless benevolent, operation. For the British it certainly was. We take pride on the so-called peaceful settlement even though it was the most fiery ordeal the country had experienced, more frightful than even the 1857 debacle.

The British salvaged with ease one fourth of their total world investments ecure in India that brought them 80% profit. Several of our seasoned leaders did not swallow the bait. They were fully conscious of the traps that were being quietly set before us. But this was of little avail, for they had little option as they showed a willingness to accept the British terms.

Before the final acceptance Gandhiji made one supreme effort to save the country from this abysmal pitfall. The continuing crisis in the Interim Government was reflected in the general destabilisation in the country. In this context Gandhiji got Jayaprakash called to the Working Committee. By now the senior leaders were so keyed up, retreat was unthinkable. One incident proved to me how completely the die was cast. After Jayaprakash vehemently opposed the British proposals, one strong voice pierced the heavy silence like a sharp knife: 'I thought there was only one mad man amidst us. I now find there are two.' The reference to Gandhiji was obvious. Deeply stung I gazed at him but his face was impassive as though he had not heard it.

By now it was becoming obvious that the Socialist Party's parting with the Congress was near. The Party was vehemently campaigning against the partition proposal. Early in 1947 the Party Executive made the first move to drop the word Congress and just call itself Socialist to make this a mass Party and abolish the compulsory membership of the Congress. As a natural corollary all mass organisational activities would be independently conducted. One crucial decision it took was to boycott the Constituent Assembly which in my opinion had very serious consequences. One of the reasons behind this negative decision was the determination to carry on a mass struggle. I personally felt this was unrealistic minus both Gandhiji and Congress.

Close on the heels of this came the British announcement of the immediate transfer of power. The reason put forth was the growing disruption in the country due to widespread communal riots. One could not but feel that actually these were generated and fanned by interested parties to serve political ends. As the Interim Government was only a pale shadow these flames could rage freely, causing untold damage. The highly aggrieved British army incensed by a streak of humiliation at having to withdraw from its privileged position, continued to add to the blazing fire.

While events moved with incredible speed like a fast moving film, those members of the Working Committee who were not in the government were outside of the arena where lightening decisions were driving the country inexorably like in a Greek tragedy, to its doom. The final plan clinched the matter by simply stating the country would be partitioned and power handed over by the British to the newly formed two dominions. V.P. Menon, Constitutional Adviser to the Viceroy, is said to have helped draft the final document. Menon would not have drafted this plan with such confidence had he not been reasonably assured by the Viceroy of its finding favour. Nor would the Viceroy have forged ahead with optimism, unless he had sufficient reason that it would work. By the time the plan was formally placed before a small gathering by the Viceroy at his house on 2nd June, 1947, it had obviously been accepted in principle. Present at thes obsequies on the Indian side were: Acharya Kripalani, Pandit Nehru, Sardar Patel, with Baldev Singh representing the Sikhs. For the Muslim side were Jinnah, Liaqat Ali, Abdur Nishtar.

Acharya Kripalani had been only too well aware of his growing humiliating position but he wanted to avoid an internal disruption while the negotiations with the British were on. But now he could contain himself no more. The resigned his presidentship.

Taking advantage of this vacancy Gandhiji suggested that either Narendra Dev or Jayaprakash be nominated for presidentship. Perhaps he hoped some of the substance of the passing India if not the core could be salvaged thereby. The senior leaders naturally rejected the suggestion. Instead Rajendra Prasad became the President.

Partitioning of a colony was the price extracted by ruling Britain as the price of 'freedom'. It has been a normal pattern of British diplomacy. Everywhere this has left an unending trail of strife, violence despair, as in Ireland, Palestine. It were as though the entire region is caught in the coils of a vicious ghost, from which it is never able to extricate itself.

True we swore we did not accept the two nation theory, nevertheless we acted on that palpable fallacy. After having lived together for centuries, we had to pretend that we could not continue to do so. The partition had to provide credibility to a lie. But the lie showed up no matter how elaborately dressed up in various political garbs like the breakaway and formation of Bangladesh later.

I could not but feel that Gandhiji could have snipped this during eht early negotiations. Why didn't he? In a kind of mental turmoil I went to Gandhiji. Dr. Mehta, the naturopath from Pune who came periodically to give Gandhiji massage, particularly when he was exhausted, met me to say Gandhiji had not come out of his room, that he had refused the massage. 'He needs it, he is rather low.' He pleaded with me to persuade him to change his mind. I went into his room in rather a stunned stage. I conveyed to him what Dr. Mehta had said. I had never seen him look so pale and dispirited. 'What for?' there was a kind of despair in his tone that I found hard to take. I feared I might break down. 'Why did you let it happen,' I almost cried out. 'You had once said we were striking at the very root of our nation. We were sure the country would be with you. Even now if you refuse to accept this monstrous decision, the people will support you. You have only to give the word,' I went on breathlessly for a while. He was silent but troubled. He made a heart-breaking figure, he who had challenged and humbled the mighty British empire. The arrogant red with which they smeared their world possessions in the maps had begun to fade. Here was the indomitable man who had shaken global foundations, looking beaten. 'It is too late. If it had been ten years earlier . . .' the voice trailed off for a while as though lost in some thought, then he resumed : 'You see my colleagues came to me when they were still in their prime of life, giving up their bright careers, plunging into an unknown destiny.' I presumed he was conveying that they too had had a stake. Many doubts, queries came surging into my mind but they were never to find expression. Dr. Mehta who had been patiently waiting at the door to be called, walked in looking enquiringly at us. Gandhiji gave him one of his sweetest smiles, but firmly shook his head negatively. My prickly doubts dangled in the air unable to find a perch. As the Working Committee had already taken the fatal decision rejecting opposition with derision as madness, the final die seemed now cast.

Though appeals to Gandhiji seemed futile, some amongst us made desperate attempts. The Socialists stubbornly insisted on active opposition by launching a country wide opposition. This however was firmly negativated by Gandhiji. We stressed that partition was not only a deep emotional atrocity that would lacerate the people for generations, it had no rationale either. The very fact that more Muslims were to stay back in what the Muslim League termed 'Hindu India', cut at the very roots of this fantasy. No wonder Gandhiji had intuitively cried out in quiet agony. 'I see only darkness before me now'. I was pretty sure that if the Khan Brothers had not boycotted the plebiscite on some obscure 'principle' in the North West, it would have stayed with India.

The final endorsement of this agreement was to be by the All India Congress Committee. Gandhiji made a special appeal to the Socialists not to raise any opposition in the Session, for he felt India must stand firmly united at this crucial hour. He had after prolonged discussion with Jayaprakash obtained his concurrence who in turn advised us accordingly, looking as heart broken as I felt. Though Jayaprakash could often melt me, this time I recoiled at the implication of this message. When the proposition was put to the vote, I could not even reconcile myself to remain neutral. Something within me warned me that if I did not record what my conscience could not reconcile itself to an act which I felt was fundamentally wrong and if I did not record my belief I would live with a sense of a heinous guilt. So I raised my hand in opposition. With that I broke my link with this political life. For by now a realisation had been growing on me that this was not my vocation.

As the deadline for the partition had approached, the Socialists had sensed more than mere 'darkness', they saw disaster involving millions on both sides. I personally fixed an immediate meeting with Pandit Nehru. We explained : we feared riots, communal attacks, for the uprooting of millions would let loose emotional tornadoes. In our opinion, the coming situation called for a total citizens' body to minimise the agonies of both the departing and the new arrivals. Finally we volunteered our services.

Pandit Nehru looked annoyed, seemed almost on the verge of temper, then controlled himself. Nevertheless there was impatience in his voice as he spoke, maybe feeling we were wasting his precious time. 'I think you people have got rather worked up, no doubt due to these disturbances here, there. But we have tried to work out an orderly system of exchange and I hope it to work.' He seems to have remarked to someone else that we always tended to dramatise situations and let our imagination run away with us.

This foolproof plan however did not work out as expected, partly because of the presence of the foreign army and all the mischief it created in its deep resentment of having to quit and lose this brightest jewel in the British Crown, as it was designated. The havoc wrought needs no repetition.

When 15th August was fixed as the day of independence, my memory harked back to Sri Aurobindo who had mentioned it as a day of special spiritual importance. It was the day of Assumption, he explained and asked me if I knew the significance of Assumption. I promptly replied that as far as my knowledge went, it was the day Angel Gabriel announced to Mary the divine spirit was entering her womb in those unforgettable words: 'The Lord is with thee. blessed art thou amongst women.' 'Ah that is only symbolic', Aurobindo interrupted. 'It implies that the physical is transferred into the divine. Mary is nature, and nature is elevated by the divine when a *jiva* takes birth in man,' was his interpretation.

The birth of freedom on this *elevated* day did not bring India any such ennobling benediction. On the contrary the country was shaken by a volcanic eruption.

All Delhi seemed ablaze waking up ghostly memories of gone by invaders who pillaged and looted this beautiful city. Fires raged right and left as bloodless hands ripped what they could lay hands on. Streets were strewn with loot. Women cried, children screamed. We rushed where we thought succour could be given. Pandit Nehru was often seen dashing into these turmoils, which provided the greatest moral boost. The very sight of him against the flames with us following, brought out even some of the timid, the wary, the doubters, the unbelievers (some of whom may have been with the evildoers in spirit. I think it was Pandit Nehru's most elevated moment, as also the darkest, when he saw the concept of secularism in tatters, its rising edifice in flames. He fought with desperation. None of us wanted this to be a rear guard action, rather, an onward leap through this very baptism. Alas the evil is still with us. Not just a shattered dream, but a haunting ghost.

Secularism was one of the concepts we wanted to wear more as a jewel on our chest with conscious pride rather than practice as an article of faith. We flaunted it rather than practise it. No wonder it came to mean so many different things to different people. But that did not worry us—each to his own. We rather puffed with pride, even though religious rituals kept intruding into so many of our national functions. We played down the fact that what are called Communal Conflicts were on the increase. In short there is hardly a time now when we are free from them.

I wonder how many can really define a true secular state as a concept of a passionate adherence to the ideal of freedom of thought, conscience, to profess and practice the faith of one's choice or even choose not to practise any faith, that the State as such would not identify itself with or be controlled by any particular faith or its laws be dictated by the fundamentalism of a particular religion. When we characterised this new state when it was formed as secular, we presupposed not an atheist or anti-religious State but to consist of people who simply believed in and accepted the spiritual dimension of each personality, to raise above his or her own narrow emotional orbit to integrate into a multi-dimensional harmonious fellow feeling.

As I watched this unbelievable turmoil descend on us at this long fought for hour of liberation, a spark ignited in the darkness. Why not make something worthwhile emerge out of this agony? I decided to apply myself to the rehabilitation of some of these uprooted families, though the very thought weighed heavily at the sheer magnitude of this colossal task.

To me the appropriate answer lay along the cooperative path. To these families torn away from their age old habitations, who now faced the challenge of remaking new homes, modelling new vocations, all in unfamiliar settings, equipping themselves to meet unaccustomed challenges, in such a context, cooperation to me was the mechanism. The resources, equipment, experimentations could all be *shared* therefore with less hazard in their struggle, and convert despair into hope and on to achievement. But for this an organisation was called for. I drew up a blue print for a cooperative body that could plan, generate action and coordinate functions.

I was at a loss whom to consult, whose aid to seek. Under this frightful emergency all concentration was on *immediate* relief. Long term plans seemed unreal. My thoughts flew to Gandhiji. So I took the blue print to him. He was one person I was confident would take it seriously. And he did, even as he glanced over it. I explained I had already initiated a few preliminary tests. I had visited some of the refugees and several of them were ready to form cooperatives if they got the land, they assured me. I would get the organising body registered as the 'Indian Cooperative Union', would he in the meantime secure land for them? He kept my draft with him to enlist supporters. I was soon called by him. He greeted me with a broad smile. I saw his old alert self again. He had liked the project, felt it should work. He had liked the project, felt it should work. In his enthusiasm he had commended it to Pandit Nehru. But the latter however characterised it as Utopian, one of these impractical new fangled plans the socialists would think up—and with this crisp comment summarily dismissed it. Gandhiji did not seem too concerned, then he proceeded. 'I shall help and identify myself with the venture. But on one condition. You and the cooperative farmers rely on your own earnest labour, and not lean on the administration. For as you know the first principle of cooperation is self-reliance.' I readily concurred, but reminded him that we would have to get some land, for all evacuee land was in government possession.

Thinking for a while he said he would approach Govind Vallabh Pant, as there are sure to be evacuee farms in U.P. bordering on Delhi. 'You go ahead with your promotional body', he ended on a most optimistic tone. That was Gandhiji. In this dark hour of his agony, caught in the cruelest turmoil of his life, he had time to spare for an ordinary worker, a novice, found time to study my fumbling project paper, try to help me. Tears trembled in my eyes.

The frame work of the Cooperative Union was unacceptable to the Delhi State Cooperative Department, as it had been independently set up. An independent cooperative body was an anachronism and a deadly challenge to its established authority.

The usual procedure was for it to sponsor it, appoint its office-bearers, give it loans, make its budget, in short, run it departmentally. Gandhiji heaved a heavy sigh when I reported this to him, then continued in a low, sad tone: 'I am glad you thought of trying to help rebuild torn lives. Because of the decisions we made, thousands of poor innocent people have to bear hardships. I myself feel it wrong to live in this palatial building. Bhangi Colony which was my chosen abode is chokeful of refugees. I am troubled by the thought of families with children out in the cold.' There was much agony on his face, his eyes, his voice.

I never realised then how much of the responsibility for this he took upon himself, that he had erred somewhere down the line for this to happen.

I went to very few of those memorable prayer meetings of his—they were truly fantastic, drawing all sorts of people like a magnet—some hardly aware why they went. At one of these I got a hint in his discourse when he confessed that he must have made a mistake somewhere and the mistake must be now having its effect.

I hesitated visiting Gandhiji frequently. Apart from the communal upheavals all over the country, there were internal political conflicts too, and I was hesitant to what I feared meant adding to his burden. When I finally went one day I was shocked by the change in him. He looked physically weaker and mentally disturbed. He was being besieged all the time by crowds in distress. There were also piles of letters, papers. I heard him say firmly he must read every single letter, and every letter must be carefully answered. The heavy air however was occasionally crackled and lightened by his unfailing witticism, mostly jokes against himself.

He finally called me by his side. 'Why have you not come for such a long time? I have spoken to Pantji and also to some private individuals. Keep your end ready.' I explained, 'I hesitated to come often as you are very busy...' He abruptly cut me short. I am never too busy to see those who wish to see me. The trouble with you perhaps is you cannot forget you are Kamaladevi, extra sensitive. Look at all the crowd here, they come when they want to.' I was shaken out of myself. Yes, I was too self-conscious. These people were may be simple. As I was ruminating, he broke in on my thoughts: 'You make amends for the past. Come when you feel you want to, just do that.' I was so emotionally moved, I leaned forward and touched his hands as I moved away, a thing I had never done before.

The next time was never to be for the very next evening he was gone. As I stood beside his body that fateful evening, I could not believe he was dead. I touched those very same hands I had said farewell to for I felt I was alone in a vast empty void, nothing I could hold onto, nothing I could look up to. I had no stomach to watch the funeral. Minoo Masani was taking Jayaprakash who had just arrived to watch the last journey and he persuaded me to join them.

As I do not listen into Radio news, I was not prepared for the sight that met me. Gandhiji's body being taken on a *gun-carriage* on its last journey—to me an unbelievable sight! It was with some effort that I could control myself. Jayaprakash and I looked at each other in painful silence. To me this was adding insult to injury. What slaves we had become to completely alien, irrelevant impacts, adopting ways and manners inimical to what the occasion demanded, outraging our finer fibres.

He died even as he had lived, adhering to his principles, no matter what the cost. He entertained an innate respect for every individual whose dignity he must not violate. To uphold that principle he had ultimately laid down his life.

What a different world we live in now. The public today is universally suspect. The more important a public function the more ferocious the display of weapons, *SECURITY* as it is called. Our innate sensitivity has by now been corroded to complete bluntness. Even the invitation, no matter how imposing its appearance, will contain stern warnings of the various *Don'ts* to be observed.

How had it all happened. As I had watched the weird funeral procession, people were standing in dead silence, too stunned, bewildered, dumb. Occasionally some voice would shriek: "Mahatma Gandhi *amar raho—Bolo,*' but the shriek would vanish into the fading light. For no answering voice would come—not even an echo. The million throats stayed dumb, making everything eerie, weird, unreal.

The past few weeks before it one had been persistently hearing of threats to the Mahatma. More tangibly while I was in Bombay. Then came the bomb explosion. Still it did not carry reality. Who would want to kill one who was an embodiment of love and compassion.

When it happened many blamed the victim himself, for he sternly forbade any *security* measures. In fact he openly condemned the very thought of it. At public places, more so at his own prayer meetings, he could not restrict peoples entry. The prayers were open to all. To him threats to those wishing to come, were abhorrant. Whoever wished to come to see him he simply would not bar. He had to be allowed to come freely. For him his life was not worth it if it was to be guarded by weapons. If such a moment came, it meant it was time for him to go. He could live only if he could serve and his service was welcomed. Those who cameto him were his honoured guests. Imposing restrictions on their entry to him was barbarous.

These were the sentiments he gave expression to. They showed up the fine fibres he was composed of. Was all that he tried to live up to in vain?

I mused over this catastrophe and wondered how it had come about. Reminiscencing over the times since the advent of the British into India, picture after picture kept floating before my eyes. Immediately preceding the gigantic revolt of 1857, the Muslims had been in the forefront of the anti-British forces. Though the various early Muslim rulers who made heroic efforts to rid India of the British grip, were those whose forefathers had originally hailed from outside, *they* had become one with this country and their patriotism was genuine and exemplary. Within our recent memories, there was Sirajuddaulah, the last independent ruler of Bengal, betrayed by his own General, Mir Jafar, who has become a symbol of treachery—Tippu Sultan, called the

Tiger of Mysore, was another uncompromising enemy of the British who fell fighting them after two months of gallant battling, whereupon the British General exclaimed that now India was theirs. It is perhaps little known that Tippu was abreast of European history, member of the radical democratic Jacobing Club, tried to build up a strong navy to keep off the European invaders; then there was the old and feeble Bahadur Shah Zafar, who lent his leadership to the last desperate bid of 1857. Somehow the Muslims were then considered the main culprits and Lord Bentinck the then Governor General wanted to avenge it by destroying the Taj and selling the blocks of marble! Twentyseven thousand Muslim rebels alone were executed in the Delhi general massacre. Then the Wahabi movement fed the anti-British revolt for the Wahabis joined hands with the anti-British elements, which built up a network of anti-British activities to intensify the revolt throughout the North. These elements were drawn from all walks of Muslim society. Even a decade before the 1857 flare up, five state trials were held when large numbers of Muslim rebels were hanged, given life sentences or exiled.

The picturesque Begum Hazrat Mahal played an active part in the 1857 war by personally leading her troops into the battle. When Queen Victoria issued her famous Proclamation announcing the British take-over of India, Hazrat Mahal issued a bold counter to it and fled to Nepal where she died in anonymity.

The Gadar Party of Indian patriots in California was studded with many Muslim luminaries like Maulana Barkatullah of Bhopal, one of its founders, who set up a network of anti-British bodies abroad. Syed Rahmat Ali Shah, also one of its members, was hanged for his part in the Gadar Party uprising in 1915. With him were noted rebels like Mohamed Bashir Khuda Bux, Zakaria Zafar Hasan, Allah Nawaz and Abdul Aziz. Mohamed Ashfaqullah Khan of Shahjehanpur, U.P. as a leader of the Hindustan Republic Army organised raids on armories and was hanged in 1927. Ali Ahmed Siddiqui of Faizabad, U.P. along with Syed Majalabra Hassain of Jaunpur, was behind the mutiny in Malaya, and Burma.

Coming to modern times Muslim leaders participated in the National Congress from its very inception. Large numbers under the guidance of the Ulema extended full cooperation on behalf of the community. A Fatwa signed by Maulana Rashid Gangohi and many leading Muslims and several religious leaders of West Asia called on the community to fully support the Congress. The 1887 session at Madras was presided over by Badruddin Tyabji. Muslims were actively involved in the revolt against the partition of Bengal led by the Central National Mohamedan Association. When the Muslim League was formed it was immediately countered by forming the Indian Mussalman Association with Nawab Syed Muhamad as President and Mohammad Ali Jinnah as one of the Vice-Presidents, to collaborate with the National movement. Several newspapers were launched by Muslims to keep up the anti-British fervour, like Al Hilal, Al-Balagh, the Comrade, Zamindar.

During World War I Shaikh-ul-Hind Maulana Mohamad-ul Hassan Deobandi sent emissaries and delegations to several important countries of Europe and Asia seeking support for Indian freedom. It may be explained that Darul-ulam of Deoband was founded as far back as 1867 by Haji Mohamad Abid as a powerful nationalist centre. Maulana Maqbulur went to China and Burma, Chaudhury Rahmat Ali to France, etc. At Medina the pro-British ruler Sharif Hussain arrested Maulana Mohamad Hassan, the Indian Emissery, and handed him over to the British. The British managed through their allies to arrest these roving messengers including Maulana Deoband, and some six of them were interned in Malta and were freed only when war ended.

In the early days of the Civil Disobedience movement under Gandhiji, a body of Muslim theologians was founded called Jamiat-ul-Ulema-i-Hind, to get all Muslim religious leaders to fight the British. Under the leadership of Maulana Hussain Ahmad Madani, the Jamiat called upon Muslims to boycott Government institutions, renounce titles conferred by government. This call was signed by nearly a thousand theologians, some eminent doctors of Islamic jurisprudence It warned serving in the British army as religiously unlawful for a Muslim. Finally it urged it as the duty of every Muslim to bring this message home to everybody. At the Madras Congress Session where Dr. Ansari presided, Maulana Mohamad Ali said that Hindus and Muslims trusted each other but they both distrusted the British.

When the Satyagraha movement was launched in 1930, the Jamiat was amongst the earliest to take the plunge, followed by the Ahrar Party of Punjab, the Shia Political Conference, the Khudai

Khidmatgar of North West Frontier, apart from a large number of citizens.

In the final 1942 movement the Muslims still played an important role. We had many precious Muslim leaders to guide us, magic names to conjure with and which still haunt us.

How then did this catastrophe occur. Now Partition hangs on our horizon like a perpetual question mark, tantalising us.

The concept of partition as a solution to multi-cultural and multi-religious problems has haunted us since that ominous partition of 1947. The British have been using this weapon wherever one of its colonies strove to come free of Britain's colonial coils. Though we in India asserted that we did not believe in the two nation theory, by acquiesing in the partition at the behest of those who forced it on us, we seemed to have accepted it.

The subcontinent was carved as a sop to one man's insatiable ambition, setting a pattern into motion, paving the way to many more splits, goaded by similar bouts of inordinate personal ambitions but under the romantic banner of linguistic states, which neither served any regional language nor developed any regional culture. The country is periodically threatened to be torn apart by such cataclysms. The chain reaction generated in 1947 still continues to spin. We have before us two similar tragedies: Ireland and Palestine.

Several world personalities were seen around after Gandhiji's funeral. How did they materialise, no one asked. It seemed natural they should be there and one kept meeting them both by design or happy accident.

There was Vincent Sheen, the noted American writer who had become a student of Indian philosophy. 'I did get here in time. Oh I was so afraid I would be late,' he exclaimed with great excitement. I threw a gaze of interrogation at him. 'Let me explain' he began. 'I was sure Gandhiji's end had come and I had to rush here before that. Do you know I was to have had an interview with him that same evening he was killed? What I feel is not superstition. My inner eye saw it as my sixth sense become keenly aware of it,' he asserted with conviction. 'But why?' I asked even more mystified. 'Because prophets like him must end as martyrs. It is inevitable.' I could not take this nor some of his other, what he termed 'intuitive' pronouncements. He went on: 'To me the average Indian has a certain inbuilt layer of consciousness, integrated in which are the universality of the spirit or god or liberation. This is an integral part of the inmost mind of everyone here. I believe that this precious self-knowledge is ineradicable; and all other learning could be termed as formal chores that formed surface layers. And what I have heard since coming here almost convinces me that my intuition is infallable. Here, this is what the Mahatma a ctually said barely twenty-four hours before he died: 'If I died of illness you should declare me a false Mahatma. But if somebody shot at me and I received the bullet on my chest, without a sigh and with Rama's name on my lips, you can say I was a true Mahatma.'

'I will give you a perfectly rational explanation for what happened and what he meant when he 'predicted' his death', I interrupted him. 'I believe in the Indian traditional faith that a great being lives only as long as he wishes. He will die when he wants to. We say he is an *Icha-Marani*—dies when he wishes—Gandhiji had lost the desire to live. So his end had to come. In my opinion this is the rational explanation. I grant intuitive knowledge is there in us, but often gets obliterated or choked by stuffing in of indigestable wasteful stuff.' Vincent Sheen's book 'Lead Kindly Light' is however a delicate interpretation of the Indian leader's personality, to whom he had come to pay his last homage.

Henri Cartier Bresson was another who attracted my attention from among the crowd that had come to see Gandhiji—a world famous photographer. He was a youthful figure, with a glowing face, he seemed all alive. He has left us some memorable pictures of that dark day.

While he had a magic touch with the camera he had also an uncanny sense of arriving at a place when some major event was to transpire. Thus he was here to witness a tragedy nobody had anticipated. Later he reached China just as the Communists were marching in. So he gave to the world the last glimpses of a China that was to be no more.

Henri Cartier Bresson had showed me an entirely new Paris that a visitor rarely sees. He drove me into the unknown twists and turns where lay the slums that gay Paris never even breathes of, down long dingy lanes, dark, dim cloistered houses, shabbily clad folk clattering around—a world on a different planet from the glittering Champs Elysee and its proud mansions. Then we floated down the river in a barge, as he showed me some unusual sights like whole families living under the huge bridges. 'This is the unseen driftwood of 'Gay Paris', 'Henri murmured in a tremulous voice, and that emotional tinge moved me. His artist's eye would be penetrating into the very depths of an ignoble scene.

Next I was transported into another world. Right outside of the city amidst scrambles were caves that had been converted into studios by artists who could not afford to hire regular studios. Several painters were busily at work. In great spirit they welcomed us and chatted with us, as though their quaint setting was perfectly natural.

As the days sped by I began to see not only new sights but old ones through Henri's eyes. It was a unique experience. Even more stirring were his comments on how he captured scenes, objects, above all *events*, for his verbal expressions were as vivid as his picture-photos. On his uncanny capturing of events he explained: 'I may show the whole world in a photograph, but it is the event itself that provokes the organic rhythm of forms.' I once asked him what were the active elements involved in photographing a person and an object. 'When I try to photograph an object, it is not integrating a bundle of details, but the essence of what has caught *me*, not just the eye.' 'That sounds so like one of the ancient Indian texts,' I interrupted him. 'I am not surprised to know that. When I photograph a person I must also take in a true reflection of that person's world. Remember this world is as much *inside* the person *as outside*. A balance has to be established between the two, for it is *this* with which I have to communicate. You may hardly believe that the expression on the man's face is more fugitive and transitory than the light playing on it,' he explained in an excited tone. 'That is why no matter how much I may study my subject, when I click the camera I can only catch what I like to call the fugitive moment. The rest goes into the melting pot.'

'Do you go through what one may crudely call an esoteric experience when handling the camera.' 'If you mean by that the reality that true perception sees. For instance I realise that it is from my own eye that space begins and slants off, enlarging itself progressively toward infinity. Photography confirms the presence of rhythm in the world.' 'Our ancestors discovered that by sensitively responding to the vibrations around, one can grasp the images created by each passing mood,' I replied 'and when you say it is from your own eye that space begins and slants off, you are repeating the very essence of Indian philosophy, something the West is just beginning to sense as new physics.'

I was most surprised however to find Edgar Snow, the star writer on China, whose sparkling book Ten Days shook the world, opened the first window on the Chinese Revolution and the new emerging China. Snow had visited India between 1941 and 1943 and lashed out at Gandhiji for refusing to aid the war effort and insisting on immediate transfer of power, had even made disparaging personal references to him. Today I listened with bated breath as he eulogised the same leader in glowing terms. Now that he had made the supreme sacrifice, he had become a martyr.

11

My cooperative project lay limp like a crumpled paper. How could I proceed, whom could I look to. I shivered with a chill inside me. Yet how could I abandon it. I had promised I would rely on my own strength. Fulfilling this pledge was my only offering to one who had given me so much, lifted me up in my moment of despair. It now became a compelling responsibility I should shoulder, for he had meant to identify himself with it, so it fell to me to complete his unfinished task. The farmers whom I had enthused waited restlessly. If they were let down, they would be doubly betrayed. I decided to make a desperate bid for the land.

The Government's Relief and Rehabilitation Secretariat was housed in an over-aged building known as the P Block which stood in the shadow of the gigantic main building. Under public health regulations, it would be easily classified in the 'slums' columns. The sun rays engaged in a perpetual guerilla war with the grim walls of P Block. They had to sneak in through chinks and crevices. When you entered you were seized with grave doubts as to whether you had not strayed into the wrong place, for you had to pick your way through storages, piled up goods, lumber of all sorts. You wondered if this was a godown or a lumber room. Rather appropriately it was given over to the Refugee Section—for in a way the refugees had become the dry leaves driven by a storm.

In this Block there was the usual reception room. It was a replica of a third class railway waiting room. I finally succeeded in pushing my way in and stood around. A gentleman rose and offered me his seat asking me to sit down. I fidgeted, I said I was in a hurry. He said 'never mind sit down'. I retorted rather impatiently 'I have really no time to sit. I am in a hurry'. He was not impressed; he continued, 'No harm in sitting down all the same. I too came in a great hurry, that was well over six months ago and you see I am still here. You better sit down'. He smiled benignly as he beckoned me once more to the seat he had vacated for me. I kept debating whether I should sit or go.

More days, weeks passed by, while I hung around up on empty promises. Finally I decided to clinch it by direct action. I located an area in Chattarpur, 12 miles from Delhi. I informed the concerned authority that if in the next three days, the allotment was not made I would simply take the refugees and settle them there. I engaged trucks, got them to select the necessary implements and whatever else they needed. The evening before the adventure, I got the allotment letter; with it came a terrific surprise.

One of the top officers in the Delhi Administration incharge of Refugees, said to me that since I was so eager to rehabilitate refugees, why don't I take on the entire job? He would provide me lists of all the available evacuee land, funds for loans, facilities for acquiring the other wherewithal. I would be given facility to visit the camps to meet the refugees and organise them into different groups where possible or individually according to their preference. As my assistant I got a worker who had been an inmate in one of the Gandhian ashrams, Ramachandra Rao, an experienced Gandhian style worker, sharp but shrewd, as a counterpoise to my bubbling enthusiasm. We both sat day after day, scrutinising the refugees with their applications as they filed past us. If they came in groups, I explained the advantages of cooperation, and where they accepted, I collected them into the Cooperative Union. Soon there were about half a dozen farms at work.

The excellent farmers coming from the Punjab were dejected to see the dry Delhi landscape. So was I, coming from the lush west coast. First we had the thrill of water bubbling out of a tube well but it was a short lived bubble. Then we fell back on the South Indian pattern of tanks.

I got a small cottage erected in Chattarpur for myself to personally share in the activities of the rural community.

We aspired to make the Chattarpur area a stimulating pattern in many-faceted community progress for this was long before the Government's launching of the community projects. Small irrigation projects were initiated together with supply of better inputs, improved cultivation techniques; a health centre; a Community hall for social gatherings, sports, games. Keen to preserve and stimulate traditional cultural forms, a noted creative artist was appointed with which we began our collection of theatre properties which has finally led up to a National Theatre Crafts Museum.

Vegetable and flower gardens were started. The cultivators were so elated with their products, quite spontaneously they landed at the Prime Minister's house and insisted he must personally accept their gifts. Good humouredly he indulged their wish, to their utter delight. Later when the Cottage Industries Emporium opened, it set up a special flower shop, Mallika.

Organising of industrial cooperatives was a natural corollary that followed. The skilled craftsmen eagerly banded themselves and could enjoy easy facilities of getting raw materials, loans, access to create a modest centre for retail sale by the Union itself for some of this.

With our limited resources, we could only set up a small sales counter in Delhi. Quality items, new and exciting objects came on this counter, attracting wide attention. Sales became brisk and popular. Pandit Nehru heard of this mini-venture and walked in one day, throwing us into confusion, and as usual with no money on him! Those aware of this would of course produce loan money to save him asking for it, and he enthusiastically picked a few items.

The Central Cottage Industries Emporium on Janpath conducted by the Commerce Ministry had been running into heavy losses troubling Pandit Nehru who had initiated it. The visit to the mini-crafts counter had made him alive to where the error lay. Handicrafts are very individual, personalised items. They could not be measured or assessed like commodities. 'No ministry can run such a shop. Ask the Refugee Crafts Counter – nay persuade it to take over the Emporium', he advised his Ministry. Thus the present Central Cottage Industries Emporium took shape. Of course the Union was only empowered to run the shop, but could claim no ownership.

Even within this parameter we were able to quickly transform the shop. With a cooperative body to manage it, the institution became the collective responsibility of the whole staff who through their membership had an equal voice in decision making. To them it became 'our emporium' in whose future fate their daily lives were interwoven. They thrashed out their own problems, made their own decisions. The Ministry was asked to set up an Advisory Board to involve public leaders in its functioning.

Training courses were started for the working cadres, the sales personnel as well as for a team of buyers. They were made to familiarise themselves with the history of crafts, production processes, special characteristics to make them more alluring and meaningful to the public. The latter went into the remotest parts of the country, sought out craftsmen, sat with them guiding them in the needed reorientation of traditional objects to adapt them to modern use and bring them into the current stream. Every single item thus got individual attention, imaginative and creative handling as handicrafts should.

The CCIE as it was popularly known, did become a centre of popular focus. As Pandit Nehru would say, it was a 'modern monument of Delhi like the Kutub of the old era and a *must* for visitors.

Almost simultaneously the All India Handicrafts Board was set up for the development of handicrafts, and I was asked to be its Chairman. It was a modest manageable board for it was composed of enthusiastic and knowledgeable members who personally applied themselves to promotional work. They travelled around, sat with craftsmen and added their own skill and knowledge to make meaningful craft objects.

To me it meant continuous travel. I combined these trips to also seek and unravel some of our vast treasury of performing arts. While it was easy enough to institute National Awards for the performing artists, it was something of a prolonged battle which was eventually won to get similar recognition for the long neglected craftsmen.

I was fairly launched on my journey through cooperation and I kept visiting the Refugee camps regularly. Once I was told of a tent town that had come up some 14 miles away. As I approached the tents the usual wild summer winds began to sweep. When we reached the tent habitat, part of it was empty, many of the tents having been blown off. Many were in tatters. I saw hundreds of families huddled together, covered all over with dust and sand, for it was open sandy land. It was a heart-rending sight. They were from the North West Frontier, the hardy Pathans, now a pathetic picture. I directly approached the President of India, Rajendra Prasad, and unfolded to him a plan I had devised to give them a township of their own, persuade them to build it themselves cooperatively and create a sense of belonging. The President set up a special board which he himself headed and the plan was launched.

These refugees to our dismay were traders, money lenders, contractors, who had never done any constructive work, certainly never with their hands. They were to be their own employers, serve themselves, they were told. But they definitely baulked at doing earth work, though were assured they would own the houses, in fact the entire township.

The womenfolk broke the deadlock, they were ready to do any work, the men shamefacedly followed. Those who had never turned a sod, nor laboured with their limbs or shouldered a burden, now gladly and willingly even broke stones till an appropriate machine for this was procured; made bricks, sawed the wood and finally made a whole city spring up in an incredibly short time as though by a wave of the magic wand. The social significance lay in the fact that traders, money-lenders, producers, shop-keepers had turned manufacturers, service-men. Cooperation is a way of life and conviction can come only through *experience* not on trust. The darkest clouds melted and happy light smiled through. They built and operated their own power house, a well fitted hospital, ran their own transport service, schools, health centres, shops, bazaar and a whole host of things.

They were more difficult than problem children. Quick tempered hasty to act, they could become quite terrifying at times. Nevertheless they were hard working, very proud, scrupulous in paying back the government the loans. The growing city was divided into a number of sectors, each to hold a self-contained community with full amenities. A properly equipped hospital was constructed, called after Badshah Khan, also a power house to supply power, internal transport system; a body to promote and conduct sports, games, recreational activities. Faridabad had its own railway station and went on the map. It became a noted model, setting the pattern for community development, which definitely strengthened the body. Soon there was a social welfare department set up to meet the growing social problems in the different communities.

The Cooperative Union was comprised of a handful of idealists with no ready resources and equally no earlier experience. What we had launched out to do was not all that easy. Everything did not alwaysrun to the pattern conceived. Experiences were equally tormenting and exhilarating. Problems of long-term rehabilitation in the existing conditions were different from normal innovative experiments that can go on through clockless days, calendarless periods, with a large dose of infinite patience and ageless faith you will get somewhere. Whereas refugee rehabilitation demanded *urgency*, quick results to create credibility in people whose faith had been cruelly shattered. We muddled alternately through heart breaks and scintillating successes.

Pandit Nehru had come to hear of the Cooperative Union and its experimental farm at Chattarpur and wished to see it. Though glad, we were in a dilemma, for there was no car road to the farm. The authorities quickly contrived one, which to us was a real boon. He was pleased with his visit. I did not spoil the day by reminding him all this was not Utopian as he had once characterised. He showed more than appreciation, confidence.

Both Faridabad and Cottage Industries Emporium were deflowered when they were blossoming, through a kind of, to my sensitivities, vandalism under the title of 'Development'. Faridabad was made into a big industrial area, completely destroying its original character of a compact small town self help. The Emporium was stripped of its independent character, and made a subordinate unit. Delhi's rapid urbanisation did the same to the farms close to the city for the city's rich moved on to them and made them the weekend holiday resorts.

Still, when I look back I feel it was worth it, a span of life dotted with herculean efforts, memorable events, beset with pitfalls, all the same a rewarding experience of infinite value.

We just seemed to be getting over the trauma of the aftermath of the partition when we were startled by the news of the raids on Kashmir. We were nearing mid-winter and the scene appeared bleak both politically and weather wise. As the 'raids' as they were called though it was a military onslaught to capture the Valley unwares, continued, it were as though my heart strings were being pulled. I decided to rush to Kashmir.

The roads were not open, for the raiders were lurking there. Air services were suspended. There was only a cargo service which also carried passengers who obtained special permits.

The internal political scene had completely changed. The Maharaja had quit. A national government as representative of the people was in operation with Sheikh Abdulla as Prime Minister.

I had come to know Sheikhsab, as he was popularly called, over a long period as he was our political contemporary. When he visited the Congress Sessions or other Congress meetings, he kept with the Socialists for he experienced a comradeship with us. So I sent him a message and got a warm response on the strength of which I secured the travel permit. I jolted along with the heavy packages and bundles, squatting amidst them on the floor.

It was a pleasure to meet Sheikhsab in his new position along with his Cabinet. It mitigated some of the gloom cast by the war. I told him that I would like to visit the war fronts. He was a bit apprehensive. 'You are sure you want to take the risk? Most of these assaulting men are marauders, not regular militarymen. They are wild and ready to run amuck.' I assured him I was prepared for any risk. 'Why would I have come if I meant to nestle cosily in the Guest House', was my answer.

The next morning I was driven to the Commander's camp where I met Major General Kulwant Singh. He was warm and friendly and put me at ease saying, 'Your first trip will be with me.' I got into his vehicle. As we drove he explained some of the features of this 'adventure,' as he termed it. The main body of raiders were recruited to come here to loot, enticed with descriptions of the wealth that could be grabbed. 'They can all handle fire arms, they start as kids playing with them. Behind this smoke screen came the army. That is what complicates the situation.'

Then we stopped. The air was occasionally rent by a boom. The Major General spoke in an apologetic tone. 'I cannot take you further, nearer the firing lines. But you can meet some of our jawans around here and share some refreshments with them.' I felt a pang of regret and rather cheated. I did not even have a token, not even symbolic, as a momento from the front.

Each day I went to a different section, as close to the firing line as I was permitted. But everywhere I met our jawans briefly, talked with them, as their searching eyes roved the horizon. I particularly visited the devastated areas. In particular the Convent that had been attacked. That seemed pure vandalism. 'What else do you expect from vandals out to loot,' said my escort contemptuously.

The Kashmir visit provided me more than an adventure, it gave me glimpses into areas that I might otherwise have been oblivious of. In the first place the Indian army had long been a distant factor to us, for it had been part of an alien element of distrust in the body of India; worse, a symbol of foreign domination. Their homeric achievements in the two world wars had roused little emotion. To us they were other people's wars, our only role being to pay for them by compulsion.

The Kashmir war was an experience and I garnered many facts about the Indian army with relish and pride. When the raiders' invasion struck the valley like a meteor, the greying military heads in Delhi were in dismay. To land a modern army in the tiny, improvised Srinagar airport appeared a frightful nightmare. Nevertheless the Indian army performed the feat, bringing hope and succour to the distraught people.

Let us first paint the fantastic setting to grasp the many adverse factors that lent a forbidding character to the operations. Winter had already pitched her snow tents and settled down for the season. The Indian army had hardly any experience of waging a battle at ten to twelve thousand feet height, that too in deep snow. Yet it magnificently pursued the raiders up the Gilgit path, cutting a road through an impossible terrain. More, it captured the hazardous Razdhainagan Pass at a height of 12,000 feet. This road constructed by our sappers and miners, from the South is one of the highest in the world and proved one of the brilliant examples of military engineering exploits. How many of our countrymen know this great story of valour and ingenuity? Who has painted the startling scenes? Who has dramatised this grand epic? A few other bright patches came to light. The antiquated myth of certain communities being labelled martial and others, non-martial had been buried once and for all. It was mainly the Southern people who had been tarred by this ignominous brush, one of the several irrational aberrations of the rulers of the day.

I felt most disheartened to note the plight of the craftsmen, whose whole existence at that time hung on the patronage of the tourists. It was for them a real long, bleak winter. Some relief action was called for. I rushed back to Delhi to place a proposal before the Indian Cooperative Union.

As the Indian Cooperative Union had brought succour and sense of fulfilment to the large number of refugee craftsmen settled in the vicinity of Delhi, I longed to carry this message to the Kashmir crafts workers, moved by their pitiable condition even though they were excellent workers. It was also tragic to see the children condemned from the time their hands can move, to earn a miserable pittance. Their vocation could be combined with general education but was not. Due to the war that had struck the picturesque valley like a shaft of lightning their lives had been made even more precarious.

The Cooperative Union set up a cooperative working Centre in Srinagar with an enthusiastic idealistic young man, Mengi in charge. His continued devotion to the workers and faith in the cooperative has been exemplary over the last three decades and I salute Mengi for it.

After partition one of the most tantalising problems and of great anguish was that of the young women abducted into Pakistan and which kept agitating the government and the public. What aggravated the problem even more was the emergence of two contrary reactions. One was that the abducted should be brought back at any cost ; the other they should not, for there was fear of a big risk lest their families reject them, which would make matters worse for the victims concerned.

Mridula Sarabhai who was the most closely involved in this problem, was a champion of bringing them back, and had persuaded the Indian government to pursue this policy. Her argument was that the women were tradition-bound, frightened to death of being rejected if they went back. They should therefore be assured of asylum, care, rehabilitation, to make it easy for them to return. She was sure none of them would really like to stay away permanently. I realised the weight behind her argument. The change of religion might also be a strong deterrent. Still I was not sure if this were the whole picture as Mridula painted it.

Shrimati Rameshwari Nehru, the Incharge for Rehabilitation, Mridula and myself were deputed by the Indian government to meet the Pakistani authorities to sign an agreement on exchange of the women forcibly taken away by either side. The negotiations were held in Lahore.

Sitting opposite, as one of the members of the Pakistan delegation, was Ara Begam Shah Nawaz. We had been very close friends, more, there seemed to be a kinship between us. I had been welcomed in the family by Sir Mohammad Shafi, her father, his wife, children. He called me and introduced me as his daughter and I called him and his wife, father and mother. The feelings on both sides were warm and genuine. Never since Pitaji's death had I known that sense of belonging. Ara was the link. When she was about to sail to England to the Round Table Conference as one of India's women delegates, we had sat in the boat and talked. She wanted to be briefed for her role. I told her it was useless discussing matters which to me were futile. Still the old affection was there. I had spent a few days with her in Lahore after my release in 1944. We had spent hours together in Simla when the Stafford Cripps Mission talks between the Congress and the British Government were going on, and which finally broke down. She had posted me before of the factors that contributed to the failure of the two major communities to put up a united front at London, and now it was being repeated here, often over petty issues. We had shared many such disappointments. After that the partition had come and we had lost touch. Now a whole life time seemed to have intervened to separate us.

At the very first glance I noticed the change in her, though she greeted me cordially. During a break she asked me to her home for a meal. A lady, resident of Lahore, looked at me with great surprise. 'Is she a friend of yours?' she asked. 'We used to be friends,' I said. 'Now she is one of the bitterest women' and she seemed about to launch out on some bitter details, I waved her away.

This visit had been a traumatic experience for me. I had cherished many pleasant and tender memories of Lahore: art, literature, warm friendly people. Today I saw just devastation, physical, emotional intellectual. That is what partition had done.

As a follow up of the Lahore proceedings I was sent to Peshawar to deal with the Frontier Province. It was headed by the much dreaded Governor, Cunningham. The Mission held no attraction for me, more so having to tackle a notorious tough like this Governor. The journey itself was a ghostly one. Occasionally a military plane took off to Peshawar to carry some personnel, goods, urgent papers and the kind. The one in which I travelled was empty, was probably carrying cargo and papers. It was strange sitting *alone* in a large plane.

The first person I contacted on arrival was Khan Saheb. He was alone, the family was away in their village Utmanzai. Sophia was away in Hazara district where her husband was posted. I felt very lonesome. I asked Khan Saheb to arrange for me to visit to Utmanzai, a place I had long wished to see, where Gaffer Khan came from. He readily agreed.

The interview with the Governor went as I had pictured it. He was a small-made, thin-lipped, cold-faced man with sharp beady eyes, what we in our vernacular terms describe as 'eyes without blood', meaning devoid of softness. He treated the subject of exchange of women as of little consequence, said we made far too much fuss over it. He agreed however to my visiting the women brought over from India and to my talking with them. He did not expect any worthwhile result. 'Any way please yourself', he barked as we ended the tiresome dialogue.

Out of the few women I met, only one from Patiala stands out as a definite personality. The others, attractive maybe to the hungry male eye, were wishy washy to me. They were frankly frightened to go back, uncertain what awaited them. I assured them protection, alternative asylum. What did it mean as against an already settled and fairly comfortable life, I asked myself. I told them they could think this over and decide, though that was not what Mridulaben wanted.

The Patiala lady was a different proposition. She explained in lucid terms the situation. In her estimation there were fewer women than men in this region. She saw men and men all the time. While the men had been imbibing something of what may be called modernism, the women were still firmly tucked away behind the old solid screen in the name of Islam. These modern young men were attracted by the young Indian women not merely by sex like the older men who were overwhelmed by brute passion, rather other elements induced by education, maybe novelty, and a sense of conquest-adventure. Her own man, she explained, had persuaded her into a marriage for he offered her the kind of life she had not known before. It was not merely in terms of money and what it could buy, he was very lavish no doubt. He confessed he was happy to be with her, enjoyed sharing the lighter side of life, a companionship she was tasting for the first time. She had a mind of her own and the adjustment had not been easy. But he had wooed her with affection and patience, he wanted her, was sure they could be happy together. The earlier husband had been a good man, kind to her, but the usual run of nice husbands. This new man had been different I could deduce. She confessed it was a hard choice to make. She had not left any children behind, if she had, the choice would have been obvious. She had all my sympathy. A radiance on her face, a sparkle in her eyes, betrayed that this man had kindled in her an element that had lain dormant within. To me the immediate choice seemed obvious for her. If she went back it was most doubtful if it would still be the same, whether the husband would be good, kind, after all she had been through. It might be either outright rejection or in the alternative one of taunts, maybe humiliations, who could say? While here was this conquerer laying his world at her feet? For her surely it was today that counted. Some of her future here she must have felt confident she could mould too. So she kept arguing to clear her mind and get my reaction. God how many messes we had created! I sat dumb, holding my hand. I had no words to say to her.

The Abdul Gaffar Khan's family had become like broken reeds. What had finally shattered them was the decision of the Pakistan Government to amalgamate into a single unit all of West Pakistan, wiping out the Constituent Units, which meant obliterating for ever from current history the very name of the land of the Pakhtuns. Gandhiji had assured them, they declared, at the time of the partition, 'We will help the Pathans to keep their honour and right of self determination'. 'But it is our misfortune he is no more', they moaned. 'If he had been alive, he would certainly have come to our rescue.'

Soon after Gandhiji's demise, the Congress decided not to allow any other party within its own body. In any event the Socialists could not have functioned any more within the Congress whose political disposition had undergone considerable change. I had already decided not to continue either in the party or the Congress.

While I had no regrets quitting the political scene, I realised I would miss many of my colleagues I had worked with over the years. I owed much to several of the personalities. It had been a rare privilege to be with them as a comrade. Most of them were idealistic, clean, sincere, completely devoted to the cause they espoused. Maybe they were not all good politicians, as the term now goes.

Thus ended the expectation of this small band of idealists offering an alternative lead, throwing out new ideas, cutting new paths, setting new directions for a new burgeoning state. Had this group come to power would India have shaped differently? I doubt it unless we started totally afresh scrapping our current political set-up. We were trapped in a Constitution which for all its grandiose garb, to me seems ill suited to this country, patterned largely on the English model when our political, social and cultural ethos are wide apart, except for our voting system over which we wax ecstatic as ours being a huge democracy. Under the Gandhian concept freedom was the establishment of a different social order which meant an alternative to both capitalism and Marxism.

The Socialist Party at the dawn of independence was still too much in the grip of Marxism. This led to its following negative policies like refusing to collaborate in the crucial constitution making process where alternative clauses could have been proposed. Even if all their measures were not accepted some breakthrough might have been possible, at least other alternatives highlighted before the people, try some break from the old rut. Jayaprakash did break out of the shell and try to initiate the long delayed revolution after the country had been rocked by the harsh winds of emergency. But by then India seemed to have grown jaded, weary, lost its early fire. The genuine democratic pattern of working up from within the rural communities was never attempted by the ruling party. The few voluntary efforts with rare exceptions, were mostly unwelcome, some suspect. From planning to execution, every state move was handed down from above, the very antithesis of democratic process. The worst was perpetrating these perversions in the name of a pro-socialist regime.

Perhaps if the original Socialists had integrated more fully with the National effort from the start, the garb of a bogus socialism may not have attained the dimension it did.

Thus with freedom came not just new problems, responsibilities, but a large share of disillusionment too.

Yusuf Meherally was my first direct link with the current political world through the Youth League. I may say he was my mentor to start with. Politically as we matured together; our political credo seemed to fuse. He showed great and continued confidence in me which was like bubbling tonic. I leaned on him for wise counsel and felt fortified when spirits were low with a cheering word from him. He was a personality after my own heart, one who dares, risks, ready for bold trials. 'Live dangerously,' was his motto but he did not write it with an empty flourish of his pen. With him it was a way of life. He was all concentration on the job in hand unmindful of what it would cost him. Fearless and sincere he inspired the young and the old alike with fire and fervour. But happily his basically pragmatic nature worked out a satisfactory balance. He gave a sturdy force and stable structure to the organisation.

He was a man of wide interests, a prodigious reader aided by a prodigious memory that enabled him to disseminate his studies with natural ease. He had a kind of magic touch in dealing with the youth. He inspired and fruitfully directed them and they felt privileged to work with him. Though essentially a man of the people, sensitive to their heart-beats, he nevertheless was as an individual, a warm and abiding friend. These qualities came out pronouncedly when he became the Mayor of Bombay which in those days was a most prestigious position. His daily morning rounds of the city when he mingled and became one with the people, particularly of the slum areas, became almost a legend. His early demise deprived the Socialist Party of the ballast, his robust practical poise, well balanced with idealism, had provided. Of all my close colleagues of the time, he was the closest. His death left for me a void that could never be filled.

I met Jayaprakash immediately after his arrival from America. He was introduced as a Marxist, a fellow traveller as the popular expression then went. His friendly genial personality soon drew me out. His basic humane approach to problems cast doubts on the label attached to him. He was essentially a humanitarian and will always be remembered and treasured as that, not a political personality. Gandhiji was the only one of that period to whom he could be compared in that respect. He instinctively and passionately stood up to any wrong or injustice being perpetrated, no matter what the cost, right up to the end of his life. It was natural he should accept a Marxist ideology, aiming as he was for radical political, social and economic changes. But disillusionment came through bitter political experiences as he tried to guide the socialist movements. Some old Comrades played him false. The arrival of freedom brought with it betrayal. He cried out in anguish that 'Partition has robbed the dawn of freedom of its glow.'

The disillusionment which had crept over me even by 1947 overtook him at a later stage. As the years rolled by we both watched with dismay the hardening stratification of the society, the lopsided development of the economy, the growing stubbornness in the ecological and demographic problems from lack of concerted purposeful action. It was to these we felt compelled to direct our attention. Though we worked apart, we kept in touch and came together at certain crucial points. My association with him continued to the end.

He was happy with my rehabilitation work after partition and a couple of the workers from the Indian Cooperation Union, worked in the rural areas with him. When I took on office responsibilities in the Handicrafts Board and the National Akademi for performing arts, he very kindly took over from me the Association of Voluntary Bodies that I had set up to coordinate the varied activities of a number of social welfare organisations. He however transformed both the basis and character of this organisation by moving it to Bihar and giving it a rural orientation. As I surveyed his earnest efforts in remote areas, trying to bring streaks of knowledge and lighten a little the heavy economic burdens of the villagers, I blessed myself for the companionship he gave me.

As my own efforts in social and economic pursuits were culture biased I watched the post-independence period of what was termed development, totally devoid of cultural elements. This was appalling since Indian life at all levels, particularly in the rural region, was fully imbued with and inextricably bound up with exquisite strands. Everything we used had to be aesthotically beautiful. There was no room for even dull and drab patches, leave alone vast areas which one now viewed with utter dismay. Why did we abandon decorating our frontage, our floors, walls? Skip over pleasure-giving festivities? When I drew Jayaprakash's attention to his, he responded fervently. I was aware of his concern for struggling artists and unknown to the world how he had helped the needy ones.

Jayaprakash agreed with my suggestion that a concerted drive be now made to revive the fading lights. To get some tangible encouragement from him, I presented him a short note in which I reminded that those whose lives the developmental efforts were to change, were the real ones still adhering to and maintaining some of the traditional culture, and by our zeal to modernise them, we squeeze dry even these lingering vestiges. Not only should these be salvaged, a strong consciousness of their need should be felt to make life pleasurable and fuller. The current attitude of 'patronisation' of those denied a life of better quality needed to be replaced by one of interdependability if cultural waves were to interact with each other.

Jayaprakash and I shared these sentiments and he wrote out a message for me: 'It is essential that all national development should include the preservation and continuation of cultural forms and pursuits. The present trend of deculturisation does great damage to our national life. The core of all progress must be based on our practising arts and crafts. Our cultural life has become sluggish and sleepy, that a powerful effort is needed to enliven it. Cultural awakening sharpens and accelerates the social development. When I had stressed on total revolution, I visualised a strong cultural force as an integral part of it. Now again I emphasise the need for a powerful cultural awakening.'

Though I pressed this on some social workers, even those from whom I expected some response, all failed us. The effort fell by the wayside.

Jayaprakash's last call to collaborate with him came to me in 1977 after the general elections. The Indian people were just recovering from the trauma of the Emergency. It was for him and the country a grand opportunity to initiate an upsurge for what he called the Total -- but I prefer to designate 'The Unfinished Revolution.' We thoughtlessly skipped it in 1947 trying to hug to our bosom a broken dream. As a result the whole sub-continent had been going through untold anguish, and humiliation. Now had come a chance for us to retrieve some of what was lost.

The organisational set up was through Peoples' Committees, the normal recognised structure, on a massive scale at various levels. They were to provide the foundation of a truly participatory democracy by enabling ordinary citizens to exercise increasing control over the local affairs and function as the instrument of popular sovereignity. For this to be meaningful and effective, large-scale, in-depth education was needed for which an army of voluntary workers and intense community cooperation was called for, to generate sensitivity to the needs of others and one's obligation towards them. Only then could equality and liberty prevail.

I was inspired and my long jaded nerves began to tingle. I could become part of a new nation in the making to wipe out the heinous scars of many iniquities.

With a frisky step I entered the hall for the inauguration of the function to launch the long-delayed Total Revolution. I was suddenly accosted by friends who informed me I was to Chair this historic gathering. I gasped with discomfiture and remonstrated, all to no purpose. Jayaprakash with his captivating smile and alluring appeals assured me I need make no speech, just a few words of blessing and good cheer. I felt privileged at this unsought honour, I literally trembled as I began to speak. I do not believe even a word was audible.

Jayaprakash was one on whom several currents had made their mark. But Gandhiji's influence predominated to the end. The two were very close even when they differed. While both were fundamentally humanitarian, Gandhiji's inner self had a stern rock-like element that mere pathos could never melt. He also possessed a sharper, more penetrating mind than Jayaprakash. Where ever Gandhiji yielded, it was not out of tender compassion, but as a political tactic. He had the seasoned politicians flair in negotiations. His famous picturesque phrase 'Seeking on bended knees' when he was seeking talks with the Viceroy on the eve of the 1932 civil disobedience movement, is typical. His knees may have been ready to bend, but not his head and heart, that ever remained erect. Jayaprakash lacked these indispensible qualities in a political leader. When his conscience was touched he would rush to the battle scene, whether it be Pakistan, Bangladesh, Nagaland. He and Gandhiji shared the same anguish however at their end: their shattered dreams.

In the common communist slang, Narendra Dev could be called the Party theoretician. But such a label would be misleading in the case. He was a Marxist by faith personally. But again he was a Marxist apart, not to be lumped together with others of his ilk. He was intellectually transparently honest, and therefore logically independent. That is his explanation for his ability to adjust and co-exist with other sincere efforts for India's freedom. In this context he accepted Gandhian thought and methods as they did not seem antagonistic to his basic beliefs. To put it in his own words: 'No injustice is done to any Marxist principle by accepting Satyagraha. Neither does it amount to a synthesis of Marxism and Gandhism. Marxism has never been fond of violent means. If the objective can be attained by using non-violent means, Marxism would give it top-most preference.' Nor did he think Bhoodan antagonistic to Socialism. This was the essence of his political faith, a broad vision and a completely nonsectarian intellect. Similarly he could never accept the Marxist volte face when they converted the World War into a Peoples' War after Russia was attacked.

Narendra Dev was essentially a savant designed to adorn an academy. Even in physique he was extra-sensitively cast, he made rather a unique figure in the motley crowd which comprised the Socialist Party of the time, which nevertheless was still moved through idealism rather than power politics. He was one of the core of the movement that made it meaningful as well as the embellishment that endowed with grace an otherwise drab exterior.

Purshottam was one of the few successful practising professionals in the Party. He was a noted lawyer. but more, had the reputation of an unusual, conscientious man. He was born not with a silver spoon, but a parental debt, that nobody would have wanted to load on him. But he assumed the burden of his own free will and would not rest until he had paid it off when he started to earn.

Though ideologically a Socialist, he had a terse practical mind, kind of 'no nonsense' type. He involved himself in a number of social welfare projects. He helped me greatly in the training camps for women that I used to run. The biggest project he initiated was the Peoples Mobile Hospital, which became an important service-giving body and still continues to offer the same excellent service to the needy public.

Politically Purshottam and I were in complete harmony. We refused to treat any 'ism' as a bible on which to base our entire edifice. We were both wary and progressively became troubled when the Communists began to undermine the Party organisation.

Purshottam as a practical politician showed keener perceptions and was therefore most sensitive to the weak spots in the Party structure and the emerging pitfalls. Being straight he generally talked right from the shoulder. He brooked no prevarications nor subterfuges. My admiration for him and confidence in him grew. When he felt the Party could no longer serve objectives he cherished, he too strayed away.

Even professionally he was unique. Though he could have earned fabulous amounts, he deliberately kept his income within required limits, just enough to serve his needs as he wanted to be free to pursue his social service avocations. As with Mehrally, death snatched him away prematurely. We had kept up our friendship which included his wife Leela, until Leela too was no more.

Rammanohar Lohia is hard to describe in simple terms. He was rather a complex personality. Comparatively, he was rather a latecomer and our acquaintance came about in a strange way. I was at a smallish gathering where a speaker was rambling on when he made a faux pas. It however seemed to have been lost on the gathering, but I could hardly suppress my smile and as I looked over the many faces, a pair of strange eyes met mine with an answering twinkle. Much later when I was introduced to a 'new comer', I looked into the same eyes and we both broke into laughter much to the discomfiture of the friend who had done the formalities. 'What is the joke? I did not know you were acquainted?' he remonstrated. I tried to assuage him in an assured tone, we were complete strangers. He was of course not mollified for that was no explanation for our hearty laughter.

So we clicked from the very first time we met. He was not only complex, he was equally unpredictable, one of the reasons that made him for me, an exciting personality. He was full of exhilarating ideas. He was daring, venturing into original avenues of thought, straying into fresh pastures of enticing schemes. With him to think was to act with no inhibitions no quirks to impede. He created a starting world, in which to function was in itself an adventure. No matter how unsettling the air around, his feet always seemed to stand on the firm earth; no matter how volatile his personality may have seemed, to me he remained the lovable individual that I first came across, gentle though tough, modest but assertive.

A change seemed to have come over him after the 1942 movement. From him I learnt of the inhuman treatment he and Jayaprakash were subjected to in the Red Fort under the guise of interrogation. The questioning would be continued ceaselessly for hours, round the clock, keeping them awake, not allowed even to drowse. They were of course kept separately.

They nevertheless communicated with each other through a novel media code, by reciting Sanskrit slokas! Thus was woven an intangible companionship between the two solitary victims of a blind cruel world.

He had an extraordinarily scintillating mind. He could speak with great skill and exactitude, for no matter what the language in which he articulated, he had a mastery over it. While a great deal of this was directed into fruitful channels to voice the agonies of the people, some spilled over into futile frothy nothingness. I once remonstrated with him about this, particularly rejected the subject matter of the themes he elaborated upon repeatedly, especially in the Parliament. 'What for instance would you want me to talk about?' he asked, rather shaken by my unusual vehemence. 'Why don't you describe what national academies should be like, repositories of knowledge, directed by real academicians, not political partymen who need to be given prestigious berths,' I replied.

To my utter and pleasant astonishment, he raised a whole debate in the Parliament, defining what a real national academy should be like. Everybody was astounded. He had spent days and nights reading up whatever he could lay his hands on to trot out an unassailable case.

That was his last speech in Parliament, a resonant swan song. In it he publicly acknowledged my rebuke as his guiding star. Within weeks he was gone, leaving a big void in the political life of the country, and a deep scar in my heart. There could never be another Lohia!

What left a bigger pang in my heart was the memory of his several arrests and being lodged in prison cells. This had particularly hurt him. I recalled the memorable letter he addressed the President of India from the Naini Central prison in 1954, when he made out a lucid and plausible case for civil resistance even in free India, when it has a specific purpose to serve. He concluded it with a pathetic confession defining one of the sad tragedies of our national life. He wrote: 'I do not like being in prison. I have always disliked prisons and I hate them now. They are a mortifying reminder to me of my impotence of justice against injustice. At least in the British days, there was the satisfaction of washing away the sins of our recent tormentors and of acquiring strength through imprisonment. There is no more such satisfaction.'

There were only two women members in the Socialist Party Executive, Satyavati and myself. She was so cast and moulded, it would have been extraordinary if one did not succumb to her soft allure. She was tall and exquisitely chiselled from face to toe, but seemed totally unaware of her quiet charm. Although she displayed an unruffled exterior, she was within herself a ball of fire. I had once teased her when she assumed another avatar as it were, that she could play the fierce Durga to perfection.

It is not surprising that she started her life in her youth as a terrorist. She was the grand daughter of Swami Shradhanand, the religious reformer who founded Arya Samaj, and some of her fire she must have derived from him, as also her consistent philosophical attitude to life. She showed an amazing degree of detatchment towards her physical problems. For by now she had got pretty battered, exposing herself to police violence, continuous prison terms, strenuous activities. Ill or well, she kept up an unbelievable poise, ready for another fray, and the prison terms came tumbling almost breathlessly.

When Gandhiji came on the scene, she abandoned the path of terrorism and joined the National Struggle. On Gandhiji's arrest during the Salt Satyagraha, she took out a huge procession. When the police officer arrived to obstruct it, he demanded the name of the leader, and Satyavati coolly stepped up, declaring herself as the one. When the processionists could not be stopped, order for firing was given. Several were wounded, some died, she however luckily escaped.

She involved herself with the lowliest ; organising the struggling individuals—in those days most labour was unorganised. With determination she got together people like cart drivers, loaders, day labourers, etc. to see that they got their dues. She worked amongst women with great passion, to encourage them to stand on their own feet, cast aside the purdah and become a part of the social mainstream. Though she had an air of sternness about her, her eyes were pools of compassion.

She was imprisoned eight times, each time she came out more shattered. But she pursued her activities with greater vigour than ever. She ventured into remote rural areas wherever anguish called her, to try to get justice rendered to victims. She addressed the peasants on the freedom movement, gathering enthusiastic recruits for the battle. She dragged on thus though her physique was rapidly deteriorating. Once when she was to address a peasant assembly she was so overcome by fatigue, she had to lie down and speak. As she was served with a quit order, she was determined to defy it. There were scores of such incidents of defiance. During one of her incarcerations, she contracted tuberculosis which kept haunting her in every imprisonment when vitality was low. The prison authorities tried to persuade her to leave, but she resolutely refused to bind herself to any undertaking that she would refrain from her activities.

During the Quit India movement she was sent to a hospital in Lahore, when she was fast deteriorating. There she heard of the death of her father and her little daughter. Though there was a ban on her entry into Delhi, she took the journey in the same defiant spirit. This was in a way her last trip. She had by now gone beyond the clutches of the police octopus, she was fast sinking. That was when I had my last meeting with her.

Her body seemed part of the white hospital sheet. But the compassionate eyes with the lurking streaks of fire still lit up her classic features. 'Don't grieve', she said holding my hand, for she must have noted an anguish I could not hide. 'You all will shoulder the far heavier and the more privileged burdens that you will need to in the days to come,' she murmured like a blessing as I bent over her.

When she passed out of my life it were as though I had lost some part of me that could never be restored. As two women we had woven a kinship between us and I had basked happily in that beautiful friendship. Now only a painful void was left.

Politicians over a period of time seem to take on a common mould which about sums up what I am trying to convey. A few who resist the moulding. stand out. Among them was Srinivas Malliah, a close compatriot of mine throughout my political career. I would like to mention some of his unusual outstanding qualities not generic to politicians. A strong personal detatchment, seeking no personal rewards or benefits even though possessed of a rare astuteness, he became a successful politician wielding considerable influence, who could have had the pick of positions.

He had a strong emotional feeling for his fellow beings. He became obsessed with plans for roads, particularly in remote rural parts. He traced it to his seeing as a youngster, fisherwomen plodding through the scorching sands under a burning sun, heavily loaded with fish, making their way to the market. He spent lots of time working out a complete network of roads and little bridges in his district. It was some achievement—that was typical of some of the silent unobtrusive services he rendered.

Nevertheless he was easily accessible to anyone who needed him, on matter how trivial it may have been. He had the same value and respect for people at all levels even as Gandhiji had. He gave so much of *himself*, his personality, his incisive mind, above all his good humour. Often those who came to weep or curse left with laughter on their lips.

A fine aesthetic sense, sensitivity to nature, to elegance is a rare trait in most involved in the hurly burly of politics. With him it was an outstanding element. He surrounded himself with choice attractive objects. He made considerable effort to foster greenery, flowers around the parliament members' houses. Many an ugly exterior with its crude angularities were sought to be covered up. He also patronised crafts, gave fruitful attention to the welfare of craftsmen, several of whom he visited in their hamlets.

Although he and I differed on political issues, he took my vehemence and assertiveness in his stride and our friendship was never allowed to be bruised.

After I quit politics we decide to create a network of social work centres throughout our district for which a District Industries Association was promoted, with emphasis on retaining the traditional skills and training in new ones.

The rich folk ritualistic drama forms prevailing in our district (already described) were showing signs of getting brash and hybrid under attempts to modernise. While I was having all these hastily documented for the archives, it seemed equally necessary that the elaborate costumes and fantastically colourful properties called for preservation. This unhappy decay was widespread, which made the need even more compelling. So we hit on a Theatre Crafts Museum. I opened it in my own house, to give it a start, converting my reception room into a mini-museum.

Malliah, however, seized with an urgency to give it a building of its own, quickly got the concerned Minister to allot a plot. Even before this could be finalised Malliah was taken away by sudden death. All one could do was to make the Theatre Crafts Museum a memorial to him. But the vicissitudes this entangled me into could fill a little volume. The battle is on, the project moves only inch by inch towards our fulfilment.

He was most unusual in several other ways. He combined a sharp agility of mind, extraordinarily keen perception, an uncanny ability to size up people with boundless enthusiasm for activity and unfailing courage to meet any situation, and grit to grapple with heaviest odds. Loaded though he was with such qualities, he had humility, unobstrusiveness and a calm gentle exterior, that rarely went with such a sharp brain. Another trait in him was a terrific sense of humour that kept the air around him sparkling. Watching him closely I would delude myself into imagining I would learn to follow the ramifications of politics, their turns and twists, but usually I came off a cropper. He would say, 'You simply don't understand politics.' If he had to meet someone for a discussion, he could narrate ahead the crucial part of the talk to come with an uncanny confidence.

Today as I look back, I am able to gauge and assess political factors that I felt too dumbfounded to express in his time, and which I admit is a precious legacy he left me.

Among our senior leaders Maulana Abdul Kalam Azad was to me someone apart, different from the other political leaders, he seemed to be living in a world of his own and I stood in awe of him. He was different from Dr. Ansari, warm, friendly, informal to whom I felt very close whose house was my home in Delhi. With Azad our acquaintance had not gone beyond formal greetings. Once when I was in Sevagram for a Congress Working Committee meeting, Pandit Nehru rather abruptly asked me why I cut the Maulana Saheb I protested. What was he aggrieved about, I asked. He explained 'Maulana wonders why you are so formal and distant and hardly speak with him.' I was plainly in awe of him. He was a great scholar, and what could I discuss with him was my simple explanation. Thereupon Panditji started a veritable dissertation on his human qualities. He was a scholar, no doubt, but a simple man at heart. He was not just a political being, he had wider interests, he was objective, free from petty prejudices. 'In fact he is one with whom you could talk freely, even if you completely disagreed with him; in other words he was a big man of vision and clarity.'

Thus was the ice between us broken. There was a rare element of respect in his manner towards others which I realised seemed to isolate him. I was very conscious of this particularly as I was so much younger to him. But as I grew to know him I realised age did not make any difference to him.

It was sometime after he took over as Minister for Education that he asked me to lunch with him. After a few preliminaries, he said: 'I propose to set up three National Academies. Here I am drawing on the Greek genesis when Plato called his school by this epithet which has since come to acquire a connonation of its own. It ideally answers what I have today in mind and breathes the full flavour of an academic body with all its dignity and stature. Only I propose to adapt the term as Akademi to conform to the Hindi pronounciation. The role of the

Akademis will be to canalise fruitfully the new cultural forces released after independence. While I believe that arts have to derive their sustenance only from the people, the Government must undertake their development and continuity as its primary duty. The Akademis will however be autonomous in their internal working and will include in their composition not only State representatives but equally representatives of important art organisations and distinguished individual artists. The Akademi of dance, drama and music will be the first to be set up. Because of your active interest in them, I wish to share my thoughts with you.' In response I expressed my pleasure and satisfaction and then added: 'I am sure you will stress in this context the spirit of assimilation and synthesis which one may say has been the core and essence of our cultural heritage. I am sure you realise the significance of this at this juncture when we have to bring our invaluable heritage into the current mainstream.'

He dilated on this at length and I realised for the first time the breadth and depth of his knowledge of these subjects, and how keenly he had applied his mind to them. Azad was never vociferous, his reticence obviously hid some rare attributes. It was therefore not easy to gauge or assess his knowledge, his cosmopolitanism, even less the quiet store of warmth and affection stored somewhere silently in the recesses of his being.

'I would like you to serve on the Executive Board of this Akademi and give all the help you can. I know it is something dear to your heart. This is a new venture and I seek your cooperation.' I expressed my pleasure to learn of the cultural Akademis and assured him of my participation. As I rose to take leave he stopped me. 'One thing more—I am just making up our delegation to the UNESCO Assembly Session at Beirut and I would like you to join it. This is our first official participation. I am asking Humayun Kabir, the Ministry Secretary to personally discuss this with you.'

At the first meeting of the newly formed Sangeet Natak Akademi I was unanimously elected Vice-Chairman. Dr. Rajmannar, the Chairman, conveyed that as he was rather pre-occupied as the Chief Justice in Madras, the Akademi needed not only someone dedicated and with the requisite knowledge of the subjects but also to give ample time to the institution to be dealt with. So for all practical purposes I had to make do for the Chairman. I was however at ease. Dr. Rajmannar was a great scholar from whom I could learn. He gave me full freedom to act as the authority on the spot. 'If you need my assistance, don't hesitate to come to me. You may trust me to give you fullest support.'

I was glad to be able to personally build up close personal contacts with performing artists all over. I drew inspiration and sustenance from this as in many cases the contacts flowered into pleasant friendships.

My abiding interest in the theatre induced me to set up a National School of Drama in the face of considerable opposition including from theatre artists, for they laboured under a comfortable feeling that anyone with talent for acting had only to join a performing company and learn as you work. To them *teaching* dramatics was an absurd idea. Anyway the School took birth, survived even though it kept on going through vicissitudes of different types, set definite standards, opened up new patterns and techniques in production, provided a new leadership for the theatre world, and attained a national status.

The other activity in which I took keen interest was documenting of the varied performing arts. The objects waiting to be documented was a never ending panorama of infinite varieties. Through the years the more one witnessed them, the more one realised one was touching just the periphery of our treasures especially the folk and the tribal, each a rich world in itself.

12

There arrived in Delhi two representatives of the Secretary-General of the Arab League, Azzam Pasha. He was one of the outstanding personalities of the Arab world and much significance was attached to the visit of his emissaries. They came to visit and we talked of my last visit to Egypt. They told me they had an invitation from Azzam Pasha who was anxious to build up close association between India and the Arab countries. He and the Arab League would be very glad if I could visit some of these countries. I was delighted and told them how appropriately this invitation had come, for I would be in Beirut very soon to attend the UNESCO session.

As we chatted Mr. Hafeez, the younger of the two wanted me to permit him to put me a question. 'We heard that you would have become the Chief Minister of a State, or a member of the Central Cabinet. Why did you decline?' I replied that I was simply not interested in political offices. The other man interposed. 'Should not more women like you assume such responsibilities and prove their abilities in the now men-dominated political arena and the rather exclusive men's domain?' This question was being posed to me often enough and I had the same answer: 'When I joined the political struggle it was not to claim a right to a high office. I began my political career as a humble volunteer. I worked as such throughout my political career. I neither sought nor held any office in the Congress organisation. I served in the Congress Executive in the last phase through sheer compulsion. I am by vocation and training a social service worker and I mean to remain so. Arts, crafts are my grammer, the medium through which to express myself. Politics as a career does not mingle with my bloodstream.'

The UNESCO gathering failed to grip me. It was too verbose, I tire quickly of too much talk. Alternately I seemed constantly ploughed under reams and reams of typed sheets, so I cut short my stay and launched out on my tour of the Arab countries.

I had been fascinated by Beirut and its very beautiful environs, and intrigued by the devices to maintain a national integrity in a multireligious land. Here I met the Druzes, visited that colourful community, met families and learnt of their exclusive faith, who later provided the Socialist leadership for this region. The air was calm, salubrious and relaxing.

All this suddenly changed as I drove into magnificent Damascus. Now it were as though stepping on hot coals, even though it was cold winter. For the formation of the Jewish State of Israel had touched off a fuse as it were and the entire region seemed to have erupted like a volcano, with splinters flying all over. In all the buzz, the name that echoed and rechoed was of King Abdullah of Transjordan—a name which had hitherto been but a distant sound now began to take on a definite form. I felt a strong compulsion to visit Jordan which had been excluded from my itinerary as the place would prove uncomfortably cold for me. I decided to convey my wish to Azzam Pasha, and hopefully-venture onward into Jerusalem.

I had come to understand he was the most outstanding personality and a rock of strength in the tumultuous Arab World. Even my little knowledge of this stormy region had made me realise that only a wizard could operate this loose body, the League, with a firm grip.

Abdurrahman Azzam Pasha was a lean courtly man with a receding chin, and despite his physical appearance and his misleading title, he also held a medical degree, and was a genuine revolutionary. He had gathered and led the Arab forces aided by the Turks against the British in the World War I while the Arabs in revolt were fighting the Turks! He was also drawn towards the Russian revolution and is said to have appealed to Lenin to help the Arab cause.

Azzam Pasha welcomed me warmly and lucidly unravelled for me each of the several strands that made up this complicated body—the

Arab League, and its Mission. 'There was the grizzly old Wahabite monarch Ibn Saud of Arabia who had mercilessly driven the Sheriff Hussein family out to hoist himself on the throne, while the exiles established their rule over Iraq and Jordan. King Abdulla was out to become the overlord of an all Arab State which the others individually and collectively opposed.

'There was one section in Syria trying for Greater Syria, a fusion of Syria and Transjordan, while the strong man Nuri-el-Saed the Prime Minister of Iraq, was manoeuvring for the Fertile Crescent by merging Syria and Iraq, which King Ibn Saud swears he will take as an aggression on his own territory. More—there is a notional independent Palestine with two veterans Ahmad Hileny Pasha and the stormy petrel, the Ex-Mufti of Jerusalem, both claiming to be the head. Opposed to all of this is Egypt which expects to be the Central power. For King Farouk dreams of becoming the new Pharaoh who will rule over the entire Arab land.' Thus he sketched this complicated drama like a master director, himself cool, unhurried. 'So you see, at the moment the Arab world is sizzling with political events from North Africa to the Gulf of Aden.' He was now the perfect spokesman of the Arab people and the words came in a slow deliberate tone. 'The concern of the Western world is understandable. They have ruled the world for better or for worse—for us for the worse,' and he swept his arms to cover our big in size but small in power, world. 'Parts of the world are in revolt and determined to assert their rights, especially as solemn promises were made to them—'. 'I am not so sure of a real free world though,' I remarked. 'If another world war overtakes us even lands that are not directly involved will once again become the battleground of other peoples quarrels and trampled upon by the same imperialist war machines, all because our planet is too small to hold more than one major power it seems.'

He replied in an indulgent tone: 'If another war comes—I shall tell you a little story to describe what will happen.' I had heard he used parables to put forth his point. 'There was once a big frog who bred a very large family. He carefully trained his progeny how to cleverly outwit others, by visualising each circumstance that would endanger them and how to circumvent it. Finally with a croak of self-satisfaction it announced the family could now face any challenge for it was fully prepared for any contingency.

'Hardly had the croak died down when a wide net descended and firmly trapped the entire family. A little terror-stricken baby frog squeaked angrily: 'Grandpapa you were boasting you have made us invincible. Why did you not teach us to elude this?' Groaned the dejected old frog, 'I had no idea of this wide net which is a new invention of modern technology and I was not prepared for it. So if our super powers insist on a war to end war, as the saying goes, all humanity will be caught in the nuclear net like the frog family. So it is the war itself that must be prevented.' He readily agreed to my visiting Jordan, 'There try to meet the King, then move on to Jerusalem where you must meet its lively Military Governor, Abdulla Tell. He is an unusual man, a sensitive intellectual still a great military hero. The youngest major in Glubb Pasha's Arab Legion, he had saved Jerusalem from falling into the hands of the Israelis at the King's personal approach to him when the city was almost lost.' To meet Abdulla Tell, the hero of Jerusalem, I felt a tingle of pleasurable excitement.

'I assume you are aware that it is a hazardous journey and you must be prepared for all risks. The situation is fluid, therefore decidedly more dangerous. Are you sure you want to risk it? I do not want to draw the wrath of your people on my head. We now enjoy their sympathy and confidence.' I assured him I was my own master, I had taken such risks before.

Palestine, once one of the central points of the world, had once more become a momentous focal spot as a storm centre. It was therefore with a tingle of expectancy that I set out on the road to Jerusalem. On the Syrian-Jordan frontier, I had a long wait. A Syrian frontier official came up to me with an apology for the delay and suggested I step in and relax with a cup of coffee. I declined, preferring to take a stroll. Very gallantly he offered to keep me company.

He spoke perfect English and soon I pricked up my ears. Naturally the topic was the continued political crisis in the region. 'It is the British and their tools for whose ambitions there are no limits and which are fed by the wily British. They always have a scheme up their sleeve to acquire a bigger British territory of influence. Every extension of the Jordan Kingdom is inevitably an expansion of British control. Nor do these plans end there. As long as we allow the Western powers to play around here, there can never be any peace. They are only designs to divide the Arab world and prevent its unity.' And so the tale went on, punctuated by the agitated waving of arms, clenching of fists, dilating of nostrils. Obviously the iron had entered these people. 'You had an audience with the King,' he tried to make his voice sound casual, but he must have been curious. 'A Jordan newspaper gave the news,' he said in explanation. We were interrupted and told I could proceed on my journey.

There is an undeniable thrill in the actual discovery of places that the Bible had made legendary—Biblical as the popular term goes. Palestine as the cradle of three great monotheistic religions and, therefore, equally holy to all of them and the centre of worship of one God is unique. More than two thousand years ago, this was obviously a well-populated, wealthy country 'flowing with milk and honey', which Moses promised his weary people. Around 2000 B.C., from Ur, the famous city of the Sumerians and centre of their resplendent culture, Abraham, the patriarch of three mighty religions, crossed the vast Arabian desert with his Semitic tribesmen and settled here. From the early Sumerian faith Abraham had brought with him the concept of the one God, which Moses later made the basis for a monotheistic creed.

1000 B.C. saw the emergence of a Hebrew Monarchy represented by a line of distinguished kings, Saul, David, Solomon. Later it was conquered by the Romans who tried to crush out the heart of the people by destroying the city of Jerusalem. But the ashes only gave birth to Jesus who tried to teach mankind a new way of life.

The next phase was the advent of Islam which recognised the Semitic tradition and prophets, and the old Jewish state became only a memory. Within four hundred years the Arab Kingdom too began to break up, and Palestine experienced intermittent invasions by European Christians known as the Crusades, who tried to maintain a precarious kingdom around Jerusalem. But by the 12th century the country reverted back to the Muslims and came under the Turks until it was conquered by the British in World War I.

As one approaches Jerusalem my school-day memories came crowding back and a clear picture of Biblical events seemed presented from the walls of the Temple overlooking the Mount of Olives whose slopes cover countless tombs. According to tradition, both Jewish and Christian, it is here that the last judgement will take place, and the rising of the dead will commence on The Mount, and therefore numerous generations have sought it for their last resting place hoping they will be amongst the earliest on hand on the day of judgement. Crossing the Kedron valley wind the roads that I ruminated, Jesus and his men must have traversed. It was from this Mount facing the Temple opposite, that he prophesied its destruction. It was from here that he had bade Peter and John go and arrange for the last supper, and descended to the quiet Garden of Gethsemane where he was taken prisoner after the betrayal by Judas. The Mount is also believed to be the scene of his ascension to heaven.

Jerusalem, known as the Eternal City, is believed to be the ancient Salem to whose King Melchizedek, Abraham paid his tithes. Antique tablets mention its existence in 1400 B.C. It is said to have been conquered thirty-six times and destroyed ten times. In A.D. 70 Titus, after razing the city to the ground, ploughed it up with salt, so nothing may grow on it! But it seems to have shown remarkable resilience unlike other ancient cities, and it continues to survive, and the devastations merely passed over it like seasonal storms.

The sunset was blazing the West with the red-orange glow that seemed to bathe the entire landscape. I was stirred as I looked upon its magnificent spread as our car reached the summit above. The same scene must have met each approaching conquerer over the rolling centuries.

The man at the wheel, beside whom I sat, turned his heavy face to me. He was a tall man of big stature and had to crouch to adjust himself to the driving wheel. Red suffused his face as though streaked by the hue from the heavens, and his eyes swam as he waved a trembling finger over the city bathed in almost an unreal light: 'This is the city of my birth, the home of my ancestors, from which I have been driven away.' He halted as his fist clenched. 'But I shall return. All my people that have been turned homeless shall return.' It sounded more like a prayer than a conviction.

All along I had seen refugees wearily trudging their way into Syria, into Jordan, into Lebanon. 'It is all the handiwork of the British,' the man at the wheel continued. They have this one technique of cutting up a country and dividing its people, thus undermining and weakening it.

Words poured out in torrents. 'And there will always be black sheep and traitors in our camp to sell out for their own petty ambitions.'

'But in the case of Palestine, it was the U.N. that intervened. And in any event I understand that the battle was going against the Arabs.'

'You are wrong,' he hotly intervened. 'You will hear the real tale by and by from the proper quarters. Let me first see you lodged safely in your quarters.'

By now we were in the vicinity of the Old City. The grim stone of the buildings only served to deepen the azure blue of the sky, the green of the cypresses and the brown and cobalt of the surrounding hills. Later as the day wore out, I noticed the colour scheme changing from the softest pastels to transparent hues of every description.

Although different invading legions had come and gone through the centuries, obviously water was still as scarce now as of yore; for one saw the water vendors carrying water in goatskin. A pipeline had been laid to meet the need but it had been disrupted by the war. I later noticed that each house had a cistern of its own.

I was totally unprepared for the Saracenic style rampart walls delicately lacing as it were the city, raised I was told, by Suleiman the Magnificent and are supposed to follow the wall of Christ's day.

As conditions in Jerusalem were disturbed and open to attacks as much by military as by non-military, I was advised to live at the Indian Mission in a Hospice, a small unostentatious affair with a quiet little couple incharge. My host told me the Military Governor of Jerusalem had invited me to a quiet lunch and we would be by ourselves. 'You can get some inside information if you try, the Governor is Abdulla Tell.'

'I am Major Abdullah Tell', the Military Governor introduced himself as he strode up to me. He looked surprisingly young with a striking young handsome face and a remarkably well-shaped head as though sensitive hands had worked skilfully on it. He wore a long white robe lined with a burning crimson material, that added distinction, nay, glamour to his personality. Strapped to his waist was a prominent revolver with a glamorous pearl handle that had become a kind of a personal hallmark. He bent low over my hand sweeping the air with his cloak as he bade me welcome to the Old City.

We were soon at his official residence, evidently once a palace, an imposing structure with large heavy doors opening into spacious salons. We went up the stairs and sat on a wide balcony overlooking the grounds.

'You may be intrigued to know that this was where Pilate tried Jesus and condemned him. This is said to be the balcony on which Pilate held court.' I was shaken by this unexpected news. 'I was always drawn to Jesus and he has always meant a lot to me. I was hoping I could visit some of the places memorable to him.' 'No hope of that' he interposed. 'They are mostly in the Israeli territory. You can't possibly cross the 'enemy' lines however much you may adore Jesus Christ.'

Far from being put off, I continued my search and found that Bethlehem was still accessible. I decided to pursue it at the appropriate time.

As we began our meal I plunged straight away into the topic which was intriguing me—how was Palestine lost, was my first question.

He hesitated and bit his lip as a deep flush suffused his face. There was much emotion in his tone as he replied in a slow measured tone. 'It is a dark and shameful tale, which had best be forgotten.' He hesitated and then continued in an uncertain tone: 'I wish I could forget—in fact I am trying to.'

'But I must know, I have come a long way to find out the truth for myself,' I pleaded.

He began. 'Briefly the facts are as follows. The British, when they realised they could not hold on to Palestine, decided on their usual formula of partitioning the country. On the one hand they negotiated with the Jews and on the other, with one section of the Arabs. Had the Arab army but entered Jerusalem at the zero hour when the British quit, the initiative would have been with us. But the Arabs came in nearly three days too late. By then the Jews had become pretty well entrenched, even then we kept pushing them out and we liberated Jerusalem that we had practically lost. The cease-fire order came just when victory lay within our grasp. Do you know what my victorious heart-broken men did when they got these fatal orders? They performed the Bedouin funeral dance to pour out their grief for voluntarily abdicating when victory lay within their grasp. That is the tragedy.' His voice trailed off into a murmur and a far way look crept into his eyes.

I waited silently intent in anticipation. He took a long breath like a deep sigh. 'Yes there was treachery behind the innocuous UN sponsored cease-fire. King Abdullah secretly got conveyed to the English Foreign Minister Bevin, that he was being pressed to call off the war by his Arab colleagues. His price: attacking the newly marked Arab Palestine territory to Jordan to expand his Hashemite Kingdom.' I gazed dumbfounded. 'It is a fact. He conveyed the cease-fire order directly to me on the telephone late one night and when I tried to remind him that victory was almost with us, he curtly reminded me it was His Majesty speaking and I as a soldier had only to carry out orders. Then to underscore this he announced he would be in Jerusalem the next day to offer prayers.'

'What of Glubb Pasha?' I asked curious to know. 'He was supposed to have reincarnated as an Arab Bedouin'. Tell, his face red again, rasped in a hoarse voice: 'He has had many incarnations in one birth. He dealt as an Arab with the King's palace, as a Bedouin with the tribes, but as Sir John Bagot which he really was, he was the most loyal officer of His Majesty's Government in London. Does that answer your question? In fact he was one of the trusted emissaries of the king to carry the secret message to London. The trouble lies in having ambitious men in our own camp. With whom did the British negotiate? An Arab leader, who was willing to march the Arab troops in late. It was a deliberate gross betrayal.' 'But why? After all if the Arabs won, Palestine would have become an Arab State,' I queried. 'Ah, that is what you think,' he retorted. 'But then you do not know our little King with his big dream of an Empire. The British were his political advisers and they taught him the familiar English rhymes, noted among them: 'Little drops of water make the mighty occan; so brick by brick the mighty Empire is being built up.'

The lunch was ending and we were joined by a group of local people. One was a lawyer, one a teacher, a couple of public workers, a magistrate and an Indian couple. One of them interposed to ask: 'What empire?'

"There is only one Empire in the making here. It is rising on the groans and moans of men, women and children,' the host retorted vehemently. 'There are thousands and thousands uprooted and adrift—driven out of this, our home city. Who cares to have them restored to their homes? All that King Abdullah bothers about is to measure the acres he can add to build his Hashemite Empire. He thinks he is going to rule over the muffled Palestine and its betrayed people. But we know better.'

'Why are the people of Palestine averse to the Hashemite Kingdom?' I queried. 'Averse', screamed one of the visiting politicians. 'They hate the very thought. But what can they do, caught between the devil and the deep sea? Their territory was occupied by the Arab Legion, which was supposed to be resisting the Jews. Any way, if the Legion withdraws the Jews would butcher them like wolves—they were warned, and they swallowed the bitter pill.'

'True they have little choice. What choice had they before? What freedom, what security have they ever known?' It was the lawyer speaking in subdued tones, but with a biting crispness in his voice : the eyes were steel cold. There was a sudden silence.

My host broke it with a sharp tone. 'The people of Palestine do not want to be under King Abdullah and be tied to the British chariot. They have had enough of slavery.' Like all other Arabs, we, too, had revolted against Turkish rule to win our freedom. And what did we get? First British imperialism, now a division of our country and finally an end to all those aspirations our people had so valiantly fought for. We want our own Government and our own leadership, not to live under the Jordan flag,' said the teacher.

'What of the other leader,' the Jerusalem lawyer came out like a spit-fire. 'Let me tell you, the people have had enough of him. You may pour scorn on King Abdullah, but he is, so many of us feel, tolerable compared to the other.'

Then he turned to me and continued. 'You know who that leader is? You may know his name, but not him. For that you have to live where his long arm can reach out to you. Ask these gentlemen sitting here, to tell you of the pretty doings of the Grand Mufti of Jerusalem. I hold no brief for the British. But nor do I hold with terrorism. Any new thought, any movement for political democracy, for civil liberties, are suspect with him. If you did not heed the warning and persisted, it was at the peril of your life. You might be waylaid in some dark lane at dusk: Or if your life were spared, you would be hounded out of public life. Ask them what happened when an attempt was made to organise the industrial labour here, when the poor tried to demand better conditions, a few amenities, a little less tyranny? Are these the leaders who are going to *liberate* Arabs ! Bah.'

'King Abdullah will decorate you for this championship of his cause,' my host interposed scornfully.

But the lawyer remained undaunted and continued. 'I need no decoration. I want to live and breathe in an uncontaminated air. The atmosphere of Jerusalem has got poisonous and it was choking us.'

The room had become stifling and I suggested taking a round of the City. We descended and ascended interminable flights of steps and soon we were standing before the Dome of the Rock, popularly called the Mosque of Omar. It is erected above the huge rock on which Abraham was to have sacrificed his son Isaac.

Islam claims that Mohamed the Prophet ascended from this very Rock to heaven on his magic horse Burak. A foot-print was pointed to me as the one made by the Prophet. It is this belief that, I was told, made the Mosque of Omar so holy to the Muslim world. Earlier, here Solomon had built the first Temple in Jerusalem, a magnificent structure and impressive. The Governor who led me in, pointed out to me its several interesting features and said in solemn tones, 'Other mighty cities have disppeared, having known their periods of glory, they have declined and vanished. Jerusalem lives on, resurrected, as it were after each death even at the end of three thousand years. Why?' He paused as though waiting for an answer, which I decided to provide by remarking: 'Greatness is probably distributed according to some unknown laws.'

'In its greatness this mosque stands apart almost as a symbol, and while the Dome of the Rock stands, Jerusalem will continue to live on. It is invincible,' thus explained the Governor, the mystery of Jerusalem's survival. 'All conquerors who came with their proud dreams had to lie here vanquished, while the eternal city lived on.' 'Does King Abdullah come here at all?' I asked.

Came the surprising answer. 'Frequently, to offer prayers, for the here lies buried his father Sherif Hassein, who should have been the man of Arab destiny. But he failed to meet that destiny. His hour struck before that. King Abdullah undaunted, believes he has inherited that role and that some day he will keep his date with destiny unlike his father.' 'Do you share that faith?' I asked.

'I don't know,' came the slow reply. 'It would be strange if he did.

He has paid too big a price with the sorrow and humiliation of men, some of them stalwarts.'

With that cryptic remark we retraced our steps back.

Very soon after this King Abdullah did keep his date with destiny and on the very spot where we had talked of it, he was assassinated and some of those suspected of implication were in that memorable gathering in which I had found myself after lunch. And among the many tales that had swiftly rolled out of Jerusalem was one which said that it was a tailor who had fired the short. He had a brother serving as an officer in the Jordan Army who, because he had been a little too enthusiastic to beat back the Israel troops, had been called alone for a supposed consultation and shot, you may guess by whose men. Whereupon the tailor had sworn vengeance. There was the other story that Riad Bey el Sonl, Lebanese ex-Premier once very close to King Abdullah had fallen foul of him. King Abdullah wanting a reconciliation with him, had got him specially invited to Amman and presented him with a distinguished decoration. Driving back to the Amman airport, he was shot. Suspecting foul play on King Abdullah's part one of El Sonl's supporters decided to wreak vengeance. Among the eight men who were tried and sentenced to death in connection with the murder was Abdulla Tell, Governor of the Old city of Jerusalem, who had however eluded arrest by going into voluntary exile. He denied any hand in the King's assassination. He remained in Cairo until 1967 when King Hussain of Jordon publicly pardoned him. What the real truth is the world may never learn.

As my visit was drawing to a close, I pressed my request when Abdulla Tell was asking me if I was pleased with my visit. I assured him I was more than pleased. But it would be perfect if I could visit Bethlehem. He explained it was a back breaking trip, a real full day's drive over hilly craggy terrain. 'In any event you won't even see the Crib lit with the Kings worshipping as at the Nativity celebration,' he said in a patient tone, with genuine concern. I wondered if I would ever visit here again, this seemed my one chance. The emotion surging within me was very different from visiting Gokul or Brindavan. Jesus to me was not the baby in the manger, he was the embodiment of human compassion, who gave so much of himself to his fellow beings.

I took the trip. It was as described, an endless travail. But over the years I had never dreamed I would have a real chance to visit this spot.

The Church of Nativity itself is simple, unostentatious. One goes down the small steep steps to where the manger had been. There had lain this child curled up in the warm straw, to rise as a man and be proclaimed one day as the Saviour. As I turned back I had a prayer in my heart for Abdulla Tell for his generosity and understanding of what to him must have seemed a woman's freakish fancy.

On our return journey we stopped for a while by the Apostles Fountain (Spring of the Sun), I was attracted by a Bedouins picturesque encampment. I wished to visit it. My interpreter rather reluctantly did some preliminary talks and we were warmly welcomed by, I presume, the leader—the Sheikh, with a rare gracious dignity. Directly the whole encampment was astir. We were invited to take our seats on rich carpets. The carpets hung around were covered with knives, pistols, swords - all gleaming. Polite concern was shown about our strenuous journey—were we fatigued, did we need to rest our head, body, so the polite enquiries went on, then gently, casually what had brought me on this long trip from far off India. The interpreter kept up the dialogue while others sat or stood around. Then as the Sheikh clapped his hands, there arrived an array of huge trays filled with fresh tropical and dried fruits and goblets of melon justices. A silent recognition of my vegetarianism. They asked about India, then related their own adventures. They were unhappy about their own war after the big war had ended.

When we tried to take leave, they bade us wait. They wanted to end the visit with a little entertainment, 'It is our desert custom,' explained the Sheikh. There was singing, strumming on stringed instruments, with drums and castanets. With deep bows we thanked each other and took leave.

As our car moved my young companion drew a long breath. 'What made you go into their camp?' she asked rather agitatedly. 'They can be terrible. You should see them in their fury, even a little feud over watering their animals at that spring can start a fierce battle with knvesi and bullets flying around.' 'Let us now enjoy the pastral scene whose serenity is not broken,' I soothed her troubled spirit.

From the time I entered this West Asian region, I had a feeling as though I was stepping on hot coals. The formation of the Jewish State of Israel had touched off a fuse as it were.

In the midst of all the turmoil, the name one heard most was of King Abdullah of Transjordan, as he was then known. It came in different keys: in anger and denunciation by the Arabs, in admiration and praise by Europeans. Transjordan began to intrigue me even as much as Palestine. Names which had seemed but distant sounds now began to take definite shape.

On a cold winter morning I set out for Amman from Damascus. As I was about to enter the car for the journey, two Palestine refugee women, with bundles and babies, approached me asking for a lift. I put them at the back and slipped into the seat beside the driver. He was a tall strapping young man, almost disturbingly handsome.

We speeded through vast stretches of desert—nothing, nothing but sand and sandy hills. Soon the driver had started a conversation with me. Why as I going to Amman? It was not a nice country. Before satisfying his curiosity, I asked him where he had learnt his English and the usual reply came, during the war from the Americans. Then I put him a counter question: Why was Amman not nice?

'King Abdullah, he no friend of the Arabs, he friend of the English' with this he spat out vehemently.

Slowly I picked up from him a lot of gossip which later I was to hear in Arab homes and circles. 'It is good you don't go to Amman: plenty trouble you will have,' he reverted back again. I asked him what trouble. 'Lots of trouble on the frontier—very strict and nasty. You see. King Abdullah very afraid. You don't like English in India, no? We also don't like the English.' I tried to find out where the English came into the picture. 'English make Abdullah King, he listen to them and now we lose Palestine. All Arabs homeless, hungry, no country, no work. Who do this? The English. They are no friends of Arabs?

It seemed simple enough logic, but I could not piece them together to make a cogent picture. Suddenly he pointed his finger ahead:—'Now you see how they give trouble—ask and ask que tions—very nasty, I tell you.'

We were at the frontier barricade. An officer came up to the car and asked for my passport: I was holding a diplomatic passport and, banking on the usual effect it had I had not been disturbed by the repeated warnings of the man at the wheel.

Then came the expected question, the purpose of my visit. I gave the usual answer: Sight-seeing. Neither my passport nor my answer seemed to make any impression. The officer went in and brought another. Again the questioning started. A third officer joined and more questions and more talks among themselves, each alternating with the other in questioning me. The longer this lasted the longer grew the frowns on their faces. This was interrupted by their retiring into the office and emerging out again.

The driver looked at me furtively as much as to say: 'I told you so.' My passport was in order, I had a visa as well as the entry permit, I pointed out. Just what was the hitch? 'Yes, yes, but you see during wartime we don't allow any casual visitors and tourists. We are very strict about this and only those on State business are allowed.' I then pointed to the women at the back: How about them?' One of the men shrugged his shoulders, then looked at the other and they all shrugged their shoulders, which, I assumed, meant it was not their concern. 'Are you suggesting I go back,' I asked. I had been there over 45 minutes. What their answer was to be I could never guess, for at this stage somebody hurriedly emerged out of the office—the only time I ever saw anybody speed—and they held an excited conversation amongst themselves. Then the new man turned to me and asked with a stern eye and commanding tone. 'Are you going to see King Abdullah?'

I was completely flabbergasted, Was this some king of a trick? Was there a catch in it? In truth the idea had never struck me though Azzam Pasha had casually suggested it. Would they let me in if I said yes or would it put me under greater suspicion that I had designs on that personality? Time was ticking by and the thought that my hesitancy would augment their suspicion made me even more fearful. I finally decided to take shelter behind the non-committal English phrase 'may be.' 'Ha' said the man who had been interrogating me: 'Why did you not tell us that before?'.

I very nearly asked if they let in anybody who simply declared that he or she was going to see His Majesty; but I decided in this delicate situation prudence was better.

The new officer then explained that they had received a telephone from the Ministry of Interior to let me in without delay and that I was to be received in audience by His Majesty.

A little further ahead I was met by a representative of the Ministry and some Arab friends so I could proceed without further adventure.

Amman looked like a toy capital of a toy Kingdom which was but an ungainly mountain patch with a tiny population of 450,000. Two main roads, a few shops, a handful of new buildings that looked like modest cottages pointed out to me as the Ministry of Justice, Ministry of Finance, Ministry of Foreign Affairs, etc., comprised the city.

Though the Hashemite Kingdom is very familiar today to the world at large, it knows next to nothing of its past history of the Petra Kingdom of the Nabatacus, fabulously wealthy and ruling over a territory as far north as Damascus from the 5th century B.C. to about the 5th century A.D., leaving behind some monumental architecture at Petra, some distance from the new city of Amman.

King Abdullah's political character began to take shape when hc acted as liaison between the Allies and the Arabs gathered under the leadership of his father, Sherifo Hassein of Mecca, during World War I. The Muslims were then exhorted by this holy leader to fight on the side of the Christian powers against their co-religionists—the Turks.

The end of the war had brought bitter disillusionment, for the Allies betrayed them. The severest blow came from their own kind. Ibn Saud of Arabia drove the Husseini family out of their country. When the Allies were dividing up their spoils, the new Kingdom of Transjordan was carved out of the area east of the Jordan by the British, when Palestine was declared the National Home of the Jews, as an alternative foothold for themselves in the event of having to pull out of Egypt and Iraq, all of which were already in ferment.

Transjordan gave British control of the pipelines from Iraq to the Mediterranean, of the Baghdad-Haifa road and the Hajaz—Damascus Railway. Therefore the British Exchequer did not grudge the subsidy to this state on which it was now mainly kept going. Actually under the Turks, it had been only a province of Arabia, tucked under the chin of the Wali of Damascus, as it had no resources to squeeze out enough to even pay a Wali of its own.

The Treaty of Alliance between it and Britain also gave the latter the right to station British troops and Air Force in the territory. In addition the British began training the Jordan youth in the trim and spectacular Arab Legion under Glub Pasha—then a romantic colourful general. Though English by birth and training he dressed like the Bedouins and identified himself with them.

On the Jordan throne was set the vibrant Amir Abdullah who, it was common knowledge, was smarting for being passed over for his brother Feisel as King of Iraq, which had added to the earlier blow to the original Husseini dream of a single Arab State under its dynastic rule.

King Abdullah, whom the West never tried to praise as a realist saw the wisdom of accepting even a tiny part of a loaf on which his heart was set, and striving for the rest.

He thus agreed to become ruler of this desert Kingdom of 4700 square miles, half of whose population was nomadic, only as a step up to that kingdom which was to stretch from the Taurus mountains to the Sinai peninsula, and from the Mediterranean to the Euphrates, some day in the near future, if he played his cards skilfully.

This ambition also became the bugbear of West-Asian politics. For extraordinarily enough, while he had the never-failing bounty from the British, each of his other several ambitions had the support of some foreign power or the other, which all in all made him a suspected personality in the Arab world.

With this background story tucked away in my bosom, I set out on a wet, drizzly morning for Jericho, a few miles from Shunet Nimrin where the King was sojourning to escape the biting winds of Amman.

I had armed myself with a reliable interpreter—an enormously important factor on all such occasions—by special request I was given a young America-travelled Arab lady, to fill this role. which, I could not but note, she accepted with some hesitation. I was to recall this later.

It was a dreary drive through grim, rocky country. As we descended into the Valley, we passed Gethsemane a small walled-in garden at the foot of Mount of Olives, slumbering under gnarled trees. Here was a last view of the Mosque of Aksa and the Dome of the Mosque of Omar in their grandeur. Then we crossed the River Jordan and I insisted on filling a small bottle with its water for devout friends in India who, I was sure, would value it, though the water was not attractive. The river becomes itself only after rains, it was explained.

We finally alighted before an unostentatious low-roofed bundgalow situated in a protected wall, forming a slightly elevated semi-circle into the mountain. We were conducted into a small room, very simply furnished, lined with touches of brocade.

King Abdulla was small made, neither warlike nor delicately cast. A small hand was extended out of the folds of his robe and as I took it I found myself gazing into a pair of beady glistening eyes set in a fat cherubic but pale and impassive face, which seemed to be sizing me up. We sat on plain silk and satin upholstered chairs as with a typical grand manner he motioned me to a seat.

I missed the characteristic warmth and friendliness of the Arab and I began to curl up inside. Then suddenly, as though sensing this reaction, his demeanour changed and with a gracious air he began to make kindly enquiries, obviously to put me at ease.

The young man with him was his English interpreter, but I intervened to say that the young lady with me would act instead. The King's eyes suddenly gleamed as though a veil had parted and the famous twinkle appeared. With a gracious air his hand moved an assent. He talked with easy smoothness and a fund of irrepressible self-confidence and we covered a fairly wide range of subjects from world politics to the Palestine situation, from Asian unity to Arab poetry. It may be mentioned here that the King is himself a writer of poetry. I tried to linger longest over Palestine, but he disposed it off more speedily than I had hoped. 'The Palestine problem is over,' and his hand made a gesture of finality.

But I was not to be stopped. 'Do you really think so? Is not this merely a seeming lull and the trouble will keep on smouldering like a covered fire, with the threat of spreading out?'

'True, feelings die slowly. But what is the use? We must face the reality of the situation. I am only too well aware of the vigour and capacity of the Israelis, especially of their youth. You have probably been (after a slight hesitation) briefed by Azam Pasha. Bah! I sometimes describe his League as a sack into which seven heads have been thrust. Personally I am not in panic over Israel as long as we keep the initiative in our hands, and that I do,' he concluded once again in a tone of finality.

It was the only time I had heard any Arab speak of the Palestine question in this self-assured manner. Usually they are overcome by emotional desperation. Still I made one more attempt: 'You don't anticipate any aggressive designs on the part of Israel?'

'Only the weak are troubled by phantom shadows,' quick came the repartee. 'After a while they tremble at their own shadows. The strong do not lose their nerve even at the spectacle of a mighty foe. Fear and and courage are one's own creation. We Arabs are nurtured by the desert, not pampered by the soft yielding earth. We are as hardy as the desert shrub, as enduring as the camel, as unvanquished as the Arab steed.' This was to stop further arguments. I had no words after that. So we turned to other topics.

We talked of the problems of Asia. 'The tragedy is our want of unity. If only we the people of this magnificant continent could stand together, we, could be the greatest people in the world. We need to bow to nobody, nor cajole anyone. We could be a power unto ourselves. It is our disunity that others exploit, it is this which makes our regions so vulnerable,' he went on.

These remarks were revealing a new personality to me. A rather faraway, pre-occupied look had crept into his eyes.

'Art and culture are easy meeting grounds that one can draw upon to get us together as they did once,' I ventured. With this topic he got into stride. It was a real pleasure to hear him on Arab literature, its sources and influence. Here was no vainglorious monarch. From this is was a short step to modern education and current social conditions.

Only too aware of the paucity of education among women, the prevalence of strict purdah, I decided to take courage and make a straight plunge. 'After all, does not social progress lie in the education and freedom of women?' was my opening remark.

There was a sudden change in the air and his demeanour. Sentences flowed out smoothly. He was now very much His Majesty, who was graciously deigning to give an audience. To speak was his right and others could do so only as a special favour shown.

'In the East, women have always been highly respected, nay almost worshipped. They have occupied the highest place in society—why, not because of any other attributes or displays, but because of that ideal of service they embodied. Their life lies in serving, looking after the husband, children, family, in thoughtfulness and care. Their evening's light lies not in clubs, but preparing for the home-coming of the family head, thinking out ways of making it a delight, offering him warmth and snug refuge from care and weariness.'

The words kept flowing on until my dainty interpreter kept getting redder in the face and paler in the eyes.

We finally rose. I felt rather sad our interview had ended on this note. I confided as much to my interpreter. 'Well, I was waiting for it. Every time a woman visitor has an audience with His Majesty, this is how it ends. The interview has to end after that, for conversation comes to an end. I feared this and was hesitant to act as interpreter. I regret I did not warn you.' I was glad she had not.

Baghdad was on the last lap of my tour of some of the Arab countries as the guest of the Arab League. I had met Nuri-el-Said, the Prime Minister. But feeling he was a seasoned pro-Britisher, I was constrained to speak freely. I made it a formal visit.

Of course the attractions of Baghdad were endless. But I accidentally learnt that it was possible to visit Babylon. In my young days Babylon to me was a bygone phantom, too ancient to have left any scraps behind. Here as I read and heard of this fantastic city and its civilising influence, I was pricked by curiousity. A Dr. D'Souza and his wife from Bombay generously offered to take me out on this journey.

I had heard that the Sumerian culture sprang into the historical view with highly civilised people living in populous cities, possesssing a written language, administered by a well established government, already full-blown. What had intrigued me was what H.R. Hall of the British Museum had told me once: 'It is by no means improbable that the Sumerians were an Indian race that passed through Persia to the Valley of the two rivers.' Descriptions of their draining of the swamps, the devising of ingenious irrigation dykes, complicated canal systems, large granaries, store houses, temples, statues, gigantic monuments, all found echoes in my heart, putting me in mind of Mohenjodaro, Harappa and that period. There was one renowned law giver amidst many wise men and rulers, Urukagina, preceding the famous Hammurabi, by several centuries.

Agriculture being the main occupation, land reclamation was crucial and vivid details were delineated on this, judging by descriptions. It is not surprising as Heredotus has expressed his astonishment, at the enormous size of the variety of their grain. Documents show that preservation of agriculture was considered more meritonous than maintenance of temples !

Irrigation became a royal pursuit and the king prided himself on his initiative and achievement in this enterprise.

It is to their law system that the world feels most indebted. For though King Hammurabi became historically the codifier of the much admired laws, it is said that these laws were mainly compiled on the basic Sumerian ones.

Considering what it once comprised, the excavation site is pretty barren as many, may be most of the objects, have been removed to the Museums of Europe's varied capitals by the different nations working on the site!

The raw materials were exciting. Asphalt, for instance, regarded as one of the modern materials, was seen lining the ground. There were double walls everywhere, the ramparts ran parallel, so was the main wall. When a deep depression was pointed out to me, I was taken aback to be told it was the spot where the town of Babel once stood.

Inspite of its paucity, the site still presents a breathless panorama, magnificently laid out with streets intersecting at right angles with meticulous precision, indications of the colossal size of the structures with tne awe-inspiring Lion of Babylon. So this was what was left of Nebuchadnezzar's proud boast. Man has and continues to be childish in his illusions of self-preservation. Even today with our name on a brickwall, we shall perpetuate ourselves. As compared with our faith, Nebuchadnezzar's delusion was more plausible, though all that is left of his old glory is only a vast expanse of rubble. 'Everything wrought of clay must pass away' sings the poet.

For those who have seen Mohenjodaro and Harappa, this site is almost nostalgic, though set apart by thousands of miles.

Time had rolled by and truce had brought relief to Kashmir. My thoughts turned to the Kashmir Valley again as I flew back home. The Cooperative Centre had been doing well. The Crafts Workers' Cooperatives had started taking root, forming a substantial part of the Crafts Sector. I felt an urge to visit and review the scene again.

As I landed in Srinagar I felt a tug at my heart as my thoughts flew to those remote heights amidst the snow-capped mountains where our jawans were guarding our ramparts.

Touching details were vouchsafed to me on their dismal lives in those far-off inhospitable regions, by Major General Thimmayya, the Commander-in-charge of Kashmir, when he met me. 'Let me tell you a quixotic thing that took place when Pandit Nehru visited Kashmir recently. As we moved around, he suddenly looked up at the heights and rather wistfully asked 'Is that where our jawans keep vigil round the clock?' When I nodded he wanted to know if it would be possible for him to communicate with them. We escorted him to the telephone booth and got him the connection. Now this is what transpired. The jawan at the other end asked who was the caller, the reply was, this is Jawharlal Nehru, I wanted to greet you. This was repeated but in answer there came only an exasperated growl and 'Don't keep on fooling me, whoever you are.' and with that click went the phone. We repeated the attempt, but he simply would not pick up, he had decided someone was pulling his leg, poor fellow.' 'I understand his reaction. We must realise that the jawan is not a mere musketeer to romanticise about. If one wants to taste the reality of their life, one should visit the army encampment oneself. That is what I would like to do.'

'No you can't,' abruptly interrupted the Major General, 'women are out of bounds.' 'Even someone of my age!' 'Women are simply not allowed to take these hazardous journeys. The roads are *kuccha*, a journey is always a risk. It becomes an added responsibility where a woman is concerned, for women are not needed. The traffic has to be restricted to those who have to travel up there,' he insisted. We kept arguing, finally in desperation I remonstrated. 'In the old days I had to steal in stealthily to escape the State police to trek, which I very much enjoyed. For the guardians of the law would be after me. Now that we have won freedom, your army will stall me, which even the Kashmir police did not succeed in doing.' When I said this, his face flushed. He rose saying, 'I shall see what can be done, I shall do my best.'

He had hit on a plan. From amongst his officers he called for a couple who would volunteer to accompany me. By coincidence the lady came from a Kanpur family I knew. So we set out in two jeeps one morning. I had selected the Gurois area as its description had tempted me.

We travelled over a track that could not even be termed a jeep road. It had such sharp turnings that where the jeep had to take a turn, it had to back to get a wide-enough berth to make the sweep, pretty nerve-wracking, for when you looked down it was into a bottomless abyss.

After a full day's drive we reached a military camp in the late afternoon. We had tea with some of the army personnel, followed by a dinner after which we sat around and chatted. They confessed they were rather excited as civilian visitors were extremely rare, except for occasional officers. Some of the jawans were shy, reticent, the younger ones curious and outgoing.

I had decided to reach the farthest heights I could attempt where the lonesome guards were ever alert and watchful. For the border at the time was still quite alive. Only pony tracts led to those spots. These minitrips on pony back took me back to my earlier forays in this region. There in those remote spots far from the normal human haunts, lived these very human jawans, so conscious of the gravity of their duties—how different from the dusty Secretariats. They could hope for no break in their monotony, no new faces to anticipate, no old ones to light up the boredom with a friendly smile. Their unfailing patron seemed to be the Moon under whose benign presence they sometimes held revelries. Their only diversion was the occasional Cinema.

Yet some of them had been at these distant bases since the Kashmir campaign opened. They sometimes got a couple of weeks at one of the Srinagar holiday homes. In dismal winter they had to just dig in. But unlike the lucky bears they could not hibernate.

I could not of course reach the lonely pickets on the mountain tops keeping ceaseless watch. Their only link with the outside world as far as I could grasp, was the telephone linked to the nearest base. From one of the lower base camps I looked up in sheer awe, picturing to myself these youthful jawans, solitary, with the weird whining winds moaning around dark ghostly shadows dancing about in the night, all the time dangerously exposed to the enemy's surprise sniping. Like the hunters of old, they had to keep the enemy at bay across the immediate border and hold the border line.

I saw some of the extreme severities endured by these mountain encampments. The relentless and continuing battles with the forces of nature gave me a sinking feeling. Getting supplies was hazardous. The convoys consisted of poines, jeeps even loaders whose limbs have learnt now to negotiate the sharp contours of the craggy mountainsides, with the agility of the monkey, the sure foot of the mountain pony and the daring of the jungle panther. As for the jeeps, they cover tracts hardly better than pony trails, who have to drive with the precision of an instrument-maker, for miscalculation of even a fraction can mean disaster. They have to move like a line of black ants amidst gaunt rocks that suddenly jut sharply across the narrow trail like a a death trap. Compared with this the tight rope walking performed to an adulating audience, seemed child's play. On the second day we had stopped briefly to see a small group looking rather distraught, to learn that a jeep from a convoy had rolled over the precipice. The man of my jeep wheel beside whom I sat, asked me if this made me nervous. 'Not with you at the wheel', and gave him a reassuring smile. He was actually the officer who had volunteered to escort me.

Small planes carried supplies to very distant corners, sometimes even to merely drop them, lacking landing facilities. Much later I often travelled about in the distant tribal areas in the border regions, in what were called *sorties*. They were tiny planes, no seats, and the embarassed crew would press me to sit on the radio operator's seat, seeing me squat on the ground with the packages. For even the jeep tracks were non-existent. In such a void even these 'birds' as we called them, assumed a spectacular personality. But in the winter months landing was normally impossible and supplies had to be parachuted, even that it was pointed out to me was a complicated affair. Different commodities called for different types of packing, like perishable goods, medical supplies, clothing, even money. Even the manner of dropping was different in each case—to me it was pretty bewildering. The engine of the Dakota which took me to Ladakh, had to keep running until it took off for the return journey, as it would not have been possible to restart it.

The army was not a mercenary organisation. I found it caring equally for the civilians. I saw excellent dispensaries and medical centres, health measures preventive and curative were both in force. I was told that the army's aid was a big factor in the build up of the cooperatives. When schools were promoted, girls were included for the first time in these far flung regions.

When I returned to the plains, I realised with a shock how completely ignorant the general public was of this panorama I had been viewing up in the mountains. It were as though they were two entirely different worlds. Those touching impulses towards the armed forces shown by a section of our society during the World War had died down. I felt it behoved me to lift up the curtain of ignorance a wee bit to give even if it be a glimpse of what I had seen.

Pandit Nehru was due back from America a few days later. I got friends in Bombay to organise a gala reception for him, ticketed, the money to go to the jawans in Kashmir for their holiday trips. So vivid descriptions were laid bare before an excited public as tumultuous crewds gathered to welcome the popular Jawaharlal and give generously towards the unknown, unseen jawans that guard our ramparts. Panditji happily accepted the substantial cheque we handed but was visibly annoyed when I asked him to return it. He protested asking, me if this was some kind of a joke we were playing on him. I explained that this cheque was earmarked for a specific cause. If the cheque was left with him it would naturally go into the Prime Minister's Fund. So it was rescued and sent to Major General Thimmaya. There came a moving acknowledgement from him. It was the first time anyone visiting the jawans had sent them a gift.

The ideal of the One World administered by an overall world government, the best talents and intellects guiding and directing its affairs, had begun to loom attractively before a war weary world. No more wars was the one cry and the plausible answer was this bright picture of one world.

Though India had not been physically ravaged, the many evil effects were tarnishing several of our old norms, values, habits. For the first time *money* began to emerge as a prime motivation and measure of evaluation. Drinking of liquor as an indispensible social custom spread rapidly. Consumerism erupted like a flaming tongue, with emphasis on show, brash, crude, vulgar facades. It was incredible how the world had changed; it seems almost overnight. Several alien elements took shape to distort the quiet culture of what was now a a bygone age.

How pragmatic or even feasible this One World was, it was hard to say. But dreams if seriously pursued do take shape. So I accepted the invitation to attend an International gathering of devotees of this ideal in Rome. The proceedings to me seemed pretty pedestrian, inspite of the obvious sincerity and seriousness of the delegates. One heard the same old phrases, trod along the same stale path. But a few other events proved stimulating.

An old Italian friend, Dr. Scarpa who once lived in India, took me to visit Professor Giuseppe Tucci, the renowned Sanskrit and Buddhist scholar, who to some of us had become a legendary personality, to me particularly because of his close personal knowledge of Tibet. His first visit to India was, he narrated, in 1926 when he lived at Viswabharathi for a year, greatly drawn by the poet. I have often wondered if anybody else had drawn as many foreign admirers as Tagore, except Gandhiji.

I wanted to know how, living in a far off corner of Italy he had got interested in these remote subjects. 'Maybe birth cycles is the answer, and India was the magnet, for nothing, nothing around me had any link with your country. I started on Sanskrit at the age of eleven, as the basic medium through which to know India. Buddhism held for me the essence of Hindu thought.' 'Is that what took you repeatedly to Tibet?' I could barely picture the severities he must have undergone—a delicately cast man—in those early days in Tibet. 'Tibet had become for me the reservoir of Buddhism after it faded out of India. Moreover, I saw it as a practising religion and not to be picked from the written word. Its visual representation gripped me as its treasures were opened out to me.' 'Can you tell me something of your delving into Tibetan archeology, for I understand you were the first to have done so.' 'There one treads on uncertain ground, for want of scientific appliances or even means. For me excavation is not a mere descent into the depths of ruins, rather it is a trial to restore to the light, imaginatively, events obscured by age. They reassure humanity of the continuing significance of the undying human values and reveal fresh evidence of the basic patterns of the human spirit. Over a period of 30 years in which I made eight trips covering 12,000 miles, and each time by a different route, I saw in several parts traces of the pre Buddhist religion, Bonpo, in people's beliefs, in some practices of the faith. What was most revealing and astonishing was to see distinct traces of Iranian, Kashmiri, Central Asian, Chinese, even whiffs of the Sassanid, in the draperies in their sculptures, even though the world imagines Tibet escaped all outside impacts.

'The world has been equally unaware of Tibet's earlier internal social and political conflicts such as between royalty and aristocracy, local overlords and peasantry, and herdsmen over grazing rights, even confrontations within monasteries. Finally the great abbeys firmly established their supreme authority over the lay people after the downfall of the Tibetan dynasty, when every activity became subordinated to the monastic power.'

'Tibetan art is lightly, described as medievl. Can I have your interpretation on it?' I asked. He thought for a moment and then began: 'It is a superficial definition. To me the Tibetans seem endowed with an innate aesthetic sensibility of their own which evolved high ornamentation as its dominant characteristic, be the object secular or sacred, as part of its Buddhist expression. I have also seen the pre-

Buddhist Bonpo art reflecting the dominant passions of those times such as man's fears of natural forces, fearsome phenomena, of spirits lurking in every object.' His words were revealing to me. I was equally cheered by his optimism over Tibet's future, the current changes notwithstanding.

I met Tucci again a few years later in India just as the latest reports of his discoveries in Nepal reached me. He looked as youthful and energetic as ever, now lit by a new radiance. 'Was this exciting trip in pursuit of Buddhism or just a voyage of discovery,' I asked infected by his bubbling emotion. 'One is indivisible from the other. In the six trips I took to Nepal I traversed the land of the little known Mallas whose empire ruled for three centuries, covering a territory larger than my Italy, in Western Tibet. In their temples the Bonpo deities co-existed with the Hindu and the Buddhist peacefully, in a single dedication to the God of Mercy.' 'Shall we close our dialogue with the ancient prayer of peace,' I queried, he nodded, and together we both hummed *Om mani padme hum.*

The other unexpected event that came my way was something that I had never even dreamt of nor would have ventured to seek. I was suddenly asked one night by our Embassy to be ready to visit the Vatican next morning. Politely I declined, I had already seen the Papal Palace. 'This is for an audience with the Pope', announced the Voice and closed the phone. I was too bewildered to make any sense of it. True in my travels I did meet heads of States, but this was a puzzle. The Pope granted audience to people, or blessed them en masse. But not being cast in that religious mould nor used to indulging in cheap curiosity, this had never crossed my mind.

The drive was through a number of fortress-like entrances, guarded by guards in dazzling uniforms. After my escort and I entered the Palace, we moved through several apartments, crowded with people, children. It was the most glittering place I had seen. Even the walls seemed sheathed in gold. Shining brocaded chairs stood about like regal figures. Overpowering the scene were the picturesque Swiss Guards, drawn from the top-most aristocracy, all lending almost an operatic touch to the scene. The figures flitted about like winged creatures in coloured plumes, each face cast in a mask as it were. Then came the array of the various Vatican officials, Cardinals, Monsignors, Bishops, each in a different colour garb, crimson, purple, red, mauve and a riot of colours, set off by sparkling cloaks and capes, all of which heightened the dramatic effect of the scene.

Finally I came to a small room where the attendant withdrew leaving me floating as it were in an eerie atmosphere. The sudden stillness after the earlier whirl and burl was creepy. It was however broken by the tinkle of a telephone, then a coloured robe stole past like a piece of rainbow wafted on the breeze. The expectant waiting was suddenly broken and without any approaching steps, a serene white figure stood facing me as though it had materialised out of the space around, and the next instant the hand with the symbolic ring was extended to me. Amidst all this glamour and glitter, here stood one of the most revered personalities of the world, clad in a simple cream coloured robe, looking by contrast unbelievably plain and simple except for the giant amethyst jewel shining on his chest. I tried to remember if I had learnt how to greet the Pope in my school days. The memory was blank. I had had occasion to greet Monsignors, Cardinals. From the Nuns I had learnt many formalities. But in one's wildest dreams coming face to face with the Pope had not been a possibility.

There was an amused expression in his eyes which watched my confusion through a plain pair of spectacles resting against a genial face. I apologised for my distraction. 'I welcome and greet you as a representative of your great country where your leader lived a true Christian life, showing to the world that the way of our Lord can still be trod, and like Him he too lay down his life. We meet today as two citizens of the world, looking to the same goal, so little formalities needs not trouble you.' The warmth in the tone was obvious. Evidently India had moved him in some special way and some of this he tried to convey. It threw a little light on the puzzle behind this visit. 'I understand you worked with the Mahatma and shared the experience. I am glad India still strives for peace in this strife-torn world.'

By now I felt emboldened to venture a question. 'Can I ask a question?' 'Of course.' 'Has the Vatican a plan for the establishment and preservation of global peace and to save the world from further repetition of world wars?' 'The Church is most concerned and takes every occasion to emphasise it.' 'Is the church content with that, does it not feel impelled to initiate a scheme of its own? The Church is powerful, wields tremendous influence,' I ventured to persist. 'The Church as you are aware has to tread cautiously to avoid giving the impression of seeming to take initiative in State affairs.' 'But the Church carries great weight', I persisted again. 'The Church uses that to influence its followers. It is trying its best to work for peace in several ways that may not always be obvious to all.' I felt disappointed and had my one last fling. 'When so much is at stake, obscure good deeds can't have the needed impact. What I had in mind was something dramatic that grips, something in the tradition of St. Francis.' He gave a wan smile My time was up and as I took leave he blessed me. I wondered if he took me for a hysterical female to talk of St. Francis in an atomic age.

When I was doing rather a longish tour of Africa, I regretted North Africa was not on my programme. I had been particularly intrigued by Ethiopia, wantonly axed by Mussolini and the subsequent humiliation of its brave midget King by the august but dead League of Nations. I had been intrigued that Ethiopia was the only territory in that huge continent to have remained free from the shackles of imperialism. But to the world, Africa was but a vast mass of black country. My extensive tour in Africa revealed to me little cracks like Benin or Zambawe where shortlived civilizations had spurted and died down. But Ethiopia was different, it was alive, free once more. From my reading, this was the land of David, of King Solomon, Queen Sheba, their son Menelik. No sooner had I got to Ethiopia, I had to add to this list our own King Rama. In a history book in schools by one Berhanu Denkie, it is recorded that when King Rama ruled in India, his influence penetrated into Ethiopia.

Though this sounded illusory, one could not but feel the evidence of close contacts between us. Obviously the native dress resembled the Indian, so did the music. Particularly when I heard it in their Church I could have sworn it was Indian.

At the crack of the Christian era there was already the flourishing kingdom of Aksum, whose adventurous people had established relations and trade with practically the entire known world of the time. The Coptic Church came only four centuries later. As a protection against the growing Islamic pressures, monasteries were carved out of the forbidding mountainsides where even a toe hold to climb was impossible. People were simply pulled up in baskets. I got there to be told no woman can enter the precincts. I wandered around and did succeed in slipping inside one of them. I was startled by the picturesque scene made by evenly shaped columns, arched vaults, elaborate friezes and walls tastefully decorated. My intrusion having been discovered, I was politely asked to leave. I asked my guide, looking sheepish, to apologise to these sensitive priests, 'I was no adventurer, and in my country my sex was not regarded as a sin that pollutes, nor is it here since the most important Shrine is of Mary of Zion where the Kings were crowned, and she is a women.' With that I quit.

Madam Senedu, principal of a girls' institution captured my interest. Through her I met some women and learnt they had always enjoyed equal rights, a common status with men and had had chances of playing important roles in national affairs, paricularly in the last struggle against the Italians. Madam Senedu explained to me, 'The Ethiopian women had always moved with the army, they cooked and fed the men, and nursed them when needed. But this time the women joined the guerillas. Here for the first time we had to face modern weapons. When the enemy bombed and gassed us, we had no protection except taking shelter in the forests. If the wind did not blow the gas away, it gave us blisters – we had neither masks nor shelter.

'But villages were easily destroyed. The crowd of the homeless grew. We sought shelter in one of our thickest forests in Kaffee, birth place of coffee, but we were pursued, arrested. When I refused to supply any information in continuous interrogation, day and night, I was sent to a tiny isolated isle off Sardinia, until the end of World War II. I returned to find great devastation here. I had lost my husband and several other members of my family. I decided to open a school for higher education of girls and start to rebuild a shattered existence.'

I was received by the King. I had had occasion to meet His Majesty earlier when he visited India. Once again he was full of assurances of the changes that he had and was initiating in the country particularly education of women. Alas, rulers encased by security cords lose touch with the wider world and come to live in an imaginary world of personal self-satisfaction, feeding on their own vanity. The changes invariably are too meagre and come too late, like feeble dykes unable to hold back the tide and then the deluge.

I asked the Indian Ambassador in Addis Ababa if I could possibly visit the graves of the Indian jawans who fought in the nearby theatre of war. August 15th was close and I thought a visit to the cemeteries might be an appropriate way of commemorating the day.

From Asmara I set out for the battlefields of Keren and Agordat, where some of the most devastating battles had been fought. The Indian losses were estimated upto sixty thousand, a figure given by the Indian community in Asmara. I walked up to the rows of graves in the cemetery but found no Indian name anywhere. I realised I was in the wrong territory, the White Man's exclusive zone. I turned to the segregated plots opposite. Most of the small cards indicating the names, had been blown away, those remaining bore only names of regiments, Punjab, Dogra, Rajput, Mahratta—below Name Unknown. For a few moments I stood bowed in grief, regret. What a waste of precious life. There were the little mounds, and I tried to conjure up little phantoms dressed in their regional costumes. Maybe he was the only bread earner in the family, the only son of aged parents, husband to a now lonely widow, all left to mourn for him, lying in a land they know not. To him the battle was his bread and butter for the family, nothing more. I felt a wave of depression sweep over me. What was man so arrogant about, still unable to make a better destiny for himself.

I showered the flowers I had brought, over the dry earth in the name of those who could never reach here.

We continued our journey in an uncertain mood. For as we drove out of Asmara, our car had been stopped by the security guard, refusing to let us proceed further, for the territory I had planned to cover was infested with 'Shiftas' who could prove a danger, atleast a threat. I had already acquainted myself with their background. They were mercenary soldiers, were capable of patriotism in repulsing invaders and had been in the forefront of the guerilla battles against the Italians; of human feeling in fighting a tyrant to set right a wrong; could also be adventurers with devilry in their nostrils. At their worst they may dispossess money bags, but protect the poor. When Ethiopia got back her freedom and Eritrea demanded a separate status, they had plumped for the Union of the two.

Nevertheless stray bands still roamed the country under the slogan of Free Eritrea, though they may have been mere adventurers, possessing arms and using them for their living or for sheer excitement. This made travelling in these areas hazardous, hence the warning. But having obtained the necessary permit to visit the war-graves, I understood I could proceed. Now I realised it meant travelling in a convoy—'Oh that means a whole day,' I protested. We assured the checkpost man we would quickly catch up with a convoy already on the way and proceed with it, not waste time. The guard was reluctant, especially seeing a foreign woman in the party. Luckily the Liaison Officer of the Government in Eritrea, Otto Amde Maccai arrived also enroute. He politely offered to take me in his car, but equally politely I declined. I did appeal to him to let me cross the city barrier which he did, with a slight frown probably for my seeming rudeness. I had however no wish to get tied up with a State car and escort, on this road of the roving adventurers. Our car belonged to one of the local Indians and he insisted on driving himself saying 'You never know if they are Shiftas or pure bandits.' I tried to put him at ease telling him of the several hair-raising situations I had known.

Unlike our friendly mountains, these were jet black, fearsome, waiting like demons to strike you. The roads literally wriggled, not zigzagged. One bend showed a branch lying across it. As we negotiated it the driver remarked it was their handiwork. As the mountains grew dimunitive, the gigantic baobah trees appeared with their strange, uncouth irregular stems, and I learnt that like with our coconut, every part of it, fruit, leaves, bark, was utilised, and is known as the Colossus of the Western lowlands. Now we could stop intermittently, meet the various tribes, watch changes in their dress and language. All had one thing in common however, terrible poverty.

At Agordat on the Sudan border, I was astounded to be greeted by a tiny local Indian community, which was equally surprised to see a woman in a sari coming out of a car. Since the Indian army came down here, no Indian had ever set foot in this deserted land, they explained. Suddenly one of the Indians remarked. 'Look here are the Shiftas.' A batch of young men in Khaki uniforms, and one in an extra smart one, stood greeting us with friendly smiles. Through an interpreter I asked if they had placed the barrier up in the passes. The extra smart one who wast heir leader, denied, 'They were our comrades,' he added. 'Did they mean to loot us?' I asked. 'No. Actually a State Minister who preceeded you, warned the comrades a freedom fighter from Gandhi's party was coming and should be treated as an honoured guest. India is and has always been a good friend of our country and thousands of your soldiers died right here liberating us. Even if we had not been warned we would never harmed you.' They laughed merrily to assure me. The leader then introduced me to all his colleagues. Seeing an Indian with the inevitable camera dangling from her shoulder impressed him that this was a momentous occasion that needed to be captured by the lens, and he did. As we took leave very warmly, a Shifta who had a comb in his hair pulled it out and held it out to me as a momento of my visit. As I accepted it he explained it would remind me that 'Bandits too are human.'

There was a call from Prime Minister Nehru to lunch; except when such occasions came, we hardly ever met now, for I neither attended social nor State functions. After the meal we would sometimes sit apart and chat or stroll out when he would talk of his travels abroad or some internal party irritations—a throw back to old days. He related his impressions of the USA, how Eisenhower had impressed him. He had been pretty excited after the China visit. The gloss had yet to be brushed off. He showed me the choice, exquisite gifts and generously persuaded me to choose some for myself.

There were at these parties two separate bulky registers in which the guests signed their names, one for official guests, the other for personal, rather unusual and amusing. Panditji's household was run by a sleek professional contractor, one of Lady Mountbatten's clever brain waves!

As usual we moved apart after the lunch and rather abruptly he said: 'Since you reject political offices, how about representing us on the Human Rights Commission?' I answered promptly that I did not know anything about it. He offered to supply papers for me to study and decide. When the literature arrived, I sought my friend Lakshmi Menon's (then Minister for Foreign Affairs) advice, she strongly pressed me to accept the offer. 'Try for a session, if you don't relish it, quit. No one can force you to stay. But as the Commission deals with very sensitive issues, and millions of people suffer through denial of fundamental rights, you should be able to help. The aftermath of the war has intensified these agonising problems.'

I sat three solid months on the Commission. So far as redressing complaints was concerned, it was worse than minus—a big zero. The atmosphere was arid though Geneva was beautiful. For weeks we wrangled over punctuation marks in our meticulous drafts on notional decisions.

Individual contacts were valuable. My old friend Harry Bridges of the Civil Liberties Union from New York was there to add spice and shocks. New innovative proposals were supposed to be referred back to New Delhi for approval, where I invariably drew a blank. Mary Lord, an important member of the American Conservative Party gave me contacts and invited me to their convention.

Our entire life revolved round the U.N. Community. The locals seemed to keep off our paths. I heaved a sigh of relief when it ended.

I spent sometime in Europe, travelling by car through several countries—my first experience of the ghostly autobahns. I made brief studies of the magnificant old Cathedrals and the spick and smart new theatre structures, learnt how theatre societies with public membership stimulated and supported the drama world in the littlest places.

One of the countries I was visiting for the first time was Turkey. Beside Halide Adeb, I had no contacts there, though I was familiar with its revolutionary history. The batch of women I met through our Embassy however nearly overwhelmed me with their warm welcome. They wanted me to tour the country and acquaint myself with its many attractions, even though Istanbul was a feast in itself.

I was keen however to see the lesser known and the more unique sights that could be more informative. I tried to brighten up my old stray memories of the Hittite empire, of the Phrygians whose fabulous King Midas figured in my English text book. Was he the man with the golden touch—obviously a symbolic metaphor. The name Hittite had puzzled me. How did these civilizations evolve, each with its own flowering. This has always stirred my appetite to learn, to know. So here I was ready for a bout. The Curator of the Ethnographic Museum at Ankara helped me draw up a fruitful itinerary to study this region. I found travelling by car the most feasible.

As I went round the Museum at Alacahoyuk, the several vague names took on shapes, forms, meaningful characters. The first pleasurable surprise was to see in the Museum garden on a door a Sphinx with the body of a lion and face of a girl. It was supposed to defend the city and one finds them in other sites as well.

The Hittite age is said to have extended from 2000 to 1200 B.C. Some of the pots and pans were stunning. Water jugs with handles and legs were beautiful and in varied shapes and colours. Some had mouths delicately carved in the shape of birds, dishes shaped liked bunches of grapes, some resting on tripods cut in the shape of animals' legs, drinking glasses like bulls' heads or heads or birds; similarly sieves, lids, in fact every single kitchen item was a work of art. I was particularly intrigued to find some vessels with pointed bottoms, which India also has where it is to be fixed firmly in the ground. Some of the jugs were of incredible size and were, I understand, carried around dangling from a pole by a number of people!

The raw material used in vessels varied from common clay to silver and gold, every one with exquisite work. I looked closely and was delighted to find every one made with meticulous care, and the workmanship of quality. The ancients never commercialised anything. Every object made was for personal use and therefore made with respect. Whole collections of finely carved deer found in the Royal tombs were most appealing. They looked so alert, with a vibrant air about them as though keenly listening for warning sounds, ready to dash off. They appeared unbelievably real!

Square bath tubs with accompanying little stools were inevitable in every household. The conclusion was the Hittites bathed more than once a day or washed themselves frequently. Polished stone was in popular use. Very striking was work on bone, making each piece into a work of art, which spoke for the finesse of their flint instruments. One saw a profusion of carved bulls and statues of lions.

In a typical Hittite temple I saw gods and goddesses carved in relief on the walls, in a strict hierarchial manner, with the name of every deity in hierogliphs.

I would like to end my description by stating the Hittites were advanced in town planning reminiscent of Mohenjodaro. Water was supplied through earthen pipes even into every room by connecting them with larger channels.

Immediately I returned to Delhi, I informed the Indian Government, I did not wish to continue to serve on the Human Rights Commission.

India has many emotional and intellectual links with Ireland even apart from our common struggle for freedom against a common conqueror, and the inspiration we drew from each other over the years. Among the political heroes who inspired us was De Valera and we watched his exploits, his last moment escape from a death sentence—as he was an American born citizen—filled us with thrill and excitement. Finally we shared the same joy and tragedy, the partition that came with our national liberation. But our knowledge of each other remained vague and in course of time grew dim.

There are several cultural similarities between the Celts and the Hindus. Comparisons are made between Manu Smriti of India and the Brehon laws of the Irish to find similarities especially pertaining to family and marriage. There are romantic comparisons between the Druids of Ireland and the Sages of India. The Celts too were divided into three sections, the Druids, Warriors and the Commoners. They also believed in rebirth. What is very striking is the image of the Celtic God with the wheel, so like Vishnu with the Chakra.

That these similarities are not imaginary, created by flimsy sentiments is proved by the fact that a person like Dr. Myles Dillon, Professor of Sanskrit and Linguistics at Dublin's Institute of Advanced Studies, worked on a fellowship at the Institute of Advanced Studies in Simla, to write a book on Celtic Hindu Culture. As he has spent more than three decades on research in Indo-European influence, his expectations carry conviction. He compares for instance the Bards of Ireland with the Bhats and Charans of India.

My own emotional ties like of others in this country of my times, are to be traced through the inspiration those of my generation and may be even an earlier one, drew from the galaxy of Irish Literary figures—of the early century into the twenties like W.B. Yeats, AE (George Russel) Lady Gregory, J.M. Synge, etc.

W.B. Yeats's close association with Tagore and his attempts to introduce the latter to the Western World resulting in the bestowing of the Nobel Prize on the Indian poet, is equally significant.

My first visit to Ireland came late which in itself shows how low our physical contacts were. When I was told I would meet De Valera, I felt a sense of privilege. He had become a legend to us since our freedom struggle days.

A tall man met me as I alighted from the car and walked me through a very silent house, tapped on a closed door and when it opened he vanished. At the door was a tall thinnish man who I took to be the Secretary, when suddenly a hand was extended to me saying 'I am De Valera, welcome' I was so astonished I had to steady myself to escape stumbling. After a few preliminaries, I asked him of his Indian visit, alas the only one. 'It was what I would call a lucky strike', he gave a tinkle of a laugh, 'incredibly well timed. When I arrived at the Viceregal palace, at least that is what it seemed to me, I found I had landed myself in a huge operation—Operation Quit!—is not that what your great leader said to the British? Quit India! Well they were moving out bag and baggage. I watched the scene with delight and satisfaction. With India gone I knew the much boosted empire would end. Some good fortune brought me on this crucial scene.' There was a faint suggestion of emotion in the voice as he ended.

'Isn't there some exciting mystery connected with your escape from an English prison. How was it contrived?' 'Yes, it was the Lincoln prison. The whole thing was rather like a detective story. A Catholic prison chaplain was given the main door key to facilitate his visits to the prison. One day the left the key absent-mindedly on a table when he went in, which an alert Sinn Feinner spotted and quickly traced on a paper. His ingenious brain conceived a novel plan. A large sized Christmas Card was cut to the exact size of the original master key. A figure was cut out in a typical reveller's pose fumbling at the lock with the caption 'Locked in Locked out'. It was sent as a greeting card by the Sinn Feinner to a friend in Manchester, but unfortunately he could not unravel the message, so wisely sent it to the Sinn Feinner Headquarters. Some bright lad there caught the point. A master key was soon made and sent in a cake to our prison but the key failed to work even after three attempts. The key watchers in Dublin finally enclosed a file which did the trick. Milroy, three others and myself escaped and got back to Ireland. My next visit to England was to sign the Peace Treaty after the Irish Free State was born! That is the grand story,' he stopped with a chuckle.

We talked for a while of the pernicious British trick of partitioning a country when they have to quit. They had bled I reland over the decades economically, politically – now this was continued emotionally, morally. He was aware of the situation in India. I related the story of my Palestine visit. I also expressed regret at the sad lack of closer contacts between our two countries. Tentatively, we discussed plans to remedy this but they went no further. De Valera was soon gone.

Inspite of the vast distances, through the twenties when those like me were only slowly becoming aware of the Irish literary and dramatic renaissance, it was further accentuated by a personal friendship for a great many of us Indians with the Cousins, James and Margaret, who when they came to live in India, seemed to bring with them a whiff of that Irish atmosphere surcharged with its upsurge. Few perhaps realise today what an important and crucial role this couple played in our country's renaissance in more than one field.'

13

At the dawn of freedom the governmental set-up in India was saddled with what was a pathetic frame work, a typical colonial one that needed to be cast away. In fact the rot had already set in. The curse of partition was the price of a negotiated peace, not the triumph of a revolution that had long been in motion. Sadly enough strong avowals had been made that the old order would be replaced, Pandit Nehru himself being most unequivocal about it.

When Pandit Jawaharlal Nehru took office with the formation of the Interim Government, he declared that one of the first things that needed to be done was to scrap the present administrative machinery. Much water kept flowing under the Jamuna carrying away in its currents so many of our long cherished hopes and ambitions, not to speak of several of Pandit Nehru's avowals and declarations, instead of scraps of that rusty old machine. Today every bureaucrat swears by his files and his aides. A leader who goes into the administration vowing to change his world soon gets entangled in the same old web, and soon gets buried under the files. In fact pretty soon questions posed for solution cease to be human problems, becoming just so many papers, notes, memorandums above all rules, a bulwark against change. It would be no exaggeration to say that were our food crops dependent on paper instead of showers, the daily papers shuffled around could easily contribute in increasing the yield of the land. For very soon we began to temporise, compromise. At that stage any change could have been wrought with the willing cooperation of most of the bureauratic personnel, who were happy and proud to be part of a national government. But the necessary will to tear down the old worm-eaten props of a structure that had become irrelevant, was missing.

In the political movement the dynamism, innovation, originality had really flowed from Gandhiji. Even the cornerstone of our foreign policy had been laid by him though it has been conveniently forgotten. True we had a band of leaders of high calibre, who could have moulded a structure in keeping with the political philosophy on which our training had been based. Gandhiji's attention and time, above all his heart got diverted to the acute situation thrown up by the partition, and which eventually engulfed him, and there seemed nobody else to ignite the much needed spark for the kind of changes the situation demanded.

In fact even several antiquated enactments still continue to blacken our legal tomes.

Speaking at the All Parties Conference at Lucknow opposing the resolution moved by Pandit Malaviya advocating Dominion Status for India as a 'practical' goal for India, Pandit Nehru said in the course of his speech: 'What does the British Commonwealth of Nations stand for? It stands for one part domineering over the other. There are England and the self-governing dominions exploiting India, and other parts of the world. When we get Dominion Status are we going to assist England and the other Dominions to go on exploiting. The thing is inevitable . . . We are told that we must be practical and here being practical is taken to mean adherence to an outworn set of ideas, regardless of the changes that have happened in the world'.

While addressing a Press Conference in New Delhi in 1949 Pandit Nehru was asked how he could declare with such confidence that the decision to keep India within the Commonwealth was for the best when several groups in the country did not agree with it, like for instance the Socialists. Prompt came a spirited reply from Panditji: 'Oh, the Socialists they are a bunch of reactionaries'. There was a dead almost uncanny silence that seemed to sting even the nonchalance of the Prime Minister and penetrate through the Nehru armour. 'No, that is not exactly what I meant' the cocksure Pandit faltered. He then paraphrased for the benefit of the Indian press and the public what he meant, as follows: 'The Socialists are so tied up in the past that they cannot see the present, much less the future. The problems of the world may change, but they only think of them in terms of a generation back. I find the Socialist Party is stuck in the old grooves of thought and is unable to get out. The biggest thing that has happened in the world is the emergence of Asia and it is quite impossible for you to judge of this in some hard and fast way, applying the same simple slogan which you might have used ten or fifteen years ago.'

Here was a repetition of the Vallabhai Patel episode and my bitterest ire was roused. Wholesale public condemnation of this nature from a responsible leader, of a whole political group that had over the years been a part of the freedom struggle, led by personalities like Narendra Dev and Jayaprakash whose cooperation he had even now been seeking. Panditji had in fact tried to get the senior leaders to agree to have one of these two above mentioned gentlemen to head the Congress after Kripalani's exit. But had no success.

I drafted what I felt was an appropriate reply to this attack which immediately went into print as a little booklet with the picture of a bunch of grapes, adorning the cover, and very soon reached M.O. Mathai's, the P.M.'s Special Assistant, hands. He was probably enraged but neither his tone nor words betrayed it when he rang me. But he firmly asked me to get this withdrawn as it was a Socialist Party publication. I declined. In return I questioned his right to make such a request. He ended up by declaring he was doing his best to keep it away from Panditji, did I mean to send it to him? I had no such intention, this was meant for the public but while in circulation it may reach him. 'You know I am only trying to spare him. You should know better than I do, how deeply hurt he will be,' he said in a conciliatary tone. 'Then he should not hurt us his colleagues,' with that I closed the telephone.

A scene rose vividly before me in Anand Bhawan when Gandhiji had expressed his surprise and unhappiness at my hitting back at Vallabhai in the tone I had. As I had left him, Panditji had joined me, looking enquiringly. 'I don't regret that I wrote it' I said. 'He could have called and scolded us, argued with us, but to publicly tarnish all of us with a dirty brush is unworthy of any leader, especially him, who was close to Bapu. No, Bapu did not scold me but it is something much worse, my language has deeply hurt him, I wish he could have been spared that. You see he must have assumed I was too delicately feminine to indulge in such harsh language, not his style. He can hit hard but with a subtlety, like an extra sharp knife but cloaked by a sleek sheath'. 'I would hate to be the target of your attack', he said and he laughed. I never imagined then it could ever happen with him. I had no sense of prophecy.

I dare say some of us have stuck to where we were a couple of decades ago. But we have not exactly been like the over-tired oxen chewing the cud and dripping saliva. Some of us have tried to cling to what now seem out of date ideas such as simplicity in living, humility in mental disposition, to serve silently those who need succour, instead of the growing pomp and show, liveried attendents decorating our halls. How much has this new resurgence the Prime Minister praised, transformed the lives of the toiling millions in their grey existence in the scattered villages?

Let us take the international scene. Is not the exploitation of the weak by the strong still an established feature? Are there not most blatant overt or covert occupations of whole countries turning the rightful citizens into pathetic refugees to wander into strange lands? Where is the U.N. and what is still its power? South Africa is an irrefutable monument to the miserable failure of the International Body. I wanted to remind the Prime Minister that the present is still an extension of the past.

There were occasions when we seemed to be straying away from the political moorings we had built up and strengthened. One was the rejection of conferring of titles on citizens by the State. This smacked too much of the ugly role this had played in winning loyalty for the Raj. So in the Constitution this was banned. Nevertheless it was sneaked in under the devious name of 'Award', though each of them was blatantly a title. The same old scramble for the awards of the British days returned. That the so-called awardees should insisting in flaunt them as titles was inevitable. So it has continued, one of several frauds we blithely keep on perpetrating on the people, blatantly violating the Constitutional clause. When it was first being introduced I instinctively felt uneasy and declined it when sounded out.

When one stands on the brink of ones life and the decades seem to be slipping behind the horizon indicating that what had once seemed like a journey on an endless highway is coming to an end, and the whole big chapter of ones life closing, events of the past seem to stand out more clearly in perspective. Now one dreams far less of the future, and the past becomes more real and somewhat compensating, for it offers a sense of surety which the future can hold out no more.

Gandhiji's humanism and the identification that he had with the common people had drawn me to him, though patriotism was strong in the air. But for me more was necessary. This Gandhiji provided by his interpretation of freedom in terms of what it should mean to all sections of the people especially the importance with which he endowed each individual in a society where the latter counted for little; his emphasis on constructive work and giving of equal opportunity to women endowed my endeavours with the necessary philosophy as a background. Politics did not come to me as a vocation or a career, it came as a great cause, the means to an end, to be able to have the opportunity and the facility to formulate a changed sense of values which can lead to a different social pattern.

Training, planning and the active fight for freedom exhilerated me, though politics as a life work was not my medium of expression. In the political organisation itself, my initiation and growth was slow and the hard way, by strenuous labour and by dint of sheer systematic work. For it was as a humble volunteer at the Belgaum Congress where I got my early training in a volunteer camp, when I took the pledge I would work for the cause of liberation until India was free. It was a stern life of severe discipline.

The idealism and selflessness permeating the atmosphere and the hope of a free India however made the hardships negligible and inconsequential. As I look back now, those years fill me with a sense of fullness, that they were worthwhile. The struggle brought out the best in us and made us feel we were the finer for having gone through these experiences. I was equally conscious of the privilege of working with many valued colleagues, devoted to the cause of freedom.

As freedom came, service was replaced by the struggle for positions of power around which the main currents of public life seemed to whirl. To me, the beacon light lay elsewhere, in the side lanes of creative and constructive work through performing arts and crafts in which I found my true vocation. Thus, I worked with the artists and artisans, those who create and produce so that mankind may not live and grow on bread alone, but on things of beauty that uplift and raise it into finer and serener realms, and experience at least moments of sublimation.

There were many all the world over who inspired, filled my life with beauty and delight. Amongst them an outstanding personality was Shankar, the noted cartoonist. Shankar to me has been in a class by himself, perhaps because of his tantalising genial personality, someone you can never get angry with even if you tried, in fact simply have to love. There is an irresistible magnetism about him. This personality I feel gives a different stamp to his cartoons, for this complex composition comes out in his drawings. 'If we are going to keep this a free world, we must go on making fun of it,' is his maxim. 'For ridicule is a powerful weapon in the service of the free world,' he once declared. He was an acid critic of what went on around, lambasting everyone from Panditji to the tiniest cog in his party and government. Shankar's Nehru was the most vivid characterisation I ever saw as he drew a childish figure often looking rather lost to depict his prevarications and indecisive attitudes.

While his cartoons were heart-warming, his warm friendship, his early morning visits when we could sit peacefully and chat, brought continuous glow into my life. There never was a time when this seemingly enigmatic person was not there to provide a sense of homely comfort, appropriately embellished by his equally delightful spouse.

My earliest close contact with a dancer was with Sitara Devi, the dancer with the magic feet as we called her. It was in a magnificent setting in a fabulous Moghul style modern mansion in Bombay. The hostess was Atiya Begam Fayzee, a colourful lady with her imperious looking sister Begam of Jenjira, who presided over this famous salon. Fayzee was an architect, spruce and smart, but being small made was rather over-shadowed by the two women. Everything about them was elegant, choice. I looked upon them and the abode as a show place to take friends from outside to, Atiya had sponsored the Three Arts Circle, under which select cultural events would take place.

During Poet Tagore's visit to Bombay, the Circle arranged a reception which included a Kathak performance by a teenaged girl who kept the audience enthralled. Gurudev was visibly moved and while blessing her called her 'Nritya Shyam Ragini.'

We clicked from that moment. Some tie drew us. She has since risen to great heights, but to me she is still the littte ball of fire which lights up our gloom by the sparkle of her dance. I have had occasion to enter a packed hall where she is enthralled in her whirl, and she has stopped for a moment to send that silent current of mutual recognition between kindred spirits.

Sitara Devi was lucky. Though born in a conservative Brahmin family, her father, a reputed musician, determined to give his daughters educatian in music and dance, abandoned his native Varanasi and moved to Calcutta. Sitara Devi later got a professional touch with its lyricism in her Kathak from the Kalka Bindadin tradition, which fused gracefully with her earlier sterner lessons of the Tandav tradition her father's original contribution to Kathak. This endowed her dance with a unique quality.

Rukmini Devi initially emerged into public prominence not as a dancer but a Brahmin girl of Madras who dared to marry an Englishman in the emerging Twenties. That chapter, long obliterated, has been covered up by a refulgent one to tell of her great contribution to the country's artistic life. By entering the then shadowy world called the domain of the devadasi, she tore down an ugly visage putrifying the face of one of India's greatest arts. Impurities may have crept into the profession, like corruption in politics. Nevertheless politics continued to be practised, not merely by the Mafia but equally decent citizens. India owes a big debt of gratitude to Rukmini Devi for this.

I was equally impressed by her ardent efforts to rescue some of our traditions. By creating Kalakshetra, a centre as a repository of the good traditional artistic forms, has become a beacon of faith and hope, for it unfolds our multifaceted cultural expressions, making them relevent in our everyday life.

I am particularly heartened by her focussing on our original dramatic form, woven into music and dance, what the west is just coming to realise—the beauty of its totality—and shut out the pseudo forms some Indian dancers indulge in like aberrations that they call 'Ballet.'

I am deeply indebted to Rukmini Devi for her continued kindness over the many years, especially as she offered the ever ready Kalakshetra to set up a laboratory for scientifically researching and promoting vegetable dyes, relating the results to her weaving centre.

I went to a Bharatanatyam recital in Madras in early thirties. It was by a new young star just emerging. Balasaraswati. Though I saw the same Nritya, padams, varnams, this was a new experience. I had rarely seen such a liquid flow of movement as though her limbs were melting under the warmth of her emotions.

Then I felt I had suddenly caught the dancer's eye and it were as though her glances would come and settle on me. But what they roused were not fires but an inner quiet that comes from a sense of fulfilment. I was no longer watching her myriad movements for they were not external. I had a sensation as though they were flooding through my own body. It was almost like two floating together. When the dance ended I had to shake myself wanting to throw off what to me was a fantasy created by an unusual experience.

In course of time Balasaraswati and I met and we soon became friends. But it was a couple of decades later that I told her when I had first seen her dance. Her answer startled me: 'I do know and I remember too.' 'But how could you in such a crowd, and we had never met,' I persisted bewildered. Then she explained that when she dances she does it with an innate conscious respect for the audience. Since it was there to receive what she had to offer, she felt she owed it to give her best. 'But I cannot quite offer it to an amorphous crowd. It sometimes gets personified in an individual with whom I can be in commune, to whom I would be directing myself. That evening you became that person and naturally you stayed in my mind, though until we met I did not know who you were.' As our friendship ripened, she took pains to show me special aspects of her dance movements, I then realised how very hard she worked, though the public thought, things came to her with great ease.

Even though Bala became a widely known star artist, she continued a very private woman. The last time I was with her, she was showing me her baby grand daugther, who danced as Bala sang. Just she, Lakshmi her daughter, and I, spent a whole morning together. She was just a woman happily watching the child trying to be the big Bala, seeking approval, a happy nod from a smiling face. That is how I like to remember the great Bala, a giant of an artist, yet at heart a sweet simple woman, savouring the little family pleasures.

I began a closer study of what lay behind the Indian picturisation when I acquired the picture album Rag Ragini by O.C. Gangoly. I was a young enthusiast and such gorgeous illustrated albums were not easy to come by in those days, they were few and far between. So I was full of a glow of pleasure like a child that has found a new toy. As I was learning music many pictures came alive. I became aware there was more to drawing than what a mere glance imparted.

As I talked with Artist Gangoly when I met him years after experiencing my youthful excitement over his Rag Ragini series, I grasped his belief that the reality lies behind the external appearance as he narrated the relationship between the two, expounding the philosophy that is pregnant in much of our Vedic teaching. But when he began expostulating that a 'landscape has in truth no reality and it is the mission of the artist to reveal the reality that lies *within, diving into the depth of eternity*', as he described it, that I interrupted him in bewilderment. 'How does one conjure up this reality.' 'Why through the very air around, by sensitively responding to the atmosphere. That is how our ancient hymns to the forests must have been composed. They convey to us a profound mystery revealed through a mystic grandeur, nevertheless carrying a strange flavour of realism. The picturisation is symbolic too. For Eternity is presented to us by the continously receding back-ground moving away from the foreground almost to a vanishing point.'

As I kept gazing at Gangoly's paintings I was startled to see how he had stripped even the words he was just uttering of their outer sheath, to let us gaze into the essence at the core. Though shaken by this realisation, I sensed equally how simple it was in a way as though some one were stripping off an obstructive curtain. 'Though the Indian tradition was not to reproduce the myriad details of physical forms, obviously the fundamental principles of depicting natural scenes were practised from early time in India,' I commented. 'True. Only Indian art drew its inspiration from a single core, the universe as a totality. For our philosophy is based on the fundamental truth or experience that there is no basic difference in the various divergent manifestations of life such as human, animal, vegetable worlds, because of a single life line running through them all. Thus a landscape does not exist in isolation, it is a part of the whole, a background that calls up the ethos.'

I turned to another nascent topic and an equally intriguing theory of his. 'You believe that a temple structure adheres to the form of the image within?' I asked. 'Every architectural form for me indicates it, whether Hindu or Buddhist. In our tradition sculpture has always been a part of architecture and the two merged naturally. A builder, according to me, is not content to just raise a roof but tries to shape it purposefully. For instance the Buddhist stupa is not a mere casket for a relic, rather it takes on the form of a seated Buddha. Taka the Mahadeo Temple at Khajuraho which with shoulders spread out looks like an image with a Mukut on the head.' I was atremble with many more queries, for he had what seemed several audacious theories. But was there an end to them, for he bubbled over with waves of bright ideas. So I fell silent.

The works of Jamini Roy in their folk grandeur touched my innermost cords and reverberated through my being in pleasant harmony. Coming as I did from a land resplendent with folk forms, his vivid imagery and earthy colours conjured up shades of my old rich environs. They even seemed to evoke the hum and rumble of the village sounds.

As I studied his works I realised that while he worked within the folk parameters, he was too creative to merely lift modes and images from the past. In some way he had simplified them, stripping them of some of the heavy trimmings and they stood out clear, fresh and alluring as though they had been through some alchemist's hands. They had no trace of any murky or stale air around.

Everything around his works was excitingly new though they put one in mind of something archaic. That was to me the magic of it all. He was original in all he did. He used clay on lime-coated cloth or wooden boards as base and like the old countryfolk tamarind seed glue for binding; above all he strictly adhered to vegetable and stone colours.

An unusual teasing quality about his works, as though each were a conundrum, kept exciting my curiosity. Apparently the figures seemed inert, but as you gazed at them they started posing questions, puzzling, speculating. Take his *Street Scene*, so empty, so gaunt, yet haunts you with uncontrolable memories. Or the cows, so immobilised, but in seconds they became alert, listening intently, and you involuntarily stretched your ears to catch the sounds. Especially with his studies in women, each to me was a question mark? There was his 'Seated Women', squatting comfortably, relaxed, then a light of expectancy starts leaping from the eyes, as though she is waiting for something and will abandon her repose. And so on, this quest of mine went on.

We both received Vishwabharati's Deshikottama award together and I waited for him at the function with a fluttering heart. But alas he was too ill to come. Much light faded out of the scene. I never got him to read his original Kalighat—inspired Pats and know I am the poorer for it.

When I met Amrita Sher-Gil she had returned from her South Indian odyssey and picturised her experiences in the new famous Trilogy. The world of the art lovers of those days was a very small one and one kept jostling against the same people at any studio hearing the same weather-beaten exclamations, the same eye brows raised skyward. Not being a connoisseur nor an art critic, it needed more than a three days' wonder to guide me to a studio. So it was by chance I saw a couple of Amrita's pictures at a private house in Delhi and was arrested by them. They seemed to come alive as I gazed at them—and their jet dark colours glistened with a myriad lights.

Someone persuaded me to visit Amrita's studio when I was in Shimla. I readily agreed. She greeted me warmly and I felt drawn to her. There was something direct and simple in her manner, contrasting with the highly sophisticated enervating social environs of the place. 'You are from the South?' was her first question. I nodded and waited for her to open up. 'I have had a most enjoyable tour there,' came the opening sentence in an emotional tone. 'I loved every bit of it—the red ochre earth, the dazzling green of the vegetation, above all the rich dark skin of the people. Everything seemed to come alive. The temples were pulsating, not deadpan as they so often are.' The words came tumbling out. 'You went further South, did you not? That is the part I come from, where the waterways and coconut groves are' I interposed. 'Yes, Yes. Rich thick vegetation, and people wearing simple white fabric pieces as a reaction I presume. And everything stark Indian—little traces of the tawdry Western blight. Have you noticed how ugly the samples of that civilization look in our midst?'

Then we began a round of her pictures. 'The South has changed my very style of painting,' she explained as she showed me the *Fruit Venders* she had painted in Cape Comorin. They seemed a part of that region as though they had sprung from the soil. I had the same feeling looking at *Brahmacharis*. They were not created externally, they just belonged there. It was a wonderful illusion she created. For me the *Elephants Bathing In A Green Pool* was another that came nearest that sensation.

'You know I feel my gift began to blossom only after I came to India, not only in emotion but even in technique,' she continued to explain. 'I feel I am interpreting this land, its people with their silent submission. I had to devise my own technique. The South has now added a new dimension. That is how in spite of Western training I react deeply to the atmosphere.' 'And which people mistakenly call rebellion,' I finished the sentence for her. 'One of the qualities in your pictures I value is their simplicity even while projecting all the essentials, you nevertheless seem to clothe them with a sense of decoration,' I remarked. She became very thoughtful then added: 'Part of my problem perhaps lies in the types I choose to depict. I don't know how much of my work you have seen but in common language what many people rave as *beautiful* to me is inspired. So what stirs me must seem to them ugly. Even the India I see, to me is bathed in a melancholy air, it is not the superficial exuberant India of the travel pictures. So some people say there is no Indian touch in my work, I am foreign.' At this stage I stopped her and explained that I was not concerned as to whether what she painted was Indian or un Indian. 'You are creating and I react to your creation and what it means to me. I am convinced you are sincere and true to your own perceptions. That is all that matters. The perceptions of no two are alike. You know that the images we see are created out of our own vibrations. There is no *one* static image, hence the concept of Maya. In this vast world there is scope for myriads of perceptions with differing reactions. It is futile agitating over this reality. All that matters is your own adherence to your creative urge unmindful of the shafts that strike your path.'

We chatted amiably for a long while as I looked deeply at her pictures, her sketches, as she rambled on. To me she seemed quite original, in her moods, her presentation and above all, her colours which seemed to me to have a life and language of their own. The forms though simple showed good draughtsmanship, probably the fruit of the early training. The ones that had power emanating from them, I valued. The rest did not mean much to me. She to me seems like a meteor that shot through our busy skies far too briefly. But I think that those who knew her will always remember her as a piece of raw sienna – a colour she revelled in.

Amongst the artists I had the good fortune to get to know, Uday Shankar stands apart. When I first met him in Bombay where he had arrived after a resounding tour of Europe and America with *his own* troupe, he did not seem a stranger. Rather it was like greeting an old friend. For I seemed to have come to know him through a number of personalities who were once his close associates. Dancer Pavlova whom I met in Calcutta during her visit, had first stirred my interest. 'How did you, a seasoned world renowned dancer, pick up a young student, an Asian learning painting and who had not even heard of Pavlova,' I asked.

'Why to gaze upon his delicate slim figure was to watch *Dance*. Every bit of him dripped rhythm. He was the concept of dance personified.' These words from Pavlova stupified me. I had watched her dance for two evenings. To me she was just that: dance. It was not a human body or its limbs moving—all I saw was a maze of rhythm. I was in a hypnotic haze, a unique experience in which I was lost. The next link in this chain that I met was Comolata Dutt whose musical compositions enabled Pavlova to create the two earliest Indian numbers: Radhakrishna and a Hindu Wedding, to partner with Shankar. Comolata was a pianist set on a passion to popularise Indian music in the Western World. I became friendly with her later when she took charge of the western music section in the AIR New Delhi. She described this adventure with some amusement. Her Indian tunes were played on forty western instruments. 'I only provided the melodies and the rhythm—they did the rest. For the public the effect was 'great' a lavish stage spectacle!

The third personality through whom Shankar came to me was Alice Boner, who truly brought Shankar's scintillating career to fruition. I met her as a scholar, a devoted indologist. By some strange trick of fate, she played the role of a modern avatar, for she took Shankar back to his roots, put him through an exhaustive study of the many manifestations of Indian traditional culture. Alice Boner's explanation was simple. 'Seeing this extraordinary artist caught in some Arabian Night's dramatics, he conjured up in my inner perception an outline in some soft substance, waiting for a master's hand to shape it to perfection. Here the master had to be himself and the mirror before which he had to perfect his image, his background, the great Indian heritage from which he had emerged, but was unaware of its grandeur. I only played an unconscious role as that of a bee which carries the nectar. Nature alone could complete the creative process.'

The public acceptance of Shankar's dance presentation in India was favourable though it was a big break from the tradition.

As I watched Uday Shankar's show, I became aware that this was a great cultural revolutionary event—the artist was making a new era for Indian dance; he had successfully melted and floated anew the traditional rigidly bound, firmly set body movements, into a current dance stream. Of course, Shankar set the tone, the direction the pattern Shankar to me gave the feeling of dripping rhythm from every little pore of his unique body. I recalled Pavlova's final retort to Rothenstein, the renowned master artist under whom Shankar was burgeoning to become his prize pupil painter: 'Look at Shankar's body—God cost it for a dancer not to wriggle with paints and brushes,' when he countered her move to take Shankar as her partner for her Indian dance pieces. Today we over the last quarter century got so used to this transformation, the public simply accepts the new format as part of the tradition. Shankar wrought this tremendous change subtly with a natural air, no fan-fare. Indian show manship owes a deep debt to him for this invaluable contribution, though rarely commended as historically most praiseworthy. True as he warmly conceded, his close collaboration with Pavlova and her company and equally crucial, his partnership with Simky for two long decades were valuable assets.

As I watched Shankar and Simky dance, I tried to analyse what made him unique, every movement of his. Every phase of his expression, was completely Indian in its *core*, though he was not following any particular pattern of Indian dance school. Shankar had created a style of his own in which the core was Indian but the outer presentation his own innovation and in keeping with the current showmanship. Every movement spoke with extraordinary simplicity yet was exuberant with a rich eloquence, something hard to put into words. Though a man, his movements were meltingly soft but no trace of the effeminate, which to many was a tantalising puzzle.

I was of course most impressed by the individuality of his creation, the extraordinary blending of the archaic with the modern.

His new piece Labour and Machinery was a startling departure from his usual delicate aesthetic pictures. It was a phase of modern Indian yet the core was the same India of our old dreams. Someone described it as a fantasy within a fantasy.

An air of radiant friendliness drew Shankar to me from our very first meeting, my mind, crowded with many vivid pictures of him imprinted by so many of his intimates. The question uppermost in my mind flew out almost involuntarily: 'What made you leap out of your sketching album into the unknown sea of dance?' 'Dance must have been dormant in every recess of my being waiting for some magic wand to bring it to life. Pavlova did that. She was herself an embodiment of dance and she seemed to electrify the air around her. Not only her gestures, even the liquid she poured into the tea cups seemed to bubble like a cascade. It is hard to find words to describe how I was shaken, like a tender tree by a gusty breeze. I really and truly found myself.' 'Yet you had no background training, how did you feel confident you could cope with someone like Pavlova, like jumping into the water without knowing even the elements of swimming?' 'I felt I was part of something in the making, like bits and pieces, and I was being made whole. I had found my mission, a rudderless boat finding its right direction. The more I composed, the more I danced, the more I became aware how loaded was the repository within me seeking release. When a dancer weaves out a dream, it is not a fantasy, it is real, permanent, not transitory. That is why those who see the form the dream is shaped into, continue to cherish it. For there is nothing transitory in creation. The artist's imagination expresses in images, in gestures, just as he or she writes a poem or sings a melody. They are all concepts that take various forms out of the same womb of creation. That is where the essence of beauty resides. Did not our ancients say that dance 'refines the mind, harmonises the emotions and uplifts the soul; that the function of dance is to ennoble and elevate mankind.' 'Though you draw your inspiration from the ancient spring, your expressions, modes, images, do not conform to the old.' 'You are right', he answered with a broad jubilent smile. 'My dance is my own. I create my own images, but the dance is genuine. It has depth for it is true to the Indian spirit, with its roots in the Indian soil. Like several Indian customs when only the dead outer crust lingers and the inner throb has long fled, the Indian dance too tends to become inane and repetitive. The creative spirit is dynamic, and forever bubbling, it is an eternal spring. I use simple techniques in a low key of my hands, feet, above all my body, which I have wrought into a very sensitive instrument to coordinate the various impulses into a perfect form.' 'What launched you forth into this adventure how did dance specifically become the touchstone to transform your life?'

'You guess right—a spark did ignite my emotion, Ananda Cooumaraswamy's description of Nataraja. This image in multiferious forms took possession of me. Even though I had never seen such shapes before, they seemed to emanate from within me. I knew I had found myself.'

I felt as though I had been listening to a fairy tale. The spell did not break.

Time slipped by. I was living in a world of storm, struggle, prisons, when suddenly in one of my quiet interludes Uday Shankar suddenly confronted me. 'I have something very important I want to talk over with you. I am going to set up a Cultural Centre in India. It is to be in Almora. I want to tell you all about it. I am excited for it is an old dream now slowly taking shape. Tell me how you feel about it.' 'I am truly most delighted and you have all my good wishes.' I was truly delighted to know the Centre he had so long hungered to establ.sh was to take shape. I wished him well. It was tragic it came to such a swift end. But Uday Shankar's stamp was so positively left on everyone of those who participated in the Centre's life, no matter how briefly. One can recognise them anywhere, any part of the country. So it had not all been in vain.

When I was involved in the search for traditional crafts that seemed worth saving and reviving, help came to me from a most unexpected quarter, the venerable Sankaracharya of Kanchi Mutt. He had become popular for not only his high piety, but even more his human relationship with people, his easy accessibility. But as I rarely visited such personalities I was unaware of this. I had however been visiting the inner precincts of several temples, especially the underground basements where lay a medley of what to me seemed rare precious treasures, from cooking vessels to the most delicate temple lamps and puja articles. Whether it simply had a leak, a torn handle, a chip off the lid, the items could not be used in the temple, no matter how insignificant the blemish. In olden times a very large variety of objects were in use in the temples, as for each occasion it was a different Kalash (pot), tray, lamp. Each design was symbolic and proclaimed the occasion to those who could recognise each individually. The temple had ample funds and I believed should replace these abandoned treasures and restore them to their rightful place in the various rituals. Yet the temple authorities seemed indifferent, shrugged their shoulders—I had been even more ambitious, I wanted even some of their rare jewellery designs to be copied for reproduction by the Handicrafts Design Centres, to restore them to the people. Somehow this struggle of mine reached Sankaracharya's ears and he called me. He said he understood my objective and he fully agreed. He explained Sanskaras sometimes tended to become mere external movements, the inner significance being often overlooked or even forgotten. Hence this indifference—'You probably are aware that each form had a symbolic meaning. Each curve, each line says some thing. These objects are pregnant with eloquence if you understand their language. The aesthetic value of its totality which as you say, you and the public appreciate, draws its quality from an inner vision'. I nodded and added: 'I completely agree. All our old texts tell us that before a man creates any objects he must meditate on it and depict the mental image he or she has conceived—Intuition is total, whereas logic is fragmentation, I believe Swamiji. That is why these objects are invaluable. I am most indebted to you for your encouragement and your readiness to help'.

The temples opened their doors. Amongst pots and pans I selected only the rarer ones. The lamps had all to be remade, for each played a special role even in the general ceremonies. They were so beautiful that it was a feast to look on them.

The courtesies were extended to allow me to have the temple jewellery copied where I thought it was worth the trial. Unfortunately there was little follow up after all these efforts. After I left the Board, the jewellery patterns so assiduously and delicately collected could never be traced in the Board's office!

I had another unique experience in my quest for crafts and craftsmen. When I was migrating from the skirt and blouse to sporting saris, my eye alert for something fresh, I stumbled on a small wayside room, proclaiming modestly Textile Dying, which for me turned out a sort of Ali Baba's cave. The quiet retiring young man at the counter responded with a bright gleam in the eye and the pale face lit up with a heavenly smile which for me soon came to be associated with colour. So I named him the Colour Man. Every time I suggested the strangest colour combinations to be tried with the fabrics I kept hauling to his counter, his almost intuitive sensing of my mental picture of the fabric to be, excited and surprised me. It were as though we were playing the same tune on an invisible instrument. Then the blow fell. I returned after a trip to final the room occupied by strangers with different commodities. I was told the dyer had just vanished one morning without a word. It left me with a strange gloom as though a streak of light that lit my pathway had suddely deserted me.

Years rolled by and I was taking a stroll in Bangalore in rather a remote deserted rocky terrain with a friend, a new comer. He asked me if I was aware of a cave in that vicinity, where he was told a yogi was staying at the time. He was keen to see him. After some local enquiries we discovered the Yogi came to the cave late in the evening. So we lay in wait and accosted him just he approached the cave. I kept gazing at him, there was something familiar about the gait, the air about him, though the face was not easy to place. Then he looked straight at me and there was the unforgettable smile—he was my long lost Colour Man. 'Kamaladevi how did you come here?' came from his lips. My friend and I both wanted to know how this transformation had taken place. He narrated briefly what I was to read in some of his books years later, particularly his 'The Vision of God.' I was seized with a sense of restlessness that drove me like a tornado far into the mountains. There I began to meditate. Then a light took shape before my mental vision which suffused me with inexpressible bliss, filling my whole being. I cannot describe the blessedness of the State." When he stopped there was a long silence which my friend broke by asking how does one get through to such a state. 'Very simple my man. Do you not get obsessed with dreams, ideas, plans? Cultivate this obsession for Him, the Being, God, call by any name. When I first experienced this ecstasy, it simply overwhelmed me with a wondrous rapture.' The ecstasy showed clearly over his face, We met a few times. Then just as swiftly as he had appeared he vanished.

Momentous decades rolled by and I was wandering about on my craft quest when I got a call from one Swami Ramdas who had started an Ashram not far from my home town. The Swami was setting up a Craft Centre and wanted my help.

The Swami was no other than my Colour Man, the Yogi in the cave, now back to the world. He greeted me with that same old inimitable smile. When I gazed enquiringly at him, he said he would explain his new phase and how he came to it. "One kind of Samadhi is sitting in one posture to meditate, entirely forgetful of the world outside. But one should not be satisfied merely with attaining this condition for oneself. One must impart the knowledge of it to others which one can do by moving in the world and serving humanity, for that too is the lila of God. This realisation occurs when the ego is entirely obliterated and constitutes the other kind of Samadhi which I have entered upon. I want your cooperation in this.'

I gladly agreed. I reminded him that the original point where our lives had first touched, had done a full circle. We were together again in Craft Work. I was excited at the prospect of working with this craftmate again. We drew up plans to concentrate on rural crafts, recruiting and training young people under master craftsmen. As this Anandashram of Swamiji's was drawing large crowds from all over the country and even from foreign lands, marketing seemed easy. For Swami Ramdas had become like a magnet. But he was not content playing the traditional Swami, a monument of the receiving end. He threw himself vigorously into enlivening the Craft Centre which soon grew into a sizeable complex, keeping to the simple rural crafts and part of the lush countryside. And I continued to ponder over the strange freaks of destiny that made my life lines keep crossing that of this great man of God who had ultimately dedicated himself to the service of the simple crafts.

To look back on the years one has left behind, nonchalantly, dispassionately and objectively, one has to reach what seems like the brink of no return when the decades have slipped by and vanished behind the horizon, indicating what had once seemed like an endless voyage is quickly coming to close. Until then the future seems to stretch itself endlessly ahead, with rosy hopes and alluring horizons to which one continues to react with optimism and excitement. The past naturally appears an embarrassing period of uncertain adolescence and wavering immaturity, when the spurt of youthful energy and growing ambitions keep relating to an unfolding future, rather than to a receding past.

Now, however, one suddenly becomes aware of an emerging end to what had seemed a continuing burgeoning. Each day, each year, one grows acutely aware, is taking that much of time out of the short span left. How long or short, it is not given to any of us to guess or know - something within only keeps warning you that it is getting shorter, quickly, fatally. Thus one dreams far less of the future, indulges less in building castles in the air. The past becomes so much surer, real and above all compensating. It offers the sense of security and satisfaction, which the future can hold out no more. So one begins to reminiscence, and try to find oneself in it.

Out of these five long years rolled wearily by within the grey walls which are called a prison. I tasted this life in six different prisons, two of them in the then Indian States. A prison brings out the worst in people is a common phrase much bandied about. No doubt confinement within a limited space has its own exasperations apart from discomforts; its capacity of irritation is limitless. Whereas in a family, traditional ties, sentiment, sometimes fear and dependence on others tone down heat, round off projections, while here there is no such common background or structural support. Here we are placed in a heterogeneous group drawn from hundreds of homes, diverse communities with different habits, speaking a babel of tongues. How can a great family be welded out of this strange nebulous mass? Though there are several individual cases of abiding friendships that that can be traced to prison companionship. Our is an unpremeditated unprepared army which literally sprouts overnight because of a patriotic call. The majority of people who are crowded into prisons in these circumstances are raw, new to any political movement, untempered by experience of working in an organization.

To me there was another side to the ugly sides of the prison; to give coherence to this incoherence, give structure to a national ideal, identity to inspiration, above all discipline the indisciplined. Though beset with hurdles it would be an exciting process interesting to develop and watch, just the tailor made training for a nation in the making. For we know that the biggest of personalities are a curious mixture of pleasing and unpleasing elements, vessels of balancing forces, mixture of idealism and pettiness, magnanimity and meanness, generosity with selfishness.

Prison to me was a trial in other ways. I am not a gregarious animal and it is a great trial to live for months on end in small crowds. And as I by nature lack small talk—in that I don't boast of being highbrow, I rather look on this as a great limitation. For often this is misunderstood. The heaviest burden to me was being locked up within a heavily crowded enclosure. It is wearing to the best of tempers, sweetest of dispositions to keep rubbing shoulders with small crowds for 24 hours over long periods. It is not surprising that one's outlook gets cramped, sense of values distorted and people are inclined to be irritated over triffles, which are exaggerated to senseless proportions.

As time-piece is allowed, one learns to observe and measure shadows to guess the time.

Life seems to have been for me a series of hurdles. Whatever I have tried to do, I have always had to contend with adverse forces. Whatever I have achieved has been the hard and rugged way. Nothing has come with ease. For every little thing at every step I have had to labour, strive and strain, and this has continued to be criss crossed by problems all the time. In fact the burdens have grown with the years, as though the challenges too have grown in dimension and intensity with age.

Whatever I have achieved has been through my own effort, and sheer hard work. I have had no godfathers nor fairy foster mothers to push me up or give me a helping hand. I am proud I began my political career as an ordinary volunteer, a very humble field worker. At heart I have stayed so.

One thing that has helped me is a cool and controlled disposition free from nerves or hysterics. I was brought up with a contempt for fear. My mother scoffed if I expressed fear. She made me travel alone even as a young girl. Fear of ghosts, spirits was unknown in my house.

Some of us can be full of contradictions. I seem bold aggressive, outgoing, having been a fighter all my life. But in reality I am shy and retiring, rather averse to facing crowds and addressing large gatherings. Left to myself I prefer to stay at home rather than go out into the highways. It is quite an effort for me to approach strangers and open a dialogue. Even if I have to ask my way around, I shrink, get some-one to do it for me. I wish I had a companion to have around or travel with me, to act as a liaison and protect me from the public. As I am careful not to show this failing, nobody guesses the struggle I am subjected to. On the whole I avoid going to functions where big crowds gather. This reticence has sharpened over the years and in some ways I am not sorry as it helps me to be selective in the way of company and conserve energy and time.

At the same time I like sharing the things that I cherish, like beautiful landscapes, particularly mountains, drama, music, exhibitions, travels and the like. A sympathetic and understanding friend beside me enhances my pleasure and adds to the enjoyment.

I discovered from an early age that my emotional responses were generally quick and deep for they were intuitive. They are too sincere to be casual. But lots of people are not serious, with the result I got continuously hurt. So gradually I have come to develop rather a stern exterior, so even if I were touched within, I would not show. Those who do not know me take me as cold, proud, and distant, none of which I really am. As I have said I am no good at *making conversation*—

I have never been convinced of the need for it. I talk when I feel that I have something to say, otherwise I can just sit quiet and not bother thinking up topics, to keep up a flow of talk.

The general belief is that a public worker becomes over the years impersonalised, drawing sufficient nourishment from the activity so as to be able to draw and enjoy a sense of contentment. With me it may be so upto a point. But it has not satisfied my whole being. It does not touch my intimate self. For me the warmth and companionship of my comrades is basic and lasting.

Nobody is altogether impervious to praise or blame of statement. But within myself I have a standard of my own and unless I have sincerely aimed at that standard, I do not feel satisfied. After all most success is in the intensity of striving, the effortone has put into the thing one is aiming at. And to that extent praise or blame does not shake me, instantly my own measuring rod comes to my rescue.

Sentimental expressions leave me entirely unaffected—those who are in the public eye receive these as frequently as showers. I am not demonstrative even where emotion is expected to be demonstrated, I feel an instinctive repugnance to provide any such expected outpouring beyond a conventional response. At such times silence seems more than sparkle.

Now in the fast drawing winter twilight when one is no more poised for a spring and one's spirit is not on the wing, there is one more the flutter and excitement of new things happening to swing one up in a fresh churning whirlpool. As I lean back and close my eyes to relax and let my memories run back the long aisles of time, to know what are the things I wanted most and discover, the same yearning remains most poignant in me still. It is the little things of life—an unhurried life of leisure to dream, to suck in the slow notes of music, to savour of the gifts of nature, the play of light and shadow so reminiscent of life with its joys and sorrows. For I am very human and it is very human to want the trifles that we usually brush or throw away.

In the ultimate an individual is a lovely soul, away and apart holding on only these little things of life while all else has faded away.

Index